THE UNITED NATIONS, PEACE AND SECURITY

Preventing humanitarian atrocities is becoming as important for the United Nations as dealing with interstate war. In this book, Ramesh Thakur examines the transformation in UN operations, analysing its changing role and structure. He asks why, when and how force may be used and argues that the growing gulf between legality and legitimacy is evidence of an eroded sense of international community. He considers the tension between the United States, with its capacity to use force and project power, and the UN, as the centre of the international law enforcement system. He asserts the central importance of the rule of law and of a rules-based order focused on the UN as the foundation of a civilised system of international relations. This book will be of interest to students of the UN and international organisations in politics, law and international relations departments, as well as policy-makers in the UN and other NGOs.

RAMESH THAKUR is Senior Vice-Rector of the United Nations University and an Assistant Secretary-General of the United Nations. He has written and edited over twenty books, the most recent being *International Commissions and the Power of Ideas* (2005) and *Making States Work: State Failure and the Crisis of Governance* (2005).

THE UNITED NATIONS, PEACE AND SECURITY

From Collective Security to the Responsibility to Protect

RAMESH THAKUR

CAMBRIDGE
UNIVERSITY PRESS

CAMBRIDGE UNIVERSITY PRESS

Cambridge, New York, Melbourne, Madrid, Cape Town, Singapore, São Paulo

CAMBRIDGE UNIVERSITY PRESS

The Edinburgh Building, Cambridge CB2 2RU, UK

Published in the United States of America by Cambridge University Press, New York

www.cambridge.org

Information on this title: www.cambridge.org/9780521671255

First published 2006

Printed in the United Kingdom at the University Press, Cambridge

A catalogue record for this publication is available from the British Library

Library of Congress Cataloguing in Publication data

Thakur, Ramesh Chandra, 1948–
The United Nations, peace and security / Ramesh Thakur. – 1st ed.
p. cm.
Includes bibliographical references and index.
ISBN 0 521 85517 9 (hardback) – ISBN 0-521-67125-6 (pbk.)
1. United Nations. 2. Security, International. 3. Pacific settlement of international
disputes. 4. International relations. I. Title.
JZ4984.5.T43   2006
341.23–dc22   2005032574

ISBN-13 978-0-521-85517-4 hardback
ISBN-10 0-521-85517-9 hardback
ISBN-13 978-0-521-67125-5 paperback
ISBN-10 0-521-67125-6 paperback

To Sanjay and Simon: may they leave this world in better
shape and condition than when they came into it,
and may they strive to make it so.

CONTENTS

vii

FIGURES

TABLES

FOREWORD

No organisation in the world embodies as many dreams, yet delivers as many frustrations, as the United Nations. Nothing could be nobler or more moving than its stated goals, not only 'to save succeeding generations from the scourge of war', but to 'reaffirm faith in fundamental human rights' and 'promote social progress and better standards of life in larger freedom'. But only sporadically and erratically has the UN been the central player in advancing and achieving these objectives. For most of its history the Security Council has been a prisoner of great power manoeuvring; the General Assembly a theatre for empty rhetoric; the Economic and Social Council a dysfunctional irrelevance; and the Secretariat, for all the dedication and brilliance of a host of individuals, alarmingly inefficient.

Of course there have been great achievements along the way. Even during the desolate Cold War years there was the management of decolonisation, which can be legitimately characterised as the largest scale redress of human rights in history; the invention of peacekeeping as a wholly new means of conflict management; the giant strides made by UN agencies in feeding the starving, sheltering the dispossessed and immunising against disease. Since the end of the Cold War, the new cooperative environment enabled major new advances in peacemaking (with more civil conflicts resolved by negotiation in the last fifteen years, for the most part under UN auspices, than in the previous two hundred), tougher-edged peacekeeping and post-conflict peacebuilding. And a far more concerted international effort has been made than ever before to set and implement new agendas on a whole range of social, economic and development issues, including women, children, the environment, indebtedness and catastrophic disease.

But the disappointments have also been immense: the failure to respond effectively to large-scale atrocity crimes in Rwanda, the Balkans and Sudan; the bypassing of the Security Council in the 2003 invasion of Iraq; the serious marginalisation of the UN and erosion of effectiveness of its major treaties in the area of arms control and disarmament; the complete politicisation and loss of credibility of the Human Rights

Commission; continued management lapses and conspicuous inefficiency in the performance of the UN Secretariat and many of its programmes and agencies; a failure to meet many of the social, economic
and development targets identified in the global agenda-setting conferences; and a general sense that the whole UN security system is still too
geared to the central preoccupation of its founders sixty years ago –
states waging aggressive war against each other – and not responding
adequately to the much wider range of human security threats and
challenges likely to dominate attention in the twenty-first century.

Although it hurts the idealists among us to admit it, it may be that
across the great spread of issues that now dominate the international
agenda we are asking more of the UN than any global intergovernmental organisation can by its very nature deliver. The UN's great
strength as a forum – that it brings together effectively all the world's
sovereign governments to address the world's problems – is its great
weakness as a decision-making and implementing body. With 191
member states, there are just too many voices and interests that have
to be accommodated. The UN is a critical instrument of global governance but is not and never can be a global government. As such, perhaps,
for all the self-evaluation and summitry of its sixtieth anniversary year,
improvements in the UN's performance can only ever be incomplete
and incremental.

But there is one area at least in which we cannot settle for incomplete
and incremental change: that of the UN's core security business. This
is the focus and core message of this book. If we are 'to save succeeding
generations from the scourge of war', the idealists have to hang in
hard, somehow finding common cause with the realists and the
cynics and pessimists, not just trying to get the system and delivery right,
but demanding that we get them right, and never resting until we do.

Only in relation to its role 'to maintain or restore international peace
and security', does the UN come close to having the kind of straightfor-
ward executive role that we associate with sovereign governments, complete with a body of manageably sized membership clearly empowered to
make legally binding decisions. The formal authority vested in the
Security Council in this respect, in effect to make peace or war, has no
precedent in international relations. But there are some very big problems, and very big issues still to be resolved, in the way in which that
authority is, and is not, exercised. It is the aim, and achievement, of
Ramesh Thakur's splendid book to systematically identify and analyse
them.

While to over-distil its core messages does no justice to the kaleido-scopic character of this work, and the multitude of interrelated issues on which the author has interesting and often provocative things to say, the two biggest such problems he addresses are the gap between authority and power in the present international security system, and the still unresolved tension in that system between the claims of national sovereignty and the demands of human security.

While the UN Security Council has always had as much formal authority as it could reasonably want, it has no legions of its own, and is never likely to acquire them. Its exercise of real coercive power – that needed for it to be a decisive force in curbing and punishing misbehaving governments – depends on the cooperation of member states. Its power is only that which the five veto-wielding permanent members allow it to exercise, and even then only as great as the acquiescence and commit-ment of resources by member states makes possible. What is new in the contemporary equation is that the gap between the UN's apparent authority and its actual power is greater than it has ever been, by virtue of the emergence of a single member state with more military power at its disposal than the rest combined (reinforced by a very substantial proportion of the world's economic power and huge cultural influence as well), and a proven disposition to use that power outside the UN collective security system.

What the UN does retain is that critical ingredient that distinguishes authority from mere power, namely *legitimacy*. While authority without real power to back it up may be weak or diminished authority, power exercised without legitimacy is not authority at all. While that consideration may not have been much of a deterrent to the exercise of raw power in times past, things are different in the globalised, interdepend-ent world we now inhabit, where we confront so many 'problems without passports', as Kofi Annan has called them – including terrorism, weapons proliferation, organised crime, environmental catastrophe and health pan-demics. And all those problems need solutions without passports, incapable as they are of resolution other than by cooperative international action. And that consideration tends to operate as a brake on the behaviour of even the most enthusiastic would-be hegemon.

But if the UN is to be able to make full use of its comparative authority advantage, and the Security Council not bypassed or marginalised again on great issues of war and peace, its legitimacy has to be real and not merely formal, and be seen by the rest of the world to be so. That is why the issue of Security Council composition – making it credibly representative of the world of the twenty-first century, not the middle of the last – cannot be indefinitely deferred. And that is why, when it comes to endorsing any form of coercion, and above all the use of military force, the Security Council's decision-making must not be ad hoc and realpolitik-driven, but be based on transparent, principled criteria of legitimacy, of the kind outlined in the reports of both the International Commission on Intervention and State Sovereignty (ICISS) and the High-Level Panel on Threats, Challenges and Change, and embraced by the Secretary-General in his own *In Larger Freedom* recommendations. None of this may be a sufficient condition for the achievement of a rule-based international order, in which the scourge of war both between and within countries no longer brings untold sorrow to mankind, but it is unquestionably a necessary condition. Thakur here makes that case powerfully and well.

The book is equally strong in its analysis of the great tension, which remains very incompletely resolved in the international security system, between the claims of national sovereignty and the demands of human security. It is difficult to overstate the extent to which the Westphalian system of sovereign independent states dominated the thinking of the UN's founders, permeated the structure and processes of the institution they created, and has impacted on the thinking of the legions of new states which have joined the UN, first during decolonisation and then with the end of the Cold War: sovereignty thus hard won, and proudly enjoyed, is sovereignty not easily relinquished or compromised. But it is also difficult to overstate the extent to which, in the modern globalised age, there is not only diminished competence in states to deal by themselves with the extraordinary problems and threats which affect them, but diminished tolerance for states being immune from scrutiny when they are unwilling or unable to deal with large-scale, conscience-shocking violations of individual and group human rights occurring within their borders.

The rapid evolution of the concept of 'the responsibility to protect' as a way of bridging the divide between these two views of the world is one of the most fascinating stories in recent intellectual history, and Thakur – very much a player himself in that story – tells it well. The idea, in a nutshell, is that sovereignty is as much about responsibility as the exercise of authority; that sovereign states have the primary responsibility to protect their own people from serious harm; that if they are unable or unwilling to exercise that responsibility it shifts to the wider international community; and that the international community's responsibility in these circumstances, to be exercised with maximum restraint but as forcefully as ultimately proves necessary, extends very much to prevention as well and, in the event of coercive intervention, to subsequent societal reconstruction. 'The responsibility to protect' is an idea of very much more than purely intellectual or academic relevance: many hundreds of thousands, perhaps millions, of lives may depend in future upon its acceptance. And it is an idea whose time has clearly come in many parts of the world – not least sub-Saharan Africa, which has suffered far more in recent times from international neglect than unwelcome engagement. But, as the author makes clear, it is one against which rearguard action can be expected to be fought, and for which forces are going to have to be rallied, for a long time yet.

There could be few persons better qualified in the world to write about all this than Ramesh Thakur. As an Indian who has researched and taught in Australia, New Zealand, Japan, Europe and the USA, and as a policy adviser to governments and international organisations, a distinguished scholar and highly articulate and visible media commentator, his personal and professional identity is, as he notes himself, 'at the intersection of East and West, North and South, and of international relations scholarship and the international policy community'. He writes, moreover, with eloquence, conviction and passion, nowhere more intensely than when describing the inequities, injustices, imbalances and institutional inadequacies of the world as it is seen by its largely voiceless majority. His analysis is often dense and multilayered, but – written from the heart as well as the head – is never dry and bloodless.

Thakur – like so many of us trying to make the world a fairer, better and above all more secure place for all its peoples – both loves and despairs of the United Nations. While this book gives us plenty of grounds for continuing to do both, its basic message, and argument, is one of optimism: new norms are emerging, new ways of thinking and acting to protect human security and to properly channel the use of force. Painfully slow and frustrating as the process may be, we are learning lessons, and gradually making progress. This book shows how and why that is happening, while also making clear how far yet there is to go. For those not only trying to understand the past and present, but to shape the future, it is eminently worth reading.

Gareth Evans
President and CEO of the International Crisis Group and former
Foreign Minister of Australia
Brussels, August 2005

ACKNOWLEDGEMENTS

I am grateful for help and helpful comments on earlier drafts of various chapters to Marrack Goulding, Ian Johnstone, Andrew Mack, David Malone, Edward Newman, John Ruggie, Shashi Tharoor and Danilo Turk, as well as to the anonymous readers for Cambridge University Press. John Haslam of the Press was wonderful to work with from start to end, and I am thankful for that.

I would also like to thank Stefano Caporaletti for assistance in collecting, collating and tabulating information on staff positions in the UN Secretariat and Department of Peacekeeping Operations; Elsje Fourie and Jasja Vander Zijde for helping out with exemplary efficiency and an accompanying smile in searching for research material and missing citation details; and Chifumi Mizutani for professional secretarial assistance. I am grateful to Hans van Ginkel, Rector of the United Nations University, for his commitment to the United Nations and dedication to academic values in a combination that has been an inspiration to the rest of us, and to my colleagues at UNU who have indulged me in the many discussions we have had on world issues big and small over eight years. Griffith University provided me with a Visiting Fellowship that helped during the final stages of revisions of the book. Finally, and most importantly, my love and appreciation to Bernadette, who has had to put up yet again with the crazed working habits of a demented academic that are so disrespectful of domestic life. Especially as, in this case, this book was written essentially after hours in my own time.

Introduction

I believe that we must embrace the responsibility to protect, and, when necessary, we must act on it.[1]

Created from the ashes of the Second World War with the Allies determined to prevent a repeat of Adolf Hitler's horrors, the United Nations for most of its existence has focused far more on external aggression than internal mass killings. Yet Nazi Germany was guilty of both. Unlike aggression against other countries, the systematic and large-scale extermination of Jews was a new horror. As the above quote from Secretary-General Kofi Annan suggests, the organisation is at long last elevating the doctrine of preventing mass atrocities against people to the same level of collective responsibility as preventing and repelling armed aggression against states. That journey is the theme of this book. Both sets of responsibility require judgements on when, how and how much force to use. This provides the leitmotif of my narrative: the procedural norm which emphasises multilateral forums and approaches for making the decision to use force, the substantive reasons justifying the recourse to force, and the manner in which both these embedded norms have come under pressure in recent times.

The second strand in my narrative is the distinction between legality and legitimacy. According to the Secretary-General's High-Level Panel on Threats, Challenges and Change, 'The maintenance of world peace and security depends importantly on there being a common global understanding, and acceptance, of when the application of force is both legal and legitimate.'[2] An international community exists to the extent that

---

[1] Kofi A. Annan, *In Larger Freedom: Towards Development, Security and Human Rights for All*. Report of the Secretary-General (New York: United Nations, document A/59/2005, 21 March 2005), para. 135.

[2] High-Level Panel on Threats, Challenges and Change, *A More Secure World: Our Shared Responsibility* (New York: United Nations, A/59/565, December 2004), para. 184.

there is a shared understanding of what constitutes legitimate behaviour. The growing gulf between lawful and legitimate use of force is evidence therefore of an erosion of the sense of international community.

To the extent that the material capacity to deploy and use force at various trouble spots around the world is concentrated in the United States while the authority to do so is legally vested in the UN Security Council (UNSC), the third strand concerns the US–UN relationship which is the central dynamic in much of the substantive discussion in the remaining chapters.

Part of the tension in UN–US relations arises from the American desire to use the organisation to prescribe justice within borders, to reach deep into the domestic jurisdictions of other states, while preserving the status quo order among states. But many developing countries reverse the priority and wish to use the UN as the forum in which to bring greater justice in relations among nations while privileging the status quo-oriented order within states.[3] The industrial–developing countries divide provides the fourth undercurrent of analysis throughout the book.

The fifth and final strand in the fabric of my analysis is the central importance of the rule of law, and hence of a rules-based order centred on the United Nations, as the foundation of a civilised state of international relations.[4]

Established to provide predictability and order in a world in constant flux, the United Nations – a bridge between power and principles, between state-based realism and universal idealism – is at once the symbol of humanity's collective aspirations for a better life in a safer world for all, a forum for negotiating the terms of converting the collective aspirations into a common programme of action and the principal international instrument for the realisation of the aspirations and the implementation of the plans. On balance, the world has been a better and safer place with the UN than would have been the case without it.

Its primary purpose is the maintenance of international peace and security. The incidence of war in human society is as pervasive as the wish for peace is universal. The use of force and the possibility of controlling it and so controlling others has preoccupied the minds of

---

[3] Mohammed Ayoob, 'Humanitarian Intervention and State Sovereignty', *International Journal of Human Rights* 6:1 (Spring 2002), pp. 98–9.

[4] For a statement of this by a distinguished UN elder statesman, see Lakhdar Brahimi, *The Rule of Law at Home and Abroad*. The 2002 Dag Hammarskjöld Lecture (Uppsala: Dag Hammarskjöld Foundation, 2002).

rulers and scholars alike since time immemorial. But so too have some of the most charismatic and influential personalities in human history reflected on the renunciation of force and the possibility of eliminating it from human relationships. The twentieth century captured the paradox only too well. On the one hand, we tried to emplace increasing normative, legislative and operational fetters on the right of states to go to war. Yet the last century turned out to be the most murderous in human history, with more dead than in all previous wars of the past two thousand years put together.

Just three years into the new century, the Iraq War roiled the UN-centred world of diplomacy as few other issues have since 1945. At the heart of the dispute was not Iraq, nor even Saddam Hussein, but the nature and exercise of American power. No one disputed the abhorrent nature of Saddam Hussein's regime, but many questioned the circumstances governing the use of force. The fragility of post-invasion Iraq confirmed that it is easier to wage war without UN blessing than it is to win the peace – but victory in war is pointless without a resulting secure peace. The crisis highlighted the urgent need for a new institutional framework and vision that can marry prudent anticipatory self-defence against imminent threats to the centuries-old dream of a world where force is put to the service of law that protects the innocent without shielding the criminals.

The evolution of institutions of international governance has lagged behind the rapid emergence of collective problems. The intergovernmental institutions that collectively underpin global governance are insufficient in number, inadequately resourced and sometimes incoherent in their separate policies and philosophies. The *problématique* of global security governance is the disconnect between the distribution of authority within existing international intergovernmental institutions, which is still fragmented and based on the assumption of a multipolar structure, and the international distribution of military power which is increasingly concentrated in just one pole.

The basis of world order has come under increasing strain in recent years due to seven major disconnects:

1. The gap between the exalted expectations of what the UN can accomplish and the modest resources given to it;
2. The growing disconnect between the threats to peace and security, and the obstacles to economic development, lying increasingly within rather than between states;

3. The persistence of policy authority and the requisite resources for tackling problems being vested in states, while the source and scope of the problems are increasingly global and require the globalisation of the process of policy-making;
4. The greater recognition given to individuals as both subjects and objects of international relations;
5. The growing gravity of threats rooted in non-state actors;
6. The growing salience of weapons of mass destruction (WMD) that, in their reach and destructiveness, challenge the basis of the territorial state and which, when acquired by non-state actors, have democratised some of the most potent means of using violence;
7. The strategic disconnect between the distribution of military, political and economic power in the real world, and the distribution of decision-making authority in the artificially constructed world of intergovernmental organisations. The most acute manifestation of this is the growing disparity between the soft as well as hard power of the USA and that of all others.

Thus the crisis over Iraq can be viewed as a symptom of underlying seismic shifts in world politics. It was doubly damaging. In the countries that waged war on Saddam Hussein, the UN was bitterly attacked for failing to give international blessing to the effort to end over a decade's defiance of world will by a particularly brutal regime. In the many more countries that opposed the war, the UN was seen as having betrayed its most fundamental of all mandates: to stop wars of aggression, particularly by major powers against small states.

The book begins with an account of the growth of international organisation, the UN's origins and nature and the conceptual roots of pacific settlement and collective security as the main instruments for the maintenance of international peace and security. The shortcomings and failures of pacific settlement and collective security were the backdrop to the emergence of a new form of international activity that came to be called peacekeeping. This too metamorphosed under the impact of changing circumstances and requirements over the decades. Not surprisingly, the most delicate and critical element in UN peace operations was the relationship between the international organisation and the dominant international power, which is taken up for discussion in chapter 2.

The UN has also been the natural home for the evolving concept of human security which links the two major items of development and security on the agenda of the global policy community. Yet this has also brought to the fore tensions – sometimes dormant, at others only too apparent, but always inherent and intrinsic to the nature of the UN – between a number of competing principles and interests: realpolitik and idealism, force and diplomacy, power and justice, efficiency and legitimacy, enforcement mandate and humanitarian agenda, wealth and equity, and so on. These comprise the substance of the discussion in Part II of the book from chapters 3–6.

The nuclear breakout by India and Pakistan in 1998, the threats of nuclear proliferation in the Middle East and the Korean Peninsula and the terrorist attacks of 11 September 2001 (9/11) put the issues of hard security back on the international agenda. So too did the examples of horrific slaughter of large numbers of people by state-sponsored killers or in conditions of state collapse and the resulting 'challenge of humanitarian intervention'. To the extent that 'rogue regimes' and non-state actors could credibly pursue the acquisition of WMD, individual states as well as the international community collectively had to confront familiar policy dilemmas with a new sense of urgency. Specifically, is the existing normative architecture of world order – at the policy, structural and operational levels – adequate to cope with the new threats? Does the fracturing of the international consensus reflect sharply and irretrievably diverging interests, priorities and preferences among the major groups of countries? Or is there a greater community of views and interests among 'We the peoples of the world' than among the member governments of the UN? These contested issues are discussed in Part III, chapters 7–12. Of these, chapters 11 and 12 are insider accounts of the work and report of the International Commission on Intervention and State Sovereignty (ICISS) and of southern perspectives on the rebalancing of the norms of sovereignty and international intervention.

In the final part of the book, chapters 13–14, I return to look at some of the critical institutional aspects of the UN system, specifically, reforms of the Secretariat, UNSC and General Assembly (GA), and the role of the Secretary-General (SG). Once again, changing context, norms, balance-of-power relations and state practice are reflected in the demands for and obstacles to reform, in the disillusionment and disenchantment with the UN on the one hand, but equally also in the continuing expectations and hopes of it on the other.

Authority, power, legitimacy

This book is not meant as a primer on the UN system. There are plenty of very good books which introduce readers to the structures, institutions and processes of the UN system with varying degrees of brevity and detail and differing degrees of sophistication of analysis and commentary. Rather, my purpose in this book is to explore the United Nations as the principal site of engagement with the great debates and controversies of the day on the issues of peace and security. The book has been completed at a time when the principle of multilateralism and the manifestations of a multilateral world order centred on the UN are under serious scrutiny. The organisation and structure of the book reflect my belief that the evolution of the UN as the principal provider of international security reflects the interplay of changing norms and state practice at this critical crossroads of world politics. The book is thus an attempt to delve into some of the major cross-cutting controversies of our times through the UN lens. Has the organisation been a central or peripheral player; what have been its strengths and shortcomings; how do we account for its successes and failures? After all, it was founded in the belief that our collective destiny is tied to its being the site for the convergence of national interests, for a congruence between interests and ideals and for the locus of diplomacy which protects the individual interests of member states while promoting global norms and values underpinning a community of states and an international society.

Inis Claude argued four decades ago that one of the UN's major political functions was collective legitimisation: 'the world organization has come to be regarded, and used, as a dispenser of politically significant approval and disapproval of the claims, policies, and actions of states.'[5] Power is the capacity simply to enforce a particular form of behaviour. Authority signifies the capacity to create and enforce rights and obligations which are accepted as legitimate and binding by members of an all-inclusive society who are subject to the authority. Authority, even when associated with power or force, necessarily connotes legitimacy; that is, authority is distinct from power to the extent that it entails acceptance of right by those to whom it is applied. While lawful authority remains vested in the UN, power has become increasingly concentrated in the USA. The brute fact is that today and in the foreseeable future

[5] Inis L. Claude, *The Changing United Nations* (New York: Random House, 1967), p. 73.

only the USA has the capacity to project power around the globe and only one standing military defence organisation, the North Atlantic Treaty Organisation (NATO), has the capacity to undertake out-of-area operations. Questions of the lawfulness and legitimacy of overseas military action by individual or groups of states in practice therefore means the USA, NATO, or coalitions of the willing with them at the core.

Ian Hurd distinguishes between coercion, self-interest and legitimacy as alternative grounds for rule obedience and argues that, precisely because there is no international government to enforce them, states' compliance with international rules is a function of the legitimacy of those rules *as perceived by the norm-conforming states*.[6] That is, they are regarded as proper or appropriate by the actors to whom they are addressed within a socially constructed system of values and beliefs. Moreover, rules internalised as legitimate, either because of the source or the procedure by which they were constituted, help to define the actors' self-interest. This in turn makes them an efficient mode of social control as habitual compliance becomes the norm and non-compliance is abnormal and deviant. If the source of legitimacy is institutions (either formal organisations or recurring and stable patterns of behaviour), then those institutions indicate the existence of an international authority even in the absence of world government. For 'the international system clearly exhibits some kind of order in which patterns repeat, institutions accrete, and practices are stable'.[7] Thus in 1994, Japan opposed the imposition of sanctions on North Korea for its clandestine nuclear programme, yet publicly stated its willingness to abide by a sanctions regime if instituted by the UNSC. That is, Japan was openly acknowledging the legitimacy of the UNSC as the source of international authority even with respect to decisions in which Japan did not have a vote and the impact of which would be more direct on Japan than on most states making the decision.[8]

---

[6] Ian Hurd, 'Legitimacy and Authority in International Politics', *International Organization* 53:2 (Spring 1999), pp. 379–408. For example, Hurd notes that many borders are undefended and indefensible, such as Canada's with the USA. Coercion or the fear of retribution is inadequate to explain US restraint in not taking over Canada. Nor does one find a continual calculation and recalculation by states of the costs and benefits of conquest as would be predicted by a rational self-interest model. Instead there is a 'taken-for-grantedness' of borders as a whole. Revisionist actors are and are seen as dangerous 'rogues' by others precisely because they approximate the self-interested model. Ibid., pp. 395–8.

[7] Ibid., p. 400.   [8] Ibid., p. 402.

The twentieth century brought many efforts to broaden the base of the institutions responsible for speaking with the authoritative voice of international society. The League of Nations and the United Nations represent the two major attempts to rationalise the institutional means for allocating international values authoritatively. The UN seeks to replace the balance of power with a community of power and represents the dream of a world ruled by reason. It is the means of outlawing war and mobilising the collective will of the world community to deter, apprehend and punish international law-breakers. 'When democrats disagree on substance, they need to agree on process', writes Michael Ignatieff.[9] UN decisions command authority because they are the outcome of an international political process of the assertion and reconciliation of national interests. It is the political process which authenticates UN resolutions and converts them into authoritative prescriptions for the common good of humanity. The UN was meant to be the framework within which members of the international system negotiated agreements on the rules of behaviour and the legal norms of proper conduct in order to preserve the society of states. Thus simultaneously the UN was to be the forum for mediating power relationships, accomplishing political change that is held to be just and desirable by the international community, promulgating new norms and conferring the stamp of collective legitimacy.

These tasks acquired particular urgency in the revolutionary conditions after the Second World War. The new power relationships were untested, revulsion against old-style management of power relationships remained strong even while the sobering experience of the interwar years had tempered the idealism associated with the League experiment, colonialism was physically on the retreat and politically on the defensive, and the incipient and inchoate sense of one interdependent community was heightened under the impact of the technological revolution in weapons of mass destruction, exploitation of the earth's resources and increasing ability to gauge ecological fragility and monitor ecological sensitivity.

Attempts to *enforce* authority can only be made by the legitimate agents of that authority. What distinguishes rule enforcement by criminal

---

[9] Michael Ignatieff, *The Lesser Evil: Political Ethics in an Age of Terror* (Princeton: Princeton University Press, 2004), p. viii.

thugs from that by police officers is the principle of legitimacy. The concept of legitimacy therefore acts as the connecting link between the exercise of authority and the recourse to power. As power reinforces legitimacy, so legitimacy expands power by buttressing its position and rendering its exercise more effective.

The UN is the only truly global institution of a general purpose which approximates universality. The size of UN voting majorities and the forcefulness of the language used are important because of the political significance attached to its perception as the closest we are able to get to an authentic voice of humanity. The role of custodian of collective legitimacy enables the UN, through its resolutions, to articulate authoritative standards of state behaviour.

For the UN to function effectively as a law-enforcing collective security organisation, states must accept two propositions regarding their own abilities to dispose of power. First, they must renounce the unilateral use of force for national purposes but, second, they must be prepared to use force on behalf of, as directed by and for the goals of the UN. The refusal of states to repudiate all possible national resort to force forecloses the possibility of the UN exercising sole international coercive authority.

In recent times, the pivotal problem is what action is permitted when no action is taken by the Security Council? Great powers play particular roles both in relations with one another and in relations between themselves and the lesser powers. Mutually, they help to promote order by preserving the general balance of power, controlling crises and containing wars; unequally, they exploit their preponderance over lesser states by unilateral intervention, tacit respect of one another's spheres of influence and concerted action. Great powers claim and are granted the right to a determining role in issues of world peace and security; but also they are burdened by the corresponding duty to modify national policies in the light of international managerial responsibilities. Permanent membership of the Security Council consecrated the special position of the five major powers in the UN scheme of helping to shape and safeguard international peace. The veto clause conferred the further competence upon the great powers to protect international encroachments upon their own vital interests. In return, as part of their obligations towards a responsible management of international order, the great powers agreed to eschew unilateral resort to force in favour of concerted action through the UN system.

Ideas and norms as drivers of policy

The debate over when and how force may be used in today's world lies at the intersection of law, politics and norms. As the worldwide turmoil in 2003 over the decision by the United States, Britain and Australia to wage war on Saddam Hussein showed, the UN is the forum of choice for debating and deciding on collective action requiring the use of military force. Similarly, contrary to popular belief, it also has been the principal forum for the progressive advancement of the human rights agenda in its totality, including group-based social, economic and cultural rights as well as individual civil and political rights.

Ideas matter and institutions matter as conduits for ideas.[10] In the broad sweep of history, empires rise and fall, kings and queens come and go. They are remembered only if they leave behind ideas, embedded in institutions or practices, for improved governance or quality of life. Ideas impart vitality to a society. A society in intellectual ferment is fertile ground for progress and advancement, provided the clash of ideas is given free play. Conversely, a society that is bereft of and represses new ideas is a society doomed to stagnation. Ideas are influential if they have strong theoretical foundations and clear policy application. The support of powerful rulers and countries helps.

Gradually over the course of the last century the idea of an international community bound together by shared values, benefits and responsibilities, and common rules and procedures, took hold of peoples' imagination. The UN is the institutional expression of that development. But, unlike the situation within countries where different political parties and civic groups can compete for public attention and political office in order to convert their contested ideas into public policy,[11] there is no world government at the international level. The UN is not run by world parliamentarians elected by the people on the basis of competing policy platforms.

How then to ensure that the clash of ideas for international security and global welfare is turned into a productive contest over international

---

[10] See Daniel Philpott, *Revolutions in Sovereignty: How Ideas Shaped Modern International Relations* (Princeton: Princeton University Press, 2001).

[11] For an example of this at the continental level with regard to the new constitution for Europe, see the three articles on one day in the *International Herald Tribune* (*IHT*), 26 May 2005: Daniel Cohn-Bendit, 'The EU constitution I: A dangerous game in France'; François Heisbourg, 'The EU constitution II: Après "non," le déluge'; and Dominique Moïsi, 'The EU constitution III: Handing the 21st century to Asia'.

public policy? One answer has been to look to 'blue ribbon' international commissions as a means of leveraging emerging new ideas into generally accepted global norms. Such commissions can be a catalyst to register norm shifts and convert them into international public policy.[12]

Human beings operate in a world of scarcity with non-identical preferences. Therefore, choices have to be made. Rules, norms and laws help to simplify choices, to impart 'rationality' by specifying the factors that must be taken into account in the process of coming to a decision through deliberation and reflection. Human beings are social actors; norms are essential to the functioning and existence of society; therefore social interaction is viewed through normative lenses. Moreover, laws and norms do not just shape decisions; the language of norms and laws permits human beings to pursue goals, challenge assertions and justify actions.[13]

A norm can be defined statistically to mean the pattern of behaviour that is most common or usual; that is, to refer to the 'normal curve': a widely *prevalent pattern of behaviour.* Or it can be defined ethically, to mean a pattern of behaviour that should be followed in accordance with a given value system; that is, to refer to the moral code of a society: a generally accepted *standard of proper behaviour.*[14] Norms are standards of appropriate behaviour; rules are specific applications of norms to particular situations, either prescribing or proscribing action to conform with the norm.

The most effective form of behaviour regulation is for complete convergence between laws and norms, for example with regard to murder. In international relations, epochal shifts in the generally accepted standards of state behaviour mean that such institutions as slavery and colonialism, common enough in earlier eras, are today proscribed in law. Conversely, the most problematic situation is when there is near-total dissonance, as with dowry and caste in India. The reason for the dissonance lies primarily in different moral frameworks of social behaviour. At the international level, one of the most likely arenas for normative

---

[12] See Ramesh Thakur, Andrew F. Cooper and John English, eds., *International Commissions and the Power of Ideas* (Tokyo: United Nations University Press, 2005).

[13] Friedrich V. Kratochwil, *Rules, Norms, and Decisions: On the Conditions of Practical and Legal Reasoning in International Relations and Domestic Affairs* (Cambridge: Cambridge University Press, 1989), pp. 10–11.

[14] The definition of a *norm* isolates a single standard of behaviour, whereas *institutions* emphasise a collection of rules and practices and do not capture the 'oughtness' of the norm definition.

dissonance is that of human rights, precisely because of alternative moral frameworks that define and locate the rights and responsibilities of individuals, community and state vis-à-vis one another.

In constructivist theories, norms shape both the goals of states (the construction of state interests) and the means employed to achieve those goals. The total range of behaviour that may be possible is wider than the range of behaviour that is conceivable in any social system; norms act as a 'cognitive energy-saver' in narrowing the total range of behaviour to manageable limits.[15] 'Shared ideas, expectations, and beliefs about appropriate behaviour are what give the world structure, order, and stability.' Moreover, 'In an ideational international structure, idea shifts and norm shifts are the main vehicles for system transformation.'[16] Just as the realist is interested in changes in the distribution of capabilities in order to explain system change, so the ideational theorist is interested in norm shifts in order to understand system change.

Collective norms constitute the social identity of actors while simultaneously constituting the rules of the game for regulating their social behaviour. The principle of sovereignty defines what a state is. The norm of non-intervention, a logical corollary of that principle, helps to regulate the interactions of states in international relations. Similarly, human rights norms increasingly constitute a 'civilised' state in contemporary international society while regulating the matrix of citizen–state interaction. The human rights norm has also encroached increasingly on the non-intervention norm. Despite that, the definition of the state still entails a necessary reference to the notion of sovereignty.[17]

We still do not have adequate conceptual tools and empirical research for a theory of international norms: how they emerge, are diffused globally, consolidated to the point of being internalised by members of the international society and embedded in international institutions. Nor is there agreement on who can legitimately claim to articulate or pinpoint 'global' norms. The crucial question is how contested norms become institutionalised both within and among nations and the interactive dynamics of the process of institutionalisation. International

---

[15] Ann Florini, 'The Evolution of International Norms', *International Studies Quarterly* 40:3 (September 1996), p. 366.

[16] Martha Finnemore and Kathryn Sikkink, 'International Norm Dynamics and Political Change', *International Organization* 52:4 (Autumn 1998), p. 894.

[17] Thomas Risse, '"Let's Argue!": Communicative Action in World Politics', *International Organization* 54:1 (Winter 2000), p. 5.

norms can be transmitted down into national politics through incorporation into domestic laws or into the policy preferences of political leaders through elite learning. By definition, collective norms are shared standards of behaviour. How many actors of a group must share a norm before we can call it a group norm? How many countries must share a norm before it is a global norm?

Finnemore and Sikkink postulate a three-stage life-cycle of norms: the emergence of a new norm and its advocacy by a norm entrepreneur; norm cascade when agreement among a critical mass of actors on an emergent norm creates a tipping point; and norm internalisation so that it becomes taken for granted and norm-conforming behaviour is routinised, requiring no further justification.[18] The UN provides an organisational platform for advocacy in the first stage, the forum of choice for cascade in the second, and the forum of choice for seeking affirmation, reaffirmation and compliance in the third and final stage.

In the first stage, human agency is critical. For norm advocacy to occur, an actor – the would-be entrepreneur – must have strong notions about appropriate standards of behaviour by fellow-actors in an inclusive social or political community and a strongly developed sense of dissatisfaction about existing standards of international behaviour. Norm entrepreneurs in international affairs – Henri Dunant for the norm of international humanitarian law, Peter Benenson for the human rights norm, Raphael Lemkin for the norm against genocide – spot gaps in the existing normative architecture of world order and engage in moral proselytism in order to fill those gaps. They use organisational platforms – including standing organisations, in particular the UN, but also ad hoc transnational and trans-actor coalitions – from which to launch their crusades; they frame issues by using powerfully resonant language and metaphor; and they lobby state actors for institutionalising the new norm in international law, in the rules of multilateral organisations, and in national foreign policies.

Norman Frolich and Joe Oppenheimer write of 'a coordinator of expectations', a political entrepreneur who coordinates the expectations of all members regarding the probable actions of all others.[19] Classical diplomacy was about national power in international relations: its location, bases, exercise by, of and for states, and distributional impact on

[18] Finnemore and Sikkink, 'International Norm Dynamics and Political Change'.
[19] Quoted in Raino Malnes, '"Leader" and "Entrepreneur" in International Negotiations', *European Journal of International Relations* 1:1 (March 1995), p. 90.

relations between states. New diplomacy is much more fundamentally about authority: its location and sources, its channelling into international norms and regimes, its exercise by states for the people, and distributional impact on the welfare and security of people. This is why norm entrepreneurship is such a useful asset in the new diplomacy of the twenty-first century.

International law as we know it was a product of the European states system and international humanitarian law too has its roots essentially in Europe. In the age of colonialism, most Afro-Asians and Latin Americans became the victims of Western superiority in the organisation and weaponry of warfare. The danger since the end of the Cold War is that they could continue to be the objects but not the authors of norms and laws that are supposedly international.[20] But a world order in which developing countries are norm-takers and law-takers while Westerners are the norm- and law-setters, interpreters and enforcers will not be viable because the division of labour is based neither on comparative advantage nor on equity. The risk is under-appreciated because the international discourse in turn is dominated by Western, in particular Anglo-American, scholarship.[21] The net result of this, in turn, is that the bulk of scholarly analyses and discourse 'privilege the experience, interests, and contemporary dilemmas of a certain portion of the society of states at the expense of . . . the large majority of states'.[22]

The changing world context

On 1 May 2004, with the entry of ten fresh members from what used to be Eastern Europe in the Cold War era, the European Union grew to a total of twenty-five countries. The single European project in its original manifestations (the European Coal and Steel Community, the European Economic Community and then the European Union) had put paid, through innovative and symbolic pan-European institutions, to the old

---

[20] See Ramesh Thakur, 'Global Norms and International Humanitarian Law: An Asian Perspective', *International Review of the Red Cross* 83:841 (March 2001), pp. 19–44.

[21] See Ersel Aydinli and Julie Mathews, 'Are the Core and Periphery Irreconcilable? The Curious World of Publishing in Contemporary International Relations', *International Studies Perspectives* 1:3 (December 2000), pp. 289–303.

[22] Mohammed Ayoob, 'Inequality and Theorising in International Relations: The Case for Subaltern Realism', *International Studies Review* 4:3 (Fall 2002), p. 29. For a rejoinder to the charge of theoretical imperialism, see Michael Barnett, 'Radical Chic? Subaltern Realism: A Rejoinder', ibid., pp. 49–62.

Europe of constantly warring states. Embedding the former satellite states of Eastern Europe into the European structures of continental governance and value systems is an equally remarkable burial of the continent's Cold War rivalries in the graveyard of history.

In the same week, on 6 May, a new audiotape, purportedly from Osama bin Laden himself, offered a bounty of 10 kg of gold each for the assassination of US President George W. Bush, the US head of the Coalition Provisional Authority in Iraq Paul Bremer, Kofi Annan and his special envoy to Iraq Lakhdar Brahimi.[23] One reading of this is to conclude that in the eyes of the resistance to foreign occupation, the UN had become just a handmaiden to US imperialism. An alternative interpretation is that the bounty was proof that the UN does indeed matter. One does not offer costly rewards to kill the chief and agents of an irrelevant organisation.

The enlargement of Europe and the bounty on offer are but two, albeit deeply symbolic, demonstrations of how the world has changed profoundly and fundamentally – in ways both good and bad – since the birth of the UN. The issues and preoccupations of the new millennium present new and different types of challenges from those of 1945. With the new realities and challenges have come corresponding new expectations for action and new standards of conduct in national and international affairs. The number of actors in world affairs has grown enormously, the types of actors have changed very substantially, the interactions between them have grown more dense and intense and the agenda of international public policy has been altered quite dramatically in line with the changing temper of the times.

The business of the world has changed almost beyond recognition over the last century. The locus of power and influence is shifting. When the UN was founded, its membership consisted of fifty-one states. Today it stands at 191. Alongside the growth in the number of states there has occurred the rise of civil society actors who have mediated state–citizen relations and given flesh and blood to the concept of 'We the peoples of the world'. The international policy-making stage is increasingly congested as private and public non-state actors jostle alongside national governments in setting and implementing the agenda of the new century.

The new actors have brought a wide range of new voices, perspectives, interests, experiences, priorities, concerns and aspirations. They have

---

[23] CNN News (www.cnn.com), 6 May 2004.

added depth and texture to the increasingly rich tapestry of international society and brought important institutional credibility and practical expertise to the policy debates. This has been especially valuable in the post-Cold War context with a new emphasis on democratisation, human rights and good governance. The revolution in information technology has heightened awareness of conflicts and disasters wherever they may be occurring with compelling visual images of the resultant suffering. This makes it possible to mobilise humanitarian assistance for rescue, relief, assistance and reconstruction in real time.

The number of armed conflicts rose steadily until the end of the Cold War, peaked in the early 1990s, but has declined since then (figure 1). The nature of armed conflict has also changed (figure 2). Until the First World War, war was an institution of the states system, with distinctive rules, etiquette, norms and stable patterns of practices.[24] In recent times the line between war as a political act and organised criminality has become increasingly blurred. The weakness of state structures and institutions in many countries has heightened the challenges and risks of nation-building and sometimes tempted armed groups to try to seize the levers of political power in order to exploit the resources of economic wealth, including 'conflict diamonds'. Internal conflicts are made more complex and lethal by modern technology and communications, and in particular by the proliferation of cheap, highly destructive small arms. Violence becomes a way of life with catastrophic consequences for civilians caught in the crossfire.

Moreover, few modern conflicts are purely internal. The networks that sustain them can involve a range of ancillary problems like trafficking in arms, drugs and children; terrorism; and refugee flows. Whole regions can be quickly destabilised. Sometimes the rich world is deeply implicated. Civil conflicts are fuelled by arms and monetary transfers that originate in the developed world, and in turn their destabilising effects are felt in the developed world in everything from globally interconnected terrorism to refugee flows, the export of drugs and the spread of infectious disease and organised crime. With '9/11' we saw elements of conceptual confusion between traditional security, challenges to state sovereignty and the threats of terrorism from 'rogue' actors, including non-state actors with access to WMD.

---

[24] See Kal J. Holsti, *War, the State, and the State of War* (Cambridge: Cambridge University Press, 1996).

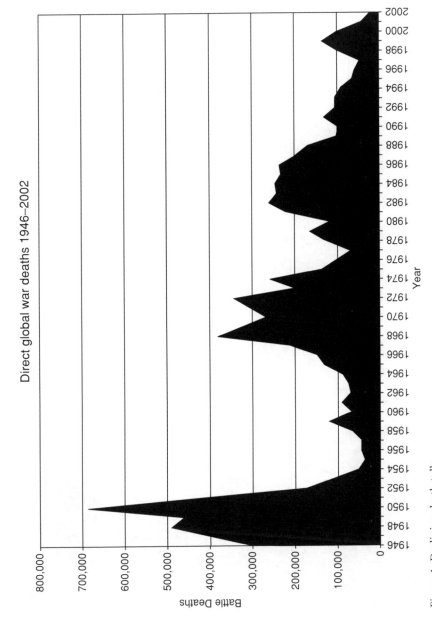

Direct global war deaths 1946–2002

Figure 1. Declining death tolls.

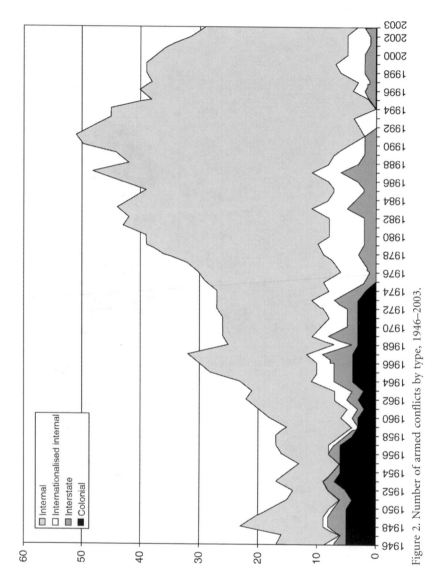

Figure 2. Number of armed conflicts by type, 1946–2003.

Reflecting the conviction that the use of force under international auspices may sometimes be necessary even in the cause of peace, chapter 7
of the UN Charter spells out many provisions in relation to collective
enforcement. Yet one of the lessons of recent times is that the UN is
not good at waging wars. By contrast, the organisation has been especially good at a slow, steady and unremitting but unglamorous effort to
find political, economic, legal and institutional alternatives to military
force as a way of tackling problems of security as well as development,
good governance and environmental protection. This ambitious project
of international institution building is far from complete. The organising principle of global governance is multilateralism, and the UN lies
at the very core of the multilateral system of global governance –
governance without global government. According to Anne-Marie
Slaughter, the glue binding the contemporary system of global governance is governing networks, both horizontal and vertical. Horizontal
networks link counterpart national officials across borders, such as
police investigators or financial regulators. Vertical networks are relationships between national officials and supranational organisations to
which they have ceded authority, such as the European Court of
Justice. The world needs global governance to combat problems without passports. Most people fear the idea of a centralised, all-powerful
world government. The solution lies in strengthening existing networks
and developing new ones that could create a genuine global rule of law
without centralised global institutions.[25]

The system of collective security proved illusory from the start and
the procedures for resolving disputes peacefully have also proven to be
generally elusive. The major UN contribution to peace and security
during the Cold War took the form of consensual peacekeeping operations. After the Cold War, this expanded to multidimensional peace
operations to reflect the more demanding complex humanitarian emergencies. In the meantime, however, the human rights and human security agenda had greatly expanded and in the 1990s was often expressed in
the form of the so-called challenge of humanitarian intervention. Increasing use was made also of sanctions as an instrument of international
statecraft. The UNSC was revitalised with the end of the Cold War, with a
jump in the number of resolutions (especially under the enforcement
chapter 7 of the UN Charter), peacekeeping missions (figure 3) and

---

[25]   Anne-Marie Slaughter, *A New World Order* (Princeton: Princeton University Press, 2004).

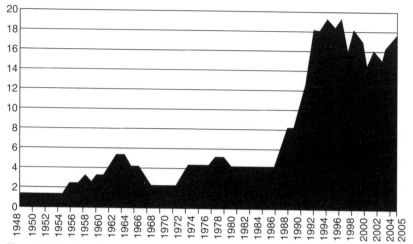

Figure 3. Number of UN peacekeeping missions, 1946–2005.

sanctions regimes, and an accompanying fall in the use of the veto by the permanent members.[26]

Often, the developing countries found themselves scrambling to resist, typically in UN forums, the fast-changing norms of humanitarian action and compulsory disarmament, even preemptive disarmament and regime change. At the same time, the rapid pace of events placed increased strains on the creaking UN system and intensified the urgency of demands for changes in the workings, structures and policy responses of the organisation. The frequent policy paralysis in the two major political organs, the Security Council and the General Assembly, also placed a premium on the political role of the Secretary-General.

This book brings together an account of these developments. It relies on a lifetime of professional studies of the UN system supplemented by an insider's perspective in recent years at the heart of some of the most important changes, including being not just Vice-Rector of the UN University, but also an ICISS Commissioner and the principal writer of the SG's second report on UN reforms. Thus, in part it is dispassionate

[26] Peter Wallensteen and Patrik Johansson, 'Security Council Decisions in Perspective', in David M. Malone, ed., *The UN Security Council: From the Cold War to the 21st Century* (Boulder: Lynne Rienner, 2004), pp. 22–7.

analysis, in part intellectual reflections,[27] in part a personal memoir. Underpinning it all is a strong normative commitment to the goals and principles of the UN and frustration with the procedural and political bottlenecks that impede its functioning and tarnish its reputation.

The book reflects my personal and professional identity at the intersection of West and East, North and South, and of International Relations scholarship and the international policy community.[28] With regard to the first and second, for example, while broadly committed to the notion of human rights that apply universally and should be embedded in international institutions, I also have some empathy and sympathy with many developing countries' charges of self-serving interpretation, selection and application of human rights norms by the powers-that-be. With respect to the third, much of the discussion in chapters dealing with some of the major contemporary controversies – Kosovo in 1999, Iraq in 2003, the threats of international terrorism and WMD, the issue of sanctions – draw on my experiences as a UN official and as an ICISS Commissioner, including its extensive outreach exercise and its follow-up activities. I have also been privileged to have had access to and to have engaged in discussions with national and international policy-makers at the highest levels from around the world, while being able to maintain active links with the global community of scholars and civil society representatives who inhabit a world less exalted but closer to everyday reality.

But does this matter? Do we really want to move to the equivalent of a quota system in scholarship and commentary? On one day in May 2004, one of the world's most influential international newspapers published three opinion articles on events in developing countries. All three were by Western authors.[29] Each by itself was of a very high quality, as one would expect from that newspaper. Nevertheless, it would be surprising to find that the paper had ever carried three opinion pieces on

---

[27] Many of the views expressed in the book have been published as newspaper op-ed articles over the past decade, in particular in the *Daily Yomiuri*, the *International Herald Tribune* and the *Japan Times*.

[28] Among other things, this might help in refraining from 'indulging the academic's tendency towards protracted definition'; Hugo Slim, *By What Authority? The Legitimacy and Accountability of Non-governmental Organisations* (Geneva: International Council on Human Rights Policy, 2002), p. 7.

[29] Philip Bowring, 'A Rural Protest is only part of India's upset', Gareth Evans, 'The world should be ready to intervene in Sudan' and R. S. O'Fahey, 'A Complex Ethnic Reality with a Long History', *IHT*, 15 May 2004.

the one day written by developing country authors but covering only affairs in Western countries. Or consider what in some ways is a more tragic example. A massive earthquake and tsunami struck southern Asia on 26 December 2004. In the three weeks following that, the *International Herald Tribune* published sixteen opinion articles on or in relation to the tragedy. Not one was by an Asian. The equally influential *Financial Times* published six articles, of which again not one was by an Asian.

This imbalance of voice in the international discourse has built up a dangerous sense of resentment by the silent majority of the world's peoples. Western commentators have their columns regularly reprinted in newspapers all over the world, which is good. Should Westerners not make a deliberate effort to read and listen to what the rest of the world might have to say? Or do we simply assume that if the rest of the world has a different opinion, they are wrong? The world-view and perspectives of Western governments, scholars and commentators changed dramatically after 9/11 with regard to the proper balance between hard and soft power, force and diplomacy, security and liberty, and unilateralism and multilateralism, compared to what their previous position had been, based on theoretical arguments rather than actual experience. There are times when, irritated by the tone of moral self-righteousness and the evident belief that one must be ethically challenged to question the need for urgent action by the powerful Western states, developing country people – even some sensitive, caring and reasonable people – ask: Who will save us from virtue run amok, from humanitarians clamouring for yet another war?[30] Hence the need to obtain a balance of points of view based on different backgrounds and formative experiences.

One final personal note. Before joining the United Nations, I was professor and head of the Peace Research Centre at the Australian National University in Canberra. The discussion in this book reflects not just an abiding commitment to the UN normative mandates, but also the perspective of the peace research community. The central problem for peace research is violence: the nature, causes, consequences, management and resolution of conflict. It seeks not just to understand violence, but to eliminate or tame it. Its task is to challenge the basic tenets of the conventional analyses of violence and offer critical alternatives.

---

[30] See Ramesh Thakur, 'Save Us From the Humanitarians for War', *Daily Yomiuri*, 9 September 2004.

At any given time, most of the countries in the world are ready to go to war if necessary. Yet most of them are also at peace and long to keep it so. Therein lies the key to the difference between peace research and strategic studies. As a general rule, strategic studies is infused with realist assumptions. International politics is seen as a struggle for power. The primary actors in world affairs are autonomous states engaged in power-maximising behaviour. National security is the ultimate and overriding goal and force is the principal instrument. In such a realist paradigm, violence is seen as endemic, inevitable and an instrument of conflict resolution. The task of strategic analysts is to predict courses of action that will enable states to maximise their own power while neutralising or minimising the national power of opponents so that the conflict is resolved on one's own terms and not on those of the enemy.

The distinct identity of the peace research community rests in the broader conceptions of 'peace' and 'violence'. Strategic studies accepts and refines the instrumentality of violence; peace research questions and rejects it. Peace research changes focus from the state downwards to individuals and upwards to the international community. Strategic studies focuses on the successful use of violence; peace research is concerned to reduce the frequency of latent and manifest use of force by human beings. For strategic studies, the most critical lesson of the interwar period (1919–39) is that pacifism and appeasement do not work against the Hitlers of the world. Few peace researchers would dispute this. But most would point to the injustice and inequity of the Treaty of Versailles and the subsequent treatment of Germany from within the realist paradigm as having spawned the rise of Adolf Hitler in the first place. For an Indian strategic studies analyst, the key question on Kashmir is how best to secure the province against the threat from Pakistan. For a peace researcher, it is equally legitimate to ask how best to protect the people of Kashmir against killings by terrorists and extrajudicial killings by Indian security forces. The threats posed by the agents of the state – whether India, Pakistan, Serbia, Bosnia or any other country – to individual and group rights are conceptually alien to strategic studies. They are central to peace research.

During the Cold War, the logic of realist analyses produced policy prescriptions of containment of the evil empire through a sustained posture of armed strength. The peace research community grew in strength, conviction and numbers in opposition to the logic of confrontation. Its adherents argued that the adversarial approach to Cold War international relations intensified mutual antagonisms, fed the conventional and nuclear arms race and increased the probability of war by design or accident. The importance of peace research increased with the end of the Cold War as the definition of security broadened substantially to embrace non-traditional notions and threats like environmental degradation and human rights violations. These are issues that are better addressed within peace research than strategic studies paradigms.

Possibilities for the breakdown of peace exist everywhere and at all times. The task for strategic studies is to identify them through the exploration of worst-case scenarios. Possibilities for building peace exist in every human crisis. The challenge for peace research is to identify them through the exploration of best-case scenarios. Under the strategic studies paradigm, states hope for the best but prepare for the worst. 'Trust, but verify', said President Ronald Reagan in the context of his historic arms control agreements with the former Soviet Union. For peace researchers, nations should be prepared for the worst but work for the best: verify, but do trust and, where possible, love thy neighbour as a means of building mutual trust.

PART I

An international organisation for keeping
the peace

1

Pacific settlement, collective security and international peacekeeping

International organisation

This chapter situates the changing peace and security role of the United Nations within the larger context of developments in international organisation and the evolution from pacific settlement and collective security to peacekeeping and peace operations. One of the most enduring if least endearing features of human history is systematic violence between members of the human family. In the modern era, this has taken the form of organised warfare between states as the basic unit of the international system. International organisation is an important means for arranging the functioning of the state-based international system more satisfactorily than had proven possible in conditions of international anarchy.

But international organisation in turn is characterised by a certain tension. On the one hand, it can be regarded as a step towards the establishment of a world government which would transcend the state system. On the other hand, international organisations are set up and managed by nation-states; the sovereign state remains the basic entity of international relations; and states have shown themselves singularly reluctant to accept significant encroachments upon their sovereignties. Thus international organisation, in addition to serving as a possible pointer to a future world government, can also be viewed as merely an agreement by, for and of states to engage in regular consultation and establish joint machinery for the formulation and implementation of collective decisions.

There was a spurt in the number and types of international organisations in the second half of the twentieth century. Their number climbed from 37 in 1909 and 123 in 1951 to about 7,000 in 2000; the number of non-governmental organisations (NGOs) increased from 176 to 48,000 in the corresponding period.[1] They have added greatly to the institutional

---

[1] *Yearbook of International Organizations: Guide to Global Civil Society Networks 2002–2003. Vol. 5: Statistics, Visualizations and Patterns* (Munich: K. G. Saur, 2002), p. 35; *Yearbook of*

complexity of international relations. In previous centuries war and peace were the mainstay of world politics. A generation ago Raymond Aron, an influential French theorist, argued that 'the *diplomat* and the *soldier. . . live* and *symbolise* international relations which, insofar as they are inter-state relations, concern diplomacy and war'.[2] Today, alongside the horde of diplomats and soldiers, the multinational merchant, international financier, World Bank technocrat, UN peacekeeper and NGO humanitarian worker jostle for space on the increasingly crowded international stage. Few issues today lie completely outside the purview of one international organisation or another.

The problem of peace and order is not new. Napoleon Bonaparte imposed temporary order and unity on Europe through conquest. The other European powers set up an alternative Concert system in reaction and transformed the original impulse of a military alliance for the single purpose of defeating Napoleon into the longer-term political goal of preventing a similar domination of Europe by any one power in the future. The Concert of Europe was the most comprehensive attempt until then to construct new machinery for keeping the peace among and by the great powers.

The Hague Conferences of 1899 and 1907 signalled the broadening of international relations in participation and agenda. They pointed to an emergent extra-European international system, in the management of which the lesser powers would demand a say; and, with their emphasis upon mediation, conciliation and inquiry, they demonstrated a rationalistic and legalistic approach to the problem of international disputes.

The two major international organisations of the twentieth century were the League of Nations after the First World War and the United Nations after the Second World War. In both instances, people horrified by the destructiveness of modern wars decided to create institutions for avoiding a repetition of such catastrophes.

The League was built around Europe as the core of the international political system.[3] It accepted the sovereign state as the central unit of

International Organizations 1974 (Brussels: Union of International Associations, 1974), p. S33.

[2] Raymond Aron, *Peace and War: A Theory of International Relations*, translated from the French by Richard Howard and Annette Baker Fox (New York: Frederick A. Praeger, 1967), p. 5; emphasis in original.

[3] Inis L. Claude, *Swords into Plowshares: The Problems and Progress of International Organization*, 3rd edn (New York: Random House, 1964), p. 49.

international affairs and great powers as the dominant participants. It did not challenge any of the fundamental principles of the traditional multistate system. It began as the embodiment of humanity's aspirations for a better world. In a sense the interwar years were witness to an increasing infusion of idealism. The League was prepared to condemn Japanese aggression in Manchuria in 1931 despite no prospect of any collective action being undertaken. The Italian invasion of Ethiopia in 1935 presented the League with its moment of greatest triumph: for the first time, the international community, acting through institutionalised channels, had condemned aggression, identified the aggressor and imposed sanctions. Their eventual failure does not negate the advancement of the ideal that the international community can take joint coercive measures against outlaws. But Ethiopia also stands as the symbol of failure to realise the high hopes held of the League at its creation, for the aggressor nation secured its ends through the means of its choice.

The League was killed by the Second World War; its legacy of international organisation lives on in the United Nations. The most important part of the legacy was the concept, by now firmly entrenched, yet revolutionary in 1919, that the community of nations has both the moral right and the legal competence to discuss and judge the international conduct of its members. An important step in the development of the idea was the Pact of Paris of 1928 (also known as the Kellogg-Briand Pact), wherein signatories condemned 'recourse to war for the solution of international controversies and renounce[d] it as an instrument of national policy in relations with one another'. The practical significance of the pact was eroded by its non-enforceability and by the many qualifications attached by various signatories, for example the extension of self-defence to embrace colonies. Yet the declaration of principle, that war was henceforth to be treated as an illegitimate method of dispute settlement, was of great symbolic significance even if it fell well short of being a contractual obligation.

The closeness with which the UN was modelled upon the League was testimony also to the fact that while the League had failed, people still had faith in the *idea* of an umbrella international organisation to oversee world peace and cooperation. While many of the Charter provisions were borrowed directly from the Covenant, others represented substantial codifications of League procedures or logical developments of nascent League ideas. Some of the other innovative ideas that were carried over from the League experiment to the UN included respect for the rights of small nations, economic and social cooperation, the habit of public debate on international crises, the formation of an international civil service, and the establishment of a world court.

Seemingly the most significant advance from the League to the UN lay in the area of enforcement. The UN incorporated the League pro-scription on the use of force for national objectives, but inserted the additional prescription to use force in support of international, that is UN, authority. As proof of the added potency of the new organisation, the UN Security Council (UNSC) was given the power to decide whether international peace was threatened, whether sanctions were to be im-posed and, if so, the nature of the sanctions, including military force. Most importantly, such decisions by the UNSC would be binding upon all the members of the United Nations, even those who had voted against the measures. The appearance of enhanced UN effectiveness was a major argument advanced in its favour in 1945 in comparison to the dis-credited and discarded League. The UNSC, it was argued, would be the equivalent of a supreme war-making organisation of the international community.

Of the principal UN organs, the General Assembly (GA) is the plenary body made up of all UN member states, each one of whom has one vote. There were 51 original members of the United Nations; by 2005 there were 191. The newest entrants, both of whom joined in 2002, were Switzerland, one of the world's oldest nation-states, and East Timor, the world's newest. The steady expansion has enabled the organisation to meet its goal of universal membership and has been helped by the fact that joining the UN is seen as conferring the final imprimatur of sovereign identity.

The UNSC has fifteen members, of whom five are permanent and known colloquially as the P5: China, France, Russia, the United States and the United Kingdom. Of the remaining ten members, five are ele-cted[4] each year for two-year terms by the GA on the basis of 'equitable geographical representation' from Africa, the Americas, Asia and Europe. No country is eligible for immediate re-election. The UNSC is the exe-cutive decision-making organ of the UN system. With virtually unlim-ited powers for the maintenance of international peace and security, it has shown the biggest gap between promise and performance. Its deci-sions are made by a majority of nine of the fifteen votes, including the concurring vote of each permanent member (Article 27.3): a requirement known as the veto power.

---

[4] Thus it would be politically more correct to call the P5 the five unelected members.

The Secretariat is a 9,000-strong international civil service headed by a Secretary-General (SG) elected for five-year terms by the GA on the recommendation of the UNSC. The Economic and Social Council (ECOSOC) has the responsibility for coordinating improvements in the social and economic conditions of the people of the world, including human rights. It consists of fifty-four members, with eighteen being elected to three-year terms each year. Immediate re-election is possible.

The legal part of the UN system is the International Court of Justice (ICJ), also known as the World Court. Its statute is an integral part of the UN Charter. It consists of fifteen judges elected for nine-year terms (and eligible for re-election) in their personal capacity, but nevertheless as a group representing the major regions, civilisations and legal systems of the world. The election takes place separately in the UNSC (where the veto does not apply) and the GA, with an absolute majority being required in each organ. The Court sits at The Hague. Its principal function is to decide cases submitted to it by states in accordance with international law. It also gives advisory opinions to the Assembly and the Council on any legal question.

Pacific settlement and collective security

The trend towards narrowing the permissible range of unilateral resort to force by nation-states has been matched by the historical movement to broaden the range of international instruments available to states to settle their disputes by means short of war. The techniques of peaceful settlement (chapter 6 of the Charter) range from bilateral negotiations between the disputants to formal adjudication by third parties. The UNSC cannot compel member states to implement resolutions adopted under chapter 6. The efficacy of UN action for the peaceful resolution of disputes is circumscribed by this retention of the principle of voluntarism. Nevertheless, the normative primacy of peaceful over forceful means is firmly entrenched. Similarly, the proposition that the international community has a stake in war-avoidance justifying its involvement in bilateral disputes between member states is no longer questioned.

UN multilateral diplomacy differs from traditional interstate diplomacy in some important respects.[5] Guided by Charter principles, it

---

[5] Javier Pérez de Cuéllar, 'The Role of the UN Secretary-General', in Adam Roberts and Benedict Kingsbury, eds., *United Nations, Divided World: The UN's Role in International Relations* (Oxford: Clarendon, 1988), pp. 67–9.

offsets the unfavourable position of the weaker party, aims to establish a just peace as well as a stable balance of power and takes into account the interests of member states as well as the disputants. Gareth Evans has drawn attention to the attractions of using UN channels and modalities for resolving disputes peacefully and to the abysmal imbalance in resources devoted to preventive diplomacy as opposed to band-aid solutions.[6]

On balance, the UN has helped states to behave less conflictually, form habits of cooperation and develop shared norms and perceptions. A substantial number of international disputes has been referred to the UN and the trend has increased in comparison to the League record in the interwar period. A majority of disputes that do not find their way to the UN involves the major powers: 'experience has paralleled the understanding implicit in the veto provision in the United Nations charter, that international organisations do not have the capacity to deal with all disputes involving the most powerful states'.[7]

After the First World War, collective security was a conscious substitute for systems of alliances and balance of power policies that were 'forever discredited'. Unlike pacific settlement, collective security is not concerned with the causes and conditions of war.[8] Only one assumption is necessary, that wars are probable; only one normative premise is required, that wars must be prevented or stopped. Predicated on the proposition that war can be prevented by the deterrent effect of overwhelming power being brought to bear against any state contemplating the use of force, collective security entails the imposition of diplomatic, economic and military sanctions against international outlaws.

Enforcement measures are outlined in chapter 7 of the Charter. Articles 42 and 43 in particular authorise the UNSC to 'take such action by air, sea or land forces as may be necessary to maintain or restore international peace and security', and require member states to make available to the UN such 'armed forces, assistance, and facilities' as may be necessary for the purpose. Thus while as a settler of disputes the UN can only recommend desirable courses of action to disputing members, as a policeman it can impose decisions upon violently erring states.

---

[6] Gareth Evans, *Cooperating for Peace: The Global Agenda for the 1990s and Beyond* (Sydney: Allen & Unwin, 1993), pp. 61–3.

[7] Harold K. Jacobson, *Networks of Interdependence* (New York: Knopf, 1979), p. 211.

[8] For elaboration of the differences between pacific settlement and collective security, see Claude, *Swords into Plowshares*, chapter 11, 'Peaceful Settlement of Disputes' and chapter 12, 'Collective Security as an Approach to Peace'.

Efforts to devise an operational collective security system have been thwarted by a fundamental tension in the concept. War between lesser states may be deplorable and unhealthy for their nationals, but cannot of itself endanger *world* peace. Only the prospect of war between powerful states directly, or their involvement on rival sides in a quarrel between minor powers, can threaten international order. Collective security, understood as the maintenance of international peace and security, is therefore superfluous in respect of small states. Equally, however, it is impossible to enforce against major powers. For any attempt to launch military measures against a great power would bring about the very calamity that the system is designed to avoid, namely a world war.

The UN sought to avoid the latter eventuality by conferring permanent membership of the UNSC upon the great powers with the accompanying right of veto. The practical effect of the veto is that 'the extensive decision-making competence' of the Security Council, necessary for the successful operation of a collective security system, is severely curtailed by the equally 'extensive decision-blocking competence' of the permanent members.[9] The mistrust between the great powers also put paid to the idea of a Military Staff Committee which was to have functioned as the UNSC's strategic adviser.

The closest that the UN has come to engaging in collective enforcement action was in Korea in 1950. Yet the collective security character of the UN action in Korea was heavily qualified. In essence, the US responded to communist North Korean invasion and the UN responded to the immediate US reaction. The initiative was American, taken in the context of the Cold War and invoking the moral support of the UN for a resort to force that would have occurred anyway. That is, the UN action in Korea was made possible by a temporary marriage of convenience between collective security and collective defence,[10] and also by a rather fortuitous combination of circumstances. The Soviet Union was absent from the UNSC in protest at an unrelated issue. Subsequent Soviet protestations that the UN action was illegal because the resolution did not meet the unambiguous criterion of Article 27.3 requiring the concurring votes of the permanent members was of limited academic interest only. The UN was helped by the fact that it had its own commission

[9] Ibid., p. 242.
[10] See Arnold Wolfers, *Discord and Collaboration: Essays on International Politics* (Baltimore: Johns Hopkins University Press, 1962), chapter 11, 'Collective Security and the War in Korea', and chapter 12, 'Collective Defense versus Collective Security'.

'on the ground' which was able to confirm immediately that aggression had occurred and identify the aggressor. The ready availability of American troops in nearby Japan allowed the UN to overcome the problems posed by the non-implementation of Article 43. An important background factor was that in this early test of the UN, member states and Trygve Lie, the first SG, were more readily inclined to adopt a firm policy towards a clear case of unprovoked aggression.

The next large-scale military action under UN mandate came four decades later in the Persian Gulf (1990–1). Its most important long-term significance lay in the crossing of the conceptual Rubicon by authorising enforcement of sanctions and military eviction of the aggressor by troops not even nominally under UN command. As in Korea in the 1950s, the advantage of the procedure was that it allowed the UN to approximate the achievement of collective security within a clear chain of command necessary for large-scale military operations. The cost was that the Gulf War, like the Korean War, became identified with American policy over which the organisation exercised little real control.

Classical peacekeeping

With the attainment of a reliable system of collective security being deferred to a distant date, states moved to guarantee national security by means of collective defence and the international community groped towards damage-limitation techniques to avoid and contain conflicts. Peacekeeping evolved in the grey zone between pacific settlement and military enforcement. It grew side by side with preventive diplomacy as practised and articulated by Secretary-General Dag Hammarskjöld. The United Nations was to aim at keeping new conflicts outside the sphere of bloc differences. The technique of preventive diplomacy was to be used to forestall the competitive intrusion of the rival power blocs into conflict situations that were either the result or potential cause of a power vacuum in the Cold War. Preventive diplomacy was a policy designed to contain a peripheral war, to achieve a kind of disengagement before the fact. It was given concrete expression by inserting the thin blue wedge of blue beret UN soldiers between enemy combatants.

While specific UN activities have been varied, the theme common to all is to promote international stability and support peaceful change outside the axis of great power rivalry. Peacekeeping operations have been diverse in function and size, ranging from a few observers (around forty) on the India–Pakistan border,[11] to a 20,000-man force in the Congo.[12] In sum, traditional or classical international peacekeeping forces could never *keep* world peace, for they lacked both mandated authority and operational capability to do so. Yet even while failing to bring about world peace, UN forces successfully stabilised several potentially dangerous situations.

The first steps towards a pragmatic contribution to peacekeeping had already been foreshadowed by the League. The earliest UN peacekeeping missions of the supervisory-observer variety were undertaken in the 1940s in the Balkans, Greece, Kashmir, Korea, Indonesia and Palestine. Their experience shows that observer groups are needed, and they work: not as a panacea, but as long-lived expedients. The UN Emergency Force (UNEF, 1956–67) first fully described the new institution of part-time soldiering for the UN and threw up difficult custodial problems in the wake of the divorce between security requirements and political issues. It established that the cardinal distinction between collective security and peacekeeping lay in their reliance upon force and consent respectively. The immediate goal of the force was to provide a fig-leaf of respectability for the withdrawal of the aggressors. Thereafter, its mission was transformed into the larger role of separating the erstwhile Egyptian–Israeli combatants. It did so not by means of the Charter formula of collective security involving the might of the major powers, but by means of a peaceful interpository force made up of contingents from the minor powers. UNEF was neither expected nor equipped to engage in hostilities; its deterrent effect was to be produced by its very presence as a symbol of the international community.

Indeed the Egyptian–Israeli border experienced more than a decade of peace and calm unlike any preceding period since the creation of Israel in 1948. The manner of UNEF's demise was as dramatic as had been its creation. SG U Thant's decision to withdraw UNEF provoked immediate political and a lingering academic controversy.[13] From a peacekeeping point of view, the most important lesson of 1967 was the demonstration

---

[11] United Nations Military Observer Group in India and Pakistan (UNMOGIP), 24 January 1949–present.

[12] United Nations Operations in the Congo (ONUC), 15 July 1960–30 June 1964.

[13] See M. Comay, 'UN Peacekeeping: The Israeli Experience', and N. A. Elaraby 'UN Peacekeeping: The Egyptian Experience', in Henry Wiseman, ed., *Peacekeeping: Appraisals and Proposals* (New York: Pergamon, 1983).

of UNEF's real significance. 'What it did during its 10 years in the Middle East was not to keep the peace. Rather it helped Israel and Egypt to implement their temporary disposition to live in peace.'[14]

The ONUC highlighted custodial problems in the Congo arising from the sudden departure of an irresponsible colonial power, with the UN dealing with the resulting authority vacuum only through floundering efforts. The force in Cyprus is a good example of time being a more likely solvent of a historical conflict than the UN – but the latter is the most likely means of gaining time. The 1970s saw a return of UN forces to the Middle East in the form of UNEF-II (1973–9), UNDOF,[15] and UNIFIL.[16] The Middle East was also the setting in the 1980s for a steady displacement of UN peacekeeping by great power multilateral peacekeeping in the Sinai MFO[17] and the Beirut MNF.[18]

One of the originators of UNEF, Canadian foreign minister Lester Pearson, aptly characterised a UN peacekeeping force as 'an intermediate technique between merely passing resolutions and actually fighting'.[19] The constraining effect of many of the core principles of classical UN peacekeeping – non-use of force because of military neutrality between the belligerents, non-intervention in domestic quarrels because of political neutrality with respect to the conflict, non-participation by great powers because of their mutual suspicions – produced controversy and frustration in the organisation. The UN refused to abandon them, however, because they represented a middle way between abdication of responsibility for management of the international order and turmoil if the organisation attempts to shake off the Charter shackles on collective military action. Impartiality becomes progressively harder to sustain

---

[14] Alan James, *The Politics of Peace-Keeping* (New York: Praeger, 1969), p. 205.

[15] United Nations Disengagement Observer Force, 3 June 1974–present.

[16] United Nations Interim Force in Lebanon, 19 March 1978–present.

[17] The Multinational Force and Observers in the Sinai, 25 April 1982–present. Somewhat paradoxically, the experience of the largely successful MFO can be said to vindicate UN peacekeeping: 'The MFO so closely resembles the UN model as to constitute an advertisement for UN peacekeeping'; Richard Nelson, 'Multinational Peacekeeping in the Middle East and the United Nations Model', *International Affairs* 61:1 (1984/85), p. 89; 'the UN can take pride in the fact that the Sinai force has been entirely organised on the basis of the UN experience in peacekeeping, that its commander is an old UN hand, and that the force was prepared, assembled and deployed with the advice of a former senior UN administrator'; Indar Jit Rikhye, *The Theory & Practice of Peacekeeping* (London: C. Hurst, 1984), p. 73.

[18] The Multinational Force in Beirut, 21 August 1982–13 September 1982, and 24 September 1982–31 March 1984.

[19] Lester B. Pearson, 'Force for UN', *Foreign Affairs* 35:3 (1957), p. 401.

with increasing use of force, for then the UN becomes a stake in the power struggle concerned. Perceptions of partial use of force erode the UN's authority and diminish the organisation's capacity to play a distinctive role in world affairs. The use of force at the behest of a UN majority is risky because majorities re-form as interests shift, and the number of minorities whose support has been lost could add up to constitute a majority. Besides, today's majority may be tomorrow's minority.

The UN cannot use force without first becoming an international enforcement machinery, capable of exerting military power against aggression and in anticipation of aggression. This could not be done without overcoming the problem of divided views and divided interests. But in order to overcome this obstacle, the UN would have to abandon the consensual approach in the plural assembly for the centralisation of authority in its executive organ. Brian Urquhart argued that 'It is precisely because the [Security] Council cannot agree on enforcement operations that the peacekeeping technique has been devised, and it is precisely because an operation is a peacekeeping operation that governments are prepared to make troops available to serve on it.'[20] There is another important implication which follows from this regarding judgements of the value and utility of peacekeeping operations. Since peacekeeping evolved as a second-best substitute for a non-obtainable collective security system, it is neither fair nor logical to assess its worth on the criterion of collective enforcement.

Peace operations

Peacekeeping has been one of the most visible symbols of the UN role in international peace and security. The number of UN operations increased dramatically after the end of the Cold War as the UN was placed centre-stage in efforts to resolve outstanding conflicts. However, the multiplication of missions was not always accompanied by coherent policy or integrated military and political responses. When the missions encountered problems, the 'crisis of expectations'[21] of the late 1980s

---

[20] Brian E. Urquhart, 'Peacekeeping: A View from the Operational Center', in Wiseman, *Peacekeeping: Appraisals and Proposals*, p. 165.
[21] The phrase is taken from Ramesh Thakur and Carlyle A. Thayer, eds., *A Crisis of Expectations: UN Peacekeeping in the 1990s* (Boulder: Westview, 1995).

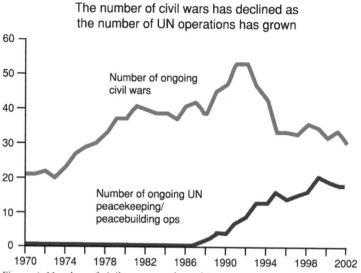

Figure 4. Number of civil wars, number of UN peace operations, 1970–2002.

and early 1990s in turn gave way to a crisis of confidence-cum-credibility in UN peacekeeping in the late 1990s, and member states began to limit their military, political and financial exposure.

Terms like 'peacekeeping', 'peace support operations' and 'peace operations' are used generically to refer to missions and operations that fall short of military combat between clearly recognisable enemies (figure 4). Traditional peacekeeping was under UN auspices, command and control. There was a reaction against UN peacekeeping because of widespread, if often inaccurate, perceptions that UN operations led to diplomatic ennui and could not be freed of the Cold War rivalry and other highly politicised antagonisms that had infected large parts of the UN system. The *second generation* of peacekeeping operations were mounted either unilaterally or multilaterally, but in any case outside the UN system, in Zimbabwe,[22] the Sinai,[23] Beirut[24] and Sri Lanka.

---

[22] See Henry Wiseman and Alastair Taylor, *From Rhodesia to Zimbabwe* (New York: Pergamon, 1981).

[23] See Mala Tabory, *The Multinational Force and Observers in the Sinai* (Boulder: Westview, 1986).

[24] See Ramesh Thakur, *International Peacekeeping in Lebanon: United Nations Authority and Multinational Force* (Boulder: Westview, 1987).

The precursor to this sort of extra-UN peacekeeping operation might well be said to have been the international control commissions in Indochina set up by the Geneva Agreements of 1954.[25] On the one hand, the non-UN operations adopted most of the principles of third-party military interposition and buffer from traditional UN peacekeeping. On the other, they expanded the range of tasks and functions that were required to beyond just military interposition.

Traditional peacekeeping aimed to contain and stabilise volatile regions and interstate conflicts until such time as negotiations produced lasting peace agreements. By contrast, the *third generation* of peacekeeping saw UN missions being mounted as part of package deals of peace agreements, for example in Namibia and Cambodia.[26] The peacekeeping mission was an integral component of the peace agreement and meant to complete the peace settlement by providing third-party international military reinforcement for the peace process. Reflecting the changing nature of modern armed conflict, UN operations expanded not just in numbers (figure 5) but also in the nature and scope of their missions. The newer 'complex emergencies' produced multiple crises all at once:[27] collapsed state structures; humanitarian tragedies caused by starvation, disease or genocide; large-scale fighting and slaughter between rival ethnic or bandit groups; horrific human rights atrocities; and the intermingling of criminal elements and child soldiers with irregular forces. Reflecting this, third-generation operations had to undertake additional types of tasks like military disengagement, demobilisation and cantonment; policing; human rights monitoring and enforcement; observation, organisation and conduct of elections; rehabilitation and repatriation; and temporary administration.

In Somalia and elsewhere the United Nations attempted the *fourth generation* of 'peace-enforcement' operations, with results that were anything but encouraging[28] – hence General Sir Michael Rose's metaphor of 'the Mogadishu Line' that peacekeeping forces dare cross only at their

---

[25] See Ramesh Thakur, *Peacekeeping in Vietnam: Canada, India, Poland and the International Commission* (Edmonton: University of Alberta Press, 1984).

[26] See Michael W. Doyle, *UN Peacekeeping in Cambodia: UNTAC's Civil Mandate* (Boulder: Lynne Rienner, 1995); Trevor Findlay, *Cambodia: The Legacy and Lessons of UNTAC* (Stockholm: Stockholm International Peace Research Institute, 1995).

[27] The Congo crisis of the 1960s, and the UN operation there from 1960 to 1964, could be said to have been precursors to the complex emergencies and third-generation missions.

[28] See Samuel M. Makinda, *Seeking Peace from Chaos: Humanitarian Intervention in Somalia* (Boulder: Lynne Rienner, 1993) and Ramesh Thakur, 'From Peacekeeping to

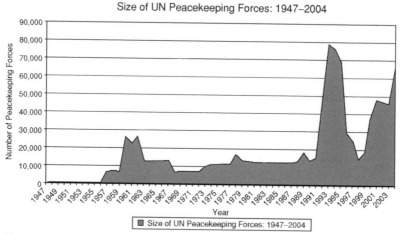

Figure 5. Number of UN peacekeeping troops, 1947–2005.

peril.[29] A peacekeeping operation in a theatre where there was no peace to keep, the UN Protection Force (UNPROFOR) in former Yugoslavia offered neither safety to the local people, solace to the displaced and dispossessed, nor even the consolation to the international community of having done the job to the best of their ability. Its failure to prevent the horrors of Srebrenica in 1995 remains a stain on world conscience for passivity in the face of the calculated return of 'evil' to Europe and a tragedy that, in the words of the official UN report, 'will haunt our history forever'.[30]

Partly in consequence of the disastrous venture into peace-enforcement, in Bosnia and Haiti UN peacekeeping underwent a further metamorphosis into the *fifth generation* of enforcement operations being *authorised* by the UNSC, but *undertaken* by a single power or ad hoc multilateral coalitions. There was not a single such operation during the Cold War (1945–89); there were fifteen such operations set up between November

Peace-Enforcement: The UN Operation in Somalia', *Journal of Modern African Studies* 32 (September 1994), pp. 387–410.

[29] Michael Rose, 'The Bosnia Experience', in Ramesh Thakur, ed., *Past Imperfect, Future UNcertain: The United Nations at Fifty* (London/New York: Macmillan/St. Martin's Press, 1998), p. 139.

[30] *Report of the Secretary-General Pursuant to General Assembly Resolution 53/35 (1998)*, New York: UN Secretariat, November 1999, para. 503.

1990 and September 2003.[31] The UN itself took back responsibility for a traditional-type consensual peacekeeping, once the situation had stabilised,[32] for a temporary period, but with the tasks of third-generation expanded peacekeeping. Modifying the Gulf War precedent somewhat, this was the pattern that emerged of UN-authorised military action by the US in Haiti, France in Rwanda, Russia in Georgia and NATO in Bosnia.

East Timor represents the evolution into the most recent, *sixth generation* of peacekeeping. A UN-authorised multinational force is prepared for combat action if necessary and is given the mandate, troops, equipment and robust rules of engagement that are required for such a mission. However, the military operation is but the prelude to a de facto UN administration, which engages in state-making for a transitional period.[33] That is, a 'nation' is granted independence as a result of UN-organised elections. But the nation concerned has no structures of 'state' to speak of. It is not even, like Somalia, a case of a failed state; in East Timor a state has had to be created from scratch. In the latter the UN finally confronted and addressed the dilemma that haunted it in the Congo in the 1960s and Somalia in the 1990s, namely that peace-restoration is not possible without the establishment of law and order. But in a country where the writ of government has either collapsed or is non-existent, the law that is made and enforced so as to provide order can only be that of the UN or of another foreign power (or coalition).

Review and reform of UN peace operations

A significant cost of the cascade of generations of peacekeeping within a highly compressed timeframe is that most of the major operations today have little real precedent to go by; each has to make and learn from its own mistakes. Secretary-General Kofi Annan appointed a high-level

---

[31] For a complete listing of the fifteen cases, see David M. Malone, ed., *The UN Security Council: From the Cold War to the 21st Century* (Boulder: Lynne Rienner, 2004), appendix 2, pp. 665–8.

[32] For an excellent analysis of the issues surrounding such a division of labour, see David Malone, *Decision-Making in the UN Security Council: The Case of Haiti, 1990–1997* (Oxford: Clarendon, 1998).

[33] For a critical evaluation of the UN's record of transitional administration, see Simon Chesterman, *You, the People: The United Nations, Transitional Administration, and State-Building* (Oxford: Oxford University Press, 2004).

international panel, chaired by former Algerian foreign minister (and subsequent special UN envoy to Afghanistan and then Iraq) Lakhdar Brahimi, to make recommendations for changes in UN peacekeeping. The Brahimi Report was unusual in the candour of its analysis and recommendations.[34] It came to the overall sound conclusion that 'when the United Nations does send its forces to uphold the peace, they must be prepared to confront the lingering forces of war and violence with the ability and determination to defeat them'. For in the final analysis, 'no amount of good intentions can substitute for the fundamental ability to project credible force if complex peacekeeping, in particular, is to succeed'.[35] Mandates, and the resources to match them, have to be guided by pragmatic, realistic analysis and thinking. The UN Secretariat 'must not apply best-case planning assumptions to situations where the local actors have historically exhibited worst-case behaviour'.[36] The UN needs to develop the professional civil service culture of providing advice that is sound, based on a thorough assessment of options, independent of what might be politically popular or fits the preconceptions of the decision-makers and free of fear of consequences for politically neutral officials. The Secretariat was urged to tell the Security Council what it needs to hear, not what it wants to hear.[37] Where clearly unimplementable missions have been approved because of confused, unclear or severely under-resourced mandates, the UN has to learn to say 'No'.

Nor should the need for impartial peacekeeping translate automatically into moral equivalence among the conflict parties on the ground: in some cases local parties consist not of moral equals but obvious aggressors and victims.[38] The panel concluded that political neutrality has too often degenerated into military timidity, the abdication of the duty to protect civilians and an operational failure to confront openly those who challenge peacekeeping missions in the field. Impartiality should not translate into complicity with evil. The Charter sets out the

---

[34] *Report of the Panel on United Nations Peace Operations* (A/55/305-S/2000/809), 21 August 2000. For an early assessment, see David M. Malone and Ramesh Thakur, 'UN Peacekeeping: Lessons Learned?' *Global Governance* 7:1 (January–March 2001), pp. 11–17.

[35] *Report of the Panel on United Nations Peace Operations*, p. viii.

[36] Ibid., para. 51.

[37] Ironically, in 2004, as the UN special envoy for Iraq, when Brahimi himself made the rather obvious point that the Palestinian conflict cast a complicating shadow over efforts at stabilising the Iraqi security situation, he was criticised for exceeding his brief.

[38] *Report of the Panel on United Nations Peace Operations*, para. 50.

principles that the UN must defend and the values that it must uphold.[39] The reluctance to distinguish victim from aggressor implies a degree of moral equivalency between the two and damages the institution of UN peacekeeping. The response of some developing-country commentators to this was that impartiality should be seen in terms of the fair application of UN mandates, not as an excuse for moral equivocation between victims and perpetrators.

In order to arrest and reverse the sense of drift, UN approaches to peacekeeping need to reflect the multifaceted nature of UN action in countries afflicted by mostly civil wars. This means promoting the rule of law and economic recovery by integrating the military, policing, institution building, reconstruction and civil administration functions of peacekeeping operations to a much greater degree than in the past. Following the Brahimi Report, the staff complement of the Department of Peacekeeping Operations (DPKO) in New York was increased to provide better support to field missions. The officers of the military and police advisers were bolstered. The old and not so well-regarded lessons learned unit was restructured into a best practices unit. DPKO's logistics base in Brindisi (Italy) received funding to acquire strategic deployment stocks. The reorganised UN Standby Arrangements System provides for forces to be made available within thirty to ninety days of a new operation. But these all amount to technical tinkering. The chief determinant of failure and success will be the quality of decisions made by member states in the UNSC, led by the P5. 'Twas ever so, and ever will be.

Conclusion

The history of UN peacekeeping is a mirror to the record of the organisation's own evolution: the initial high hopes, the many frustrations on the ground and the sometimes bitter disappointments in the end. Another thread that is common to both the UN and its peacekeeping ventures is the failure of states to make full use of the international machinery available to them for the avoidance of war and the peaceful resolution of conflicts.

---

[39] The language and the argument of the Brahimi Report here borrowed from a speech of Kofi Annan himself to the Council on Foreign Relations in New York in 1999; see Ian Johnstone, 'The Role of the UN Secretary-General: The Power of Persuasion Based on Law', *Global Governance* 9:4 (October–December 2003), p. 444.

Traditional peacekeeping operations do not enforce the peace, but they do buy time. Given the intensity of conflicts and depths of distrust between local belligerents, peace would be even more tenuous in the absence of international forces. Moreover, they can help to contain sporadic incidents that are not meant to initiate a large-scale war. The deficiencies in the machinery of peacekeeping merely highlight the fact that such forces cannot be self-sustaining. It is perhaps more accurate, therefore, to speak of war-dampening rather than peacekeeping forces.

The tenets of classical UN peacekeeping came under sustained challenge under the impact of changed circumstances and demands with the end of the Cold War. The UN became involved increasingly in post-conflict reconstruction, 'building' peace in order to prevent a relapse into conflict. Where the UN suffered from a lack of credibility and a crisis of confidence during the Cold War, it was afflicted by a lack of resources and a crisis of expectations with the end of the Cold War. It had to address the resulting problem of being overloaded with tasks while remaining seriously under-resourced and spread far too thin. The zeal to intervene everywhere had to be tempered with caution about entering into entangling commitments. The UN's dilemma is that it must avoid deploying forces into situations where the risk of failure is high; not be so timid as to transform every difficulty into an alibi for inaction; and be flexible and agile enough to be able to adapt missions to fast-changing political requirements and operational environments.

The need for UN peacekeeping remains and will continue. How can we reconcile 'the temporary nature of specific operations with the evident permanence of peacekeeping and other peace operation activities as core functions of the United Nations';[40] that is, the imperative of ad hoc missions with the persisting reality of permanent engagement?[41] Modern peacekeeping demands a very broad range of skills and competence, including 'innovation, flexibility, initiative and moral courage'.[42] Peacekeepers have to determine the application of relevant domestic, international humanitarian and human rights law to their conduct and operation. Civilian, police and military elements have to cooperate

---

[40] *Report of the Panel on United Nations Peace Operations*, p. xiii.

[41] Ramesh Thakur and Albrecht Schnabel, eds., *United Nations Peacekeeping Operations: Ad Hoc Missions, Permanent Engagement* (Tokyo: United Nations University Press, 2001). See also Alex J. Bellamy, Paul Williams and Stuart Griffin, *Understanding Peacekeeping* (Oxford: Polity Press, 2004).

[42] *Challenges of Peace Operations into the 21st Century: Concluding Report 1997–2002* (Stockholm: Swedish National Defence College, 2002), p. 17.

willingly and coordinate effectively with one another and with NGOs in the pursuit of common objectives. They have to be adaptable as the focus changes from security in one mission to humanitarian assistance in another and peacebuilding in yet a third. The last has led to growing recognition of the importance of instilling and institutionalising the rule of law and justice systems that avoid a 'one-size-fits-all' approach on the one hand, and encompass the entire criminal justice process on the other – from police, prosecutors and defence lawyers to judges, court officials and prison officers – in a whole-of-legal-chain approach. The older certitudes of traditional peacekeeping no longer apply when peacekeepers find themselves operating with the executive authority of transitional administrators inside societies characterised by criminality, corruption, political instability and armed power struggles. They have to ensure their own security in an environment in which, far from being an emblem of safety, the blue helmet can be a target. They must learn to use modern information and communications tools to their advantage while being conscious of hostile elements also exploiting the newer opportunities to maximise mayhem. All this and more must be done in harmony with professional colleagues in a truly multinational, multicultural and multilingual effort operating in highly localised and particularised theatres.

Countries with large financial and military resources are reluctant to deploy either to address African conflicts (figure 6).[43] This also will have to change if the UN's credibility on peacekeeping is to be restored. In order to reoccupy its niche as a major actor in international security, the UN requires consistency of purpose, the resources to give it substance and a convincing attention span. One of the remarkable trends of recent years has been the falling incidence of organised armed conflict alongside a rising number of peace agreements that are actually holding. But for UN peacekeeping, this has produced a paradox: 'The military resources needed to help keep the peace are being strained by so much peace to keep.'[44]

---

[43] For a collection of essays examining the peacekeeping requirements for Africa, see Jakkie Cilliers and Greg Mills, eds., *From Peacekeeping to Complex Emergencies: Peace Support Missions in Africa* (Johannesburg and Pretoria: South African Institute of International Affairs and Institute for Security Studies, 1999).

[44] Jean-Marie Guéhenno (UN Under-Secretary-General for Peacekeeping), 'A Plan to Strengthen UN Peacekeeping', *International Herald Tribune*, 19 April 2004.

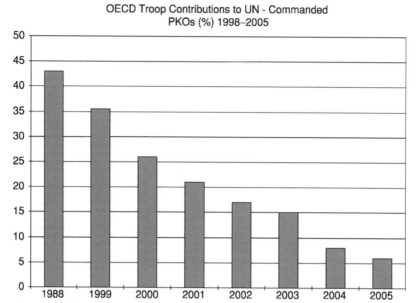

Figure 6. OECD troop contributions to UN peace operations, 1998–2005.

Kofi Annan has appealed to member states to ensure that the UN has effective peacekeeping capacity commensurate with the demands placed on it. He urged the creation of strategic reserves that can be deployed rapidly and welcomed the development of regional capacities by the African and European Unions. He added that 'the time is now ripe for a decisive move forward: the establishment of an interlocking system of peacekeeping capacities that will enable the United Nations to work with relevant regional organisations in predictable and reliable partnerships'.[45]

The challenge of peacekeeping shows no sign of abating. Compared to just sixteen missions during the 1945–90 Cold War period, forty-one new missions were established during 1990–2003. By April 2004, 130 countries – two-thirds of UN member states – had contributed personnel to UN peacekeeping operations. In March 2005, over 65,000 UN peace-keepers (soldiers and police officers) from 103 countries – over half the total UN membership – were deployed in 17 missions around the

[45] Kofi A. Annan, *In Larger Freedom: Towards Development, Security and Human Rights For All*. Report of the Secretary-General (New York: United Nations, document A/59/2005, 21 March 2005), para. 112.

world.[46] The total number of fatalities in peacekeeping operations from 1948 to March 2005 was 1,941. The annual cost of UN peacekeeping operations stood at US $3.9 billion in 2005, and the cumulative cost from 1948 to 30 June 2004 was a surprisingly low $31.5 billion.

Is this value for money? How do we judge? One benchmark could be that governments spend one trillion dollars on arms every year. The UN's peacekeeping budget is less than New York City's annual budget on its fire and police departments. More positively, some of the recent UN successes include the operations in Bosnia-Herzegovina, the most extensive police reform and restructuring project in the UN's history; East Timor, where the UN guided a traumatised people to independence through a ring of fire and helped to lay the foundations of democratic governance; Sierra Leone, where a UN force facilitated the transition to democratic governance by a much improved security environment; and Liberia, where a UN force was dispatched in record time to help in the implementation of a comprehensive peace agreement. In a recent article, the Under-Secretary-General for Peacekeeping noted that in Burundi over the past year, with UN help, a new constitution has been approved, an election held and a new president sworn in in a peaceful transfer of power. In East Timor and Sierra Leone, peacekeepers are packing up and going home, their jobs done. And UN workers are helping Afghanistan to prepare for its first parliamentary elections since the overthrow of the Taliban regime.[47]

Peacekeeping is a circuit breaker in a spiralling cycle of violence. The problem with traditional peacekeeping was that it could at best localise the impact of conflicts and then freeze them. The UN can do the job, sometimes, but only if given all or most of the right tools: uniformed soldiers and police officers from industrial and developing countries, specialised military support services from countries with modern military forces, financial resources, strategic force reserves, political support in the Security Council and sustained commitment. The last requires time and patience, for building sustainable peace has no instant solution. The community of states must be willing to work with local partners and institutions to create enduring structures of liberal democratic governance, the rule of law, market economy and civil society.

---

[46] Up-to-date figures can always be found by navigating through the UN home page on the web (www.un.org).

[47] Jean-Marie Guehénno, 'Putting the Warlords Out of Business', *International Herald Tribune*, 11 September 2005.

2

Peace operations and the UN–US relationship

The Iraq War in 2003 brought to a head a sometimes troubled and uneasy relationship between the world's premier international organisation and its most important member state. The whole affair generated heated controversy about the system of multilateral governance centred on the United Nations and the capacity and propensity of the USA to embark on unilateral adventures. The tension between the competing imperatives to unilateralism and multilateralism in US foreign policy has long bedevilled relations between the UN and the USA with respect to international peace operations, well before the advent of the administration of President George W. Bush. This chapter will seek to demonstrate that the critical UN–US relationship in fact soured over the course of the 1990s with respect to a range of peace support operations.[1] This forms the necessary backdrop to understanding the ill-tempered UN–US exchanges of 2002–5.

The UN Security Council (UNSC) is the proper locus of authorising and legitimising the creation, deployment and use of military force under international auspices. The major powers were given permanent membership of the UNSC and the veto power in recognition of their special role and responsibility in underwriting world order and collective security. When collective security proved unattainable and peacekeeping emerged as a substitute technique for keeping the major powers out of competitive involvement in armed conflicts, direct military involvement by the five permanent members (P5) of the UNSC was not welcome. But they still had to consent to the creation, deployment and financing of UN peacekeeping missions. When the nature of the types of crises into which UN peace operations were deployed changed after the Cold War, the blue berets were often confronted with the challenge of military

---

[1] This is a revised and updated version of 'UN Peace Operations and US Unilateralism and Multilateralism', in David Malone and Yuen Foong Khong, eds., *Unilateralism and US Foreign Policy: International Perspectives* (Boulder: Lynne Rienner, 2003), pp. 153–79. Reprinted with permission of the publisher.

enforcement. It did not take long for the realisation to sink in that the UNSC is singularly ill-suited to being the proper locus of the command and control of fighting forces. The UN's own panel on peacekeeping concluded that 'the United Nations does not wage war'.[2]

If the UN is the font of legitimate international authority, the USA has unparalleled capacity for the maintenance of international peace and security. What is the optimal 'mode of articulation' between the UN as the authoritative custodian and the USA as the de facto underwriter of international peace and world order? For many US decision-makers, it is difficult to understand why those who do not contribute a fair share of the military burden should be given any determinative role in deciding on the deployment of US military forces. One of the main reasons for the US rejection of the League of Nations was fear of an automatic requirement to use military force as decided by the League. The symbolic shift of the world organisation's headquarters from Geneva to New York after the Second World War did not lessen the innate suspicions of overseas entanglements at others' behest. For defeated and pariah states like Japan and Germany, UN peacekeeping was helpful in the 1990s in providing the legitimising framework of multilateralism for hesitant and tentative participation of military units in overseas missions. Unlike them, the USA has not needed international organisations as the vehicle and imprimatur of reintegration into the community of nations. Instead the UN remains a lightning rod for many American concerns about distracting entanglement of American forces overseas.[3] The US Congress was careful to enunciate that decisions by the UNSC could not encroach upon the internal constitutional distribution of war-making power in the USA.

Operation Desert Storm (1990–1) generated unwarranted and unsustainable optimism about the centrality of the UN in the new world order and of the USA in the UN scheme of things. This was ephemeral because it was based on a unique confluence of circumstances that had produced a fortuitous conjunction of US national and international interests. President George Bush left office on a cautiously optimistic note with regard to US–UN relations in international peace operations. The Clinton

[2] *Report of the Panel on United Nations Peace Operations*, UN doc. A/55/305-S/2000/809, 21 August 2000, para. 53.

[3] Sarah B. Sewell, 'Multilateral Peace Operations', in Stewart Patrick and Shepard Forman, eds., *Multilateralism and US Foreign Policy: Ambivalent Engagement* (Boulder: Lynne Rienner, 2002), p. 209.

administration came in with an initial blush of enthusiasm that faded as the reality of peace missions in the complex environment of civil wars put paid to naïveté and enthusiasm for ever-enlarging US involvement in ever-expanding UN missions.

The USA remained essentially multilateral throughout the 1990s. What did change over the course of the 1990s was the centrality of the UN in the US scheme of multilateralism. Learning from experience in a world no longer riven by the Cold War blocs, yet facing messy internal conflicts, Washington progressively divided its multilateral impulse between the UN as the global mobilising and legitimising organisation, and NATO as the strategic enforcement arm for peace operations in Europe. Outside Europe, Washington progressively retrenched from direct participation but not necessarily all forms of involvement in UN peacekeeping. By the end of the century, the peacekeeping effort was channelled through the UN, the security response through NATO or coalitions of the willing, and diplomatic efforts through the European Union or other regional organisations. Multilateralism remains important to US foreign policy and the USA remains the pivot of multilateral action in the maintenance of international peace and security.

The USA and traditional peacekeeping

During the Cold War the USA was not among the ranks of the major UN peacekeepers. The core mission of the US military was considered to be the defence of the USA at home and abroad; its core task was war-fighting; ancillary tasks like disaster relief operations could be accepted on an ad hoc basis; but peacekeeping was a distraction and carried the baggage of too many unnecessary complications, with the potential to infect and undermine the core task of waging and winning wars. US political support in the UNSC was necessary and generally forthcoming, its specialised technical support was irreplaceable and welcome, and its financial support was substantial and unmatched. But the USA neither wanted to be nor was wanted as a UN peacekeeper.

The traditional UN operations underwrote in-theatre stability while the major powers were diplomatically engaged (or not) in efforts to resolve the underlying conflict. The non-P5 peacekeepers did the first part of the equation while the P5 diplomats engaged in the second part. The thin blue line was used to contain and quarantine essentially local conflicts. As a P5 member, the USA had to consent to the establishment of any peacekeeping mission; its national interests were protected through avoidance of military entanglement in a conflict without major significance; yet the maintenance of stability was helpful to its role as the underwriter of world order. In addition, because the P5 were not in fact required to underwrite world order militarily as had been the expectation in constructing the UN system, they were instead asked to assume a disproportionately large share of the financial burdens of UN peacekeeping; other major powers bore a fair share, and the poor countries a disproportionately low share. Washington willingly acquiesced in this set of agreements and arrangements. While the US financial contribution to the UN's regular budget is capped at 25 per cent, its assessed share of UN peacekeeping bills has been 30 per cent.

Thus the UN's universal-multilateral forum was useful as the conduit for minimising and constraining the risks of international engagement in a bloc-divided world. The first substantial UN peacekeeping operation was launched in the Middle East in 1956 as a means of extricating US allies Britain and France from a reckless military adventure strongly opposed by Washington. In Congo in 1960 robust peacekeeping by the UN mission largely furthered US goals and interests. The Cyprus operation in 1964 was at the request and with the participation of loyal ally Britain and a means of keeping NATO members Greece and Turkey from each other's throats. The principle of UN peacekeeping therefore continued to receive diffuse US support until the mid-1960s. But the acquiescence by Secretary-General U Thant to Egypt's request for the withdrawal of the UN Emergency Force (UNEF-I) from the Middle East in 1967, and the manner in which the withdrawal became the curtain raiser to the Six Day War, produced some disillusionment. This was deepened by perceptions of the rise of anti-Americanism and anti-Zionism in a UN (and UNESCO, from which Washington withdrew in disgust in 1984 and did not rejoin until 2003) that was seen to have been captured by radical Third World countries who were determined to pursue a fundamentally illiberal agenda. Nevertheless, Washington itself returned to the UN instrument of peacekeeping after the Yom Kippur War of 1973 as UNEF-II was established; and another traditional mission was established in southern Lebanon in 1978 at American request-cum-insistence and with full American backing.

Post-Cold War optimism

The breadth and depth of US involvement with UN and other multilateral peace missions increased dramatically during the closing days of the

Cold War as the number and complexity of such missions rose. With the end of the Cold War, at the UNSC summit in January 1992, the US administration supported the British call for Secretary-General Boutros Boutros-Ghali to prepare a position paper on how the UN could play a more enhanced and effective role in maintaining international peace. The report was presented in July.[4] The administration also initiated a parallel review in Washington of ways and means by which the USA could help the UN execute an expanded security role.[5] The outcome of the review formed part of the president's address to the UN General Assembly on 21 September where Bush announced that the USA was prepared to introduce a peacekeeping curriculum in US military schools; to train combat, engineering and logistical units for international peace-keeping duties; and to open US military bases for multinational training and field exercises.[6]

There was intense disagreement in Washington over whether the US military should actually participate in UN peacekeeping operations. Some argued that peacekeeping was integral to the new security archi-tecture and US participation would be helpful to the UN and important to the USA in cementing its post-Cold War leadership role. Others regarded UN peacekeeping as a threat to the mission clarity of the task-oriented US military and insisted that the US contribution should be limited to unique capabilities like lift, command and control and intelligence capabilities. Nor was the military hierarchy prepared to accept US troops serving under the operational command of UN officers. The generally more sceptical approach prevailed.

The end of the Cold War, at the same time as it enhanced the potential for more UN peacekeeping operations, made US participation in them more problematical.[7] The abatement of the Soviet threat destroyed the doctrine of containment that had underpinned an unprecedented US engagement with the international order. The absence of a 'clear and present danger' from the Soviet menace made it more difficult to justify

---

[4] Boutros Boutros-Ghali, *An Agenda for Peace: Preventive Diplomacy, Peacemaking and Peace-keeping* (New York: United Nations, 1992).

[5] See Ivo Daalder, 'Knowing When to Say No: The Development of US Policy for Peace-keeping', in William J. Durch, ed., *UN Peacekeeping, American Policy, and the Uncivil Wars of the 1990s* (New York: St. Martin's Press for the Henry L. Stimson Center, 1996), pp. 35–67.

[6] George Bush, *Address to the United Nations General Assembly*, 21 September 1992.

[7] See William J. Durch, 'Keeping the Peace: Politics and Lessons of the 1990s', in Durch, ed., *UN Peacekeeping*, pp. 15–16.

the dispatch of US service personnel to risky foreign conflicts. The transition from the end of the Bush senior administration to the end of Clinton's second term also marked the shift from the new world order optimism at the start of the final decade to the new world disorder pessimism by the close of the twentieth century. The net result was to privilege domestic over international concerns even more in structuring the decision incentives of the administration and Congress.

UN peacekeeping missions were used in Namibia, Cambodia and other places to legitimise the transition from Cold War conflicts to post-Cold War stability, and to (re)integrate these communities into the international community. Washington subscribed to both goals and could not have achieved either on its own. Equally, given the magnitude, range and heavier call on human, technical, logistical and financial resources of the more ambitious missions, the UN would have been hard pressed to achieve anything without active US support and participation.

Later-generation peacekeeping missions required deeper engagement of the UN, and of the USA as its most influential member, in nation-building and peace-building tasks like creating structures of governance and administration alongside military functions like disarmament and demobilisation of combatants. The presence of many inter- and non-governmental organisations with overlapping and competing functions and agendas added to the complexity, untidiness and risks of the operation. Mission creep (where the mandate and tasks expand well beyond the original limited functions) and the lack of credible exit strategies were crucial to the steady erosion of US support for UN operations. The fear of mounting public and Congressional opposition heightened the risk-aversion of US administrations. But the increased casualty aversion of the USA, as it became widely known, merely added to the danger of US personnel being deliberately targeted by hostile elements determined to wreck a peacekeeping mission through severing its weakest link which, ironically, was the strongest member state of the UN.

Events in Europe and Africa tested the limits of the new complex peace support operations and the US–UN division of labour. The escalating crisis in the Balkans in the 1990s had its roots in the inability of Joseph Tito's successors to pursue policies that would keep Yugoslavia united in the changed circumstances of the post-Cold War period. As the republic disintegrated, Washington faced conflicting pressures to support Yugoslav territorial integrity, recognise the independence of newly formed countries seceding from the former republic, support the principle of multiethnic countries, resist systematic and pervasive violations of human rights and resist any hint of embarking down the slippery slope of military intervention. Maintaining a delicate balance between different members of NATO with competing interests in the Balkans was always fraught with difficulty. Yet another complicating factor was the US effort to draw Russia into some sort of partnership for the peace and prosperity of Europe and avoid antagonising it in its geopolitical backyard.

US policy under George Bush was to treat it essentially as Europe's problem. He was prepared to support humanitarian peacekeeping by the UN, provide relief supplies for delivery by UN peacekeepers and financial and logistical support for the operation, but otherwise limit US military and diplomatic exposure by handing over responsibility to the Europeans and the UN. Given the bloody history of the Balkans, the complexity of the conflict, the inhospitable topography and the rugged terrain, Washington effectively regarded the conflict as a no-win quagmire. As the scale of the atrocities being committed became clearer, the clamour for more US involvement grew, but the administration's response remained restricted to substantial financial support and transport and logistical assistance for the UN to airlift relief supplies to Sarajevo. In-theatre military risks were transferred wholly to the UN.

In the Horn of Africa, by contrast, the level of US cooperative involvement with UN peacekeeping did grow rapidly, substantially and disastrously. Ironically, both in Bosnia and Somalia the argument of US exceptionalism,[8] used to telling effect by the administration in mobilising domestic as well as global support for the multinational operation in the Gulf in 1990–1, was turned against its reluctance to respond. Critics of US passivity in the face of evil in Europe and tragedy in Africa recalled and reiterated the argument that US leadership – military, moral, diplomatic and financial – was critical to catalyzing the world into doing whatever was necessary. Intimidated by the difficulties in Bosnia, the administration responded to the pressures in Somalia on the adage that it should if it could.

A humanitarian emergency in Somalia in 1991 snowballed into a crisis of state authority in 1992 and brought forth many calls for active involvement by the international community. Sentiment in Congress, humanitarian

---

[8] For the importance of the sense of exceptionalism in US foreign policy, see Samuel P. Huntington, 'American Ideals versus American Institutions', in G. John Ikenberry, ed., *American Foreign Policy: Theoretical Essays* (New York: Longman, 1999, 3rd edn), pp. 221–53.

relief organisations and the media intensified the pressure for US intervention in the rapidly deteriorating situation in Somalia.[9] The public debate on the appropriate US response to the unfolding crisis in Somalia was mirrored in the discussions within the administration. The State Department was more responsive to calls for greater involvement in relief and rescue efforts. The defence establishment was more concerned to limit US exposure to uncontrollable events.[10] The complexity and intractability of the conflict made them sceptical with regard to the clarity and exit point of any operation, fearing instead mission creep and an open-ended commitment to an ill-defined 'nation-building' mission.

Agreement was reached to commit US troops to securing the environment in Somalia for the delivery of relief supplies to those most in need. But in a concession to the sceptics, it was decided that the US military would mount its own operation, authorised by UNSC Resolution 794 (3 December 1992) but separate and independent from the ongoing UN operation, with a defined end-point and an exit strategy in the form of handing over the mission to the UN once a secure environment for humanitarian relief operations had been established. This was the mandate for the UN-authorised but US-led Unified Task Force (UNITAF). In this low-risk and low-cost concept of US-UN cooperation in multinational peace operations, the risks, burdens and costs would be shared between the USA and the UN based on comparative advantage. The USA would secure the environment by military means in a time-bound mission and then hand over responsibility for nation-building and restoring political stability to the UN in early 1993.

---

[9] The thesis of the so-called 'CNN factor' holds that the US government can be propelled into foreign adventures on the basis of active but selective attention to particular crises by the main US media. The case of Somalia, like those of others, shows that the relationship between the selective attention devoted to foreign events by public authorities and the media is more nuanced and mutually reinforcing: the media will cover stories where US personnel are involved more than other stories. But the prospect of US involvement increases if the US media covers a foreign crisis in a big way. Thus Mohamed Sahnoun, the Special Representative of the Secretary-General for Somalia at the time, actively courted the major Western media in 1992 in order to increase Somalia's attention span in the minds of the principal policy-makers. Private discussions, 2001.

[10] One of the best accounts of the US story with respect to Somalia is by ambassadors John Hirsch and Robert Oakley, *Somalia and Operation Restore Hope: Reflections on Peacemaking and Peacekeeping* (Washington, DC: US Institute of Peace, 1995). See also John Bolton, 'Wrong Turn in Somalia', *Foreign Affairs* 73:1 (January/February 1994), pp. 56–66.

At the end of 1992 it appeared that the UN framework had provided the means to avoid the destiny of becoming a hyper-power, engaged and entangled everywhere: the UN provided the administration with the means to purchase a leveraged buy-out of unilateral US responsibility for world order. In President Bill Clinton's first term, the initial euphoria of working through the UN system in order to pursue US interests and promote US values generated enthusiasm for the established cooperative framework and legitimating authority of the international organisation. The administration pursued a policy of 'assertive multilateralism', meaning not just multilateral engagement, but American leadership within collective organisations in order to infuse them with American values and ideology.

The US retreat from multilateralism

Somalia

The initial Clinton world-view was addressed through Presidential Review Directive 13 (PRD-13) designed to bolster the capabilities and efficiency of UN peacekeeping. However, under charges of handing over control of the US national security agenda to the UN, weakening US ability to defend its own interests and entangling the USA in UN-led action, the administration steadily retreated from early positions. The transformations were not unrelated to the rapidly evolving situations on the ground in Somalia and Bosnia. UNOSOM-II, the follow-up operation to UNITAF, had a mishmash of humanitarian, disarmament and state-building objectives throughout Somalia.[11] Most crucially and without precedent, it was established under Chapter 7 of the UN Charter pertaining to collective enforcement – the significance of which was not apparent to the USA at the time. Their naïveté was dispelled within a few months. The command and control relationship between US troops and UNOSOM-II was fuzzy. In reality the US troops never took operational orders from

---

[11] For analyses of the Somalia failure as a peacekeeping operation, in addition to Hirsch and Oakley, *Somalia and Operation Restore Hope*, and Bolton, 'Wrong Turn in Somalia', see William J. Durch, 'Introduction to Anarchy: Humanitarian Intervention and "State Building" in Somalia', in Durch, ed., *UN Peacekeeping*, pp. 311–65; Robert Patman, 'The UN Operation in Somalia', in Ramesh Thakur and Carlyle A. Thayer, eds., *A Crisis of Expectations: UN Peacekeeping in the 1990s* (Boulder: Westview, 1995), pp. 85–104; and Ramesh Thakur, 'From Peacekeeping to Peace Enforcement: The UN Operation in Somalia', *Journal of Modern African Studies* 32:3 (September 1994), pp. 387–410.

the UN Force Commander. Instead, the logistics unit was under the command and control of the US Central Command (CENTCOM), and the civilian head of UNOSOM-II was US Admiral Jonathan Howe, appointed at Washington's request.

The US–UN politics of these complicated command and control arrangements created confusion and generated mutual suspicion and anger in the field. They proved simply unworkable once crisis struck. When Pakistani peacekeepers were killed on 5 June, the UNSC author-ised 'all necessary measures' on the 6th to deal with their attackers and US forces took part in the ensuing operations. The heightened US military involvement turned US soldiers into targets for retaliatory attacks and four were killed in a landmine explosion in August. This in turn awakened Congressional and media interest in and questioning of US involvement in a conflict devoid of vital national interests. Another 400 US soldiers were dispatched, but the special troops were to serve directly under CENTCOM command. In October, without prior UN knowledge or approval, they launched a raid on a suspected hideout of Somali warlord General Mohamed Farah Aideed. On 3 October 1993, eighteen US Rangers were killed – the largest single combat casualty for the US military since Vietnam – and one dead American soldier was paraded through the streets of Mogadishu by the very people that Americans had supposedly risked their lives to help.

The footage of the incidents, broadcast repeatedly throughout the world, sapped any remaining US resolve to stay the course in Somalia. Sensitive to the charge of having ceded control of US foreign policy to the UN,[12] the administration did little to discourage Congressional, press and public attribution of the blame to the world organisation. The impression was left to fester that the operation had been ordered, directed and controlled by the UN and that the fiasco was the result of UN incapacity to fight wars and keep the peace. The alienation of responsibility from the USA to the UN helped to shore up the adminis-tration's crumbling credibility in domestic politics but only at the ex-pense of lasting damage to US–UN relations. The decision to pull out the US troops from UNOSOM, after a suitable grace period for the sake of appearances, was made in Washington free of any encumbering consult-ations with the UN. The announcement of a withdrawal by the end of

---

[12] One of the most influential op-ed articles of the time was former UN ambassador Jeanne Kirkpatrick's 'Where Is Our Foreign Policy?' *Washington Post*, 30 August 1993.

March 1994, and a scaling down of the operation to focus solely on humanitarian delivery, forestalled Congressional calls for an immediate end to the US participation in the Somalia mission.

The new Washington consensus held that the complexity of tasks in modern peace operations was beyond the institutional capacity of the UN to manage, too dynamic and fluid for rigid criteria and guidelines to be of much practical use, too uneven in the manner in and extent to which they cut across US political and security interests, and too divisive and fractured for any international consensus to hold in the UN system. In his address to the UN General Assembly on 27 September 1993, Clinton spoke more of the limits to multilateralism in shaping US foreign policy than its potential for externalising the costs while internalising the benefits of international engagement.

The administration now made a distinction between offering political support and military contributions. US comparative advantage lay in specialised areas like logistics, training, intelligence, communications and transportation (air and sea lift capability). When the drawn-out review of US policy on UN peacekeeping was finally completed and signed in May 1994 as Presidential Decision Directive 25 (PDD-25), the emphasis was far more on making UN peacekeeping efficient, cost-effective and selective ('It will be easier for the US to say Yes if the UN learns when to say No'[13]) than on enthusiastic US participation in UN peacekeeping.[14] The most immediate and most tragic price was to be paid by almost a million Rwandans when the US in general, and Ambassador Madeleine Albright in particular, rejected calls for a modestly expanded UN operation to defeat, contain or avert the genocidal killings.[15] The conviction grew in the UN community in turn that the USA was becoming an irresponsible member state prone to making illegal and unreasonable demands on the organisation in return for less than full financial support. American public opinion in the 1990s

---

[13] That was an interesting experience, Bill Clinton telling the UN to learn to say No.

[14] For a study of PDD-25, see Michael G. MacKinnon, *The Evolution of US Peacekeeping Policy Under Clinton: A Fairweather Friend?* (London: Frank Cass, 2000).

[15] See Michael Barnett, *Eyewitness to a Genocide: The United Nations and Rwanda* (Ithaca: Cornell University Press, 2003); Roméo Dallaire, *Shake Hands with the Devil: The Failure of Humanity in Rwanda* (New York: Random House, 2003); Mahmood Mamdani, *When Victims become Killers: Colonialism, Nativism, and the Genocide in Rwanda* (Princeton: Princeton University Press, 2002); Linda Melvern, *A People Betrayed: The Role of the West in Rwanda's Genocide* (London: Zed Books, 2000); and Samantha Power, '*A Problem from Hell*': *America and the Age of Genocide* (New York: Perennial, 2003).

favoured the channelling of US overseas military action through the UN. The distancing of the USA from the UN by the Clinton administration was less a response to public hostility than an attempt to pre-empt political opponents from making it a damaging issue in the internecine domestic squabbles between a Democratic White House and a Republican Congress.[16]

The Balkans

As the Somalia intervention turned to disaster, Washington found it expedient not to allay the gathering impression that the major policy decisions leading to the débâcle in Somalia were the fault of the UN, and that US troops killed in Mogadishu had been under UN operational command who had thus implicitly failed to assure the safety of US soldiers. The USA found it similarly expedient not to dispel the illusion that a passive UNSC was preventing a more active US engagement in Bosnia.

Bill Clinton had pressed George Bush hard on Bosnia during the election campaign in 1992 and entered office believing that to be the most urgent foreign policy issue. The complexity of the conflict and the limited nature of US interests convinced the new administration to stay essentially within the parameters of the previous administration: to mitigate the humanitarian crisis and contain the Bosnian conflict without getting the USA directly involved in 'another Vietnam'.

But Washington, NATO and the UN could neither contain the Bosnian conflict nor mute the humanitarian catastrophe. Calls grew more insistent in Congress and the press for Washington to do something, including ending the arms embargo which was disproportionate in its impact on the Muslims. But a unilateral lifting of a UN-imposed embargo would complicate efforts to maintain the increasingly fraying international coalition with regard to sanctions on Iraq and undermine the authority of the UNSC more broadly. As the Serbs grew ever bolder in challenging UN-imposed limitations on their activity, the UN and NATO worked out dual key arrangements whereby the Special Representative of the Secretary-General could authorise NATO air strikes against designated targets. This neither intimidated, deterred nor defeated Serb territorial ambitions and increasingly brazen atrocities. When reports of ethnic cleansing could no longer be credibly denied

---

[16] The two competing hypotheses are explored and evaluated in MacKinnon, *The Evolution of US Peacekeeping Policy Under Clinton.*

and Serb troops were engaged in massacring civilians who had sought shelter in UN 'safe areas' that had been overrun by Serb troops, leading NATO members began in 1995 to contemplate pulling out of the increasingly ineffectual UNPROFOR.

At this point Washington faced the choice between a fatal erosion of NATO authority and credibility as the guarantor of European peace in the post-Cold War Europe; the defeat of UN peacekeeping in the Balkans and a resulting loss of US credibility as alliance and global leader; and increased direct exposure to the Balkan conflict. The authority to launch air strikes was progressively detached from the UN, assumed directly by NATO and used more forcefully and effectively, while the UN mission was scaled down to humanitarian and traditional peacekeeping activities. In addition, diplomatic negotiations were also taken outside the UN framework, although the UN was kept informed (and in any case, NATO members dominate the UN Security Council), and culminated in the Dayton Accords of November 1995.

One item of unfinished business at Dayton was Kosovo. The growing lesson of the Balkans in the 1990s had been that for decisive and effective action against President Slobodan Milošević, the political solidarity and military cohesion of NATO was a more congenial multilateral framework for collective action than the UNSC. In the early 1990s, the UN framework had enabled Washington to disclaim responsibility for the tragedy in the Balkans. The scale of the tragedy had magnified to such an extent that it threatened to destabilise the entire region, destroy the credibility of NATO and diminish the authority of the UN. Sickened by Milošević's record of brutality in the Balkans and evasions and deceit in dealings with the Europeans and the UN, in 1999 the US decided on 'humanitarian intervention' in Kosovo through the multilateral framework of NATO but without prior UNSC authorisation.[17]

Somalia and Rwanda became metaphors in the US political discourse of the UN as a failed international organisation, and that perception helped Washington to rally support for action outside the UN framework in Kosovo. Yet the USA bore significant responsibility in both, through acts of commission in Somalia where US troops went on a hunt for General Aideed like cowboys beyond UN control, and of omission in Rwanda where any possible timely action by the UNSC was stymied by US refusal to get involved in, or even support, enforcement action at any level in Africa in the post-Somalia atmosphere.

[17] This is discussed in chapter 9 below.

Relative gains and costs of unilateralism and multilateralism

At times US power and international authority can be in isolation from each other, for example with respect to the MNF in Beirut in the early 1980s[18] or the international control commissions in Indochina in the 1950s.[19] Or force and authority can work in tandem. Using the metaphor in its exact sense, the UN can lead and America support, which is the preferred US model today with respect to peacekeeping duties in Africa; or Washington can lead and the UN can support, as in Korea in the 1950s, the Gulf War in 1991 and allied troops in the Balkans today.

The USA had no peer competitor in the drafting and construction of the normative architecture of the multilateral machinery for the maintenance of international peace and security. The UN system was the forum and instrument for externalising American values and virtues like democracy, human rights, rule of law and market economy, and embedding them in international institutions. Nor does the USA have a peer competitor today in operating and driving the multilateral machinery for the maintenance of international peace and security. The UN helps to mute the costs and spread the risks of the terms of international engagement. It is a means of mediating the choice between isolationism – disengagement from the world – and unilateralism, or going it alone; between inaction through refusing to be a cop and intervention through being the world's only cop. But in order to maximise these benefits, Washington needs to instil the principle of multilateralism itself as a norm in its own right: states must do X because the UN has called for X, and good states do what the UN asks them to do.

In the First Gulf War in 1990–1, the language used to construct Iraq as a major threat to international peace (as distinct from US material interests) emphasised the danger of Iraq's action to the system of codified order (the so-called 'new world order') whose basic tenets were being challenged and violated. An international consensus was forged and maintained and US national interests were subsumed within that international consensus. Moreover, being the virtuous power, the USA, and no one else, had both the moral standing and the material capacity to provide international leadership and galvanise the UN into action.

---

[18] See Ramesh Thakur, *International Peacekeeping in Lebanon: United Nations Authority and Multinational Force* (Boulder: Westview, 1987).

[19] See Ramesh Thakur, *Peacekeeping in Vietnam: Canada, India, Poland and the International Commission* (Edmonton: University of Alberta Press, 1984).

Conclusion

There are by now enough cases for a preliminary comparative assessment of UN and US experience in peace operations. Rand undertook just such an exercise.[20] Its results make for very interesting reading and certainly reinforce the need for complementary operations based on comparative advantage. The UN is better at low-profile, small footprint operations where its soft power assets of international legitimacy and local impartiality compensate for hard power deficit. The quality of UN peacekeeping troops, police officers and civilian administrators is more uneven and has become worse with the retrenchment of Western nations from UN operations, and their arrival on the scene is often tardy. But military reversals are less consequential for the UN because military force is not the source of its credibility, whereas they strike at the very heart of the basis of US influence. In order to overcome domestic scepticism for overseas missions, American policy-makers define the mission in grandiloquent terms and make the operations hostage to their own rhetoric, while UN missions are outcomes of highly negotiated, densely bureaucratic and much more circumspect documents. Because member states are unwilling to contribute more manpower or money, UN operations tend to be under-manned and under-resourced, deploying small and weak forces into hopefully post-conflict situations under best-case assumptions. If the assumptions prove false, the forces are reinforced, withdrawn or rescued. Washington deploys US troops under worst-case assumptions with overwhelming force to establish a secure environment quickly. The USA was spending $4.5 billion per month just in Iraq in 2004, compared to under $4 billion per year for all the seventeen UN missions combined. This does not mean that the UN could do the job in Iraq better, more efficiently or more cheaply, but it did mean that there were at least seventeen other places where Washington did not face calls to intervene because the UN was already doing the job.

UN missions have been the more successful – a higher proportion of local countries were left in peaceful and democratic conditions than with

---

[20] James Dobbins, et al., *America's Role in Nation-Building: From Germany to Iraq* (Santa Monica: Rand, 2003), and *The UN's Role in Nation-Building: From the Congo to Iraq* (Santa Monica: Rand, 2005). Dobbins presented a paper summarising the main conclusions at a conference in Hiroshima; 'The UN's Role in Nation Building: From the Belgian Congo to Iraq', UNITAR/IPS Conference on United Nations as Peacekeeper and Nation-Builder, Hiroshima, 28–29 March 2005.

US operations. This could be a statistical artifice, in that a different selection of cases might have produced different results. Or it could indicate that the American operations have been intrinsically more difficult, requiring larger forces, more robust mandates and greater combat weight. Or it could even be that the UN has been better at learning lessons. Dobbins notes that Secretary-General Kofi Annan kept many of his staff from his days as Under-Secretary-General for Peacekeeping with him in New York in key advisory positions, thereby offsetting many institutional discontinuities. By contrast, Washington 'tends to staff each new operation as if it were its first, and is destined to be its last'.[21] In sum, non-UN operations tend to be more costly, as with US or EU missions in Europe, or less competent, as with regional organisations other than European. The US and UN roles complement each other in managing the messy conflicts around the world. The total number of UN peacekeepers – 65,000 in 2005 – may be modest by the standards of American expeditionary capability but is more than any other country or coalition can field. But neither the UN nor the USA has been able to move successfully from initial stabilisation and the re-establishment of local institutions for governance to the more demanding goal of self-sustaining structures of state that can implement rapid economic growth and social transformation.

Peace operations enlarge the spectrum of capabilities available to the international community to respond to threats of chaos in the periphery. But the UN does not have its own military and police forces and would be hard-pressed to achieve anything of note without active US engagement, let alone against its vital interests and determined opposition. UN operations permit Washington to choose its preferred mode of articulation between international/UN responses and US engagement on a spectrum of the level and geographical theatre of international involvement. Participation in them symbolises solidarity and encapsulates shared responsibility. At the end of the spectrum, if the UN is unable or unwilling to honour its responsibility to protect victims of genocide, ethnic cleansing or other egregious humanitarian atrocities, Washington can forge multilateral coalitions of the willing to lead military interventions to stop the atrocities. The Brahimi Report reinforced the importance of the formula of a UN-authorised force under the active leadership of a significant military power. For while the UNSC can validate the legitimacy of a peace

---

[21] Dobbins, 'The UN's Role in Nation Building', p. 16.

support operation, the UN does not have enough professionally trained and equipped troops and police forces of its own. Successful operations that need robust mandates might still have to depend on coalitions of the able, willing and duly authorised.

For decades, UN peace operations have served US security interests in the Middle East, southern Africa, Central America, Southeast Asia and Haiti. By their very nature, they cannot produce conclusive results either on the battlefield – they are peace operations, not war – or around the negotiating table – they are military deployments, not diplomatic talks. Criticisms levelled at UN peace operations can be fundamentally mis-conceived, intentionally ill-conceived, grossly exaggerated or designed to deflect criticisms from the failures of the administration.[22] Conversely, the disengagement of the USA from UN peacekeeping has had a spill-over effect in eroding partially the legitimacy of UN operations, and therefore the effectiveness of the UN as the primary manager of inter-national security. In turn, this has reduced US leverage in spreading the burden of providing international security and lessening the demands and expectations on the USA to take up the slack. At the same time, scapegoating the UN has produced a backlash among other nations and so reduced the US ability to use the UN in pursuit of US goals.

Because the world is essentially anarchical, it is fundamentally inse-cure, characterised by strategic uncertainty and complexity because of too many actors with multiple goals and interests and variable capabil-ities and convictions. Liberal institutionalists believe that multilateral organisations externalise such bedrock US values as respect for the rule of law, due process and human rights. Multilateralism – the coordination of relations among several states in accordance with certain principles[23] (such as sovereign equality) – rests on assumptions of the indivisibility of the benefits of collective public goods (peace, telecommunications, transportation, etc.) and diffuse reciprocity (whereby collective action

---

[22] See, for example, the systematic rebuttal of persistent US criticisms of UN peace operations by a former New Zealand Secretary of Defence who is anything but anti-American, having been pilloried in the second half of the 1980s in his home country for having been too pro-American; Denis McLean, 'Peace Operations and Common Sense', in Chester A. Crocker and Fen Osler Hampson with Pamela Aall, eds., *Managing Global Chaos: Sources and Responses to International Conflict* (Washington, DC: United States Institute of Peace, 1996), pp. 321–32.

[23] John G. Ruggie, 'Multilateralism: The Anatomy of an Institution', in John G. Ruggie, ed., *Multilateralism Matters: The Theory and Praxis of an Institutional Form* (New York: Columbia University Press, 1993), pp. 8–11.

arrangements confer an equivalence of benefits, not on every issue and every occasion, but in aggregate and over time[24]).

US power, wealth and politics are too deeply intertwined with the cross-currents of international affairs for disengagement to be a credible or sustainable policy posture for the world's only superpower. Unilateralism – what Richard Haass, Director of the Policy Planning Unit at the State Department, called 'à la carte multilateralism',[25] or what some others in private call, even more dismissively, disposable multilateralism – cannot be the strategy of choice either.

Because peacekeeping is likely to remain the instrument of choice by the UN for engaging with the characteristic types of conflicts in the contemporary world, the US approach to peace operations will continue to define the nature of the US engagement with the UN. Perceptions of US disengagement will in turn erode the US ability to harness UN legitimacy to causes and battles that may be more important to the USA than peacekeeping in messy conflicts in far-away countries whose names can neither be pronounced nor remembered by US voters and members of Congress, and sometimes even by presidents. Because the USA will remain the main financial underwriter of the costs of UN peacekeeping, it will continue to exercise unmatched influence on the establishment, mandate, nature, size and termination of UN peace operations. At the same time, the level of informed interest about the UN is so low in the American body politic that any administration will always be able to distance itself from spectacular failures of UN peacekeeping.

UN peacekeeping rests on a conjunction of interests in overseeing peace. That consensus has difficulty surviving any effort to transform the mission into keeping the peace by force. There is the requisite convergence of wishes to supervise peace in the larger interests of the international security. Force cannot be used effectively without the participation of major powers. The international consensus collapses because the use of force by great powers is inseparable from calculations of national interest. As this reality was internalised by US decision-makers in the 1990s, they progressively shifted the task of enforcement from the UN to NATO, while retaining the UN framework for legitimising multilateral enforcement operations.

---

[24] Robert Keohane, 'Reciprocity in International Relations', *International Organization* 40:1 (Winter 1986), pp. 1–27.

[25] Quoted in Thom Shanker, 'Bush's Way: "A la Carte" Approach to Treaties', *International Herald Tribune*, 1 August 2001.

Any US president must grapple with five interlinked and challenging questions on when and how Washington should:

1. offer political support to UN missions;
2. provide military assistance to them;
3. participate in possible combat operations through them;
4. enhance the peacekeeping credentials of the UN; and
5. opt for military action outside the UN framework.

The five-item menu of options means that the dichotomy between unilateralism and multilateralism in American foreign policy with respect to international peacekeeping is false. UN peace operations are only one of many foreign policy tools available to the USA, others being multilateral action through standing alliances like NATO, or an ad hoc multinational coalition as in the Gulf War, or even unilateral US action if truly vital interests are involved. In the case of non-UN operations, the USA would prefer to obtain the legitimating approbation of the United Nations if possible, in the form of enabling UNSC resolutions authorising the operations. But Washington will not accept a prior UNSC resolution as a mandatory requirement. The problematic element in this comes from the equally compelling US interest in promoting the norm of the UN being the only collective legitimator of international military action for everyone else. Washington thus faces an unresolved and irreconcilable dilemma between instilling the principle of multilateralism as the world order norm and exempting itself from the same principle because of the sustaining and enduring belief in exceptionalism, in its identity as the virtuous power.

Peacekeeping is but one item on the full menu of the multilateral meal. 'Cherry picking' or 'forum shopping' with regard to multilateralism risks generating normative inconsistency (different applications of the same norm) and incoherence (incompatibility between cognate norms). Being the only superpower is seen as having encouraged the USA to set the rules of globalisation, choose some parts (trade liberalisation) and reject others (globalised decision-making), lecture others on the rule of law while refusing to accept international criminal jurisdiction, and promoting the rhetoric of pluralism and diversity when the world is concerned about the concentration of multimedia power in a few US hands, etc.[26] This provokes normative contestation. Those who

---

[26] See, for example, Philip Bowring, 'Bush's America is Developing an Image Problem', *International Herald Tribune*, 31 May 2001.

are unhappy with an existing norm begin to question its validity or point to US rejection of one norm as justification for their own rejection of another norm. Over time, extensive contestation over specific norms risks chipping away at the foundations of the normative architecture. In the end, a collapse of the normative architecture would be more damaging to US national interests than to the national interests of any other country in the world.

PART II

Soft security perspectives

3

Human security

'Although the United Nations gave birth to the notion of human security,
it proved poorly equipped to provide it'.[1]

The challenge posed by the massive earthquake and devastating tsunami
of 26 December 2004 was a vivid illustration of the advantages of conceptualising security within the inclusive framework of human security. The
natural disaster caused catastrophic loss of life in many countries around
the perimeter of the Indian Ocean, including thousands of Westerners
vacationing in the pleasure resorts. Mother Nature did not discriminate
between Muslim and Christian, Tamil and Sinhalese, poor and rich, native
and foreigner. She claimed them all equally to her bosom in the sea to
bring forcefully home the realisation that we are indeed one human
family. We inhabit the same planet Earth, and artificially constructed
enmity and rivalry based on the competitive and exclusionary concept
of national security can be irrelevant to securing citizens against the real
threats to their safety. The very symbol of 'us against them' national
security – military forces – was used cooperatively in the international
effort to provide disaster relief and assistance to the victims.

At the same time, the general expectation was that the lead responsibility for organising international rescue and relief operations belonged
properly to the United Nations. Thus even when nominated to the select
core group of four aid coordinators, India demurred, saying that the UN
should lead.[2] President Susilo Bambang Yudhoyono of Indonesia, the
worst-hit nation, said that 'We must ensure that we benefit from the
experience of the United Nations in establishing and managing special
emergency funds and relief efforts.'[3] US Secretary of State Colin Powell

---

[1] High-Level Panel on Threats, Challenges and Change, *A More Secure World: Our Shared Responsibility* (New York: United Nations, A/59/565, December 2004), para. 13.
[2] *Hindu* (Chennai), 4 January 2005.
[3] *Japan Times*, 7 January 2005.

confirmed that the four-nation core group to coordinate tsunami relief (Australia, India, Japan and the USA) would be disbanded and folded into broader UN operations. A number of UN agencies swung immediately into action as soon as the world awoke to the magnitude of the disaster: the Office for the Coordination of Humanitarian Affairs (OCHA), the children's fund (UNICEF), the World Food Programme (WFP), the World Health Organisation (WHO), etc.

As the tsunami example illustrates, the concept of security has been stretched both horizontally, to embrace issues beyond just the military, and vertically, moving up to embrace regional and global structures and down to local and individual identities.[4] In the traditional framework, security is viewed in relation to wars between countries. In order to defend the nation, to pursue national security, many governments have called on citizens to make the ultimate sacrifice. This puts the individual at the service of the state, including killing others and being killed oneself, as and when called for duty by the government of the day. By contrast, human security puts the individual at the centre of the debate, analysis and policy. He or she is paramount, and the state is a collective instrument to protect human life and enhance human welfare. The fundamental components of human security – the security of *people* against threats to personal safety and life – can be put at risk by external aggression, but also by factors within a country, including 'security' forces. The reformulation of national security into the concept of human security is simple, yet has profound consequences for how we see the world, how we organise our political affairs, how we make choices in public and foreign policy, and how we relate to fellow human beings from many different countries and civilisations.

One 'leg' of human security is in the human rights tradition which sees the state as the problem and the source of threats to individual security.[5] The other is in the development agenda that sees the state as the necessary agent for promoting human security. Both are reflected in UN policy discourse, and indeed may well explain why the human security discourse first arose within the United Nations and was popularised by the 1994 *Human Development Report* published by the UN Development Programme (UNDP). Human security was said to include

---

[4] The distinction between horizontal and vertical dimensions of security was drawn by Emma Rothschild, 'What is Security?', *Daedalus: Journal of the American Academy of Arts and Sciences* (Summer 1995).

[5] See Bertrand Ramcharan, *Human Rights and Human Security* (The Hague: Kluwer, 2002).

the seven dimensions of economic, food, health, environmental, personal, community and political security.

In general, and despite some overlaps[6] as in the Ottawa Treaty banning anti-personnel landmines,[7] Canada and Japan have each emphasised a different leg of human security. Canadians have given priority to protecting citizens at risk of atrocities arising from failed or perpetrator states and set up an international commission to try to reconcile the imperative to render effective protection to at-risk populations with the persisting reality of state sovereignty. Japan has prioritised the developmental leg of human security, and set up its own World Commission on Human Security. The Canadian-sponsored commission defined human security as 'the security of people – their physical safety, their economic and social well-being, respect for their dignity and worth as human beings, and the protection of their human rights and fundamental freedoms'.[8] The Japanese-sponsored commission defined it as protecting 'the vital core of all human lives in ways that enhance human freedoms and human fulfilment'. It means 'creating political, social, environmental, economic, military and cultural systems that together give people the building blocks of survival, livelihood and dignity'.[9] The emotional rod that connects both the protection and well-being agendas is solidarity across borders, the sense of shared affinity with fellow human beings qua human beings regardless of differences in nationality, race, religion or gender.

The reality of human insecurity cannot simply be wished away. To many poor people in the world's poorest countries today, the risk of being attacked by terrorists or with weapons of mass destruction is far removed from the pervasive reality of the so-called soft threats – hunger, lack of safe drinking water and sanitation and endemic diseases – that kill millions every year, far more than the so-called 'hard' or 'real' threats to security. The 2005 *Human Development Report* has some telling – and grim – comparative statistics. For all of India's economic successes in the

---

[6] For a comparison of the two, see Kanti Bajpai, 'The Idea of Human Security', *International Studies* 40 (2003), pp. 207–16.

[7] See Ramesh Thakur and William Maley, 'The Ottawa Convention on Landmines: A Landmark Humanitarian Treaty in Arms Control?', *Global Governance* 5:3 (July–September 1999), pp. 273–302.

[8] *The Responsibility to Protect*. Report of the International Commission on Intervention and State Sovereignty (Ottawa: International Development Research Centre for ICISS, 2001), p. 15.

[9] *Human Security Now* (New York: Commission on Human Security, 2003), p. 4.

past decade, its child mortality reduction rates have not matched those of its poorer neighbour Bangladesh. *Had India matched Bangladesh, 732,000 fewer Indian children would have died in 2005.*[10] Among children aged 1–5, girls are 50 per cent more likely to die than boys. That is, 130,000 girls are discriminated to death every year in India.[11] Globally, on 2005 trends, the shortfall in the Millennium Development Goal target for reducing child mortality will lead to *4.4 million avoidable deaths* in 2015.[12] Some 2.3 million children could be kept alive through preventive and curative neonatal interventions at a cost of $4 billion – just two days of military spending in the developed countries.[13] More than one billion people in the world lack access to clean water and 2.6 billion to sanitation. These deficits could be overcome through a decade-long annual investment of $7 billion – less than what Europeans spend on perfume – which would save 4,000 lives *each day* from the resulting reduced exposure to infectious diseases.[14]

The soft threats are neither unconnected to peace and security, nor can they be ignored until the hard threats have been taken care of. For, in the words of Kofi Annan, 'we should have learned by now that a world of glaring inequality – between countries and within them – where many millions of people endure brutal oppression and extreme misery, is never going to be a fully safe world, even for its most privileged inhabitants'.[15] Neither development nor security can be achieved without the other and enjoyed without respect for human rights. The UN must work to ensure that 'all people have the freedom to choose the kind of lives they would like to live, the access to the resources that would make those choices meaningful and the security to ensure that they can be enjoyed in peace'.[16]

This is why human security can be regarded as a foundational value from which flow other individual and social values.[17] This helps, too, to

[10] UNDP, *Human Development Report 2005. International Cooperation at a Crossroads: Aid, Trade and Security in an Unequal World* (New York: Oxford University Press, 2005), p. 29.

[11] Ibid., p. 31.

[12] Ibid., p. 41.

[13] Ibid., p. 33.

[14] Ibid., p. 93.

[15] Kofi A. Annan, 'Defining a New Role for the United Nations', *International Herald Tribune (IHT)*, 4 December 2003.

[16] Kofi A. Annan, *In Larger Freedom: Towards Development, Security and Human Rights For All.* Report of the Secretary-General (New York: United Nations, document A/59/2005, 21 March 2005), para. 17.

[17] Hans van Ginkel and Edward Newman, 'In Quest of "Human Security"', *Japan Review of International Affairs* 14:1 (Spring 2000), pp. 59–82.

explain why the African Union has adopted the expansive definition of human security.[18] Africans' security is threatened more by state weakness, incapacity and absence of control over its territory, people and resources than by conventional threats of armed attack by other countries. At the same time, individuals cannot be secure in conditions of anarchy at the state level. The state must be efficient in the provision of law and order and other public goods. Thus secure and stable countries and a body of law that mediates the exercise of power between citizens and the state are prerequisites of human security. But so, too, is human development, *which is not synonymous with but contributes to human security* by tackling the long-term structural causes of conflict and by converting the choices available to people from merely theoretical to effective (as in effective demand in economics). Only so can people exercise effective choice to pursue a safe life and livelihood on equal terms with others.

In this chapter, I will argue that security is a contested concept and there are several ways of constructing it. The choice may reflect trade-offs between precision of meaning and breadth of coverage or between different value clusters. By the same token, framing security as human security facilitates a particular set of policies directed at protecting and prolonging the lives of individual human beings.

Security as a contested concept

One of the UN's early great achievements was to oversee the decolonisation of large parts of the human family. Emerging from colonial rule in the shadow of the Cold War that was transcendental as well as global, many of the new countries were less interested in the Cold War rivalry than in development. This meant that the UN soon acquired two great mandates: peace and security, and growth and development. The linkage between the two great agendas of security and development became clearer and more widely accepted after the end of the Cold War in the form of peace-building.

We tend to assume that the phrase 'national security' has been around forever. In fact it was only in 1945 that Secretary of Defense James Forrestal invoked the concept as a guiding principle of US foreign

---

[18] See Jakkie Cilliers, *Human Security in Africa: A Conceptual Framework for Review* (Pretoria: African Human Security Initiative, 2004), p. 8.

policy.[19] Its immediate and lasting popularity was the result of the way in which it encapsulated a world-view. The utility of 'human security' lies in the way in which it is a similar shorthand for an elegant new analytical lens for framing policy choices and 'a very powerful concept around which practical policies and concrete initiatives can be developed and promoted'.[20]

During the Cold War, the central balance was dominated by the highly militarised and ideologically transcendental confrontation between Moscow and Washington. Both because the threat of actual war was real and its scope would have been total, military concerns dominated the security agenda. That particular bipolar relationship has ended and the dominance of the military factor has gone with it. What has not changed is the dominance of the English-language security literature by British and US analysts and a resulting conflation of international security concerns into Anglo–US security preoccupations. As most of them are insular in their reading, they remain uncontaminated by the real world of political choice in developing countries.[21] As Kolodziej observed, 'Those concerned with comparative security studies or with regional conflict – and with the end of the Cold War the latter is what we will have in abundance – dismiss the thinking and behavior of non-Americans only at the peril of both their scholarly credentials and policy relevance.'[22]

After the end of the Cold War, there was a spurt of ethnonational conflicts, complex humanitarian emergencies and even genocide with massive civilian deaths. The intensification of conflict and human vulnerability blurred the Westphalian line between the domestic and international spheres of human activity and the dominant paradigm of national security, with its narrow focus on territorial integrity, state sovereignty and political independence, weakened under assault from the broader concept of human security.

---

[19] Keith Krause, 'Is Human Security "More than Just a Good Idea"?', in *Promoting Security: But How and For Whom?* (Bonn: Bonn International Center for Conversion, Brief 30, October 2004), p. 43.

[20] Ibid.

[21] Unlike Western academics, Western diplomats do have to come into contact with non-Western counterparts on a regular basis and have less capacity to impose their hegemonical views.

[22] Edward A. Kolodziej, 'Renaissance in Security Studies?: Caveat Lector!' *International Studies Quarterly* 36:4 (December 1992), p. 434.

The concept of 'security' is politically powerful, weakly conceptualised and intensely contested:

1. Who are the objects or referents of security: *for whom* is security intended – individuals, groups, nation, state, region, world?
2. What are the instruments of security: *by what means* is security to be achieved – military, nuclear, political, diplomatic, economic, cultural (e.g. a war over ideas, or for the soul of Islam)?
3. What are the costs of security: *at what price* to the economy and to the social and political values can security be achieved?

Our answers to the three questions have been changing since the end of the Cold War when there occurred 'an explosion of activity around the concept of human security'.[23] The very fact of raising these questions suggests, too, the need to explore the phenomenon of securitisation: who securitises an issue, how and for whom? The 'sociology of securitisation' situates the definition and pursuit of security within their particular, but over time shifting and evolving, context. The states system, and the focus on state security, is a characteristic of the Westphalian system that emerged as the answer to the problem of order and violence in seventeenth-century Europe. The consolidation of the primacy of the state in the eighteenth–nineteenth centuries was accompanied by the monopolisation of security by the state. The state provided the solution to the security dilemmas of individuals who sublimated their quest for personal safety to the identity and security of the state.

By the same token, once the underlying assumption began to fray, the fusion of individual and state security began to unravel. MacFarlane and Khong attribute the rise of human security in the twentieth century to six factors.[24] First, the participants in armed conflict broadened from a narrow elite to mass conscripts. Second, the consequences of the industrial and scientific revolutions dramatically increased the range, lethality and accuracy of firepower, meaning that the state had to accept growing numbers of its own people being killed in the effort to protect them. The ultimate paradox came with nuclear weapons and strategies of mutually assured destruction. Third, many regimes took to murdering

---

[23] S. Neil MacFarlane and Yuen Foong Khong, *Human Security and the United Nations: A Critical History* (Indiana University Press for the UN Intellectual History Project, 2006), p. 269.

[24] Ibid., pp. 6–9.

large numbers of their own people,[25] for example in the Holocaust. Fourth, in the wake of decolonisation, many states emerged lacking the capacity to assure their citizens' security or exert authority over the resources which were then captured by predatory groups who used the principle of sovereignty and the norm of non-intervention to shield themselves from external pressure. Fifth, the collapse of the Soviet empire and the end of the confrontational, militarised and state-centric Cold War opened space for alternative conceptions of order and security. And finally, globalisation has helped to reduce the salience of the state and of military threats and defences.

Analysts of the security problematique are likely today to be grappling simultaneously with problems of internal social cohesion, regime capacity and brittleness, failed states, economic development, structural adjustment, gender relations, ethnic identity, external threats, and transnational and global problems like AIDS, environmental degradation, drug trafficking, terrorism and so on. For example, malaria kills more than one million people around the world every year, 90 per cent of them in Africa: 3,000 people, or the equivalent of 9/11, per day. It accounts for one-fifth of all child deaths.[26]

War lies at the heart of traditional security paradigms and military force is the sharp edge of the realist school of International Relations. At any given time, most countries are at peace but ready to go to war if necessary. National security policy is usually based on the dictum of prudence that, given an adversary's capabilities, preparations must be made against the possibility of aggression: hope for the best, but be prepared for the worst. Yet 'national security' is more of a slogan for political mobilisation than an analytically useful concept. The consolidation of state power can be used in the name of national security and law and order to suppress individual, group or even majority demands on the government, and to plunder the resources of a society. In many countries the state is a tool of a narrow family, clique or sect preoccupied with fighting off internal and external challenges to its closed privileges. Internal security bureaucracies of many countries are dedicated to the protection of the state against dissident threats from within and can pose a major threat to the human security of the citizens of that state.

---

[25] See Rudolph Rummel, *Death by Government* (New Brunswick: Transactions Press, 1994).

[26] *Malaria: A Major Cause of Child Death and Poverty in Africa* (New York: UNICEF, 2004).

Human security directs our attention to the rationale, forms, techniques and measures of state and societal coercion: from the Holocaust and the gulags to the death squads and disappearances in Latin America and the killing fields of Cambodia. The threats posed by the administrative, judicial, police, paramilitary and military structures to individual and group rights are central, not incidental, to human security studies. This can be shown by a simple but stark statistic. The number of battle deaths for *all international and civil wars* in the twentieth century was 30 million and 7 million respectively; the total number of civilians killed by governments (excluding wars) was 170 million.[27]

Once a state is appropriately disaggregated, security threats can be seen to be sector-specific. Ethnic minorities may perceive threats differently from majority communities. The Sinhalese and Hindus of Kashmir look to the state to provide them with security against Tamil and Islamic fighters in Sri Lanka and India respectively. To the Tamils and Kashmiri Muslims, by contrast, the state is itself the principal source of threat to their security. Not many Chechnyans are likely to view the Russian state as their protector.

Ethnonationalism is the assertion of rights to sovereignty by ethnic nationalities and, by implication, a reconstruction of the international order on the basis of a system of nations. This makes 'nationalism' a key threat to state security. But this is just another way of saying that the sanctity of state sovereignty and its accompanying tenet of territorial integrity are the key threats to 'national' security: witness the fate of former Yugoslavia over the last decade, or the conflict between the nation of Palestine and the state of Israel, or East Timor and Indonesia, or the Kurds and the many states across which they are divided.

Thus national security is an artifice of the realists' imagination, a politically constructed concept, not an objective analytic tool. There are other ways of slicing the security cake. From the perspective of *economic security*, economic competition can be a cause of conflict. Entities suffering economic deprivation, or denied access to critical economic resources or markets, can decide that the costs of inaction outweigh the costs of military action. There is at least an observable empirical coincidence of poverty and insecurity. An ILO study concluded that only 8 per cent of the world's people live in countries providing favourable economic security; about three-quarters live in circumstances

---

[27] *The Economist*, 11 September 1999, Survey on 'Freedom's Journey', p. 7.

of economic insecurity that foster a world full of anxiety and anger.[28] Wealth is important to the realist security analyst not in its own right, but because it enables the purchase of power. Are arms races fuelled by the needs of military–industrial complexes in the arms manufacturing countries? Do heavy expenditures on arms amount to stealing from the poor? Some countries are worried, still, that the forces of globalisation are going to impinge adversely on their economic sovereignty, cultural integrity and social stability: 'interdependence' among unequals is tantamount to the dependence of some on international markets that function under the dominance of others. Economic insecurity can be manifested in inability to feed one's population, volatility in earning capacity based on the exports of primary commodities where developing countries are essentially price-takers, and vulnerability to exogenous policy pressures. Economic collapse can also be the precursor to political collapse.

Regional economic integration can ameliorate conflict. A principal original impulse to West European integration was the political motive of avoiding another major war in Europe.[29] However, the general relationship between conflict and integration is curvilinear. Initially conflicts seem to increase as countries come into greater contact but then, beyond an unspecified threshold of integration, conflicts peak and begin to decline as the costs to either side of disrupting the relationship begin to outweigh possible gains.

As for *environmental security*, previously we sought security *from* the environment, trying to tame and control the environment through technology in order to increase net human welfare. Now we seek security in harmony *with* the environment. We worry about the threats posed to delicately balanced ecosystems by human activity and the consequential threat to human existence. Scarce or strategic resources can be causes, tools or targets of warfare. They can be the source of political disputes which degenerate into violent conflicts within as well as between states.[30]

---

[28] International Labour Organisation, *Economic Security for a Better World* (Geneva: ILO, 2004). The book is described as exploring the social and economic dimensions of human security: www.ilo.org/public/english/support/publ/xtextsp.htm#b6117.

[29] J. S. Nye, *Peace in Parts: Integration and Conflict in Regional Organizations* (Boston: Little, Brown & Co., 1971), p. 117.

[30] For accounts of the internationalisation of environmental concerns, see Peter M. Haas, Robert O. Keohane and Marc A. Levy, eds., *Institutions for the Earth: Sources of Effective International Environmental Protection* (Cambridge: MIT Press, 1993).

Still, environmental factors, whether rooted in scarcity or degradation, do not generally cause wars directly. Rather, they are catalysts to war.[31]

The concept of *common security* was articulated by the Palme Commission in 1982 in the context of disarmament.[32] *Comprehensive security* entered the international political lexicon under the impact of the Brundtland Commission.[33] *Cooperative security* was offered as an all-embracing, multidimensional concept which incorporates common security and collective security yet progresses beyond them.[34] On closer inspection, cooperative security was remarkably similar to *collective security*, not an advancement on the UN Charter.[35]

Two conclusions follow. First, security is an essentially contested concept because it is an intellectual and cognitive construct, not an objective given.[36] We already have many different ways of conceptualising security, depending on the context and analytical or policy purpose. Second, the standard referents of security are faced by many internal inconsistencies. 'National security' is itself riddled with conceptual confusion and policy problems stemming from its integral link to the state. Putting human welfare at the centre of security concerns – the securitisation of individual life as a deliberate artifice of the liberal imagination – helps us to resolve some of these tensions. The rise in the proportion of internal wars, the use of small arms as weapons of choice and the emergence of irregular forces as the major combatants make today's violent conflicts less centralised and more brutal. Civilian casualties and displacement are no longer 'collateral damage', unintended by-products of warfare, but often the deliberate war aims of the fighting. At the same time, norms, instruments and regimes have proliferated for the advancement of human rights and humanitarian laws. The intersection of the

---

[31] Thomas Homer-Dixon, 'On the Threshold: Environmental Changes as Causes of Acute Conflict', *International Security* 16 (Fall 1991), pp. 88–98.

[32] *Common Security: A Programme for Disarmament.* Report of the Independent Commission on Disarmament and Security Issues under the Chairmanship of Olof Palme (London: Pan, 1982).

[33] *Our Common Future: World Commission on Environment and Development* (London: Oxford University Press, 1987).

[34] Gareth Evans, *Cooperating for Peace: The Global Agenda for the 1990s and Beyond* (Sydney: Allen & Unwin, 1993).

[35] See Ramesh Thakur, 'From Collective to Cooperative Security? The Gareth Evans Vision of the United Nations', in Stephanie Lawson, ed., *The New Agenda for Global Security: Cooperating for Peace and Beyond* (Sydney: Allen & Unwin, 1995), pp. 19–38.

[36] See Edward Newman, 'Human Security and Constructivism', *International Studies Perspectives* 2 (2001), pp. 239–51.

two trends – of civilians as direct targets of warfare and rising standards of military behaviour during armed conflict – has created new and higher expectations regarding enforcement of human rights and humanitarian norms.

Human security also takes us more self-consciously into the world of values. Security studies which ignore the normative questions associated with the control, threat and use of organised violence rest on shallow foundations and are isolated from the central question of their legitimation.[37] The great wars (the American civil war, the Cold War) and revolutions (French, American, Russian, Chinese) are those fought over first-order values. It was their normative element that gave them global reach and transcendental importance. All were concerned with the primary legitimising principles of state order.

The intensional–extensional trade-off

The definition of any concept involves a trade-off between precision and inclusiveness. The more complex the social reality, the greater the need for analytical parsimony in social science. The multidimensional concept of security introduces extra elements of *complexity* (that is, a greater number and variety of actors, elements and interactions) and *uncertainty* (due to lack of knowledge and information).[38] Realists could legitimately argue that only a 'lean' conception of security can provide an honest and effective policy tool to cope with the 'mean' enemies that prowl the international jungle.

There is a political agenda behind the efforts both to advance and resist a broader definition of security. The high politics of 'national security' has traditionally ensured government attention and resources to military security. External military threats hold a number of significant advantages for governments. They feed on 'us–them' dichotomies; their harm can be demonstrated in easily grasped terms; sacrifices can be readily demanded of citizens to deal with them; dissenters can be more summarily silenced; and extraordinary measures can be justified for reasons of state. But the military is only one of several competing

---

[37] Kolodziej, 'Renaissance in Security Studies?', p. 429.

[38] For critical comments on the dangers of broadening the concept an attribute (or two) too far, see MacFarlane and Khong, *Human Security and the United Nations*, chapter 7 and Roland Paris, 'Human Security: Paradigm Shift or Hot Air?', *International Security* 26:2 (2001), pp. 87–102.

interest groups vying for a larger share of the collective goods being allocated authoritatively by the government. Other dimensions of security have suffered from the 'attention deficit disorder' syndrome: lower priority, less resources and a softer commitment of resources in times of tightening budgetary constraints. In part the original 1994 UNDP agenda was to influence the 1995 Copenhagen Social Summit, to capture the peace dividend by diverting resources from the military during the Cold War to more productive ends afterwards.

Thus there are competition, tension and conflict among major value clusters. The militarised and statist concept of security serves to disguise the reality of intervalue competition; a multidimensional concept highlights the need for integrative strategies that resolve or transcend value conflicts. Most individuals, societies and countries hold core values in addition to territorial integrity and there are domains of social activity in addition to the military which should be factored into the concept of security. As well as trade-offs, there are opportunity costs: allocation of resources to cope with military security is at the cost of promoting socio-economic security. A multidimensional conceptualisation of security compels scholars and policy-makers alike to explicate value trade-offs. This was starkly and tragically illustrated with Hurricane Katrina in New Orleans in September 2005 when it became clear that because of Iraq, the region had been starved of funds that could have strengthened the levee flood protection system and had about one-third fewer National Guards available to help with the disaster rescue and relief operations.

One possible solution to the dilemma is to focus on security policy in relation to crisis,[39] short of which it is more accurate to assess welfare gains and losses rather than increased security and insecurity.[40] Even if we limit 'security' to anything which threatens the core integrity of our

---

[39] This is suggested by Eric K. Stern, 'Bringing the Environment In: The Case for Comprehensive Security', *Cooperation and Conflict* 30 (September 1995), p. 225. Taylor Owen, in a valiant attempt to find points of agreement among twenty-one divergent authors, suggests a similar threshold-based conceptualisation; 'Human Security – Conflict, Critique and Consensus: Colloquium Remarks and a Proposal for a Threshold-Based Definition', *Security Dialogue* 35:3 (September 2004), pp. 373–87.

[40] This is why I am not persuaded by the definition adopted by the Commission on Human Security: 'to protect the vital core of all human lives in ways that enhance human freedoms and human fulfilment'; *Human Security Now*, p. 4. This is too amorphous, especially as the Commission acknowledged that what people consider to be vital 'varies across individuals and societies'; ibid. As Hampson and Hay point out, this definition is difficult to distinguish from that of human development offered by UNDP back in 1994;

unit of analysis (individual life), many non-traditional concerns merit the gravity of the security label and require exceptional policy measures in response. Traditional security threats are not necessary to destroy the lives and livelihoods of very large numbers of people. The annual mortality correlates of poverty – low levels of life expectancy, high levels of maternal and infant mortality – run into several million. When rape is used as an instrument of war and ethnic 'impurification', when thousands are killed by floods resulting from a ravaged countryside and 280,000 are killed by an earthquake and the resulting tsunami, and when citizens are killed by their own security forces: the concept of national security is policy-irrelevant and of zero analytic utility.

The realists should get real. Annual deaths, even on this scale, cannot be accommodated within the analytical framework of 'national security'; they can in 'human security'. To insist on national security at the expense of human security would be to trivialise the concept of security in many real-world circumstances to the point of sterility, bereft of any operational meaning. The primacy of the goal of state security does not withstand rigorous scrutiny, for it does not have privileged claim over such other needs for human beings as food, water and air. Instead, it is more satisfactory to conceptualise security in terms of the 'marginal value' approach: 'security is only one of many policy objectives competing for scarce resources and subject to the law of diminishing returns . . . Rational policy-makers will allocate resources to security only so long as the marginal return is greater for security than for other uses of the resources.'[41]

A template for policy and action

The operationalisation of human security in the practice of state and international organisations during the 1990s was evident in the changing and toughening mandates of peace operations, the training of personnel for such operations, the prohibition of particular types of weapons, the norm against the use of children in armed conflict, the terms of peace agreements, the international interventions in Kosovo and East Timor and the changed priorities of donors and humanitarian actors. Human

---

Fen Osler Hampson and John B Hay, 'Viva Vox Populi' (review essay), *Global Governance* 10 (2004), p. 248.

[41] David Baldwin, 'The Concept of Security', *Review of International Studies* 23 (January 1997), pp. 19–20.

security thus gives us a template for national policy and international action, and that is its attraction for the United Nations both in peace and security, and in development.[42] This can be usefully illustrated by examples from health, violence against women, children in armed conflict and human trafficking.[43] All of these are important to the UN and the UN has been a central player in all of them.

Health and security converge at three intersections.[44] First, the withdrawal of the state from the public health domain can be both a symptom and a cause of failing states. Second, there has been a marked trend in recent internal armed conflicts to manipulate the supplies of food and medicine. Indeed the struggle to control food and medicine can define the war strategies of some of the conflict parties. And third, the use of biological weapons represents the deliberate spread of disease against an adversary. Human security implies policies for correcting state failures of policy and governance that fail to secure people against the most commonly prevalent as well as infectious and pandemic diseases.

In the words of Kofi Annan, 'A world in which every year 11 million children die before their fifth birthday and three million people die of AIDS' is not a secure world.[45] The UN Security Council held a summit meeting on HIV/AIDS and adopted Resolution 1308 (17 July 2000) declaring it a threat to international peace and security. AIDS is a human security issue because of the vicious chain of infection, communal devastation and social-national disintegration.[46] It is a *personal security* issue in that as prevalence rates reach 5–20 per cent, gains in health, life expectancy and infant mortality are wiped out, agricultural production and food supply fall and families and communities start breaking apart.

---

[42] This leads a foreign affairs official in Canada, who deals with human security at the policy level, to comment that 'One might have thought that it was only French philosophers who rejected concepts that "worked in practice, but not in theory." Recent academic debates on human security suggest, however, that this affliction is rather more widespread'; Don Hubert, 'An Idea that Works in Practice', *Security Dialogue* 35:3 (September 2004), p. 351.

[43] See *Empowering People at Risk: Human Security in the 21st Century*. Report of the Human Security Track of the Helsinki Process on Globalisation and Democracy (December 2004).

[44] *Contagion and Conflict: Health as a Global Security Challenge*. A Report of the Chemical and Biological Arms Control Institute and the CSIS International Security Programme, Washington, DC, Centre for Strategic and International Studies, January 2000.

[45] Annan, *In Larger Freedom*, para. 26.

[46] International Crisis Group, *HIV/AIDS as a Security Issue* (Brussels: Issue Report No. 1, 19 June 2001).

It is an *economic security* issue in that a 10 per cent HIV/AIDS prevalence rate can reduce the growth of national income by one-third, while a 20 per cent infection rate will cause GDP to fall by 1 per cent per year. It damages *communal security* by breaking down national and social institutions and decimating the ranks of the educated and mobile like civil servants, teachers, health professionals and police. It damages *national security* by enfeebling the security forces and corroding the pillars of economic growth and institutional resilience that protect nations against external and internal conflict. And it is an *international security* issue both in its potential to exacerbate international security challenges (disintegration of any one state has potential cross-border implications for neighbours through economic dislocation, refugee flows and communal violence), and to undermine international capacity for conflict resolution, for example with respect to peacekeeping. In Darfur, around 35,000 people were killed directly in the fighting, but around 10,000 more died every month from malnutrition and disease. (Over the twenty-six-month period to April 2005, using a sampling survey methodology, the numbers estimated to have been killed by fighting range up to 140,000, and those through starvation and disease up to another 250,000.[47])

HIV/AIDS infection rates are still rising in many countries and defeating the pandemic has the world's highest health priority. Sadly, in sub-Saharan Africa women make up the majority of victims and face additional risks of poverty, stigmatisation and social ostracism. These are failures not of science but of policy, politics and governance. An internationalised human conscience should find it intolerable that while life expectancy in the rich countries is 80 years and rising, in parts of sub-Saharan Africa it is half that and falling. Poverty contributes to epidemics of infection and curtails access to health professionals and medicines. More than half a million women die every year in pregnancy and childbirth, 99 per cent in developing countries. Failing health in turn exacerbates family poverty and retards national development, thereby fuelling a vicious cycle that destroys the lives and livelihoods of millions around the world every year. The policy responses include adequate and fully funded anti-retroviral therapies, speedy resolution of negotiating deadlocks on intellectual property rights to provide affordable medicines to the poor people in the poorest countries, the creation of globally

---

[47] See Marc Lacey, 'Tallying Darfur Terror: Guesswork With a Cause', *IHT,* 11 May 2005.

interlinked national disease surveillance systems and improved access to public health care.

The placement of gender on the security agenda can easily be justified by recalling the role of rape as a weapon of war.[48] Women can confront insecurity that is direct (for example, honour killing), or rooted in structural and cultural violence.[49] Human security entails the enactment of protective laws and the creation of effective policing and enforcement machinery to ensure their implementation. While men suffer from the public violence of criminality and wars, the violence inflicted on women is mainly in the private realm of the household. Even war-related violence directed at women takes the form of public shaming and humiliation and is mostly suffered in silence. '"Teach the bitch a lesson. Strip her in public." As one of the police officers told me, these were the orders issued by their bosses.'[50] The 'bitch' concerned was not just anybody; she was Asma Jahangir, head of the Human Rights Commission of Pakistan and the UN special rapporteur on freedom of religion. The UN action in this regard includes the Declaration on the Elimination of Violence against Women, the Beijing Platform for Action and Security Council Resolution 1325 (2000) on women, peace and security. The policy measures include increasing state capacity to monitor and enforce laws against women-specific violence like rape, national implementation machinery for international commitments signed by states and priority attention by humanitarian agencies to women's recovery from wartime violence.[51]

Like women, children have become even more acutely vulnerable to abuse with the shift in armed violence to internal wars. While civilians have always been 'collateral' targets of interstate warfare, in many of the most destructive internal conflicts of recent times they have become prime targets and prizes of war. Children are forcibly recruited as child soldiers or sex slaves. They are more vulnerable to death caused by disease and starvation, especially when access to medical help and food aid become deliberate tactics of war. They have the right to be protected

---

[48] See Radhika Coomaraswamy, 'Violence against Women: Sexual Violence during Wartime', in Helsinki Secretariat, ed., *Helsinki Process Papers on Human Security* (Helsinki: Foreign Ministry's Publications, 2005), pp. 103–19.

[49] See Johan Galtung, 'Cultural Violence', *Journal of Peace Research* 27 (August 1990), pp. 291–305.

[50] Ali Dayan Hasan, 'Pakistan's Moderates are Beaten in Public', *IHT*, 15 June 2005.

[51] See Noeline Heyzer, *Women, War and Peace: Mobilising for Peace in the 21st Century.* The 2004 Dag Hammarskjöld Lecture (Uppsala: Dag Hammarskjöld Foundation, 2004).

by their own government. Where national governments fail, the international community cannot abdicate from its responsibility to protect them. Treaty law, the UN Convention on the Rights of the Child and a series of explicit Security Council resolutions outline the duties of states. Resolution 1539 (22 April 2004) reiterates the obligations of governments to protect children in armed conflict. The national, regional and global machinery for enforcing laws and norms for protecting the rights of children could be strengthened still further.

Around 800,000 people are trafficked internationally every year and large numbers are trafficked internally, to service the sex trade, the adoption industry, the begging for alms industry, the market for domestic and industrial servitude or trafficking in brides and organs. Amnesty International believes that 'the trafficking of women into forced prostitution is one of the most widespread and pervasive forms of violence against women'.[52] Even after they have been rescued by the authorities, trafficked women are vulnerable to violations by law enforcement, criminal justice and other agencies. A UNICEF study concluded that human trafficking is a problem in almost every African country, with children, its biggest victims, twice as likely to be trafficked as women.[53] In January 2005, in the wake of the earthquake and tsunami, the Indonesian government and UNICEF stepped up efforts to account for tens of thousands of children still missing because of their vulnerability to local human trafficking networks. National performance lags behind international law-making in combating the threat. The dominant national security paradigm tends also to treat the problem as a crime against the state; it would seem more fruitful to view this as a crime against the individual person within the framework of human security.[54] For then the trafficked person can be treated by the police, immigration and criminal justice system as the victim and the focus of prosecution can shift to where it really belongs: the buyers and sellers and the corrupt officials who collude with them. The requisite policy responses include ratification of the UN protocol against human trafficking, its incorporation into

[52] *Protecting the Human Rights of Women and Girls Trafficked for Forced Prostitution in Kosovo* (London: AI, document EUR 70/010/2004, 2004), Summary, p. 1.

[53] *Trafficking in Human Beings, Especially Women and Children, in Africa* (Florence: UNICEF Innocenti Research Centre, September 2003).

[54] See Edward Newman and Joanne van Selm, eds., *Refugees and Forced Displacement: International Security, Human Vulnerability, and the State* (Tokyo: United Nations University Press, 2003).

domestic legislation and the criminalisation of trafficking in national law.[55]

Human security can also provide a template for policy in Africa.[56] One attempt to apply it to the continent posits five conditions.[57] The first is the shift from a personal-patrimonial to a rational-legal bureaucracy that exercises effective control over the territory of the state and thus can provide order. Second, the emergence of an independent commercial class which helps to split patronage between politics (power) and economics (wealth). Third, the transformation of people from subjects to citizens by incorporating them within an inclusive ideology of nationalism. Fourth, democratisation which helps to institutionalise the transfer of sovereignty from ruler to people. And fifth, because of the persisting weakness of the state in Africa, the regionalisation of security and development. One can always of course quibble with any such lists, adding, deleting and modifying to suit the preferences and prejudices of the analyst concerned. That is not at issue. The larger point is that human security permits policy-makers to adopt a particular agenda for action that is distinct from alternative ways of conceptualising security. Jakkie Cillier's list confirms that human security is not intrinsically opposed to state security.

Finally, human security can provide a policy template for other regional organisations as well. The Barcelona Report of the Study Group on Europe's Security Capabilities, for example, argued that there is a gap between current security capabilities consisting mainly of military forces and real security needs. 'A human security approach for the European Union means that it should contribute to the protection of every individual human being and not only on the defence of the Union's borders, as was the security approach of nation-states.'[58] Arguing that the EU has 'a critical interest in developing capabilities to make a

---

[55] On 29 October, the United Nations brokered a landmark agreement in Yangon among Cambodia, China, Laos, Myanmar, Thailand and Vietnam, the first of its kind in the world, to fight human trafficking in the region; 'Asian Nations Sign Agreement to Battle Human Trafficking', *Japan Times*, 31 October 2004.

[56] With respect to East Asia, see Shin-wha Lee, *Promoting Human Security: Ethical, Normative and Educational Frameworks in East Asia* (Seoul: Korean National Commission for UNESCO, 2004).

[57] Cilliers, *Human Security in Africa*, pp. 12–13.

[58] Mary Kaldor et al., *A Human Security Doctrine for Europe* (presented to EU Secretary-General Javier Solana in Barcelona in September 2004), p. 5. The group comprised Mary Kaldor (London School of Economics and Political Science, convenor), Jan Pronk (Special Representative of the UN Secretary-General in Sudan), General (retd) Klaus

contribution to global human security', it outlined seven principles for a new European security doctrine: the primacy of human rights, clear political authority, multilateralism, a bottom-up approach, regional focus, use of legal instruments, and appropriate use of force. Importantly and explicitly, the report did not seek to replace existing national forces and multilateral structures.[59]

Conclusion

Kanti Bajpai has argued for the possibility of an annual human security audit consisting of an accounting of the growth or decline (a) in threats and (b) in capabilities to meet those threats.[60] The best guarantee of human security is a strong, efficient, effective, but also democratically legitimate state that is respectful of citizens' rights, mindful of its obligations and responsibilities and tolerant of diversity and dissenting voices. States that are too strong or, at the other end of the spectrum, weak and failing, cannot provide human security to their citizens. At the same time, states by themselves cannot provide the full measure of human security, but instead must act in partnership with robust market forces and resilient civil society.

The shift from 'national security' to 'human security' is of historic importance. It would be strange to accept 3,000 killed by terrorists on 9/11 as a security threat with the full range of responses that Washington embarked on in defence thereafter, but insist that 30,000 annual hand-gun casualties is not a security issue. But rather than a wholesale replacement of one security concept by another, it may be more profitable to accept a pluralistic coexistence. Human security is neither in opposition to national security nor a substitute for it. In certain contexts, 'national security' may still prove more durable and satisfying as the analytical prism through which to view security threats and responses. In other contexts, the security problematique may be better framed in the conceptual vocabulary of human security.[61] The comment of Walter Maestri,

Reinhardt (former commander, Kosovo), Narcis Serra (former Minister of Defence, Spain), and Christine Chinkin (University of London).

[59] Ibid., pp. 9–16, 25–6.

[60] Kanti Bajpai, *Human Security: Concept and Measurement*. Kroc Institute Occasional Paper 19 (Notre Dame, Indiana: Joan B. Kroc Institute for International Peace Studies, 2000).

[61] For a discussion of the different operationalisations of national, environmental and human security with respect to environmental damage, see Ramesh Thakur, 'Threats

the emergency management chief in Jefferson Parish, to the Times-Picayune of New Orleans in 2004 was widely reported in the aftermath of Hurricane Katrina: for New Orleans locals, he said, the levee was part and parcel of security because it helped protect them 365 days a year.[62] Katrina thus joined the devastating earthquake and tsunami of 26 December 2004 in the need to reframe security in human terms.

The United Nations has been instrumental in the shift in security thinking in three ways.[63] First, as an incubator and generator of new ideas on key aspects of human security thinking, most notably through the 1994 *Human Development Report* and the UNDP's Human Development Report Office thereafter. Second, a number of UN organs, including the humanitarian actors like the High Commission for Refugees under Sadako Ogata's leadership, were used as forums for debating, articulating and advocating alternative conceptions of security by states and non-governmental organisations. The UN was used also as a forum for forming complex coalitions of civil society and state actors on particular issues like landmines and international criminal justice. And third, parts of the UN system embedded the new concept in their operations and practices, again including the UNHCR but also Secretary-General Kofi Annan in the way in which he pushed the envelope of international intervention to protect civilians at risk of mass deaths. In doing so, the UN system was a key legitimising device for the new concept of human security.

The safest and most peaceful communities are composed of individuals who have their basic needs and aspirations met. We will not be able to live free of fear, will not be able to secure a sustainable future, so long as over a billion people live in servitude to want. The mark of a civilisation is not the deference and respect paid to the glamorous and the powerful, but the care and attention devoted to the least privileged and the most vulnerable. Children in particular need and should have the most protection in any society. Many hazards to children's survival, healthy growth and normal development, in rich as well as poor

---

without Enemies, Security without Borders: Environmental Security in East Asia', *Journal of East Asian Studies* 1:2 (August 2001), pp. 161–89.

[62] Maureen Dowd, 'The United States of Shame', *IHT*, 5 September 2005; Andrew Sullivan, 'Earth to the President: Warnings Ignored at Your Peril', *Australian*, 5 September 2005; and Jim Vandehei and Peter Baker, 'Critics say Bush Undercut New Orleans Flood Control', *Washington Post*, 2 September 2005.

[63] MacFarlane and Khong, *Human Security and the United Nations*, pp. 9–10, 16–18.

countries, constitute a critical and pervasive threat to human security. Over the last decade, 2 million children have been killed, 1 million orphaned, 6 million disabled or otherwise seriously injured, 12 million made homeless and 10 million left with serious psychological scars. Large numbers of them, especially young women, are the targets of rape. The steps taken in defence of the rights of children remain small, hesitant and limited. The biggest danger is compassion fatigue: we will get so used to the statistics that they will cease to shock us, and we will learn to live with the unacceptable.

4

Human rights: civil society and the United Nations

The rise and diffusion of human rights norms and conventions and the extension and diffusion of international humanitarian law (IHL) were among the truly great achievements of the last century. The United Nations was at the centre of that effort, led in particular by individuals and non-governmental organisations (NGOs). The 'first-generation negative rights' emerged from constitutional traditions that prevented the state from curtailing the civil rights and political liberties of citizens; the 'second-generation positive rights' reflected the agenda of many newly independent but poor countries to prescribe an activist agenda of social and economic rights for their citizens; and the 'third-generation solidarity rights' pertain to collective entities rather than individuals based on notions of solidarity.[1]

The human rights machinery in the UN system works in three areas: information, analysis and policy development; provision of support to human rights bodies and organs; and promotion and protection of human rights. For all this to be sustainable, robust human rights institutions have to be built at the country level. The Office of the High Commissioner for Human Rights (OHCHR) has developed the practice of assigning human rights advisers to country teams. The challenge is to build on the progress achieved by helping countries to advance the protection of human rights at home through legislative, judicial and other enforcement measures and mechanisms. Improvements to human rights should be related to human rights capacity-building and be attentive to strains on the limited resources of developing countries. The UN must pay particular attention also to countries emerging from conflict.[2] It must maintain efforts to modernise the human rights treaty system, enhance the role of the special procedures for fact-finding and

---

[1] Thomas G. Weiss, David P. Forsythe and Roger A. Coate, *The United Nations and Changing World Politics*, 4th edn (Boulder: Westview, 2004), p. 142.

[2] See Shale Horowitz and Albrecht Schnabel, eds., *Human Rights and Societies in Transition: Causes, Consequences, Responses* (Tokyo: UN University Press, 2004).

strengthen the capacity of OHCHR to support these efforts. The OHCHR was created by the UN General Assembly as late as December 1993 and has suffered from a vague mandate and a weak authority: weaknesses that the late Sergio Vieira de Mello had hoped to rectify before he was tragically killed in Baghdad in August 2003.

The Commission on Human Rights is a vital part of the organisation. Its history includes the drafting of the Universal Declaration on Human Rights. The Millennium Declaration affirmed the continuing centrality of that mission. Yet the UN record and reputation are decidedly mixed. Critics can all too easily find any number of sticks with which to beat the UN record on human rights, including the election of some of the most abusive regimes to human rights committees and even chairmanships. Considerable progress has been achieved during the lifetime of the UN's existence, but this is due to active partnerships with the far more robust civil society organisations (CSOs) than to direct UN action.

In this chapter, I will first outline the progress on the human rights front, then look at the rise of CSOs as international actors and examine and explain their comparative performance with the UN on the promotion and protection of human rights. I will also address the rising concerns about the abusive behaviour of UN peacekeepers.

Human rights

A human right, owed to every person simply as a human being, is inherently universal. Held only by human beings, but equally by all, it does not flow from any office, rank or relationship. 'Human rights is the language that systematically embodies' the intuition that the human species is one 'and each of the individuals who compose it is entitled to equal moral consideration'.[3] The debate in US circles on whether under some circumstances torture – the prohibition of which 'appears on every short list of truly universal standards'[4] – can be justified if it leads to preventing mass terrorist attacks, and may therefore be authorised by judges through 'torture warrants',[5] mirrors long-argued positions

---

[3] Michael Ignatieff, *Human Rights as Politics and Idolatry*, edited and introduced by Amy Gutmann (Princeton: Princeton University Press, 2001), pp. 3–4.

[4] Diane F. Orentlicher, 'Relativism and Religion', in Ignatieff, *Human Rights as Politics and Idolatry*, p. 150.

[5] And not just in the USA. In Australia, too, a law professor at Deakin University has argued the case for torture, saying that if torture can produce information that will save innocent

on cultural relativism. Human beings do not inhabit a universe of shared moral values. Instead, we find diverse moral communities cohabiting in international society.

Consider the case of a cross-clan murder in some kinship systems. If a chiefly person has been killed by a commoner, then the revenge death of the original killer may not be appropriate retribution, that of a person of chiefly rank may. The original killer can go scot-free, an outcome that is alien and abhorrent to the Western concept of individual guilt and responsibility. In most such societies with an eye for an eye and a tooth for a tooth philosophy, the underlying principle of retributive justice was a means of limiting violence: take your tooth and be done with it. A second mechanism for containing violence, which also horrified some Europeans, was blood money or the compensation principle: the kin-group which initiated the killing could escape retribution in kind by compensating the victim kin-group with appropriate payment.

Equally, though, we should be suspicious of the self-serving and spurious claims of ruling elites that their rejection of external criticism is based on an alternative social consensus. Relativism is often the first refuge of repressive governments. The doctrine of national security has been especially corrosive of human rights. It is used frequently by governments, charged with the responsibility to protect citizens, to assault them instead. Under military rule, the instrument of protection from without becomes the means of attack from within.

A posture of moral relativism can be profoundly racist, proclaiming in effect that 'the other' is not worthy of the dignity that belongs inalienably to one. By contrast, human rights advocacy rests on 'the moral imagin-ation to feel the pain of others' as if it were one's own, treats others as 'rights-bearing equals', not 'dependants in tutelage', and can be viewed as 'a juridical articulation of duty by those in zones of safety toward those in zones of danger'.[6] Relativism requires an acknowledgement that each culture has its own moral system and that institutional protection of human rights must be grounded in historically textured conditions and local political culture. But just because moral precepts vary from culture to culture does not mean that different peoples do not hold some values in common. International relations is a domain of moral choice where diversity does not vitiate or preclude efforts at moral reasoning. Human

---

lives, then 'it is verging on moral indecency to prefer the interests of the wrongdoer'; Mirko Bagaric, 'A Case for Torture', *Age* (Melbourne), 17 May 2005.
[6] Ignatieff, *Human Rights as Politics and Idolatry*, p. 163.

rights protection embedded in particular cultural traditions can be compatible with moral pluralism. For every society, murder is always wrong. But few proscribe the act of killing absolutely under all circumstances. At different times, in different societies, war, capital punishment, abortion or euthanasia may or may not be morally permissible. So the *interpretation and application* of the moral proscription of murder varies from one time, place and society to another. All societies require retribution to be proportionate to the wrong done. All prize children, the link between succeeding generations of human civilisation; every culture abhors their abuse.

Human rights can adjudicate conflicts between individual and group rights, including the right of exit for individuals from groups.[7] Thus sensitivity to cultural variation and specificity need not collapse into deferring to difference. It means respecting the right of individuals to choose between membership and exclusion from the group if their claims to free agency are denied from within the group. Few non-Westerners asserting claims to international human rights norms seek a wholesale replacement of their cultures by Western belief and value systems. Rather, they – the *dalit* in India, the girl in Afghanistan, the Muslim in Australia – seek protection of their rights *within* their own cultures.

That said, Africans and Asians are neither amused nor mindful at being lectured on universal human values by those who failed to practise the same during European colonialism, and now urge them to cooperate in promoting 'global' human rights norms. The superiority of Western ways has remained a constant theme over the past few centuries, only the universal truths of Christianity have been replaced by the universal rights of humankind. Western countries are quite happy to use Amnesty International (AI) and Human Rights Watch (HRW) reports as a stick with which to beat other countries on human rights. But they are outraged at the idea that their own human rights record, for example with respect to the condition of their indigenous peoples or the racial bias in the death penalty, might merit independent international scrutiny. This is in addition to the cynical belief by many that 'American democracy requires the repression of democracy in the rest of the world'[8] – and in international organisations like the UN, one might add. Many Asians dismiss Europe's expressions of concerns on human rights as

---

[7] Ibid., pp. 68–9.

[8] An Asian human rights activist quoted in Jeffrey C. Goldfarb, 'Losing Young Allies in the War on Terror', *International Herald Tribune* (*IHT*), 21 August 2002.

based on the twin recurring refrains of arrogance and hypocrisy. The Europeans want to dictate whether or not Myanmar should be permitted in the Asian delegation for the annual ASEAN-Europe (ASEM) meeting in protest at Aung San Suu Kyi's house arrest, but ingratiate themselves with the leaders of China whose former pro-reform leader Zhao Ziyang was under house arrest for longer (fifteen years), until his death on 17 January 2005.[9]

Diane Orentlicher asks 'By whose lights does one determine which rights are "*prima facie* universal" and what local variations in interpretation are permissible?. . . *Who decides?*[10] Who indeed?

Civil society and the United Nations

Governments can satisfy only a small and diminishing proportion of the needs of human beings as social animals. Citizens look more and more to civic associations to channel a growing range and variety of social interactions. 'Civil society' refers, broadly speaking, to the social and political space where voluntary associations (as distinct from the automatic, binding and compulsory membership of a state) attempt to shape norms and policies for regulating public life in social, political, economic and environmental dimensions.[11]

Like national society, international society, too, is becoming more plural and diverse. There has been an exponential growth in the number of civil society actors and in the volume of transnational networks in which they are embedded.[12] They bridge the 'disconnect between the political geography of the state on the one side and the new geography of economic and social relations on the other'.[13] The expanding worldwide civil society networks embrace almost every level of organisation, from the village community to global summits; and almost every sector of public life, from the provision of microcredit and the delivery of paramedical assistance, to environmental and human rights norm promotion and activism.

[9] Philip Bowring, 'EU Lectures on Human Rights Ring Hollow', *IHT*, 26 June 2004.
[10] Orentlicher, 'Relativism and Religion', p. 144; emphasis in original.
[11] See Michael Edwards, *Civil Society* (Cambridge: Polity Press, 2004).
[12] See Mary Kaldor, *Global Civil Society: An Answer to War* (Cambridge: Polity Press, 2003), and John Keane, *Global Civil Society?* (Cambridge: Cambridge University Press, 2003).
[13] Thorsten Benner, Wolfgang H. Reinecke and Jan Martin Witte, *Shaping Globalisation: The Role of Global Public Policy Networks* (2002), p. 4; downloadable from:www.globalpublicpolicy.net/.

Civil society actors can play one or more of the following roles: research; outreach education; advocacy and norm promotion; agenda setting; lobbying governments and intergovernmental organisations to adopt and police laws, policies and courses of action; implementing programmes and delivering services and humanitarian assistance; monitoring implementation of international commitments; and direct action. With respect to multilateralism specifically, CSOs have contributed in three ways: by advocating multilateral solutions to global problems, cultivating popular constituencies for multilateralism, and connecting local and national struggles to global norms and international institutions.[14]

Nevertheless, NGOs face many challenges to their legitimacy as they are often seen as unelected, unaccountable, unrepresentative, self-serving and irresponsible. Can they claim to speak on behalf of anyone but themselves? What mechanisms exist to hold them accountable to their constituents? Hugo Slim writes of 'voice accountability': the reliability and credibility of *what* they say (an empirical question: can you prove it?), and the *locus of their authority* for saying it (a political question: from where do you get your authority to speak?).[15] They can behave like 'five star activists' indulging their pet causes without taking responsibility for trying to effect changes. According to Chidi Odinkalu, in Africa, 'Far from being a badge of honour, human rights activism is . . . increasingly a certificate of privilege.'[16] UN engagement with unelected civil society actors can sometimes cut across and undermine the role of democratically elected representatives.[17] Recipient countries, for example Afghanistan, can resent the NGO community as competitors for siphoning off aid from governments.[18] In their unrestrained eagerness to capitalise on worldwide public sympathy after the earthquake and tsunami of 26 December 2004, NGOs paid little heed to how much they could actually do by way of relief work that could not be done better by governments

---

[14] Jackie Smith, 'Social Movements and Multilateralism', in Ramesh Thakur, Edward Newman and John Tirman, eds., *Multilateralism under Challenge: Power, International Order, and Structural Change* (Tokyo: UN University Press, forthcoming).

[15] Hugo Slim, *By What Authority? The Legitimacy and Accountability of Non-governmental Organisations* (Geneva: International Council on Human Rights Policy, 2002), p. 6. Available at www.ichrp.org.

[16] Quoted in ibid., p. 2.

[17] For an uncompromising statement of this thesis, see Gary Johns, 'Relations with Nongovernmental Organizations: Lessons for the UN', *Seton Hall Journal of Diplomacy and International Relations* 5:2 (Summer/Fall 2004), pp. 51–65.

[18] Don D'Cruz, 'Tracking Aid Dollars', *Canberra Times*, 31 December 2004.

and the UN system. 'For all the talk of coordination and accountability, the need to maintain market share continues to trump sound humanitarian practice – at least in crises like the tsunami, where the Western public and Western donor governments are attentive and engaged.'[19]

Recognising the validity of many of the complaints, civil society groups have begun to address the need for a system of self-regulation that rejects violence and lawlessness. Accountability and transparency will be better ensured through adoption of codes of conduct and common principles of behaviour. And they have been trying to broaden their membership to incorporate people from developing countries.

The United Nations is fundamentally an organisation of member states. But it is also the natural focus of 'We the peoples' and civil society groups who wish to be heard on issues that affect their lives and livelihoods. How can the organisation give voice to civil society without drowning out the voice and diluting the vote of governments? Member states are wary of the constant pressure to make more room for NGOs in their deliberations, and sometimes even in delegations, while NGOs feel they are not allowed to participate meaningfully. Questions about the accountability and representativeness of NGOs, as well as concerns about foreign political agendas being pursued through the powerful Western-based 'international' NGOs, further complicate the picture.

The Cardoso Panel urged the UN to promote 'networked governance' by fostering greater interaction between governments and citizens.[20] It noted that many CSOs had become frustrated at being able to speak in the UN but not heard, with their participation producing little impact on outcomes.[21] In his response to its report, the Secretary-General noted that extending and deepening the UN's relationship with NGOs will strengthen the organisation and enrich the quality of intergovernmental debates and policy analysis in its forums, and so enhance the UN's impact in a world vastly changed from 1945.[22]

---

[19] David Rieff, 'Tsunamis, Accountability and the Humanitarian Circus', *Humanitarian Exchange* 29 (March 2005), p. 50.

[20] *We the Peoples: Civil Society, the United Nations and Global Governance.* Report of the Panel of Eminent Persons on United Nations-Civil Society Relations (New York: United Nations, document A/58/817, 2004). The chair of the panel was former Brazilian president Fernando Henrique Cardoso.

[21] Ibid., p. 7.

[22] *Report of the Secretary-General in Response to the Report of the Panel of Eminent Persons on United Nations-Civil Society Relations* (New York: United Nations, General Assembly document A/59/354, 13 September 2004), paras. 3–4.

Three major human rights and humanitarian CSOs are the International Committee of the Red Cross (ICRC), AI and HRW, each one of which has a global footprint and a sizeable staff and budget. The ICRC, headquartered in Geneva, has a permanent mandate under international law to take impartial action for prisoners, the wounded and the sick, and civilians affected by conflict.[23] AI, headquartered in London, is a worldwide voluntary activist movement working to promote and defend human rights.[24] Independent of any government, it neither supports nor opposes the views of victims whose rights it seeks to protect by mobilising volunteer activists. It neither seeks nor accepts funds from governments for its work investigating and campaigning against human rights violations. HRW began in 1978 as Helsinki Watch to monitor the compliance of Soviet bloc countries with the provisions of the Helsinki Accord.[25] Americas Watch followed in the 1980s to counter the notion that only one side was guilty of human rights abuses in the conflicts in Central America. Subsequently the different branches were amalgamated into HRW with its global headquarters in New York. It monitors developments in seventy countries, conducting and publicising fact-finding investigations into human rights abuses by governments and non-state actors, and meeting with national governments and international organisations to urge changes in policy and practice.

AI, HRW and the ICRC have access to national delegates and Secretariat officials, provide a range of information from a broad cross-section of sources and lobby for their preferred solutions. Each is a limited actor in its own right. While the UN is a sovereignty-bound actor, they are sovereignty-free actors.[26] The lofty proclamations of human rights in the UN Charter suggest an expansive interest; the enabling clauses reveal a more restrictive authority. The powers of CSOs, although no more extensive, can be utilised more effectively because they are free of some of the types of inhibitions that impede the functioning of the UN which

---

[23] See www.icrc.org.

[24] See www.amnesty.org.

[25] See www.hrw.org.

[26] The terminology is borrowed from James N. Rosenau, *Turbulence in World Politics: A Theory of Change and Continuity* (Princeton: Princeton University Press, 1990), p. 36. However, Rosenau uses sovereignty-bound to refer to state-actors, and sovereignty-free to refer to non-state actors. Thus in his definition international organisations are explicitly included in the sovereignty-free category. I find his terminology useful, but not his usage. In the sense in which I am using it, the United Nations is constrained by the sovereignty of its member states, but AI, HRW and the ICRC are not so bound.

is subject to capture by member governments. While the UN and many NGOs deal with states' international behaviour, AI and HRW are concerned principally with states' internal behaviour and the ICRC with both. AI and HRW are less constrained than the UN in holding states to norms that have been declared in forms other than legally binding instruments.

Standard setting and norm generation

The UN–civil society partnership in human rights has meant that the international organisation takes the lead in standard setting and norm articulation while NGOs are the more effective monitors and watchdogs. The most appropriate forum for efforts to reconcile divergent moral traditions into common public policy is the UN as a universal organisation. Civil-political human rights are an outgrowth of Western liberalism; the UN is a meeting ground for all the world's civilisations.[27] Human rights puts the welfare of individuals first; the UN puts the interests of member states first. AI and HRW are of, by and for individuals; the UN is of, by and for governments. They are single-purpose NGOs; the UN is a general-purpose IGO. UN resolutions are the most commonly cited and widely acceptable code of conduct and metric of state compliance with internationally prescribed behaviour.

'The promotion and protection of human rights is a bedrock requirement for the realisation of the Charter's vision of a just and peaceful world.'[28] International concern with human rights prior to the Second World War dwelt on the laws of warfare, slavery and protection of minorities. The experience of Fascism-Nazism strengthened the concern and enlarged its scope. In 1948 the UN adopted the Universal Declaration of Human Rights. On a par with the other great historical documents like the French Declaration of the Rights of Man and the American Declaration of Independence, the Universal Declaration was the first *international* affirmation of the rights held in common by all.[29]

---

[27] The Western-universal dichotomy should be qualified. The UN Charter is itself indebted politically and philosophically to Western civilisation: politically, due to the fact that the Western countries dominated the UN Conference in San Francisco in 1945; philosophically, in that the Charter embodies the dominant Western values of the time.

[28] *Strengthening of the United Nations: An Agenda for Further Change. Report of the Secretary-General* (New York: United Nations, A/57/387, 23 September 2002), para. 45.

[29] See Johannes Morsink, *The Universal Declaration of Human Rights: Origins, Drafting and Intent* (Philadelphia: University of Pennsylvania Press, 1999).

The simplicity of the language belies the passion of conviction under-pinning it. Its elegance has been the font of inspiration down the decades; its provisions comprise the vocabulary of complaint. Its origins in the experiences of European civilisation are important, not for the reason that most critics cite but its opposite. It is less an expression of European triumphalism and imperial self-confidence than a guilt-ridden Christendom's renunciation of its ugly recent record; less an assertion of the superiority of European human nature than revulsion at the recent history of European savagery; not an effort to universalise Western values but to ban the dark side of Western vices like racial and religious bigotry.[30]

The two Covenants in 1966, on civil-political and cultural-social-economic rights, added force and specificity, affirming both civil-political and social-economic-cultural rights, without privileging either set. Together with the Declaration, they comprise the International Bill of Rights that mapped out the international human rights agenda, estab-lished the benchmark for state conduct, inspired provisions in many national laws and international conventions, and provided a beacon of hope to many whose rights had been snuffed out by brutal regimes. They are our 'firewalls against barbarism', 'a tool kit against oppression', a source of power and authority on behalf of victims.[31] The UN has also adopted scores of other legal instruments on human rights.

UN efforts are greatly helped by activists and NGOs who use the Declaration as the concrete point of reference against which to judge state conduct. The utility of the two Covenants lies in the requirement imposed on signatories to submit periodic reports on the human rights situation in their countries. Therefore, ratifying and bringing the Coven-ants into force does not simply connote acceptance of internationally proclaimed standards of human rights. It also entails the creation of long-term national infrastructures for the protection and promotion of human rights.

The most recent advances on international human rights are the progressive incorporation of wartime behaviour and policy within the prohibitionary provisions of humanitarian law, for example in the Ottawa Treaty which subordinated military calculations to humanitarian

---

[30] Jack Donnelly, 'Human Rights and Asian Values: A Defense of Western Universalism', in Joanne R. Bauer and Daniel A. Bell, eds., *The East Asian Challenge for Human Rights* (Cambridge: Cambridge University Press, 1999), p. 68.
[31] Ignatieff, *Human Rights as Politics and Idolatry*, pp. 5, 57–8.

concerns about a weapon that cannot distinguish a soldier from a child, and in the establishment of the International Criminal Court (ICC). The US absence from both shows the extent to which human rights have moved ahead of their strongest advocate in the past, and how the former chief champion of human rights has in some respects become one of its most prominent delinquents or 'outlier'.[32]

Monitoring and verification

Responsibility for human rights oversight was given to the Economic and Social Council (ECOSOC) under the general auspices of the General Assembly. ECOSOC set up a Commission on Human Rights in 1946. The United Nations has also set up special committees to oversee implementation of the human rights covenants. But international teams have little formal power to monitor or carry out independent investigations of state compliance with UN norms, such as spot-checks and on-site verifications with unfettered freedom of movement for UN inspectors. The UN 'monitoring' machinery is little more than a system of international information exchange, some of which can be plain farcical. The result is 'normative strength and procedural weakness'.[33]

While human rights means putting people first, the UN remains a creature of member governments. AI, HRW and the ICRC, too, put people first. Their reports carry a ring of authority because they have not been wilfully myopic in the UN mould in investigating and judging human rights abuses around the world. Contrast their reports on sensitive subjects like Chechnya, Tibet and Abu Ghraib with UN silences. The UN is a multipurpose organisation. This means that many considerations in addition to the human rights record have to be taken into account in deciding what to do about the errant behaviour of a member state. A permanent member of the Security Council can veto any draft resolution critical of its human rights records. It can also veto other resolutions where its help may be urgently needed. Such broader considerations of trade-offs are extraneous to the decision calculus of single-issue NGOs like AI and HRW.

UN activities have been severely affected also by the fluctuations of its finances, the refusal of major member states to pay their assessed share of

---

[32] Weiss, Forsythe and Coate, *The United Nations and Changing World Politics*, p. 145.
[33] Jack Donnelly, 'International Human Rights: A Regime Analysis', *International Organization* 40:3 (Summer 1986), p. 614.

costs, the refusal of some to pay for particular UN activities or agencies which offend their political sensibilities and the insistence of others that they be given a larger say in some decisions. Guaranteed financing of the core budget of OHCHR has fallen to less than half. With more than half its budget coming from extra-budgetary allocations from key member governments, it is inevitably going to be restricted in its capacity to investigate allegations of abuses by those governments.

Unlike the UN, the three CSOs maintain a scrupulous neutrality with respect to international ideological conflicts. They have assisted prisoners of all political stripes and investigated the actions of governments from across the political spectrum. AI's neutral stance has been helped by the deliberate tactic of precluding national chapters from investigative and lobbying activities in home countries. Impartiality is buttressed with veracity. The long-term credibility of AI, HRW and the ICRC would be badly damaged if their reports and statements could be shown to be false. The structure of the three is designed to collect, distribute and use information that has been cross-checked and will withstand efforts by governments to discredit it.

The United Nations is required to be impartial and neutral. Human rights activism requires having to take sides, typically against abuser governments, and mobilising powerful constituencies to force them to stop their abuses. The UN's members are territorially bounded states claiming exclusive competence. Human rights is ineluctably extraterritorial in its moral activism, and that is a task better suited to civil society.

Compliance and enforcement

States are less eager to create enforceable police and judicial machinery than to endorse human rights in the abstract, and less open to effective UN enforcement of rights than to weak UN supervision of policies. Consequently, the UN instruments and techniques for the implementation of human rights norms and standards range from encouragement and coaxing to naming and shaming, but usually without any sanctions.

While the UN is better qualified to set international human rights standards, AI and HRW are better able to investigate human rights abuses at the grass-roots level and the ICRC has a better record of investigating compliance with IHL. Measuring success is difficult, perhaps even impossible. No government is going to admit having given in to external pressure. In many cases there may well be several influences at work simultaneously on a government. For the UN, AI, HRW or the ICRC to claim success could be boastful, only partially true and possibly counter-productive in future cases. The fact that they cannot demonstrate success in every instance does not diminish the worth of their efforts. Between them, NGOs and the UN have achieved many successes. National laws and international instruments have been improved, many political prisoners have been freed and some victims of abuse have been compensated.

Examples could be chosen from virtually any continent and every decade since the Second World War to illustrate the twin thesis that CSOs and the UN play complementary roles. A good contemporary example is Darfur. Cynicism among Western governments, people and media about UN habits increased when the government of Sudan, under intense scrutiny for its atrocities in the south and in Darfur in the west, was chosen by the African countries for re-election to one of Africa's slots on the fifty-three-member UN Human Rights Commission in 2004. The US ambassador to ECOSOC where the election took place, Sichan Siv, walked out in protest, saying that the USA 'will not participate in this absurdity'.[34] When the General Assembly refused to vote on a resolution denouncing human rights violations in Sudan, US Ambassador John Danforth gave vent to his anger and frustration: 'One wonders about the utility of the General Assembly on days like this', he remarked.[35] The draft resolution had been sponsored by thirty-eight Western nations but was opposed by developing countries, including nearly all Islamic and African countries and China. In effect African states decided to vote against a Western-sponsored resolution condemning an African state. Yet the UN was among the earlier and more consistent critics of abuses committed in Darfur by or with the connivance of the government of Sudan. This is a good example of the need to distinguish between the UN officials and UN member governments when criticising 'the United Nations'.

Since 9/11 AI, HRW and the ICRC have led the international push to hold the Bush administration's feet to the fire of international humanitarian law. To be fair, the UN High Commissioner for Human Rights, Mary Robinson, claimed that the Bush administration had blocked her from remaining at her post because she had had the temerity to criticise

---

[34] 'Sudan keeps seat on UN Rights Commission; US walks out', *UN Wire* (www.unwire. org), 5 May 2004.
[35] 'US Castigates UN Assembly on Sudan Human Rights', Reuters, at www.alertnet.org, 25 November 2004.

these policies.[36] Theo van Boven, the UN special rapporteur on torture, also sharply criticised several US practices in the war on terror – but he is not a UN official.[37] Under American pressure, the UN eliminated the job of its top investigator on human rights in Afghanistan, American scholar Cherif Bassiouni, because of his temerity in repeatedly criticising the US military for detaining Afghans without trial and for barring human rights monitors from US prisons in the country.[38]

The ICRC paid detention visits to prisoners in Afghanistan, Guantá-namo Bay and Iraq, reported discreetly to US authorities the nature and scope of the prisoner abuses its delegates witnessed, and in mid-2003 it went public with its concern about the effects on the mental health of detainees held in indefinite detention in Guantánamo without charge or trial.[39] It was the ICRC which insisted that with the transfer of sover-eignty from the occupation authorities to an interim Iraqi government on 30 June 2004, Saddam Hussein and many others had either to be released or charged with specific crimes.[40]

AI and HRW in their annual reports and in several more focused reports have tried to document continuing abuses in the name of the war on terror and to mobilise opinion against such practices.[41] In a toughly worded report issued in October 2004, Amnesty argued that the US response to 9/11 'has resulted in its own iconography of torture, cruelty and degradation.'[42] Interestingly for the thesis being argued in this

---

[36] Brian Knowlton, 'UN Rights Chief Cites US Role in Departure', *IHT*, 1 August 2002.

[37] John H. Cushman, 'UN Condemns Harsh Methods in Campaign against Terror', *New York Times*, 28 October 2004.

[38] For the extraordinary story, see Douglass Cassel, 'The US and the UN: See no Evil', *Chicago Tribune*, 29 May 2005; reprinted in the *Daily Yomiuri*, 4 June 2005.

[39] The ICRC policy on the balance between discretion and publicity is to make representa-tions about violations of international humanitarian law discreetly to the authorities concerned, give them reasonable time to make the necessary changes, but reserve the right to go public if adequate changes are not forthcoming and if public comment is likely to help the prisoners. For a critical yet respectful study of the ICRC, see David P. Forsythe, *The Humanitarians: The International Committee of the Red Cross* (Cambridge: Cambridge University Press, 2005).

[40] Jonathan Steele, 'Red Cross Ultimatum to US on Saddam', *Guardian*, 14 June 2004; Edward Wong, 'Saddam's Status Raises Legal Complications', *IHT*, 16 June 2004.

[41] *Amnesty International Report 2004* (London: AI, 2004). *World Report 2005* (New York: Human Rights Watch, 2005), downloaded on 14 January 2005 from www.hrw.org/wr2k5. From Human Rights Watch, see also 'The Legal Prohibition against Torture', 1 June 2004; 'Guantánamo: Detainee Accounts', *Background Briefing*, 26 October 2004; and 'US: Did President Bush Order Torture?', 21 December 2004.

[42] *Guantánamo – an Icon of Lawlessness* (London: AI, document AMR 51/1002/2005, 6 January 2005).

chapter, AI praised statements by Kofi Annan emphasising the absolute prohibition on torture and other cruel, inhuman or degrading treatment.[43] AI's 2005 report drew attention to rights violations, among others, by the governments of Afghanistan, Australia, China, East Timor, Egypt, India, Israel, Malaysia, Nepal, the Philippines, Russia, Singapore, Thailand and Uzbekistan.[44] In her Foreword to the report, AI Secretary-General Irene Khan wrote that 'The detention facility at Guantánamo Bay has become the gulag of our times, entrenching the practice of arbitrary and indefinite detention in violation of international law. Trials by military commissions have made a mockery of justice and due process.' She added that 'When the most powerful country in the world thumbs its nose at the rule of law and human rights, it grants a licence to others to commit abuse with impunity.'[45] The Gulag 'hyperbole is wrong – but that's cold comfort to those of us who believe America should hold itself to a higher standard than "we're better than the gulag"'.[46]

In its annual survey of the state of human rights in 2004, HRW argued that abuses committed by the USA in Guantánamo and Iraq significantly weakened the world's ability to protect human rights. When a country as dominant as the USA openly defies the law, it invites others to mimic its policy. It also reduces US leverage over others, since Washington cannot call on others to uphold principles it itself violates. HRW called on the administration to set up a fully independent investigative commission to look into the Abu Ghraib prisoner abuses. At the same time, it criticised China and Russia in particular for contributing to the world's callous disregard of the large-scale deaths in Darfur in order to protect oil contracts and arms sales.[47] When the military investigations exonerated US generals of direct or command responsibility over the prisoner abuses

---

[43] *USA: Human Dignity Denied. Torture and Accountability in the 'War on Terror'* (London: AI, AMR 51/145/2004, 27 October 2004).

[44] *Amnesty International Report 2005: The State of the World's Human Rights* (London: AI, 2005).

[45] Irene Khan, 'Foreword', downloaded from http://web.amnesty. org/report2005/message-eng. Although effective, the soundbite may also be deeply flawed in equating two phenomena that are simply not comparable in their scale and historical significance. See Pavel Litvinov (a dissident and human rights activist in the former Soviet Union), 'Far from a Soviet "Gulag"', *Japan Times* (reprint of a *Washington Post* article), 24 June 2005. The spectre of moral equivalency between a flawed democracy and Stalin's totalitarian dictatorship trivialised the Soviet gulags, allowed the administration to deflect attention from the US abuses to AI's hyperbole, and risked diminishing AI.

[46] Cathy Young, 'Guantánamo is not the Gulag', *IHT*, 10 June 2005.

[47] *World Report 2005*.

despite the similarity in the pattern of abuses from Guantánamo to Afghanistan and Iraq, HRW called on the Attorney-General to appoint a special prosecutor and urged Congress to launch a bipartisan and independent investigation into the roles of senior officials, including the president, the defence secretary and the former CIA director.[48]

Policing UN peacekeepers?

If the UN is to maintain its human rights credibility, soldiers committing abuses in its name must face investigation and prosecution by effective international machinery. Over a decade ago AI argued that the time was overdue for the UN to build measures for human rights promotion and protection into its own peacekeeping activities.[49] Among other things blue-helmeted troops are alleged to have patronised brothels containing captive Croat and Muslim women in Bosnia and paid for sex with children in Mozambique.[50] In what has been described as a kiss-and-tell book, three UN staffers write of things like Bulgaria recruiting prisoners to fill their quota for peacekeepers to be sent to the UN mission in Cambodia, who drank too much, raped the Cambodian women and crashed their landcruisers with remarkable regularity; and UN peace-keepers being more concerned to save their own lives than to protect their wards.[51] Equally, though, the book is an account of the alienation and sense of betrayal felt by many idealistic recruits who are disillusioned by the realities of power, politics, greed and bureaucracy surrounding the machinery of international organisation in the midst of many long-running conflicts and their deeply traumatised victims.

The UN Office of Internal Oversight Services (OIOS) conducted a probe of seventy-two allegations of sexual abuse in Bunia (eastern Congo) in 2004. They fully substantiated abuses of underage girls in six cases, where UN peacekeepers procured girls aged 12–14 for sex in return for $2–3 or its equivalent in food. There have also been cases of rape. Many of the allegations are difficult to prove in a court of law. Worse, the UN has no power to try the offending soldiers, who are subject to the disciplinary authority of their own military. The South

---

[48] 'Rights Groups Reject Iraq Prison Findings', *Japan Times*, 25 April 2005.
[49] Amnesty International, *Peace-keeping and Human Rights* (London: AI, 1994).
[50] *IHT*, 26–27 February 1994.
[51] Kenneth Cain, Heidi Postlewait and Andrew Thomson, *Emergency Sex and Other Desper-ate Measures: A True Story from Hell on Earth* (New York: Miramax Books, 2004).

African government decided to take action against two of its soldiers, and a French civilian with pornographic pictures and video of his victims was arrested in Paris pending prosecution.[52] There were even suggestions that the existence of photographs could potentially mark this as the UN's 'Abu Ghraib'.[53] But the abuses are not confined to UN peacekeepers. Amnesty concluded that 'the international community' (that is, NATO peacekeepers as well as UN civilian personnel) made up around 80 per cent of the clientele of women trafficked into prostitution in Kosovo.[54]

In his package of reform proposals, Annan admitted to being 'especially troubled by instances in which United Nations peacekeepers are alleged to have sexually exploited minors and other vulnerable people', repeated his policy of zero tolerance of such offences, and reaffirmed the UN's commitment 'to respect, adhere to and implement international law, fundamental human rights and the basic standards of due process'.[55] Annan appointed Prince Zeid al-Hussein, Jordan's ambassador to the UN with personal civilian peacekeeping experience in Bosnia, to study the abuses and make recommendations on improving the accountability of UN peacekeeping missions. Prince Zeid's report, submitted in March 2005, concluded that sexual exploitation of women and girls by UN security and civilian personnel in Congo was significant, widespread and ongoing. His recommendations included withholding the salary of guilty peacekeepers and putting the money into a fund to care for their victims, requiring troop-contributing countries to prosecute perpetrators identified by UN investigative teams, and making soldiers financially liable for 'peacekeeper babies' they have fathered as determined by DNA testing.[56] Annan concurred with the analysis and recommendations with respect to the investigative processes; the organisational, managerial

---

[52] 'Sex Abuse by UN Peacekeepers in Congo Largely Unpunished', *Japan Times*, 9 January 2005.

[53] Jonathan Clayton and James Bone, 'UN Officials in Sex Scandal', *Weekend Australian*, 24–26 December 2004; Maggie Farley, 'Sex-for-food scandal: the UN's "Abu Ghraib"', *Japan Times* (reprinted from the *Los Angeles Times*), 27 December 2004; Thaddeus Hoffmeister, 'Policing Those who Police the Peace', *IHT*, 31 December 2004.

[54] *Protecting the Human Rights of Women and Girls Trafficked for Forced Prostitution in Kosovo* (London: AI, document EUR 70/010/2004, 2004).

[55] Kofi A. Annan, *In Larger Freedom: Towards Development, Security and Human Rights for All.* Report of the Secretary-General (New York: United Nations, document A/59/2005, 21 March 2005), para. 113.

[56] Prince Zeid Ra'ad Zeid al-Hussein, *A Comprehensive Strategy to Eliminate Future Sexual Exploitation and Abuse in United Nations Peacekeeping Operations* (New York: United Nations, document A/59/710, 24 March 2005).

and command responsibility; and individual disciplinary, financial and criminal accountability.

Implementing the recommendations will require resources being voted for them by the General Assembly. Before doing so, the Assembly might want to ask why, when the problem of peacekeepers as sexual predators has been known at least since the Namibia and Cambodia operations, no action was taken earlier and who has been held accountable for the lapse.[57] Interestingly, in a UN report commissioned from DeLoitte Consulting, UN staff reported that the infrastructure to support ethics and integrity is already in place but accountability is not.[58] Another major lesson has to be the importance of educating and training UN peacekeepers – soldiers, police and civilian officials – in international humanitarian and human rights laws, with a particular focus on gender protection laws and norms (both local and global).

Conclusion

UN leadership on human rights has helped to change the public policy discourse in all parts of the world.[59] 'Those whose rights have been trampled are no longer alone; the state's monopoly on international affairs has been broken, and literally hundreds of organizations watch for human rights abuses by whoever might commit them.'[60] As a universal organisation, the UN provides a unique institutional framework to develop and promote human rights norms and practices and to advance legal, monitoring and operational instruments to uphold the universality of human rights while respecting national and cultural diversity. But 'the juridical, advocacy and enforcement revolutions' in human rights[61] rest on a partnership between the intergovernmental and non-governmental actors with regard to standard setting, rule creation, monitoring and compliance. The world needs NGOs so that they can put pressure on states on a variety of fronts such as human rights and the environment.

---

[57] See, for example, Peter Dennis, 'The UN, Preying on the Weak', *New York Times*, 12 April 2005.

[58] Deloitte Consulting LLP, *United Nations Organizational Integrity Survey 2004: Final Report* (New York: United Nations, 2004).

[59] See Sarah Zaidi and Roger Normand, *The UN and Human Rights Ideas* (Bloomington: Indiana University Press for the UN Intellectual History Project, forthcoming).

[60] Thomas W. Laqueur, 'The Moral Indignation and Human Rights', in Ignatieff, *Human Rights as Politics and Idolatry*, p. 129.

[61] Ignatieff, *Human Rights as Politics and Idolatry*, p. 17.

Only governments can implement changes, so CSOs need governmental forums for the pursuit of their single-interest agendas. On the other hand, human rights claims are claims by citizens on governments. They can be abused most systematically, pervasively and widely by governments. This is why the UN is ill-suited to the task of being the guardian of human rights and why NGOs are so much better at monitoring human rights abuses and state compliance with international standards of human rights treatment. The UN and the CSOs acting in concert have helped to establish the principle that states are responsible for the protection of the human rights of their citizens and internationally accountable for any failures to do so. Conversely, CSOs set the standard against which UN efforts at censuring and preventing human rights abuses are often measured. There is now a symbiotic relationship between the UN and CSOs in the establishment of new human rights standards and the implementation of existing ones.

Is the UN system overloaded with respect to human rights – too many treaties and norms, too many monitoring mechanisms with confusing and overlapping jurisdictions, and at too high a financial cost? In some ways the Human Rights Commission became a victim of the world body's growing success in promoting human rights and monitoring abuses. As the international community aimed the searchlight of critical scrutiny more directly on the human rights abuses of governments, many regimes decided that the best defence was to join the Commission. It became morally bankrupt and an embarrassment to the UN system. To reverse growing cynicism about the hypocrisy of existing institutions and practices, and noting that states often seek membership in the Commission to shield themselves from scrutiny, Annan has recommended the creation of a smaller Human Rights Council to facilitate more focused debate and discussions.[62] Based in Geneva, it could be a principal organ which would give it more status as one of the three Councils but would require Charter amendment; or a subsidiary body of the General Assembly. But it is not clear just how the Council could escape the trap of deep politicisation that plagues the Commission, or how much it would downgrade the authority of the High Commissioner for Human Rights. The 2005 summit document expressed agreement on a new Human Rights Council but dropped the requirement for a two-thirds majority in the General Assembly for election to it and delegated the task of

---

[62] Annan, *In Larger Freedom*, paras. 140, 182 and 183.

constructing one to the Assembly.[63] But it did double the budget of the High Commissioner for Human Rights over the next five years.[64]

Finally, AI and the ICRC are living proof that individuals matter. Distressed by the horrors of war he witnessed in the Battle of Solferino (1859), a young Swiss businessman named Henri Dunant became the driving force behind the establishment of the Red Cross movement which continues to play a major role in the development and dissemination of international humanitarian law. Writing in the *Observer* on 26 May 1961, Peter Benenson called for a one-year campaign for the release of 'The Forgotten Prisoners' – people imprisoned for political or religious beliefs and then forgotten by the media, the public and even the authorities. The campaign goes on. The first effort at neutral research into political imprisonment, the 1961 article sowed the seeds of an idea whose time had come. Sceptics doubted the impact of the John and Jane Smiths of the world writing directly to government leaders and expected the initial impetus to flag. Instead they have watched AI grow from an idea to an organisation to an institution. Its continuance is made necessary by the persistence of human rights abuses by governments; its continuing vitality is proof that people, ordinary people, are no longer prepared to accept the abuses as a permanent blot on the human race anywhere in the world. Just one private citizen with a good idea can make a visible impact on world affairs by bringing joy to some and hope to many.

---

[63] Draft Outcome Document, 13 September 2005, paras. 157–60.
[64] Ibid., para. 124.

5

International criminal justice

'The International Criminal Court is now operational in The Hague. The United Nations is proud to have played an important role in its establishment and in making arrangements for the commencement of its operation.'[1]

'No UN institution – not the Security Council, not the Yugoslav tribunal, not a future ICC – is competent to judge the foreign policy and national security decisions of the United States.'[2]

The world has made revolutionary advances in the criminalisation of domestic and international violence by armed groups and their individual leaders.[3] The 128-article Statute of the International Criminal Court (ICC) was adopted at the conclusion of the UN Diplomatic Conference on the Establishment of the ICC held at the Food and Agriculture Organisation in Rome from 15 June–17 July 1998. The final vote was 120–7 (including China and the USA, two permanent members of the UN Security Council), with 21 abstentions (including India, representing one-sixth of humanity). Participants included representatives from 160 countries plus 33 observers from intergovernmental and 236 observers from non-governmental organisations (NGOs). The ICC Statute received its sixtieth ratification in April 2002 and came into effect in July 2002. On 22 April 2003 Luis Moreno Ocampo of Argentina, who helped to put his country's former military rulers on trial, was elected as its first

---

[1] Kofi A. Annan, *Report of the Secretary-General on the Work of the Organization* (New York: UN, 2004, document A/59/1), para. 207.

[2] Senator Jesse Helms in an appearance before the UN Security Council on 20 January 2000, quoted in Raju G. C. Thomas, 'Prologue: Making War, Peace and History', in Raju G. C. Thomas, ed., *Yugoslavia Unraveled: Sovereignty, Self-determination, Intervention* (Lanham, MD: Lexington Books, 2003), p. xii.

[3] See Steven R. Ratner and Jason S. Abrams, *Accountability for Human Rights Atrocities in International Law: Beyond the Nuremberg Legacy* (Oxford: Clarendon, 1997) and Aryeh Neier, *War Crimes: Brutality, Genocide, Terror, and the Struggle for Justice* (New York: Times Books, 1998).

prosecutor. By the end of 2004, 135 countries had signed and almost 100 had ratified the Rome Statute.

Its adoption marked the culmination of a decade-long process initiated by the General Assembly in 1989 when it requested the International Law Commission to study the subject of the establishment of an ICC. Georg Nolte has argued that the Rome Statute was the most important treaty in public international law since the 1982 Law of the Sea Convention, that the USA played a key role in its negotiations, and that the decision to adopt it was the most serious US diplomatic defeat since the end of the Cold War.[4]

This chapter examines the dynamic interaction between law and politics in the search for universal justice, a search rooted in the growing recognition that perpetrators and victims alike are real and identifiable individuals, not just abstract entities.[5] I will begin with a look at international judicial machinery and international humanitarian law, then discuss the evolution of and problems with international criminal justice, and finally look at alternative forms of transitional and restorative justice.

International law and international criminal accountability

The role of human rights organisations, discussed in the previous chapter, points to an interesting phenomenon, namely the globalisation of the process of making and implementing international policy. There has been a matching decentralisation of international judicial authority, with the International Court of Justice (ICJ) standing alongside the ICC, international criminal tribunals, the Law of the Sea Tribunal, the World Trade Organisation (WTO) Panel, regional human rights courts, and so on.

The ICJ is the judicial arm of the United Nations and its Statute is an adjunct of the UN Charter. Successor to the Permanent Court of International Justice under the League system, the ICJ has its seat in The Hague and comprises fifteen judges elected to renewable nine-year

---

[4] Georg Nolte, 'The United States and the International Criminal Court', in David Malone and Yuen Foong Khong, eds., *Unilateralism and US Foreign Policy: International Perspectives* (Boulder: Lynne Rienner, 2003), pp. 71–93.

[5] Paul G. Lauren, 'From Impunity to Accountability: Forces of Transformation and the Changing International Human Rights Context', in Ramesh Thakur and Peter Malcontent, eds., *From Sovereign Impunity to International Accountability: The Search for Justice in a World of States* (Tokyo: United Nations University Press, 2004), pp. 15–41.

terms. UN organs and specialised agencies can seek legal advice from the world court and states can (and should, according to the UN Charter[6]) refer their disputes to it. But while the Court is available to states for settling their disputes, they cannot be compelled to use it. Serbia's case against NATO in 1999 was rejected by the Court on the procedural ground of lacking jurisdiction, not on the merits of the case.

The world court's history confirms that peaceful relations facilitate advances in international adjudication more than the latter being an instrument to prevent war. Its intersection with politics is most clearly illustrated with contrary examples involving the USA. Following the capture and holding of American diplomats in the US embassy in Tehran as hostages in November 1979, Washington took Iran to the world court. The ICJ, noting that the authorities had done nothing to stop the attack and some organs of the state had endorsed it, found against Iran in 1981. But in 1986, when Nicaragua instituted proceedings against the USA alleging responsibility for military and paramilitary activities in and against it, and the Court found against the USA, Washington withdrew from the Court's jurisdiction. The only recourse for enforcement of the Court's decisions is the UN Security Council (UNSC) – where the USA is a veto-wielding permanent member. If the UNSC bends to the will of the sole superpower, can the world court discharge the function of judicial review and be the ultimate guarantor of the legality of UNSC decisions vis-à-vis the Charter – not just with respect to procedural regularity, but also, and more importantly, with respect to the compatibility of the decisions with the objects and purposes of the Charter?

The law of the Charter governs *when* force may be used; international humanitarian law (IHL) governs *how* force may be used. The ICJ is independent and autonomous. But it is nonetheless one of the main organs of the United Nations and therefore must support its principles and purposes. It is and must be apolitical, but it cannot be innocent of the political context in which a ruling or advisory opinion is sought. The roots of IHL are to be found in the tradition of 'just war', which focused not simply upon the circumstances leading to the initiation of hostilities (*jus ad bellum*) but also the conduct of hostilities themselves (*jus in bello*).[7] While the ICJ deals with justice among states, the increasing

---

[6] Article 36.3: 'legal disputes as a general rule should be referred by the parties to the International Court of Justice'.

[7] See Michael Walzer, *Just and Unjust Wars: A Moral Argument with Historical Illustrations* (New York: Basic Books, 1992); and Geoffrey Best, *Humanity in Warfare: The Modern*

attention and sensitivity to human rights abuses and humanitarian atrocities raise questions of individual criminal accountability in a world of sovereign states. The international community has responded to barbarism by drafting and adopting international legal instruments that ban it.[8] In these days of post-Enlightenment Europe, we tend to forget that the phrase 'crimes against humanity' was coined by the African-American George Washington Williams to describe Belgian atrocities against the natives of Congo in the last two decades of the nineteenth century.[9] Similarly, 'genocide' (the crime of crimes) was coined by Raphael Lemkin to describe Nazi German atrocities against the Jews in the first half of the twentieth century.

As with human rights and IHL, progress in codifying international accountability for mass crimes can be attributed to one individual's moral engagement. Having petitioned the League of Nations to outlaw 'acts of barbarism and vandalism' in his youth, as a Jew in occupied Poland Lemkin fought in the underground resistance and in late 1944 published one of the most fateful (and, at 712 pages, voluminous) works of political thought of the last century: *Axis Rule in Occupied Europe: Laws of Occupation, Analysis of Government, Proposals for Redress*.[10] On the occasion of his birth centenary, Secretary-General Kofi Annan recalled that to describe an old crime, Lemkin had coined the new word 'genocide' in 1943, two years before the world became familiar with Auschwitz, Belsen and Dachau, and 'almost single-handedly drafted an international multilateral treaty declaring genocide an international crime, and then turned to the United Nations in its earliest days and implored Member States to adopt it'.[11] The Genocide Convention, adopted by the General Assembly on 9 December 1948[12] (one day before

---

History of the International Law of Armed Conflicts (London: Weidenfeld & Nicolson, 1983).

[8] See Robert Gellately and Ben Kiernan, eds., *The Spectre of Genocide: Mass Murder in Historical Perspective* (Cambridge: Cambridge University Press, 2003), and Martin Shaw, *War and Genocide: Organized Killing in Modern Society* (Cambridge: Polity Press, 2003).

[9] For an account of the scale of humanitarian atrocities committed by Belgium in its African colony, see Adam Hochschild, *King Leopold's Ghost* (Boston: Houghton Mifflin, 1999).

[10] Reissued in 2005 by Lawbook Exchange.

[11] United Nations, *Press Release* SG/SM/7842, 13 June 2001.

[12] Lemkin was discovered weeping in a UN corridor at the news and described the convention as an epitaph for his mother who had been among many members of his family killed in the Holocaust; Michael Ignatieff, 'The Legacy of Raphael Lemkin', lecture

the Universal Declaration of Human Rights), was indeed a milestone in defining genocide as a crime against humanity and thus a matter of universal criminal jurisdiction. Nevertheless, Annan continued, 'article VI of the Convention, which binds the Parties to try persons charged with genocide before a national or international tribunal, has for all practical purposes remained a dead letter'. But recent developments give hope: the crime of genocide was included in the statutes of the International Criminal Tribunals for Rwanda (ICTR),[13] the former Yugoslavia (ICTY)[14] and the ICC.[15]

In a brilliant essay on Lemkin's legacy, Michael Ignatieff notes that the fatally seductive appeal of genocide 'lies in its promise to create a world without enemies . . . a world without discord, enmity, suspicion, free of the enemy without or the enemy within'.[16] The Holocaust in which several million Jews were systematically killed in the Nazi programme to exterminate them – the familiar cycle of pogroms modernised into industrialised and highly efficient mass slaughter – retains a unique emotional resonance. But repeating the slogan of 'Never Again' requires chutzpah after the repeats of the horror of mass killings in Rwanda, Srebrenica, Darfur and elsewhere. As an old joke has it, you commit one murder, you get sent to trial and prison; commit ten, you get sent to an insane asylum; commit 10,000, you get sent to Geneva for peace talks.

Writing in 1946 to her former professor Karl Jaspers of Heidelberg University, Hannah Arendt questioned how one could comprehend what the Nazis had done within the existing compass of criminal law. 'The Nazi crimes . . . explode the limits of the law; and that is precisely what constitutes their monstrousness', she wrote. 'We are simply not equipped to deal on a human, political level, with a guilt that is beyond crime and

---

delivered at the US Holocaust Memorial Museum Washington, 13 December 2001, available at www.ushmm.org/conscience/ events/ignatieff/ignatieff.php.

[13] See Kingsley Chiedu Moghalu, *Rwanda's Genocide: The Politics of Global Justice* (New York: Palgrave Macmillan, 2005).

[14] See Roger S. Clark and Madeleine Sann, eds., *The Prosecution of International Crimes: A Critical Study of the International Tribunal for the Former Yugoslavia* (New Brunswick, NJ: Transaction, 1996).

[15] See William A. Schabas, *An Introduction to the International Criminal Court* (Cambridge: Cambridge University Press, 2001); and Bruce Broomhall, *International Justice and the International Criminal Court: Between State Consent and the Rule of Law* (Oxford: Oxford University Press, 2003).

[16] Michael Ignatieff, 'The Danger of a World without Enemies', *The New Republic*, 4:493 (26 February 2001), pp. 25–8.

an innocence that is beyond goodness or virtue.'[17] Objecting that such a moral vocabulary would endow Nazi crimes with 'satanic greatness', Jaspers insisted on seeing them instead 'in their total banality'[18] – a phrase that Arendt famously used in the subtitle of her book published almost two decades later.[19]

The way to apprehend and punish the perpetrators of conscience-shocking crimes on a mass scale is through an international legal framework that establishes the notion of 'universal jurisdiction', where jurisdiction in respect of such crimes depends not on the place where they are committed, but on the nature of the crime itself. If they are truly 'crimes against humanity', they can properly be prosecuted before the courts of any country. The Geneva Convention of 1949 established a new category of war crimes called 'grave breaches' which could be prosecuted in the courts of all countries that have ratified the Convention. The arrest and transfer of former Serbian strongman Slobodan Milošević to the ICTY in The Hague in 2001 was but one of several dramatic twists and turns in the last few years in the search for universal justice.[20]

The UN Charter was never meant to be a tyrant's charter of impunity or his constitutional instrument of choice for self-protection. Nevertheless, as worrisome as the challenge to national sovereignty posed by international judicial accountability is the unpredictability of the potent new weapon as an instrument of the new international order. Its potential for abuse for mischievous, vexatious and vindictive purposes is vast. After the Iraq War in 2003, British Prime Minister Tony Blair and some of his cabinet colleagues (such as the defence and foreign ministers) were accused of crimes against humanity by Greek lawyers who lodged a case with the ICC on 28 July 2003.[21] The doctrine of universal jurisdiction was employed also to threaten prosecution against President

---

[17] Hannah Arendt, letter to Karl Jaspers, 17 August 1946, in Hannah Arendt and Karl Jaspers, *Hannah Arendt Karl Jaspers: Correspondence, 1926–1969*, edited by Lotte Kohler and Hans Saner and translated from German by Robert and Rita Kember (New York: Harcourt Brace Jovanovich, 1992), p. 54.

[18] Jaspers, letter to Arendt, 19 October 1946, ibid., p. 62.

[19] Hannah Arendt, *Eichmann in Jerusalem: A Report on the Banality of Evil* (Harmondsworth: Penguin, 1963).

[20] See Rachel Kerr, *The International Criminal Tribunal for the Former Yugoslavia: An Exercise in Law, Politics and Diplomacy* (Oxford: Oxford University Press, 2004).

[21] Helena Smith, 'Greeks Accuse Blair of War Crimes in Iraq', *Guardian* (London), 29 July 2003.

George W. Bush and General Tommy Franks (commander of the US forces in Iraq).[22] Defense Secretary Donald Rumsfeld retaliated by warning that if US officials could no longer travel to Brussels without fear of prosecution, then the NATO headquarters would clearly have to be relocated to another country.[23] In July 2003 Belgium amended its controversial law on universal jurisdiction and restricted trials in Belgian courts to crimes committed or suffered by its citizens or residents.

The International Criminal Court

As we move from the restrictive culture of sovereign impunity of previous centuries to an enlightened culture of international accountability more suited to the modern sensibility, it is worth making three arguments about the relationship between justice being done (the domain of law), and being seen to be done (the realm of politics): justice can be seen not to have been done; justice may not be seen to have been done; and in some cases justice may not be done despite being seen to have been done.[24]

The Hague and Arusha ad hoc tribunals were set up as *substitutes* for effective action to halt the atrocities in the two regions:[25] they were alibis for no action, not indicators of toughening new standards of international judicial accountability. Their policy utility lay in the fact that indictments isolated the offending leaders diplomatically, strengthened rivals in the domestic power struggle and helped to pave the way for economic sanctions and even the use of military force.[26]

If a leader – Adolf Hitler, Augusto Pinochet, Slobodan Milošević, Saddam Hussein – is deemed criminal only with convenient hindsight,

---

[22] See George Monbiot, 'Let's Hear it for Belgium', *Guardian*, 20 May 2003.

[23] Noell Knox, 'Rumsfeld Warns Belgium about War-crimes Law', *USA Today*, 13 June 2003. Not for the first and probably not for the last time, US officials ignore the directly equivalent practice of US courts in subjecting foreign officials and officers to the jurisdiction of American courts. See Robert H. Bork, 'Judicial Imperialism', *Wall Street Journal Europe*, 18 June 2003.

[24] For elaboration, see Ramesh Thakur, 'Dealing with Guilt Beyond Crime: The Strained Quality of Universal Justice', in Thakur and Malcontent, eds., *From Sovereign Impunity to International Accountability*, pp. 272–92.

[25] Philippe Kirsch, John T. Holmes and Mora Johnson, 'International Tribunals and Courts,' in David M. Malone, ed., *The UN Security Council: From the Cold War to the 21st Century* (Boulder: Lynne Rienner, 2004), p. 281.

[26] Michael Scharf, 'Indicted for War Crimes, Then What?', *Washington Post*, 3 October 1999.

what is the element of complicity of foreign governments who engaged in full diplomatic intercourse with that leader? The ICTY is sited in a NATO country, was set up by the UNSC in which NATO countries are disproportionately dominant and its expenses are met mainly from them. The indictment of Milošević in the middle of the war, on the basis of evidence supplied by NATO, meant that tribunals had progressed from being victors' justice after the war into an instrument for ensuring and accelerating victory during war. The enforcement of the tribunal's indictment of Milošević and cronies as war criminals has been totally dependent on the same NATO powers.

In a stinging indictment of the ICTY, Robert Hayden argued that it delivers biased justice: prosecutorial decisions are based on the national characteristics of the accused rather than on an objective assessment of the available evidence with regard to cluster bombs and war crimes, wanton destruction of property, intentional targeting of civilian infrastructure which caused civilian deaths in a policy designed to avoid casualties among one's own military that would have resulted from attacking enemy military assets, etc.;[27] the supposedly independent ICTY prosecutes only those whom Washington wants prosecuted; Washington in turn uses the threat of ICTY prosecution to secure compliance from political actors in the Balkans; its judicial decisions trample on the rights of accused to obtain a fair trial; and it has shown a lack of interest in investigating prosecutorial misconduct.[28] There is also the troubling element of the chief prosecutor who issued the indictment being appointed to her country's highest court very shortly thereafter.[29]

And yet it is highly probable that justice will be done with regard to Milošević. There is no question but that Milošević was at the centre of the most murderous decade in Europe since the second World War. The

---

[27] See also 'NATO/Federal Republic of Yugoslavia "Collateral Damage" or Unlawful Killings?', *Amnesty International Report* (London: AI, 6 June 2000); and 'Civilian Deaths in the NATO Air Campaign', *Human Rights Watch* 12, no. 1(D), February 2000.

[28] Robert M. Hayden, 'Biased Justice: "Humanrightism" and the International Criminal Tribunal for the Former Yugoslavia', in Thomas, ed., *Yugoslavia Unraveled*, pp. 259–85.

[29] See John Hagan, *Justice in the Balkans: Prosecuting War Crimes in the Hague Tribunal* (Chicago: University of Chicago Press, 2003), chapter 4. According to Hagan, Louise Arbour's Supreme Court appointment was approved but undisclosed on 26 May 1999, the day before her announcement of the Milošević indictment; normally such appointments are announced in the week they are made; at her request, the official announcement was delayed until 11 June. Ibid., p. 127. Arbour became a Judge of the Supreme Court of Canada effective from 15 September 1999, and five years later she became the UN High Commissioner for Human Rights.

ICTY was established before winners and losers had emerged from the various conflicts sparked across former Yugoslavia.[30] Its judges, like their counterparts with the ICTR in Arusha, have come from many countries, some not involved in the conflicts at any stage. Their proceedings demonstrate high standards of fairness in evidential matters,[31] and their verdicts have represented exciting developments in the extension, deepening and broadening of international humanitarian law and international criminal justice. Crucially, unlike the Tokyo Tribunal after the Second World War, the new ad hoc tribunals have eschewed the death penalty – which may perhaps have influenced the decision calculus of some indictees from countries where capital punishment is still an option for national criminal prosecutors.

Nevertheless, the international criminal tribunals have been ad hoc and ex post facto, set up to try limited numbers of individuals for specific activities, in specific situations and specific regions. The tribunals are not merely ad hoc; they also suffer from particularism. An international criminal court with universal jurisdiction has been the missing link in the system of international criminal justice.[32] The ICJ handles cases between states, but not between individuals. Without an international criminal court that holds individuals responsible for their actions where governments fail or are not able to do so, acts of genocide and egregious violations of human rights often go unpunished. In the last sixty years there have been many instances of crimes against humanity and war crimes for which no individuals have been held accountable.

The ICC's permanence, institutionalised identity and universal jurisdiction will enable an escape from the tyranny of the episodic and

---

[30] See M. Cherif Bassiouni, *Justice in a Time of War: The True Story behind the International Criminal Tribunal for the Former Yugoslavia* (College Station: Texas A&M University Press, 2004).

[31] Bert Swart, 'International Criminal Courts and the Admissibility of Evidence', in Thakur and Malcontent, eds., *From Sovereign Impunity to International Accountability*, pp. 135–53.

[32] See Yves Beigbeder and Theo van Boven, *Judging War Criminals: The Politics of International Justice* (New York: St. Martin's Press, 1999); Steven R. Ratner and Jason S. Abrams, *Accountability for Human Rights Atrocities in International Law: Beyond the Nuremberg Legacy*, 2nd edn (Oxford: Clarendon Press, 2001); David Scheffer, 'The United States and the International Criminal Court', *American Journal of International Law* 93:1 (January 1999), pp. 12–22; and Sarah B. Sewall and Carl Keysen, eds., *The United States and the International Criminal Court: National Security and International Law* (Lanham, MD: Rowman & Littlefield, 2000).

attenuate perceptions of politically motivated investigations and selective justice. Only universal liability can arrest and reverse the 'drift to
universalism'[33] from the Nuremberg and Tokyo to the Yugoslavia and
Rwanda tribunals, along with such other way-stations as the detention
of Pinochet in Britain. Permanence also helps to cumulate and build on
precedents. The ICC will be an efficient and cost-effective alternative to
ad hoc tribunals with respect to money, time and energy, and may also
provide sensible alternatives to dubious sanctions and unilateral military
retaliation. Yet Washington has led a determined campaign against the
ICC. The Clinton administration was engaged in a contradictory two-
level game: international negotiations to build an effective multilateral
institution for international criminal justice; and negotiations with domestic constituencies strongly opposed to putting the USA under any
such institution. The US campaign against the ICC by the Bush administration – not simply refusing to sign itself, but working actively to
undermine the ICC – led to the novel situation where some countries
found themselves the target of US sanctions for trying to advance and
promote the rule of law in world affairs.

Subjecting prosecutorial investigations and indictments to UNSC
authorisation, one of the key US demands, would have politicised the
process and tainted its impartial credibility from the very start: it would
have been born in sin. The five permanent members (P5) would be able
to veto any action against themselves while pressing charges against all
others. The international community has been concerned for some time
to limit the scope of the P5 privileges, not extend the veto's application
still more. The notion that US personnel should enjoy blanket exemption from any possible investigation is such an egregious example of
double standards, of exceptionalism rooted in the self-definition of the
USA as the virtuous power that cannot be held to account to standards
that must nevertheless apply to everyone else, that it was never taken
seriously even as a negotiating ploy.[34] There are real safeguards for all
countries against whimsical and idiosyncratic abuse of the ICC procedures. The ICC is being set up as a court of last resort, complementary to
national courts that are unable or unwilling to dispense justice. The

---

[33] Gary Jonathan Bass, *Stay the Hand of Vengeance: The Politics of War Crimes Tribunals*
(Princeton: Princeton University Press, 2000), p. 283.
[34] On the importance of exceptionalism in US foreign policy, see Samuel P. Huntington,
'American Ideals versus American Institutions', in John G. Ikenberry, ed., *American
Foreign Policy: Theoretical Essays*, 3rd edn (New York: Longman, 1999), pp. 221–53.

prosecutor will be accountable to a panel of judges exercising due oversight. The world court's experience with respect to the election of international judges is essentially a positive story.

Washington heaped insult on injury when it vetoed a routine extension of the UN's peacekeeping mission in Bosnia in 2002 because of the failure to get a blanket and permanent immunity from prosecution of its peacekeepers by the ICC. Stung by the fierce criticism from even its diehard European friends and allies, the USA softened its position slightly and won a renewable twelve-month exemption for the peacekeepers of all countries that had not ratified the ICC Statute. This damaged the integrity of the court and treaty negotiations and the credibility of the UNSC itself. Lloyd Axworthy, who as Canada's foreign minister had been a powerful voice in the campaign to establish the ICC, cautioned that 'the compromise acquiesces to the Security Council's questionable right to amend by interpretation a treaty arrived at in open discussion by representatives of more than 100 nation states in a founding convention.'[35] It was the searing images of US soldiers abusing Iraqi prisoners in Abu Ghraib that finally put an end to the annual exemption in 2004.

Washington seems to have been tripped in the end by its own 'curious mixture of American idealism and Stalinist opportunism'[36] that led it to support the establishment of ad hoc tribunals. By keeping them under the jurisdiction of the UNSC, the USA made sure that it controlled their destiny. But they generated an unstoppable momentum for a permanent ICC with genuinely universal jurisdiction. In a fitting symmetry, the driving force behind the US rejection of the ICC is an equally curious mixture of exceptionalism and power politics.[37] Washington may preach universalism, but it practises national particularism and cultural relativism. The real difficulty could come not with *rogue* prosecutors, but with *responsible* ones. From the world court's pronouncements against the USA with regard to Nicaragua in the 1980s, to NATO's choice of targets

---

[35] Lloyd Axworthy, 'Stop the US Foul Play', *Globe and Mail* (Toronto), 17 July 2002.

[36] Geoffrey Robertson, *Crimes Against Humanity: The Struggle for Global Justice* (London: Penguin, 1999), p. 211. Quoted in Michael D. Biddiss, 'From the Nuremberg Charter to the Rome Statute: A Historical Analysis of the Limits of International Criminal Accountability', in Thakur and Malcontent, eds., *From Sovereign Impunity to International Accountability*, p. 44.

[37] See David Forsythe, 'International Criminal Justice and the United States: Law, Culture, Power', in Thakur and Malcontent, eds., *From Sovereign Impunity to International Accountability*, pp. 61–79.

and armaments in the Balkans and the actions of the US military in Afghanistan and Iraq, it is possible to imagine circumstances in which the domestic political atmosphere is too hostile within the USA to permit national investigations and prosecutions and a conscientious ICC prosecutor decides to take up the case.[38] Similarly, the problem may lie not so much with regard to junior and middle-ranking military personnel as with generals and defence secretaries and even presidents: those with command responsibility making policy and issuing the orders, not the foot-soldiers merely carrying out orders.

In a damning end-of-year indictment of international justice, Eric Posner, professor of law at the University of Chicago, used some telling statistics.[39] The ICJ had ruled on only three cases during the year: against Israel on its barrier to keep out terrorists, which Israel duly rejected and ignored; against the US violation of the Vienna Convention on diplomatic relations (which Washington used successfully against Tehran in the 1979 hostages case) because US police often fail to inform foreign citizens under arrest of their consular rights; and on a claim brought against NATO countries by Serbia and Montenegro, on which the Court ruled it lacked jurisdiction. Over sixty years, the ICJ has ruled on fewer than 100 cases, compared to several hundred rulings from the WTO Panel in less than a decade, and several thousand from the European Court of Justice in its fifty years of existence. The number of cases heard each year has remained constant even as the number of states has tripled, leading to a two-thirds decline in the cases per nation. Similarly, the proportion of countries putting themselves under the Court's compulsory jurisdiction has declined from two-thirds to one-third, with Britain the only one of the permanent members of the UNSC in the group. Moreover, judges tend to vote some 90 per cent of the time with their home countries if they face judgement at The Hague, and to vote sympathetically with countries like their home countries in political system, wealth or poverty.

Nevertheless, there are three respects in which the US fears about the ICC may be well founded: the rule-of-law standards, the integration of criminal justice within an overarching framework of governance and issues of transitional justice.

For a trial to be authentic, the possibility of acquittal must be as much an inbuilt requirement as the possibility of conviction. The US criminal

---

[38] Ibid., pp. 69–70.
[39] Eric A. Posner, 'All Justice, Too, is Local', *New York Times*, 30 December 2004.

justice system goes about the farthest in the world in protecting the rights of the arrested and accused. International criminal law, by contrast, has shifted the focus from the defence to the prosecution. The ICTY 'does not always respect the rights of the criminal defendant in ways consistent with international human rights norms or national constitutions'.[40] The UN has to ensure that any process of trial and prosecution is credible, meets international standards on the independence and impartiality of prosecutors and judges, and respects the rights of victims as well as defendants.[41]

Second, the ICC is not embedded in a broader system of democratic policy-making, there is no political check on it, and therefore its authority to overturn policy established by national democracies is questionable. In a national system, the office of the prosecutor functions within a well-established structure of state governance, while the ICC 'is not established as part of a centralized system of international governance that can govern the entire international community'.[42] The ICC, 'insofar as it provides for jurisdiction over non-party nationals, displaces the state as the conduit of democratic representation and provides no alternative mechanism for democratic governance'.[43]

Transitional justice[44]

Third, international criminal justice takes away from domestic authorities the options of alternative modes of healing and restitution with a view to reconciliation that puts the traumas of the past firmly in the

---

[40] Jose Alvarez, 'The UN Security Council: Are There Checks to Provide Balance?', *Law Quadrangle Notes* (University of Michigan Law School) (Fall 1994), p. 43.

[41] Annan, *Report of the Secretary-General on the Work of the Organization* (2004), para. 223.

[42] Hisashi Owada, 'The Creation of the International Criminal Court: A Critical Analysis', in R. K. Dixit and C. Jayaraj, eds., *Dynamics of International Law in the New Millennium* (New Delhi: Manak, for the Indian Society of International Law, 2004), p. 101. Prof. Owada was a member of the Japanese delegation to the Rome conference and has since been elected as a judge of the ICJ.

[43] Madeline H. Morris, 'Democracy, Global Governance and the International Criminal Court', in Thakur and Malcontent, eds., *From Sovereign Impunity to International Accountability*, p. 191.

[44] See Kofi A. Annan, *The Rule of Law and Transitional Justice in Conflict and Post-conflict Societies*. Report of the Secretary-General (New York: UN, document S/2004/616, 23 August 2004). See also Priscilla Hayner, *Unspeakable Truths: Confronting State Terror and Atrocity* (London: Routledge, 2001); Neil Kritz, ed., *Transitional Justice: How Emerging Democracies Reckon with Former Regimes* (3 volumes) (Washington, DC: US Institute of Peace, 1995); A. James McAdams, ed., *Transitional Justice and the Rule of Law in New*

past.[45] The legal clarity of judicial verdicts sits uncomfortably with the nuanced morality of confronting *and overcoming*, through a mix of justice and high politics, a jointly troubled past. Studies for the New York-based International Center for Transitional Justice concluded that lack of political will, local capacity and social trust, combined with the absence of a comprehensive and effective approach to transitional justice issues, had stymied progress in addressing the past and laying the foundations for a Balkans future based on justice and the rule of law.[46]

In South Africa, building on the Chilean model,[47] this was done by means of the Truth and Reconciliation Commission (TRC).[48] In both cases, the final reports summarised the findings, put them in their proper political and historical contexts and disseminated the facts of past atrocities to their own public and the world. The South African case is especially interesting and instructive because the criminal apartheid state was such an international *cause célèbre* for such a long time, and also because the TRC became such a celebrated case of the genre.[49] In addition, in South Africa the *process* was at least as important as the final

---

Democracies (Notre Dame: University of Notre Dame Press, 1997); Robert I. Rotberg and Dennis Thompson, eds., *Truth versus Justice: The Morality of Truth Commissions* (Princeton: Princeton University Press, 2000); and Ruti G. Teitel, *Transitional Justice* (Oxford: Oxford University Press, 2000).

[45] The growing literature on the subject includes Bass, *Stay the Hand of Vengeance;* Richard J. Goldstone, *For Humanity: Reflections of a War Crimes Investigator* (New Haven: Yale University Press, 2001); Martha Minow, *Between Vengeance and Forgiveness: Facing History After Genocide and Mass Violence* (Boston: Beacon Press, 1998).

[46] Mark Freeman, *Serbia and Montenegro: Selected Developments in Transitional Justice,* and *Bosnia and Herzegovina: Selected Developments in Transitional Justice* (New York: International Center for Transitional Justice, 2004).

[47] With total costs of $1 and $35 million respectively, the Chilean and South African truth commissions were also incredibly inexpensive in comparison to the ad hoc international criminal tribunals in Rwanda and former Yugoslavia that have cost one hundred million dollars per year on average.

[48] See Madeline Davis, ed., *The Pinochet Case: Origins, Progress, Implications* (London: Institute of Latin American Studies, University of London, 2003); Naomi Roht-Arriaza, *The Pinochet Effect: Transnational Justice in the Age of Human Rights* (Philadelphia: University of Pennsylvania Press, 2005); and Alex Boraine (vice-chair of South Africa's TRC), *A Country Unmasked: Inside South Africa's Truth and Reconciliation Commission* (Cape Town: Oxford University Press, 2000). In a remarkably prescient letter that anticipated the truth and reconciliation commissions, Jaspers wrote in 1960 that for mass crimes, 'a process of examination and clarification' was preferable to a criminal trial. 'The goal would be the best possible objectification of the historical facts.' Letter to Arendt, 16 December 1960, in Arendt and Jaspers, *Correspondence*, p. 413.

[49] See Traggy Maepa, ed., *Beyond Retribution: Prospects for Restorative Justice in South Africa* (Pretoria: Institute for Security Studies Monograph Series No. 111, February 2005).

product. South Africa opted for a statutory body set up by parliament, not merely a presidential commission; it had subpoena powers that carried the carrot of full amnesty and the stick of criminal prosecution; and it held public hearings under shady trees in villages as well as in churches (with the attendant symbolism of repentance and forgiveness) that were televised to a large national and international audience. Moreover, women testified in large numbers, and for many it was the first opportunity to tell their stories. For most of its thirty months, the commission was *the* national story: compelling, gripping, poignant – and cathartic. It remains the gold standard for transitional justice.

Rwanda's version of transitional justice operates through the local *gacaca* system of people's courts whose overriding goal is not to determine guilt but to restore harmony and social order.[50] An estimated one million people are expected to be tried in the *gacaca* system launched in 2002.[51] The *gacaca* system has arguably been more productive and efficient, whereas the international criminal tribunal track has been slow, hesitant, time-consuming, money-intensive, and with very little to show for it all at the end of the day. Ten years after the genocide, the ICTR had indicted eighty-one, convicted twenty and acquitted three people.[52]

Mozambique offers equally successful examples of communal healing techniques. The South African, Mozambican and Rwandan cases were all deliberate efforts through social and political channels to *escape* cycles of retributive violence coming out of decades of tumultuous political conflicts congealed around communal identity; the purely juridical approach to transitional justice traps and suspends communities in the prism of past hatreds. Their record of bringing closure to legacies of systematic savagery in deeply conflicted societies is superior to that of institutions of international criminal justice. They fall in the tradition of 'restorative justice'[53] systems rather than retributive justice systems.

In a similar vein, three years after Indonesian-backed militias had laid waste to his country, East Timor's president-elect Xanana Gusmao declared that justice for the perpetrators of the violence would be subordinated to the need for development and social justice. 'We fought, we

---

[50] See Helena Cobban, 'The Legacies of Collective Violence: The Rwandan Genocide and the Limits of Law', *Boston Review* 27:2 (April/May 2002), pp. 4–15.

[51] Arthur Asiimwe, 'Rwanda Estimates 1 Million Face Genocide Charge', Reuters, www.boston.com/news, 14 January 2005.

[52] Ibid.

[53] See Wesley Cragg, *The Practice of Punishment: Towards a Theory of Restorative Justice* (London: Routledge, 1992).

suffered, we died for what?', he asked. 'To try other people or to receive benefits from independence?'[54] After being elected president, he met General Wiranto in Bali, even though Wiranto had been indicted for war crimes in East Timor; Foreign Minister Jose Ramos Horta expressed public disagreement.[55] East Timor's prosecutor-general asked for a revision of the case against Wiranto and questioned the timing of the UN-backed court warrant for the former military chief's arrest issued on 10 May 2004.[56] The Truth and Friendship Commission set up jointly by East Timor and Indonesia in March 2005 is the first example of such a bilateral (not merely internal) body: hence its name. The ten-member panel, based in Bali, will be given access to legal documents and is expected to conduct interviews in both countries. But its remit is to reveal the truth and promote reconciliation, not to recommend prosecution of offenders. Ramos-Horta explained that East Timor was bending over backwards because of the futility of pursuing perpetrators outside its jurisdiction in a context of complete non-cooperation by Indonesian authorities. Academic experts who refuse to come down to earth from their stratospheric heights might express distaste for compromises based in realism. But since East Timor's destiny was tied to good relations with its powerful neighbour, the Commission inquiry would bring closure by telling the truth, acknowledging responsibility and apologising to the victims.[57] Human rights groups and the Catholic Church in East Timor have criticised the Commission as an attempt to bury the past rather than to pursue justice. On the same reasoning, a UN panel of legal experts recommended that Indonesia should be given six months to bring perpetrators of atrocities in East Timor to justice under international supervision, failing which the UNSC should refer the matter to the ICC.[58] The governments of East Timor and Indonesia, both of which are the democratically elected governments of the two countries, rejected this.

As almost all these examples show, the logics of peace and justice can be contradictory. Peace is forward-looking, problem-solving and

---

[54] Quoted in Don Greenlees, 'East Timor Puts justice to One Side', *Weekend Australian*, 4–5 May 2002.

[55] 'East Timor's Horta Hits Gusmao's Meeting War Crimes Indictee Wiranto', *Japan Times*, 31 May 2004.

[56] 'East Timor Prosecutor Files for Revision in Wiranto case', *UN Wire* (www.unwire.org), 12 May 2004; Sian Powell, 'Wiranto Arrest in Doubt', *Australian*, 13 May 2004.

[57] Personal conversation, Brisbane, 15 August 2005.

[58] John Aglionby, 'UN Pressures Jakarta over East Timor Trials', *Guardian*, 29 June 2005.

integrative, requiring reconciliation between past enemies within an all-inclusive community. Justice is backward-looking, finger-pointing and retributive, requiring trial and punishment of the perpetrators of past crimes. Religious leaders from northern Uganda – home to Africa's longest running war – argued that the ICC threat to indict the top commanders of the rebel Lord's Resistance Army would only serve to scare the rebels from peace talks and prolong the war.[59] There were fears that the possible indictment for war crimes of Kosovo's Prime Minister Ramush Haradinaj, a former Kosovo Liberation Army (KLA) commander, could push Kosovo over the edge. But if he was not indicted, already grudging Serbian cooperation with the ICTY would be further jeopardised.[60]

The trial of Saddam Hussein could easily be seen as victors' justice.[61] When Iraq's interim leaders asked for help in training about thirty judges and prosecutors to try Saddam, the UN turned down the request, in part because Iraq has the death penalty which the UN opposes.[62] A survey in mid-2003 revealed nuanced and sophisticated perspectives among Iraqis on the balance between trial and punishment, and truth and reconciliation.[63] There was a strong desire to bring perpetrators of past human rights abuses to justice, but concern that the process should be fair and legitimate without being overly lengthy. There was lingering suspicion of the USA for its past support for Saddam and as an occupying power, but also of the UN for its past tolerance of Saddam and the maintenance of sanctions. The idea of an official truth-seeking and memory-preservation process was strongly supported in order to reveal the truth to the outside world as well as to Iraqis, to prevent a repetition of the past, and to mediate personal experiences through a national narrative. But there was also anxiety about reopening old wounds alongside opposition to the idea of granting amnesty to perpetrators of

---

[59] Abraham McLaughlin, 'Africa to World: We Can Handle War Justice Ourselves', *Christian Science Monitor*, 18 March 2005.

[60] Simon Tisdall, 'War Crimes Indictment Could Push Teetering Kosovo to Edge', *Guardian*, 5 January 2005.

[61] See Neil MacDonald, 'Saddam Tribunal Struggles for Credibility', *Financial Times*, 10 June 2005; William Pfaff, 'Hussein Trial Already Flawed', *Japan Times*, 11 July 2004; Samuel Loewenberg, 'Trying Saddam', *Nation*, 5 April 2004, pp. 6–7.

[62] 'UN Won't Train Iraqi Judges', *Daily Yomiuri*, 24 October 2004.

[63] *Iraqi Voices: Attitudes toward Transitional Justice and Social Reconstruction* (New York: International Center for Transitional Justice and Human Rights Center of the University of California, Berkeley, 2004).

serious crimes like genocide, war crimes and crimes against humanity, but not lesser ones.

The point is not to deny that the choice may be a painful one, the government and the people may be divided on the issue, and the public policy that results may turn out to be flawed and wrong. Rather, the point is that these are *profoundly political* choices that may involve complex trade-offs, not primarily and simply legal decisions. For that very reason, the choice is one that only the country concerned can make. Only the previously traumatised and war-torn societies can make the delicate decisions and painful choices between justice for past misdeeds, political order and stability today, and reconciliation for a common future tomorrow.

Conclusion

The establishment of the ICC as a permanent and universal international criminal court marks one of the most significant advances in international law. Yet the negative vote by two of the P5, and the abstention by India, were testimony to a significant division of opinion in the international community. In the battle over the ICC, reasonable US demands were listened to and accommodated. But gradually the conviction grew that objections were being raised and arguments were being framed to fit a predetermined policy of opposing the very idea of a credible and independent ICC with universal jurisdiction. 'The perceived demand to remain beside or even above the law ultimately hardened' the resistance to US intransigence.[64] Cherif Bassiouni, chair of the Rome Statute's drafting committee, wrote later that most delegations concluded that 'it would be better to stop giving in to the United States; they believed the United States would never be satisfied with the concessions it got and ultimately would never sign the Treaty for completely unrelated domestic political reasons'.[65]

The untenability of the US position became clear over Darfur. Fearing that the perpetrators of the atrocities against the people of Darfur would go unpunished by the government in Khartoum, the European members of the UNSC, supported by Annan,[66] opposed any thought of an ad hoc

[64] Nolte, 'The United States and the International Criminal Court', p. 74.

[65] Cherif Bassiouni, 'Negotiating the Treaty of Rome on the Establishment of the ICC', *Cornell International Law Journal* 32:3 (1999), p. 457.

[66] Evelyn Leopold, 'Annan: Sudan Suspects Should Go to Global Court', Reuters, www.alertnet.org, 19 January 2005.

court and wanted to refer the issue to the ICC.[67] A UN inquiry chaired by Judge Antonio Cassesse reported that massive atrocities, conducted on a widespread and systematic basis on a large scale, which continued even during the Commission's inquiry, had been committed by the Sudan government and the Janjaweed militia in Darfur.[68] It concluded further that 'The Sudanese justice system is unable and unwilling to address the situation in Darfur', and as Sudan was not a party to the ICC, the best course of action was for the Security Council to refer the matter to the ICC under Article 13(b) of the ICC Statute.[69] In April 2005 the UNSC resolved to refer the Darfur atrocities to the ICC. In return for its agreement through abstention (which by common understanding does not translate into a veto), Washington managed to get a blanket exemption for US personnel serving in Sudan from ever being brought before the ICC. A leading Indian newspaper condemned 'the strong scent of double standards' that made 'a complete mockery of the ideals that informed the setting up of a permanent international criminal court to try perpetrators of the gravest crimes against humanity'.[70]

Nuremberg and Tokyo were instances of victors' justice.[71] Yet by historical standards, both tribunals were remarkable for giving defeated leaders the opportunity to defend their actions in a court of law instead

---

[67] In a prescient passage, Nolte had written that 'When international crimes arise, other members of the Security Council will press for a referral of the situation to the ICC. At that point it will be difficult for the United States to justify its veto (and general opposition to the ICC). . . . It will therefore be increasingly difficult for the United States to pressure other states into establishing ad hoc tribunals, like the ICTY, instead of employing the ICC'; Nolte, 'The United States and the International Criminal Court', p. 86.

[68] *Report of the International Commission of Inquiry on Darfur to the United Nations Secretary-General Pursuant to Security Council Resolution 1564 of 18 September 2004* (Geneva: Office of the High Commissioner for Human Rights, 25 January 2005), para. 271. Available online at http://www.ohchr.org/english/docs/darfurreport.doc. Resolution 1564 was adopted under chapter 7 of the Charter.

[69] Ibid., p. 5.

[70] 'Duplicity on Darfur', editorial, *Hindu* (Chennai), 12 April 2005.

[71] This still casts a shadow over East Asian regional relations. The annual visit by Prime Minister Junichiro Koizumi to Tokyo's Yasukuni Shrine to honour Japan's 2.4 million soldiers killed in war arouses fierce opposition from China and the Koreas because fourteen Class A convicted war criminals are also interred there. Defenders of his visit retort that the convictions were based on victors' justice. See 'Separation of War Criminals "Will Never Happen": Yasukuni', *Japan Times*, 5 June 2005. Parliamentary Secretary Masahiro Morioka asked 'What tribunal was the Tokyo tribunal? Both sides do wrong in a war. It is erroneous to label only countries that win as right and nations that lose as wrong'; 'Morioka Again Slams War Tribunal', *Japan Times*, 23 June 2005.

of being dispatched for summary execution. The ad hoc tribunals of the 1990s are important milestones in efforts to fill institutional gaps in the original central mission of the UN, viz. to control group violence. They have been neither unqualified successes nor total failures. While the international criminal tribunals have primacy over the operation of domestic court systems,[72] the ICC has been constructed to give primacy to domestic systems and become operative only in the event of domestic unwillingness or incapacity. With the US refusal to join the universal justice of the ICC, many developing countries view the moral imperialism of human rights as the handmaiden to judicial colonialism in the form of ad hoc tribunals that leave the process of international criminal law vulnerable to the pursuit of power politics.

Yet the landscape of international criminal justice has changed dramatically over the last fifteen years. In 1990, a tyrant could have been reasonably confident of the guarantee of sovereign impunity for his atrocities. Today, there is no guarantee of prosecution and accountability; *but not a single brutish ruler can be confident of escaping international justice.* The certainty of impunity is gone. The credit for the dramatic transformation of the international criminal landscape belongs to the ad hoc tribunals set up by the UN.

The problematic element of tribunals – the infection of judicial processes with politics – can be seen with regard to Serbia.[73] What was most needed was an open trial within Serbia that brought home to the Serbs, beyond any reasonable doubt, the crimes that were committed in their name. They are the ones who need to confront the recent ugly past, punish the guilty in their midst and move on with their lives. Only an open trial conducted inside Serbia would hold up a mirror in which the collective past can be seen in all its ugliness.

In his response to the reform package proposed by his high-level panel, Kofi Annan emphasises that 'every nation that proclaims the rule of law at home must respect it abroad and that every nation that insists on it abroad must enforce it at home'. Nowhere 'is the gap between rhetoric and reality – between declarations and deeds – so stark and deadly as in the field of international humanitarian law'. The UN cannot

---

[72] For a study of the issue, see Yuval Shany, *The Competing Jurisdictions of International Courts and Tribunals* (Oxford: Oxford University Press, 2003).

[73] For a broader critique, see Jackson Nyamuya Maogoto, *War Crimes and Realpolitik: International Justice from World War I to the 21st Century* (Boulder: Lynne Rienner, 2004).

just stand by and let genocide or massive human rights abuses unfold to the end. Annan encourages all states to ratify and implement all treaties relating to civilian protection and to cooperate fully with the ICC and other international or mixed war crimes tribunals.[74]

Truth commissions provide a halfway house between victors' or foreigners' justice and collective amnesia. The ethic of conviction would impose obligations to prosecute people for their past criminal misdeeds to the full extent of the law. The ethic of responsibility imposes the countervailing requirement to judge the wisdom of alternative courses of action with respect to their consequences for social harmony in the future. While the ad hoc tribunals have helped to bring hope and justice to some victims, combat the impunity of some perpetrators and greatly enrich the jurisprudence of international criminal and humanitarian law, they have been expensive,[75] time-consuming and contributed little to sustainable national capacities for justice administration. Truth commissions take a victim-centred approach, help to establish a historical record and contribute to memorialising defining epochs in a nation's history. The ICC offers hope for a permanent reduction in the phenomenon of impunity.

Christine Chinkin quotes from one of the international criminal cases, referring to the Bosnian Muslim women victims of war-related sexual violence, that consent could not be freely given when the women had nowhere to go and no place to hide.[76] We will perhaps have made our transition from barbarism to culture when the burden of that haunting phrase is transferred from the victim to the perpetrators and would-be perpetrators: 'know that henceforth, you will have nowhere to go, no place left to hide'. Then, but only then, instead of being footnotes to history, international criminal justice will bear daily witness to history.

---

[74] Kofi A. Annan, *In Larger Freedom: Towards Development, Security and Human Rights for All*. Report of the Secretary-General (New York: UN, document A/59/2005, 21 March 2005), paras. 133–8.

[75] The two tribunals for Rwanda and former Yugoslavia cost the equivalent of more than 15 per cent of the UN's total regular budget; ibid., para. 42.

[76] Christine Chinkin, 'Gender-related Crimes: A Feminist Perspective', in Thakur and Malcontent, eds., *From Sovereign Impunity to International Accountability*, p. 128.

6

International sanctions

The international community should be under no illusion: . . . humanitarian and human rights policy goals cannot easily be reconciled with those of a sanctions regime.[1]

Coercive economic sanctions developed as a conceptual and policy bridge between diplomacy and force for ensuring compliance with UN demands. Recourse to sanctions – diplomatic isolation, restrictions on international travel, trade and financial transactions, arms embargoes[2] – increased dramatically in the 1990s.[3] Compared to sanctions having been imposed only twice until 1990 (in Rhodesia and South Africa), more than a dozen have been imposed since then by a sanctions-happy UN Security Council (UNSC) against Afghanistan, Angola (on rebel forces), Ethiopia, Eritrea, Haiti, Iraq, Liberia, Libya, Rwanda, Sierra Leone, Somalia, Sudan and former Yugoslavia.[4] The United Nations has played a central role in the imposition and implementation machinery of sanctions because of its defining characteristic as the dispenser of international legitimacy.

Although once seen as an attractive non-violent alternative to war, sanctions became discredited for their harsh humanitarian consequences on the civilian population.[5] Instead of the authority of the UN

---

[1] Kofi A. Annan, *Partnerships for Global Community: Annual Report on the Work of the Organization 1998* (New York: UN, 1998), para. 64.

[2] See W. Andy Knight, 'Improving the Effectiveness of UN Arms Embargoes', in Richard M. Price and Mark W. Zacher, eds., *The United Nations and Global Security* (New York: Palgrave Macmillan, 2004), pp. 39–55.

[3] See David Cortright and George A. Lopez, *The Sanctions Decade: Assessing UN Strategies in the 1990s* (Boulder: Lynne Rienner, 2000).

[4] An up-to-date list can be found at http://www.un.org/Docs/sc/committees/INTRO.htm.

[5] See Thomas G. Weiss, David Cortright, George A. Lopez, and Larry Minear, *Political Gain and Civilian Pain: Humanitarian Impacts of Economic Sanctions* (Lanham, MD: Rowman & Littlefield, 1997), and Tim Niblock, *Pariah States and Sanctions in the Middle East: Iraq, Libya, Sudan* (Boulder: Lynne Rienner, 2001).

legitimising sanctions regimes, the baleful effects of sanctions began to erode the legitimacy of the UN. This was exacerbated by the paucity of intellectual and institutional foundations for the organisation's sanctions policy. Interest shifted to incorporating carefully thought-out humanitarian exemptions or looking for 'smarter' alternatives to comprehensive sanctions that put pressure on regimes rather than peoples. But even when much improved from a moral, political and technical point of view and conceptually compelling, smart sanctions remain unproven in actual practice. And the larger question remains: are sanctions a substitute for, complement to or precursor to war? That these are not empty questions was clear with the dilemmas confronting the international community with respect to the humanitarian crisis in Darfur in 2004–5.

Sanctions have a bad history. They inflict undeniable pain on ordinary citizens while imposing questionable costs on leaders. Indeed, often the leaders are enriched and strengthened on the back of their impoverished and oppressed people by the law of perverse consequences. In response, the international community has been trying to refine and improve the tool in both design and implementation. In this chapter, I begin by looking at why the tool remains attractive. Then I argue that sanctions all too often are a poor alibi for, not a sound supplement to, a good foreign policy. They are ineffective, counter-productive, harmful to the economic interests of those imposing sanctions, damaging to relations with allies, morally questionable, yet difficult to lift once imposed. The general arguments are buttressed by appropriate historical and contemporary examples, with particular attention being paid to the Iraqi oil-for-food scandal as exemplifying many of the problems inherent in sanctions as a tool of UN policy. Finally, I look at efforts to refine the tool by making it smarter.

The limited utility of sanctions

Sanctions are imposed to punish or deter foreign military adventurism, punish regimes for providing safe sanctuaries for international criminals (drug runners and terrorists), penalise such specific acts as nuclear testing and humanitarian atrocities, destabilise and bring down target regimes by isolating and weakening them, stigmatise or contain 'states of concern' (also known as 'rogue states') and prevent and deter undesirable behaviour by copycat states or groups in the future.

Yet the track record of sanctions in ensuring compliance with UN resolutions is 'uneven'.[6] In a debate in the UNSC in April 2000, not one member was prepared to offer unqualified support for the existing system and practice of sanctions. France and Russia issued a call for sunset clauses that would require complete reviews rather than periodic rollovers of sanctions once imposed by the Council. Britain and the USA argued that sanctions should remain in place until the target regime changes behaviour,[7] else it could simply adopt a 'hunkering down' strategy of waiting out the sanctions regime rather than complying with UNSC demands.

This was more of a power play than a doctrinal disagreement. Controversies over sanctions camouflage competing visions over the role and enforcement powers of the UNSC dominated by the five permanent members (P5). On the Franco-Russian version, which has prevailed since 2000 because the two are prepared to risk no sanctions rather than impose open-ended ones, any attempt to renew sanctions is subject to the veto. On the US–UK version, any attempt to lift sanctions once imposed would be subject to veto. Considering that the USA imposed sanctions 120 times over the last century,[8] this was not surprising. What is surprising is that Washington should persist with a policy of trying to destroy economies and destabilise governments by resorting to a tool that has never worked: a triumph of hope over experience indeed.

Remarkably for a tool of national and international statecraft that is so common, there is still not a single major comparative study which establishes their efficacy. Part of the difficulty is definitional and methodological: what constitutes success and how does one establish a conclusive link between sanctions and the successful outcome? Sanctions have multiple impacts and outcomes can be traced back to multiple causes. For example, what respective roles did sanctions and air strikes play in inducing compliance by Slobodan Milošević at Dayton in 1995? Sanctions did force Libya into releasing its agents to stand trial for the Lockerbie bombing. But was it sanctions or the demonstration effect of the Iraq War that led to Libya's abandonment of the pursuit of weapons of mass destruction? By contrast, there are many studies that

---

[6] Kofi A. Annan, *We the Peoples: The Role of the United Nations in the 21st Century* (The Millennium Report) (New York: UN Department of Public Information, 2000), p. 49.

[7] Barbara Crossette, 'UN to Take a Hard Look at Sanctions', *International Herald Tribune* (*IHT*), 19 April 2000.

[8] Thomas J. Donahue, 'A China Sanctions Plan Needs to Be Headed Off', *IHT*, 11 July 2000.

point to the limitations in their utility as diplomatic tools. Johan Galtung long ago postulated the naïve theory of sanctions, empty of empirical support, according to which economic pain in the target countries would mysteriously produce political gain for the sanctions-imposing countries.[9]

Sanctions are tied to the interests of major powers. The generic theory of sanctions views them as being a useful tool of statecraft for certain purposes. They may successfully stigmatise a norm-violating regime and so signal the international community's disapprobation of particular patterns of behaviour; they may thereby deter such behaviour by others; they may contain a transgressor regime even without changing its unacceptable behaviour; or they may ease the transition to the use of force as the ultimate resort. The instrumental goals of sanctions include changing the behaviour of target states through deterrence or compellence; overthrow of the regime of target states through economic deprivation which leads to massive social dislocation and political revolt; and symbolic protest which registers disapproval of certain kinds of behaviour. The calculus of the majority of countries should be different from that of major powers. Yet the discourse on sanctions in middle power countries like Canada and Australia is indistinguishable from that in the USA.[10] Countries that lack the power to bully or the wealth to bribe resort to sanctions not for instrumental but largely for symbolic purposes. The target of symbolic action can be the citizens of the country imposing sanctions, so that they feel good at the thought that 'something' has been done. In addition to symbolism, maintaining alliance solidarity is an important consideration underlying the imposition of sanctions by middle powers.

Ineffectual

Sanctions were discredited in the 1930s when imposed on Italy in punishment for its invasion of Ethiopia and again when applied against the Ian Smith regime in Rhodesia in the 1960s. An influential study of the 115 cases between the First World War and 1990 concluded that sanctions achieved only 'partial success' – where the target regime

[9] Johan Galtung, 'On the Effects of International Economic Sanctions: With Examples from the Case of Rhodesia', *World Politics* 19:3 (1967), pp. 378–416.
[10] Kim Richard Nossal, *Rain Dancing: Sanctions in Canadian and Australian Foreign Policy* (Toronto: University of Toronto Press, 1994).

changes behaviour, and the change can be traced to the effects of sanctions – in a mere one-third of the cases.[11] The success rate declined even further after 1970 as the global economy became more open. The study was faulted for being too generous. Using more rigorous criteria of success, only 5 per cent of sanctions regimes in that study were successful.[12]

Sanctions do not work because the target country can choose from a range of sellers in the international marketplace. It is virtually impossible to secure universal participation in and policing of embargoes. The incentive to make large profits by circumventing sanctions is usually more powerful than the motive for enforcing them. A variety of means and routes exist to camouflage sanctions-busting contacts. Traders find ways and means for evading sanctions and carrying on profitable commerce with regimes under international boycott: there is a market clearing price for any good or service. While enforcement authority vests in the UNSC, enforcement capacity rests with the major powers, so that sanctions on regimes whose behaviour is a challenge to the interests of major powers (Iraq, Serbia) have better prospects of serious enforcement efforts than others.

The 1998 South Asian nuclear tests

The 1998 nuclear tests by India and Pakistan were a direct challenge to the exclusive status of the P5.[13] But that which has been tested, no matter how intensely detested, cannot be de-tested. The dilemma faced by outsiders was this. A moderate response would have been self-negating. The nuclear hawks in the domestic debate would have felt vindicated, saying that India was now being treated with respect because it had nuclear weapons, so these should be openly deployed in numbers. To accept India and Pakistan as nuclear-weapons-states (NWS) would

---

[11] Gary C. Hufbauer, Jeffrey J. Schott and Kimberley Ann Elliot, *Economic Sanctions Reconsidered: Supplemental Case Histories*, 2nd edn (Washington, DC: Institute for International Economics, 1990). See also their *Economic Sanctions Reconsidered: History and Current Policy* (Washington, DC: Institute for International Economics, 2003).

[12] Robert A. Pape, 'Why Economic Sanctions Do Not Work', *International Security* 22 (Fall 1997). For other methodological criticisms, see A. Cooper Drury, 'Revisiting *Economic Sanctions Reconsidered*', *Journal of Peace Research* 35 (1998).

[13] See Ramesh Thakur, 'The South Asian Nuclear Challenge', in John Baylis and Robert O'Neill, eds., *Alternative Nuclear Futures: The Role of Nuclear Weapons in the Post-Cold War World* (Oxford: Oxford University Press, 1999), pp. 101–24.

reverse three decades of non-proliferation policy and victimise many countries that had signed the Non-proliferation Treaty (NPT) and the Comprehensive Test Ban Treaty (CTBT) on the understanding that the number of NWS would be limited to five. On the other hand, a harsh response would be self-fulfilling. The hawks would argue that a friendless India that is the target of hostile international attention needs an arsenal of nuclear weapons to defend its interests.

Outsiders' self-interest lay in assisting South Asia's economic growth. India's size, resources and depth give it the resilience to withstand sanctions to a much greater extent than Pakistan. At a time when the world community was mounting emergency rescue efforts in countries besieged by currency and stockmarket collapse, it made little sense to try to push Pakistan towards the same precipice of economic, social and political meltdown.

Then there was the question of moral equivalence. The five nuclear powers preach non-proliferation but practise deterrence. Their nuclear stockpiles are in defiance of the World Court's opinion of a legal obligation to nuclear disarmament; India and Pakistan breached no international treaty, convention or law by testing. For the five NWS to impose sanctions on the nuclear gatecrashers was akin (on this issue) to outlaws sitting in judgement, passing sentence and imposing punishment on the law abiding.

For the UNSC, dominated by the P5 who are also the five nuclear powers, to condemn eleven Indian and Pakistani tests – when not one of the over 2,000 previous tests had been condemned – inflamed opinion in the subcontinent. The official Indian response was to point out that no other nuclear power had supported the World Court Advisory Opinion on the illegality of nuclear weapons; India's record of restraint on export of nuclear technologies and commodities was better than that of some of the five NWS; unlike India's unconditional commitment to a nuclear weapons convention, they were not prepared to commit themselves to decisive and irreversible steps towards nuclear disarmament; and India's tests had been restricted to 'the minimum necessary to maintain what is an irreducible component of our national security calculus'.[14]

The sanctions imposed on India and Pakistan were especially egregious because both countries had already crossed the nuclear threshold and announced unilateral moratoria on further testing. Any serious

[14] Government of India, 'Evolution of India's Nuclear Policy', paper tabled in parliament on 27 May 1998, para. 18.

analysis of relative bargaining levers would have quickly concluded that the probability of coercing even Pakistan, let alone India, into restoring the status quo ante was close to zero. The point of sanctions therefore could only be symbolic expression: registering international disapprobation of the tests, communicating similar displeasure to any future would-be proliferators abroad and signalling resolve and leadership to an approving public at home.

A study by the US International Trade Commission concluded that in the year following the imposition of US sanctions, their cost to India's economy had been a mere $320 million and to Pakistan's $57 million.[15] Russia refused to terminate long-established defence links with India. By September 1999, France had initiated a 'strategic dialogue'. By the end of October, Britain was edging back towards re-establishing links. In November, Washington eased most sanctions. Documentation and analyses by US intelligence sources in 2000 showed that China had accelerated the sale of missiles to long-time ally Pakistan after the 1998 tests.[16] In 2004 Pakistan was designated a major non-NATO ally of the USA and in 2005 the Bush administration decided to lift restrictions on assistance to India's civilian nuclear industry even without requiring New Delhi to sign the NPT.

Counter-productive

Sanctions are counter-productive through two effects: political and economic. The political goal is to reduce the support for sanctioned leaders by their own people. While this may indeed happen in exceptional cases, the more general reaction is one of 'rallying around the flag'. 'Far from imposing on the Italian people a desire to reverse their government's policy, sanctions made the Ethiopian war popular.'[17] Sanctions offer an easy scapegoat for ruinous economic policies. Economic pain is simply blamed on hostile and ill-intentioned foreigners and coping with sanctions is portrayed as patriotic duty. Dissent is stifled and political opposition muted, silenced or liquidated for bordering on treason.

---

[15] Adam Entous, 'Sanctions Have Boomeranged, says US Commission', *Times of India*, 25 September 1999.

[16] David E. Sanger and Eric Schmitt, 'China Missile Aid to Pakistan Goes On, US Suspects', *IHT*, 3 July 2000.

[17] George W. Baer, 'Sanctions and Security: The League of Nations and the Italian-Ethiopian War, 1935–1936', *International Organization* 27 (Spring 1973), p. 179.

In the late 1950s, the former Soviet Union tried a range of coercive economic measures to bring Josef Tito's Yugoslavia to toe Moscow's line. Not only did Soviet efforts prove ineffectual, despite Belgrade's economic dependence on the communist bloc; in fact they proved counter-productive, for Yugoslavia turned to the West for alternative supply and market sources and helped to establish the Non-aligned Movement as a more congenial political grouping.[18]

Probably the best continuing example of the counter-productiveness of sanctions is the history of US sanctions on Fidel Castro's Cuba. A small neighbouring country that was almost completely dependent on the USA for its economic health was subjected to increasingly harsh and all-encompassing sanctions that left it with little choice but to turn to Soviet bloc countries for alternative suppliers and markets and so become the forward base of communism in the Western hemisphere: a case of self-fulfilling prophecy. Far from dislodging Castro from power, the sanctions helped him to consolidate power by delegitimising domestic critics, scapegoating Washington for the disastrous consequences of bankrupt economic policies and acquiring the stature of a mythic hero throughout Latin America for repeatedly tweaking Uncle Sam's nose. Conversely, any opening of Cuba to the world immediately around it would expose its people to the infectious effects of freedom, democracy and prosperity.

Sanctions create shortages and raise prices in conditions of scarcity. The poor suffer; the middle class, essential to building the foundations of democracy, shrinks; the ruling class extracts fatter rents from monopoly controls over the illicit trade in banned goods. Family cliques surrounding dictators under international sanctions monopolise the black market spawned by the imposition of sanctions and the resulting scarcities and shortages of goods in the open market. The more profitable the trade, the richer the leaders become and the greater the vested interest they have in perpetuating sanctions while using state-controlled media to scapegoat the West or the 'US-controlled' UN. Scarcity also increases the dependence of the population on the distribution of necessities by the regime, so

---

[18] On the other hand, during the same period Moscow did succeed in achieving its objectives through measures of economic coercion against Finland. See K. J. Holsti, 'Strategy and Techniques of Influence in Soviet–Finnish Relations', *Western Political Quarterly* 17 (1964), pp. 63–84. It could also be argued that the oil weapon was used to some effect by the Arabs after 1973, in that many countries moderated their previously unqualified support of Israel.

leaders gain yet another tool with which to exercise control and leverage over their people. Alternatively, the besieged country itself can actually emerge stronger overall, or in strategic sectors like defence, by pursuing a determined policy of import-substitution.

Self-damaging

Sanctions are market distorting. Altruism has little role to play when firms engage in hard-nosed commercial calculations on what to trade, in what volume, and with which firms, regardless of their geographical location. Countries trade on the basis of comparative advantage. Even 'foreign aid' rests on a mixture of strategic, commercial and altruistic motives. Efforts by governments to introduce political impediments to trade inflict damage on home country traders. The real question is not whether sanctions impose costs on domestic sector interests, but the severity, magnitude and lasting effects of the damage. A related question is the ameliorative measures that can be instituted to shelter or soften the blow to domestic producer groups. In addition, because of the frequency with which a country resorts to sanctions, the long-term reliability of its suppliers becomes suspect, with the result that foreign purchasers may not switch back to its products even after sanctions are lifted.

Countries are in a much stronger position to impose sanctions if targets are asymmetrically dependent on sanctions-imposing countries while the latter are relatively insulated from the effects of the sanctions and relatively invulnerable to retaliatory counter-measures. A good illustration of this was provided in the 1980s in the dispute involving France and New Zealand. On 10 July 1985, the Greenpeace boat *Rainbow Warrior* was sunk in Auckland harbour by bombs planted by French secret service agents who were caught, tried and imprisoned in New Zealand, only to be released under the impact of French sanctions on New Zealand's trade with Europe.[19]

Strained relations with third parties and allies

When the pain of economic sanctions is borne chiefly by countries in the neighbourhood of the target regime and little help is available from

---

[19] See Ramesh Thakur, 'A Dispute of Many Colours: France, New Zealand and the "Rainbow Warrior" Affair', *The World Today* 42:12 (December 1986), pp. 209–14.

the international community to offset the pain, enthusiasm for monitoring and enforcing the sanctions wanes. They either connive to make the sanctions regime porous or tolerate such an outcome brought about by sanctions busters, and this puts them in conflict with the global policies of major powers. US sanctions against the former Soviet Union, for example with respect to the construction of a gas pipeline to Western Europe, often strained relations between Washington and other NATO capitals. The long history of US sanctions on Cuba has many times brought Washington into conflict with some of its major allies who resent having their international morality and foreign economic interests defined by Washington, and resent even more strongly attempts to expand the extra-territorial jurisdiction of US laws.

Questionable morality: a weapon of mass murder in slow motion?

The imposition of sanctions is frequently accompanied by sentimentality and sanctimony. Public and hence political support for sanctions rests in their image as a humane alternative, and perhaps a necessary prelude, to war which is increasingly regarded as a tool of the very last resort. Yet in contrast to wars, sanctions shift the burden of harm solely to civilians, mainly women and children. They cause death and suffering through 'structural violence' (starvation, malnutrition and disease) on a scale exceeding the 'cleaner' alternative of war.

If sanctions were imposed because of gross, pervasive and persistent human rights violations by the government, then its hapless citizens are doubly damned. Moreover, large and diversified economies are immune to sanctions because they can pay higher costs in the short term and make structural changes in the long run. The weaker and more vulnerable an economy, therefore, the more susceptible it is to sanctions: an uncomfortable moral conclusion.

The just war doctrine imposes the ethical obligation to discriminate between combatants and non-combatants. Sanctions do indeed discriminate between them, but spare the combatants and target the rest in inflicting methodical and comprehensive deprivation of food, water and fuel. Regimes typically respond by shifting remaining resources to the political, bureaucratic and security elite. Because this is a typical response, it can be predicted. Because it is a predictable response, sanctioners cannot evade ethical responsibility for the consequences of their actions. Attempts to shift the burden of agency to the recalcitrant target regime are simply not credible in the light of the overwhelming historical record of how despots behave when under siege.[20]

According to John Mueller and Karl Mueller, sanctions caused more deaths in the twentieth century than all weapons of mass destruction throughout history and should be relabelled 'economic warfare' in order to bring them within the purview of the laws of warfare.[21] As Gordon notes, 'If sanctions were indeed peaceful, there would be no ethical dilemma. If, on the other hand, they were flatly understood as an act of aggression, the framework of the rules of war would offer guidance for their use.'[22]

Termination trap

The motives for the imposition and continuance of sanctions have more to do with domestic politics than trying to effect changes in the behaviour of target regimes. It becomes difficult to lift sanctions even when the target regime's behaviour has changed appreciably because the domestic electoral cost may be too high. The cost is much greater if the target actor has not changed behaviour, that is even if sanctions are clearly not working. Once an offending leader has been successfully demonised, rivals for office in domestic politics seek to reap electoral advantage by depicting opponents as 'soft' on the enemy. Sanctions on Cuba are a historical artefact of the Cold War that ended over a decade ago. They remain in place not because they serve any purpose or are achieving the original goals,[23] but because of the power of a domestic electoral lobby. The geographical concentration of Cuban exiles in Miami gives them a crucial swing vote role in determining the outcome of Florida's electoral votes, which in turn is important in influencing the outcome of presidential elections. UN-centred multilateral sanctions regimes are less clearly rooted in domestic politics than unilateral sanctions. Partly

[20] Joy Gordon, 'A Peaceful, Silent, Deadly Remedy: The Ethics of Economic Sanctions', *Ethics & International Affairs* 13 (1999), pp. 123–42.

[21] John Mueller and Karl Mueller, 'Sanctions of Mass Destruction', *Foreign Affairs* 78:3 (May/June 1999), pp. 43–53.

[22] Gordon, 'A Peaceful, Silent, Deadly Remedy', p. 124.

[23] In an on the record interview in 2004, Larry Wilkerson, chief of staff of US Secretary of State Colin Powell, pointed out that they had not worked for forty years and described the Cuba sanctions as the 'dumbest policy on the face of the Earth'; Gary Younge, 'Powell Aides Go Public on Rift with Bush', *Guardian*, 6 May 2004.

because of this, the UN record is much better. Between 2001 and 2003, the UN terminated seven sanctions regimes.[24]

Sometimes sanctions are lifted for exogenous reasons. Having imposed sanctions on India and Pakistan for their 1998 nuclear tests, Washington found itself imprisoned in the classic termination trap: how to lift sanctions without appearing to back down, on the one hand, or reward 'bad' behaviour on the other. In the end the impact of the terrorist attacks of 11 September 2001 on US foreign policy included the lifting of sanctions against India and Pakistan in return for their support in the higher priority war on terrorism.

How can we offer a mixed strategy of punishment and inducements without falling into the moral hazard trap of rewarding bad behaviour? One solution may be to offer a graduated series of partial lifting of sanctions in return for good behaviour. One of the problems with Saddam Hussein was that he believed, probably rightly, that London and Washington would not be satisfied with anything short of his ouster from power, and therefore there was no incentive for him to cooperate.

Iraq and the oil-for-food programme (OFFP)

Many of the contradictions, inconsistencies, perverse consequences, moral costs and impassioned differences over the lifting of sanctions came to a head with respect to the sanctions imposed on Iraq by Security Council Resolution 661 in the aftermath of the first Gulf War. The human rights of the Iraqi people were violated by their own leadership. Perversely, their humanitarian plight was worsened with the imposition of sanctions by the international community. An estimate from the International Federation of Red Cross and Red Crescent Societies concluded that 80 per cent of the civilian population of Iraq was adversely affected by the UN sanctions.[25] Then the leadership enriched itself by cornering the black market for goods in the resulting scarcity. The humanitarian costs of the sanctions regime maintained indefinitely on Iraq slowly but surely destroyed the fragile consensus in the UNSC, which in turn spilled over into other business conducted by the Council.

Mueller and Mueller report estimates of a net increase per year of 40,000 deaths of children under five and of another 50,000 older Iraqis

---

[24] For the list of these, see http://www.un.org/Docs/sc/committees/INTRO.htm.
[25] Cited in Barbara Crossette, 'UN to Take a Hard Look at Sanctions', *IHT*, 19 April 2000.

due to the effects of sanctions.[26] This is comparable to the 100,000 people killed by the atomic bombings of Hiroshima and Nagasaki and the 50,000–100,000 Iraqi soldiers killed in the Gulf War. The spread of diseases was accelerated by the breakdown of sanitation, sewage and electrical systems. The capacity to mitigate the effects of disease was sharply diminished by restrictions on imports of food and medicines. The supply of syringes was stopped for fear of their being used in the creation of anthrax spores; chlorine, a common enough water disinfectant, can also be used for making chlorine gas; nuclear medicine was banned under the sanctions regime; fertilisers and insecticides are obvious dual-use products.

Slowly but surely, Baghdad was winning the international propaganda war even while Saddam Hussein remained defiant of UN resolutions. The Iraqi leaders inflated casualty statistics in order to embarrass Western capitals, while the USA and UK had a matching interest in minimising them. Some deaths were unreported, especially in outlying parts of the country, either because parents knew that the local hospital could no longer cope or because survivors could go on collecting valuable food rations. If a leader is known to be prepared to make children and the old the primary victims of sanctions, does the UN have any moral responsibility for their fate by persisting with the sanctions? The right to life, dignity and livelihood of a people should not be forfeit to the international community because their leaders have violated international norms.

The methodological difficulty of assigning weights to sanctions as causes of success was replicated in assigning blame to sanctions for humanitarian suffering. The widely cited UNICEF estimates of half a million child deaths caused by the sanctions relied on extrapolation of trends (table 6.1). It (1) assumed that without sanctions, Iraq would have maintained the pace of progress achieved on the reduction of infant and under-five mortality rates, (2) calculated the extra number of deaths resulting from the failure to maintain the same reducing mortality rates, and (3) assumed that this counter-factual number of 'excess deaths' could be attributed to the effect of sanctions. Each assumption may be queried separately; the two together are hotly contestable. But what is not deniable is that sanctions did cause the deaths of more innocent Iraqis than the number of soldiers killed during the Gulf War

---

[26] Mueller and Mueller, 'Sanctions of Mass Destruction', pp. 49, 51.

Table 6.1. *Iraq child mortality rates, 1960–1995*

	1960	1970	1980	1990	1995	1998
No. of deaths under 5 years old per 1000 live births	171	127	83	50	117	125
Deaths at birth per 1000 live births	117	90	63	40	98	103

Source: Child Mortality: Iraq (New York: UNICEF, 26 August 1999), document GJ-99.8 (available at http://www.childinfo.org/cmr/cmriq.html).

proper.[27] This is why the international community lost the appetite for imposing comprehensive open-ended sanctions again.

In 2004, the oil-for-food scandal gave fresh life to critics who could not forgive the UN for having been proven right about Saddam Hussein's weapons of mass destruction. Allegations flew thick and fast well in advance of investigation and substantiation. While some of the charges were ill-informed, some ill-intentioned (the timing coincided with efforts to transfer authority for Iraqi nation-building and reconstruction from the US-led coalition to the UN), and some based on genuine and legitimate questions, many critics treated all allegations as fact.

Two separate scandals were rolled into one: smuggling and bill padding.[28] The oil-for-food programme (OFFP) ran from 1996 to 2003 with the goal of relieving the misery inflicted on Iraqis by Saddam Hussein. It was created to ensure that Iraq's oil money was used to meet the basic needs of the people and not for rearmament. In return for being allowed

---

[27] The more scientifically reliable studies include A. Ascherio et al., 'Effect of the Gulf War on Infant and Child Mortality in Iraq', *New England Journal of Medicine* 327:13 (1992), pp. 931–6; Richard Garfield, *Morbidity and Mortality among Iraqi Children from 1990 to 1998: Assessing the Impact of Economic Sanctions*, Occasional Paper Series 16:OP:3 (Joan B. Kroc Institute for International Peace Studies of the University of Notre Dame and the Fourth Freedom Forum, March 1999); and Mohamed M. Ali and Iqbal H. Shah, 'Sanctions and Childhood Mortality in Iraq', *Lancet* 355 (May 2000), pp. 1837–57.

[28] The two best published accounts that I have read are Maggie Farley, 'All Players Gained from "Oil-for-Food"', *Los Angeles Times*, 3 February 2005, and James Traub, 'The Security Council's Role: Off Target', *The New Republic Online*, 21 February 2005. For an effective presentation of the UN case, see John G. Ruggie, US House of Representatives, Committee on International Relations, Hearings on 'The United Nations Oil-for-Food Program: Issues of Accountability and Transparency', 28 April 2004; available online at http://wwwa.house.gov/international_relations/108/rug042804.htm. Ruggie was Assistant Secretary-General in the Office of the SG from 1997–2001.

to export oil, Iraq would be required to transfer all revenues earned into a UN-controlled escrow account in Paris which would pay for the purchase of food and medicines. Saddam rejected this as an infringement of sovereignty. After five years of stalemate, with the increasingly devastating impact of the sanctions regime on the ordinary people, a deal was struck giving Baghdad the power to determine who bought the oil and supplied the relief goods.

Financial skulduggery is a predictable outcome of sanctions. In the distribution of responsibility, what should be the respective blame on the Secretariat, the UNSC and member states? In an analogous situation in national governments, how would we apportion blame between bureaucrats and ministers?[29] The General Accounting Office (GAO) of the US Congress estimated that the Saddam regime got $10.1 billion in illegal revenues from the OFFP. Of that, $5.7 billion came from oil smuggled out in violation of UN sanctions during and before the OFFP. Washington turned a blind eye to extensive sanctions-busting in the pre-war sale of Iraqi oil, according to a Senate investigation. US oil purchases accounted for 52 per cent of the kickbacks paid to the regime in return for sales of cheap oil – more than the rest of the world put together and dwarfing the amounts allegedly paid to UN officials and European politicians.[30] The US administration 'was not only aware of Iraqi oil sales which violated UN sanctions and provided the bulk of the illicit money Saddam Hussein obtained from circumventing UN sanctions', the report said. 'On occasion, the United States actually facilitated the illicit oil sales.'[31] The OFFP worked much better in the northern Kurdish region where the UN was directly responsible and did not have to work through Saddam's henchmen and Iraqi government agencies.

---

[29] Indeed the US federal watchdog agency for Iraqi reconstruction concluded that the US-led Coalition Provisional Authority that governed Iraq until mid-2004 did not properly monitor the spending of $8.8 billion in Iraqi money, opening the door to possible corruption. Erik Eckholm, 'Occupation Authority Did Not Properly Monitor Spending of Iraqi Money, US Audit Says', *New York Times*, 31 January 2005.

[30] In an analysis in one of the major US newspapers, the US role was mentioned in three paragraphs towards the end (paras. 17–19 of a twenty-paragraph report). The focus on France and Russia seemed out of proportion to the fact that 'US imports of Iraqi oil helped finance 52 percent of the secret deals made under the oil-for-food program'; Peter Grier and Faye Bowers, 'Oil-For-Food Probes Expose Cultural Gulfs', *Christian Science Monitor*, 18 May 2005 (www.csmonitor.com/2005/0518/p03s01-usfp.htm).

[31] Julian Borger and Jamie Wilson, 'US "Backed Illegal Iraqi Oil Deals"', *Guardian*, 17 May 2005.

The remaining $4.4 billion can be accounted for in two ways: underpricing Iraqi oil and overpricing goods purchased in return. UN overseers raised concerns about price discrepancies and apparent surcharges in oil sales to the UNSC's Iraq sanctions committee in 2000. The UN's Office of Internal Oversight Services ordered fifty-nine audits of the OFFP between 1996 and 2003. Seven of its reports identified 'a variety of operational concerns involving procurement, inflated pricing and inventory controls'.[32] The Iraq sanctions committee decided whether or not to approve contracts. The USA and the UK acted in March 2001 on concerns raised by the UN officials and put on hold thousands of contracts. These related mainly to concerns about dual-use technologies, not price padding, bribes and kickbacks. Not one of the 36,000 contracts was ever cancelled. Why not? We can take an educated guess. The 661 committee (named after the resolution which set up sanctions in the first place) reflected the competing priorities of the Security Council and especially of the USA and the UK.[33] Their chief concerns were to disarm Saddam Hussein, starve him of resources to rearm in the future and minimise the collateral harm to his people. These goals were achieved. They probably chose to overlook pricing irregularities in the OFFP in order to keep the sanctions regime going and stop Saddam from acquiring dangerous weapons.[34]

The OFFP worked. Over the life of the world's largest humanitarian aid programme delivering $31 billion worth of food and medicines, a basic food ration was provided for the 27 million Iraqis, the average caloric intake jumped by 83 per cent from 1,200 to 2,200 kilocalories per day, malnutrition among Iraqi children was halved, and the mortality rate of children under five plummeted.[35]

In response to the scandal, Annan acted with alacrity in seeking a full investigation – which only the UNSC could authorise – and appointed

---

[32] Quoted in Barbara Crossette, 'No Simple Place to Pin Blame for Iraq Oil-for-Food Problems', *UN Wire*, www.unwire.org, 10 May 2004.

[33] See Claudio Gatti, 'US Ignored Warning on Iraqi Oil Smuggling', *Financial Times*, 13 January 2005.

[34] As the *New York Times* noted in an editorial, the blame for the rip-off of the oil-for-food programme lies either with the UN bureaucracy or with the UNSC. 'It makes a big difference which explanation is right.' For if UN officials are to blame, then the UN's troubles are 'immense enough to justify its bitterest critics'. But if the UNSC is the primary culprit, then 'most of the current UN bashing would look off target'. 'The Oil-for-Food Audits', *New York Times*, 17 January 2005.

[35] UN data. See also George A. Lopez and David Cortright, 'Containing Iraq: Sanctions Worked', *Foreign Affairs* 83:4 (July/August 2004), pp. 90–103.

people of impeccable integrity for the purpose: former Federal Reserve Chairman Paul Volcker (chair), former special prosecutor from the Hague Tribunal Richard Goldstone and Swiss Professor Mark Pieth, an internationally recognised specialist on money laundering. In its interim report, the committee described the scandal as a painful episode and revealed some institutional weaknesses in the area of procurement of some UN contractors.[36] In 'a tainted procurement process', prescribed rules and regulations were overridden for essentially political considerations. But it also confirmed that the major source of illicit funds to the Iraqi regime were sanctions violations outside the OFFP framework, namely smuggling to Jordan, Turkey, Syria and Egypt. And it failed to find evidence of any systematic misuse of funds dedicated to administration of the OFFP. The final report of the Volcker Committee was expected to be published in November 2005. There were some suggestions that the committee's interest had widened to include the activities of the Secretary-General's brother and son, as well as yet another family friend from Ghana who works in the UN procurement department.[37]

The committee's main report, published on 7 September 2005, came to the less than flattering conclusion of not proven rather than exoneration of the Secretary-General.[38] He had been chosen more for his widely admired political and diplomatic than for his managerial and administrative skills. Thus failures of administrative and managerial oversight by the SG and the Deputy SG were lamentable but perhaps not so surprising, especially as differences among member states in the UNSC 'impeded decision-making, tolerated large-scale smuggling, and aided and abetted grievous weaknesses in administrative practices within the Secretariat'. The committee repeated the 'real accomplishments', both humanitarian and disarmament, of the OFFP. But it also confirmed the reality of 'waste, inefficiency, and corruption'. It concluded that the UN requires 'stronger executive leadership, thoroughgoing administrative reform, and more reliable controls and auditing'. No organisation other

---

[36] Paul A. Volcker, Richard J. Goldstone and Mark Pieth, *Interim Report of the Independent Inquiry Committee into the United Nations Oil-for-Food Programme* (New York: 3 February 2005).

[37] Claudio Gatti, 'Annan Family Friend Linked to Oil-for-Food Investigation', *Financial Times*, 30 June 2005; David Nason, 'UN Chief Orders Procurement Audit', *Australian*, 17 August 2005.

[38] Paul A. Volcker, Richard J. Goldstone and Mark Pieth, *The Management of the United Nations Oil-for-Food Programme*, 4 volumes. The Report of the Independent Inquiry Committee (New York: IIC, 7 September 2005). Available at www.iic-offp.org.

than the UN may be available or appropriate for taking on complex missions cutting across national boundaries and diverse areas of competence. The organisation simply has to be able to respond 'promptly and effectively to the responsibilities thrust upon it by the realities of a turbulent, and often violent, world'.

Smartening up the sanctions act

Many of the problems associated with sanctions can be minimised through the imposition of 'smart' sanctions that target members of the ruling elite and are limited in their application.[39] Examples include restrictions on overseas travel and financial transactions and a freeze on foreign assets. All UN sanctions since 1994 have been targeted rather than comprehensive, such as financial sanctions against designated individuals and entities (such as the Taliban), oil and conflict diamond embargoes against the National Union for the Total Independence of Angola (UNITA) in Angola, and the sweeping counter-terrorism measures of Resolution 1373 adopted after 11 September 2001. Humanitarian impact assessments and impact missions, involving the use of such indicators as public health and population displacement, are now standard practice in sanctions policy. Designated humanitarian agencies can be given blanket exemptions from sanctions.

Smart sanctions help the UN to mitigate the subversion of humanitarian goals and efforts. Their costs to third-party countries are negligible. They reduce perverse incentives and consequences such as enrichment of the elite by black market manipulation alongside impoverishment of the general population. They deny regimes the use of aid as a tool for establishing control over people by controlling its delivery. They avoid long-term damage to the social, educational, health and physical infrastructure. Above all, they make clear to the people that the international community does discriminate between the sins of the leaders and the distress of the people. 'They are politically easier to

[39] See David Cortright and George A. Lopez with Linda Gerber, *Sanctions and the Search for Security* (Boulder: Lynne Rienner, 2002); David Cortright and George A. Lopez, eds., *Smart Sanctions: Targeting Economic Statecraft* (Lanham, MD: Rowman & Littlefield, 2002); Daniel W. Drezner, *The Sanctions Paradox: Economic Statecraft and International Relations* (Cambridge: Cambridge University Press, 1999); and *Report of the Panel of Experts on Violations of Security Council Sanctions against UNITA* (Fowler Report) (New York: UN, Document S/2000/203, 10 March 2000).

initiate and to sustain in the long run and less likely to bring the sanctions instrument into disrepute.'[40]

The difficulties associated with the imposition, monitoring and enforcement of 'smart' sanctions will only become known with experience. With respect to arms embargoes, for example, the well-intentioned effort ran into the problem of a buyer's market. Another problem is that UNSC sanctions resolutions need to be translated into national legislation,[41] which requires technical drafting competence for enacting relevant laws, competent surveillance and regulatory mechanisms and corruption-free regulatory and law enforcement personnel to monitor and enforce the laws. Violent conflicts increasingly are internal and involve rapacious and criminal behaviour in a regional environment of failed or criminalised states and warring and profiteering factions exploiting a shadow economy.[42] On whom are the sanctions to be imposed, how are they be to enforced, where is the financial incentive for the armed factions to comply with international demands instead of simply absorbing the extra costs? Where are the border control mechanisms and state institutions for regulating and controlling the flow of goods that are subject to sanctions? The people at large, already victims of war, dispossession and dislocation, are further victimised by warlords, black marketeers and armed gangs. The most marked effect of sanctions in such circumstances may be to disrupt relief efforts and activities. This is why all UN sanctions 'should be effectively implemented and enforced by strengthening State capacity to implement sanctions, establishing well resourced monitoring mechanisms and mitigating humanitarian consequences.'[43]

There were three parallel efforts to study how the technical elements of sanctions regimes could be strengthened: the Interlaken (1998–9), Bonn–Berlin (1999–2000) and Stockholm (2001–3) processes.[44] The

---

[40] Andrew Mack and Asif Khan, 'UN Sanctions: A Glass Half Full?', in Price and Zacher, eds., *The United Nations and Global Security*, p. 119.

[41] See Vera Gowlland-Debbas, ed., with the assistance of Djacoba Liva Tehindrazanarivelo, *National Implementation of United Nations Sanctions: A Comparative Study* (Leiden: Martinus Nijhoff, 2004).

[42] See Carolyn Nordstrom, *A Different Kind of War Story (Ethnography of Political Violence)* (Philadelphia: University of Pennsylvania Press, 1997).

[43] Kofi A. Annan, *In Larger Freedom: Towards Development, Security and Human Rights for All.* Report of the Secretary-General (New York: UN, document A/59/2005, 21 March 2005), paras. 109–10.

[44] See Michael Brzoska, ed., *Design and Implementation of Arms Embargoes and Travel and Aviation Related Sanctions – Results of the 'Bonn–Berlin Process'* (Bonn: Bonn International Centre for Conversion, 2001); Peter Wallensteen, Carina Staibano and Mikail

Swiss were behind the first, which looked at the implications for the financial and banking sectors of sanctions regimes targeting financial assets and transactions. Germany followed with a study of sanctions focusing on arms embargoes and travel restrictions. Then the Swedes focused on implementation-related issues: guidelines on implementing arms, financial, commodity (like conflict diamonds), and travel sanctions, and improvement of the UN sanctions committees themselves.

A sanctions committee is created by the UNSC whenever sanctions are imposed with the main task of granting or denying exemptions and exclusions. It is a committee of the whole: all fifteen UNSC members are members of the sanctions committee, represented at deputy permanent representative level. The chair of the committee is usually the permanent representative of a non-P5 country and acts in a personal capacity, taking instructions only from the UNSC, unlike his or her duty on the UNSC proper where instructions are taken from the home government. As with most UN bodies, sanctions committees are typically under-resourced and inadequately staffed with regard to technically competent personnel. An exception was the committee in charge of monitoring sanctions against UNITA in Angola. Chaired by Canada's ambassador Robert Fowler, with the full backing of his government, it produced a revolution in UN affairs by 'naming and shaming' sanctions busting countries and leaders. But the 2000 report was disputed with respect to some of its findings, ignored with respect to many of its recommendations and provoked hostility in some developing countries already critical of aid conditionality by donor governments and international financial institutions.

On 17 April 2000, the UNSC established a working group to develop recommendations on improving the effectiveness of UN sanctions. The group, chaired by ambassador Anwarul Chowdhury of Bangladesh, reached broad agreement on many items but failed to agree on a final report. Nevertheless its draft contained many interesting recommendations. These were divided into three clusters. With respect to the administration of sanctions, for example, the group recommended additional staff, expertise and resources for upgrading the Secretariat's capacity and

Erikson, eds., *Making Targeted Sanctions Effective: Guidelines for the Implementation of UN Policy Options* (Uppsala: Uppsala University, Department of Peace and Conflict Research, 2003); and *Targeted Financial Sanctions: A Manual for Design and Implementation. Contributions from the Interlaken Process* (Providence: Brown University Watson Institute, 2001).

the establishment of a database of outside experts. On the design of UNSC resolutions, it recommended the use of standardised language developed by the Interlaken and Bonn–Berlin processes, the exemption of specific items and designated humanitarian agencies, the specification of conditions to be fulfilled for sanctions to be lifted and actions short of sanctions termination to reward partial compliance. With regard to monitoring and assessment, it suggested such measures as urging states with the relevant expertise to provide technical and legal assistance to requesting states and analyses of third-party effects in sanctions assessment impact reports.

The two issues on which consensus could not be reached were time limits for sanctions termination and whether sanctions committees could move to making decisions by majority voting. The USA and the UK argued strenuously for retaining the consensus rule. In other words, politics trumped consistency and equity in the debate on how to move forward with more carefully calibrated sanctions regimes. In a similar vein, efforts to use the UNSC as the enforcement arm of the international community in order to uphold global norms are undermined, to some extent, by the lack of transparency and democratic norms in the decision-making procedures of the Council. Given that sanctions are mandatory on everyone, the closed-door method of making decisions does grate.

Often the threat is more effective than the actual imposition of sanctions. Target regimes respond to threats with gestures and offers of concessions and partial compliance, although it is not always clear whether these are delaying tactics or negotiating gambits. By contrast, the imposition of sanctions produces a hardening of positions: perhaps the moderate, pro-compromise factions are discredited by the rejection of the peace offerings?[45]

Another recent notable trend is the use and involvement of expert working groups, academic specialists, private sector firms and NGO advocates and field workers in designing and evaluating sanctions.[46] In the Kimberley Process designed to halt the trade in conflict diamonds, for example, the enthusiasm and energy of NGO activists have been combined with UN legitimacy and the technical expertise of De Beers to come up with a standardised and credible system for certificates of origin

---

[45] See Cortright and Lopez, *Sanctions and the Search for Security*, pp. 13–15.
[46] See Susan Burgerman, *Moral Victories: How Activists Provoke Multilateral Action* (Ithaca, NY: Cornell University Press, 2001).

for the export of legitimate diamonds, alongside the threat of exposure (the high value-added diamond industry would be devastated if diamonds became associated in the public mind as objects of shame) and forfeiture of contraband conflict diamonds.

Still, major problems remain. 'While smart sanctions may seem logically compelling and conceptually attractive . . . [t]he operational problems – due to persistent technical inadequacies, legal loopholes, institutional weaknesses, budgetary and staff scarcities, and political constraints – are daunting.'[47] Thus the UNSC sanctions committee concluded that sanctions imposed against al Qaeda and the former Taliban by Resolution 1267 (1999) had had little impact on the groups' operations.[48] There remains a pressing need, therefore, for serious studies of the compliance and transaction costs of targeted, well thought-out sanctions regimes with built-in monitoring and enforcement mechanisms that are as effective as they are credible. For example, how to impose secondary sanctions on sanctions-busting countries on the one hand while supporting states adversely affected by sanctions on the other. Or the criteria and ground rules for exceptions and exemptions. Or the question of time limits and sunset clauses. Or even the criteria for smart sanctions: should they be established on the basis of efficacy; if they are not proving efficacious, should they be lifted, expanded to comprehensive sanctions or lead to military enforcement? As we shall see in the next chapter, some of these dilemmas on how to enforce compliance with international norms and treaties by striking the right balance between force, diplomacy and sanctions haunts the international community with particular urgency in combating the threat of and from nuclear weapons.

---

[47] Quoted in Michael Brzoska's very good review essay, 'From Dumb to Smart? Recent Reforms of UN Sanctions', *Global Governance* 9:4 (Oct.–Dec. 2003), pp. 519–35, at pp. 530–1.

[48] Letter from Heraldo Munoz, chairman of the committee, dated 25 August 2004, document S/2004/679.

PART III

Hard security issues

The nuclear threat

'We are approaching a point at which the erosion of the non-proliferation regime could become irreversible and result in a cascade of proliferation.'[1]

'One cannot worship at the altar of nuclear weapons and raise heresy charges against those who want to join the sect.'[2]

This book began with the assertion by the High-Level Panel on Threats, Challenges and Change that a common understanding on the use of force is necessary for revitalising the role of the United Nations in the twenty-first century. The most lethal force known to mankind so far is nuclear weapons. As the above quotes show, the subject of nuclear arms control and disarmament is back on the international agenda with a vengeance. The triple crisis arises from non-compliance with obligations of the Non-proliferation Treaty (NPT) by some states engaged in undeclared nuclear activities and others that have failed to honour their disarmament obligations; states that are not party to the NPT; and non-state actors seeking to acquire nuclear weapons. The list of concerns includes North Korea's weaponised nuclear capability,[3] worries expressed by the International Atomic Energy Agency (IAEA) about Iran's nuclear programme,[4] reports that Saudi Arabia may be contemplating an

---

[1] *A More Secure World: Our Shared Responsibility*. Report of the High-Level Panel on Threats, Challenges and Change (New York: UN, document A/59/565, 2 December 2004), para. 111.

[2] Brazilian statement, quoted by Douglas Roche (former Canadian ambassador for disarmament), 'At the Unholy Altar of Nuclear Weapons', *Toronto Star*, 19 April 2005.

[3] See International Institute for Strategic Studies, *North Korea's Weapons Programmes: A Net Assessment* (London: Palgrave Macmillan, 2004); Wade Huntley, 'Ostrich Engagement: The Bush Administration and the North Korean Nuclear Crisis', *Nonproliferation Review* (Summer 2004), pp. 1–35; and *North Korea: Where next for the Nuclear Talks?* (Brussels: International Crisis Group (ICG), Asia Report No. 87, 15 November 2004).

[4] See *Iran: Where Next on the Nuclear Standoff?* (Brussels: ICG, Middle East Briefing, 24 November 2004).

off-the-shelf purchase of nuclear weapons,[5] reports of mild misdeeds by South Korea,[6] Taiwan[7] and Egypt,[8] apprehensions of a new uranium enrichment plant that would give Brazil a nuclear breakout capability,[9] anxieties about the 27,000 nuclear warheads with a total yield of 5,000 megatons held by the five nuclear powers (with just Russia and the USA accounting for more than 26,000 warheads), fears that Washington is lowering the threshold of normative barriers to the use of a new generation of nuclear weapons, evidence of an extensive multinational nuclear black market that demonstrated the inadequacy of the existing export controls system,[10] and the prospect of terrorists acquiring nuclear weapons. The only good news stories are that Libya walked away from that path in December 2003[11] and that Iraq does not have them.

[5] See Jonathan Power, 'Turning a Blind Eye to Nukes: The US and Saudi Arabia?', *International Herald Tribune* (*IHT*), 4 August 2004.

[6] 'South Korea Says it Enriched Uranium Four Years Ago', *Japan Times*, 3 September 2004; 'Top Scientist Acknowledges Uranium Tests', *Japan Times*, 5 September 2004; 'ROK Enrichment Tests Conducted "3 Times"', *Daily Yomiuri*, 5 September 2004; 'Seoul Admits Scientists Extracted Plutonium in '82 Experiment', *Japan Times*, 10 September 2004; James Brooke, 'Report Details South Korean Cover-up', *IHT*, 25 November 2004; 'S. Korea Chided for Nuclear Tests', *BBC News* (http://news.bbc.co.uk), 11 November 2004.

[7] 'Taipei Held Nuke Experiments as Late as Mid-1980s', *Japan Times*, 14 October 2004 and 'Concern over Taiwan Nuclear Ambitions', *Japan Times*, 17 October 2004.

[8] 'Egyptian Scientists Produced Nuclear Material: Diplomats', *Japan Times*, 6 January 2005.

[9] Larry Rohter, 'If Brazil Wants to Scare the World, It's Succeeding', *New York Times*, 31 October 2004.

[10] 'Nuclear components designed in one country could be manufactured in another, shipped through a third, and assembled in a fourth for use in a fifth'; Mohamed El Baradei, 'Preserving the Non-Proliferation Treaty', *Disarmament Forum* 4 (2004), p. 5. See also Christopher Clary, 'Dr. Khan's Nuclear WalMart', *Disarmament Diplomacy* 76 (March/April 2004), pp. 31–5.

[11] The Bush administration was quick to claim the Libyan renunciation of the nuclear option as a tangible success of its Iraq war policy. It is just as plausible to link the Libyan decision to domestic political compulsions, the adverse impact of the international sanctions imposed on it in the 1980s, and the trend line for a negotiated end to the stalemate visible since the Clinton administration. See Thomas E. McNamara (a former ambassador and assistant secretary of state who developed and implemented the UN sanctions policy against Libya as a special assistant to President George H. W. Bush in 1991–2), 'Why Qaddafi Turned his Back on Terror', *IHT*, 5 May 2004; and Geoff D. Porter, 'The Faulty Premise of Pre-emption', *New York Times*, 31 July 2004. Many Arabs believe that as a result of the difficult insurgency in Iraq after the war, it is Washington that became more receptive to long-standing Libyan overtures and signals for an end to the confrontation. Thus both versions agree on the war being the deal maker, but for opposite reasons.

Weapons can be sought for one or more of six reasons:[12] deterrence of enemy attack; defence against attack; compellence of the enemy to one's preferred course of action; leveraging adversary and great-power behaviour;[13] status; and emulation. Specific causes of proliferation are many, diverse and usually rooted in a local security complex. On the supply side, a major challenge is the globalisation of the arms industry, the flooding of the global arms market and a resulting loosening of supplier constraints. Under modern conditions of globalised trade, instantaneous and voluminous electronic information exchanges, interlinked financial systems and the sheer diversity of technology, the control of access to nuclear-weapons technology and material has grown vastly more complex and challenging.

The UN Charter was signed two months before the first use of atomic weapons and the first session of the General Assembly (GA) was held two months after. The organisation has been engaged with the topic of nuclear arms control and disarmament from the start. The very first GA resolution (1/I, January 1946) called for the newly established UN Atomic Energy Commission to make proposals for the elimination of atomic weapons and other weapons of mass destruction (WMD).

The goal of containing the spread and enlargement of weapons and arms stockpiles has rested on three pillars, each of which has been crumbling in the last few years: norms, treaties and coercion. In this chapter, after reviewing the three pillars, I will posit a symbiotic link between nuclear non-proliferation and disarmament and conclude with suggestions for the way forward.

Norms

One of the most powerful norms since 1945 has been the taboo on the use of nuclear weapons. There have been many occasions since 1945 when nuclear weapons could have been used without fear of retaliation

---

[12] This is developed more fully in Ramesh Thakur, 'Arms Control, Disarmament, and Non-Proliferation: A Political Perspective', in Jeffrey A. Larsen and Thomas D. Miller, eds., *Arms Control in the Asia–Pacific Region* (Colorado Springs: USAF Institute for National Security Studies, US Air Force Academy, 1999), pp. 39–61.

[13] Many of the newer proliferating materials and processes are 'leveraging' technologies that allow poorer countries to offset high-technology advantages. By demonstrating the acquisition of just a few key capabilities, developing countries can affect the perceptions and alter the decision calculus of diplomacy and war of the advanced military powers.

but were not, even at the price of defeat on the battlefield.[14] Norms, not deterrence, have anathematised the use of nuclear weapons as unacceptable, immoral and possibly illegal under any circumstance – even for states that have assimilated them into military arsenals and integrated them into military commands and doctrines. The force of the norm is buttressed by operational disutility: the enormous destructiveness of nuclear weapons does not translate easily into military or political utility. The most spectacular Soviet territorial and political advances were made between 1945 and 1949, when the Americans had a monopoly of atomic weaponry; the Soviet empire disintegrated after attaining strategic parity with the USA. The nuclear equation has been irrelevant in determining the outcomes of recent conflicts in the Balkans, the Congo, Rwanda and Sudan.

If the UNSC is the geopolitical centre of gravity, the GA, with universal membership, is the normative centre of gravity. It is the unique forum of choice for articulating global values and norms and the arena where contested norms can be debated and reconciled. Such a role was true for it historically in delegitimising colonialism, even though decolonisation resulted from policy decisions taken in national capitals. It was the UN more than any other institution or organisation which proclaimed racial equality as a global norm and delegitimised apartheid as an ideology and system of government. And it is to the GA that civil society actors look and member states go when they wish to proclaim and reaffirm arms control and disarmament norms. This is the chief explanation for so many declarations and resolutions first being adopted in the UN before producing conventions and treaties – norms followed by laws.

Ireland in particular sponsored GA Resolutions 1380 (1959), 1576 (1960), and 1665 (1961) calling for a non-proliferation treaty. In 1965, the Soviet Union presented a draft treaty to the GA which also adopted Resolution 2028 outlining five principles of non-proliferation submitted by eight non-aligned countries. Resolution 2346A (19 December 1967) requested the Eighteen-Nation Committee on Disarmament (the

---

[14] Richard Price and Nina Tannenwald, 'Norms and Deterrence: The Nuclear and Chemical Weapons Taboos', in Peter J. Katzenstein, ed., *The Culture of National Security: Norms and Identity in World Politics* (New York: Columbia University Press, 1996), pp. 114–52. Price and Tannenwald ascribe non-use by the USA to its essentially democratic government and its self-conception as a moral actor in world affairs (pp. 139–41), yet fail to see the anomaly of their explanation with the equally compelling example of non-use by the Soviet Union.

predecessor of the Conference on Disarmament, CD) for a full report on the NPT negotiations. After receiving this, on 12 June 1968 the GA commended the draft text of the NPT (Resolution 2373) and the NPT was opened for signature on 1 July 1968 in London, Moscow and Washington (capitals of the three designated depository countries). The treaty entered into force on 5 March 1970, at which time the IAEA established its safeguards system for NPT parties.[15]

The GA's First Committee is charged with considering disarmament and international security. Many of its resolutions are mere repeats from previous years, but new resolutions are introduced every year and serve as a litmus test of progress or lack of it and weathervanes of current international thinking. The UN Disarmament Commission, too, is a deliberative body where all UN member states can come together to set the framework for disarmament. However, it is effectively moribund.

A norm cannot control the behaviour of those who reject its legitimacy. India had argued for decades that the most serious breaches of the anti-nuclear norm were being committed by the five nuclear powers who simply disregarded their disarmament obligations under Article 6 of the NPT. The imbalance of reporting, monitoring and compliance mechanisms between the non-proliferation and disarmament clauses of the NPT, India insisted, had in effect created nuclear apartheid.[16]

In 1996, India's opposition to the Comprehensive Test Ban Treaty (CTBT) at the CD in Geneva forced Australia into a constitutional stratagem to seek endorsement by the GA in New York. Sometimes it is possible to be mesmerised by the illusion of a numerical majority in the UN for the weight of national security calculations in the real world. The resulting hardening of India's nuclear stance was predictable: 'Faced with US-led UN coercion, an isolated, sullen and resentful India is more likely to respond with an open nuclear programme, including a . . . series of nuclear tests.'[17] For in Indian eyes the issue was no longer the clauses

---

[15] In 2005 a total of 908 facilities were under the IAEA routine safeguards inspections in 152 countries that had safeguards agreements with the Agency. Moreover, 65 NPT states had ratified the IAEA Model Additional Protocol.

[16] The use of the word 'apartheid' by critics of the NPT is especially unfortunate. The emotive word entails entirely negative connotations. But in fact apartheid referred to a system where a minority imposed its order on a majority by coercion. The NPT has been signed by a majority of the world's countries exercising their free choice.

[17] Ramesh Thakur, 'Nuclear India Needs Coaxing, Not Coercion', *Australian* (Sydney), 6 September 1996. The GA vote on the CTBT was held on 10 September and India tested nuclear weapons in May 1998.

and substance of the CTBT. Rather, its passage by the GA was taken as proof that the international environment had deteriorated alarmingly against the security interests of the country.[18]

Treaties

Arms control and disarmament agreements are negotiated outcomes among governments entailing difficult technical and political judgements on reciprocity, mutuality and relative balance. A large number of treaties and conventions regulate the use and spread of armaments. The WMD trinity is regulated by the Chemical Weapons Convention (CWC), the Biological Weapons Convention (BWC), the NPT, the CTBT,[19] several regional nuclear-weapons-free zones (NWFZ), and a whole series of bilateral and multilateral treaties and agreements. There are even more agreements imposing curbs and controls on conventional weapons including, for example, the Ottawa Convention on anti-personnel landmines which has the distinction of banning a class of weapons already in widespread use.[20]

The NPT is the centrepiece of the global non-proliferation regime which codified the international political norm of non-nuclear-weapons status. China and France among the NWS and Argentina, Brazil and South Africa among the rest joined the NPT quite late. The former Soviet republics, too, transferred nuclear weapons inherited from the former Soviet Union to Russia and signed the NPT as non-nuclear states. Progress in multilateral forums includes the indefinite extension of the NPT in 1995,[21] negotiation of the CTBT and agreement on thirteen steps

---

[18] For elaboration of the argument that the CTBT stratagem at the UN increased domestic pressure and determination to proceed with testing, from a range of other people, including opponents of that option, see: K. Sundarji, 'India's Best Option', *Hindu* (Madras), 17 September 1996; K. Subrahmanyam, 'The World after CTBT', *Economic Times* (Delhi), 19 September 1996; K. K. Katyal, 'Gujral Defends Pokhran Tests', *Hindu*, 26 September 1998; and Jaswant Singh, 'Against Nuclear Apartheid', *Foreign Affairs* 77: 5 (September/October 1998), p. 46.

[19] As of January 2005, 174 states have signed and 120 ratified the CTBT. But 11 of the 44 whose ratification is necessary for the Treaty to enter into force have not done so, including China, the USA, India and Pakistan.

[20] The interesting thing about the Ottawa Treaty is that it may be better viewed as advancing the humanitarian norm than as an arms control treaty; see Ramesh Thakur and William Maley, 'The Ottawa Convention on Landmines: A Landmark Humanitarian Treaty in Arms Control?', *Global Governance* 5:3 (July–September 1999), pp. 273–302.

[21] For an account of that by the president of the conference, see Jayantha Dhanapala with Randy Rydell, *Multilateral Diplomacy and the NPT: An Insider's Account* (Geneva: UN

to non-proliferation and disarmament at the 2000 review conference. These are supplemented by such technology-denial regimes as the Nuclear Suppliers Group and the Australia Group, and unilateral initiatives like the Cooperative Threat Reduction initiative for securing Russia's 'loose nukes'.

There is a widespread sense today that the UN has become dysfunctional and moribund as a forum for negotiating arms control and disarmament treaties. The machinery and the programme of action for disarmament in the United Nations was established at the first UN Special Session on Disarmament (UNSSOD I) in 1978. The sixty-six-member CD is in the paradoxical position of being the UN's sole disarmament legislative forum while not being a true UN body. Consensus decision-making means that every treaty is hostage to the veto of any one of its sixty-six members. Hence the alienation of public support from the intergovernmental forums of international arms control agreements. The preference for and success of the Ottawa Treaty on landmines was evidence of mounting frustration with the painfully slow rate of progress in the CD as the interstate negotiating forum. In 2004 both the CD and the Disarmament Commission failed to agree on a work agenda. A number of states are proposing radical overhauls of the way in which business is done in the First Committee.[22] Kofi Annan has acknowledged openly that the CD 'faces a crisis of relevance resulting in part from dysfunctional decision-making procedures and the paralysis that accompanies them'.[23]

The UN has often been the forum for negotiating new international instruments and the depositary organisation for many treaties negotiated outside the UN framework. The GA can adopt resolutions that initiate new negotiations on arms control and disarmament, and also adopt treaties negotiated in the CD as with the CTBT. The NPT was negotiated outside the UN framework, but its conceptual origin lies in an Irish resolution introduced in the GA in 1958. Multilateral treaties do not have to be negotiated within standing international machinery. Even if

---

Institute for Disarmament Research and the Stockholm International Peace Research Institute, 2005).

[22] See Patricia Lewis and Ramesh Thakur, 'Arms Control, Disarmament and the United Nations', *Disarmament Forum* 1 (2004), pp. 17–28.

[23] Kofi A. Annan, *In Larger Freedom: Towards Development, Security and Human Rights for All.* Report of the Secretary-General (New York: UN, document A/59/2005, 21 March 2005), para. 97.

negotiated outside UN forums, treaties are often submitted to the UN machinery for formal endorsement that has no bearing on the legal standing of the treaty but does substantially enhance its moral weight. This has been true, for example, of the various regional NWFZ.

Of late, Washington has made policy pronouncements, engaged in some preparations and retreated from a series of arms control and disarmament agreements, including the anti-ballistic missile (ABM), NPT and CTBT treaties.[24] Senator Dianne Feinstein notes that 'our own new nuclear posture could provoke the very nuclear-proliferation activities we are seeking to prevent'.[25] Indonesia's Foreign Minister cautions that 'The most dangerous force eroding the [NPT] treaty's credibility is the inclination of some nuclear-weapons states to reinterpret at will the package of agreements reached in the past'.[26] In the words of a former Assistant Secretary of Defense in the Republican Reagan administration, in the Nuclear Posture Review, 'the administration made it clear that it would be prepared to use nuclear weapons against non-nuclear states, including launching preemptive attacks with nuclear weapons against nations that were close to acquiring nuclear arsenals. This new strategy may well have led North Korea and Iran to accelerate their own nuclear programs.'[27]

The net effect has been to soften some existing arms control regimes and restraints. In doing so, Washington is caught in the twin trap of alienating allies and worsening the proliferation challenge. This is why Robert McNamara, the former Secretary of Defense (1961–8), has argued that the current US nuclear policy is 'immoral, illegal, militarily unnecessary, and dreadfully dangerous'.[28] It is difficult to convince others of the *futility* of nuclear weapons when some demonstrate their *utility* by the very fact of hanging on to them and developing new doctrines for their use. That is, *treaty* setbacks contribute to a weakening of *norms*, which

---

[24] See Thomas Graham Jr. and Damien J. Lavera, 'Nuclear Weapons: The Comprehensive Test Ban Treaty and National Missile Defense', in Stewart Patrick and Shepard Forman, eds., *Multilateralism and US Foreign Policy: Ambivalent Engagement* (Boulder: Lynne Rienner, 2002), pp. 225–45.

[25] Dianne Feinstein, 'Dangerous for US to Lower Nuclear Threshold', *Straits Times* (Singapore), 8 January 2004.

[26] N. Hassan Wirajuda, 'Keep Nonproliferation from Going to Seed', *Japan Times*, 4 May 2004.

[27] Lawrence J. Korb, 'Bush's Policy Endangers US Security', *IHT*, 9 August 2004.

[28] Robert S. McNamara, 'Apocalypse Soon', *Foreign Policy* (May/June 2005), p. 29. See also Jimmy Carter, 'Erosion of the Nonproliferation Treaty', *IHT*, 2 May 2005.

then sets in train a vicious cycle, since the heightened risk of proliferation is used to justify a further scaling back of treaty or voluntary commitments like no testing. According to two people who once had the responsibility for the US and British foreign policies, a failure by the nuclear powers to do more to reduce their own nuclear arsenals 'would encourage states that do not have nuclear weapons to rebel against nonproliferation norms out of dissatisfaction with what they perceive to be a double standard: some states get nuclear weapons, while others do not'.[29]

Compliance and coercion

Norms and laws are complementary mechanisms for regulating social behaviour. Within countries, there are many social and legal mechanisms to ensure compliance and punish outlaws. Among countries, the universe of compliance-enforcing tools is slighter, more contentious and divisive, and usually less efficacious. Compliance is especially problematical in relation to the production, exchange and use of arms, for it lies at the very heart of national security.

There are several international bodies set within the UN framework as part of the implementation mechanism for treaty regimes: the IAEA (Vienna), the OPCW (the Organisation for the Prohibition of Chemical Weapons in The Hague) and the CTBTO-PTS (Vienna). Although autonomous, the IAEA is a member of the UN system and reports annually to the GA on its work. It is the centrepiece of international efforts to combat proliferation from within the NPT regime. The agency's three-pronged strategy to combat nuclear security risks is prevention of illicit and non-peaceful use of nuclear material, the timely detection of any such efforts, and swift and decisive response by the international community to all such efforts.[30] Its database recorded 630 confirmed incidents of trafficking in nuclear and other radioactive material from 1993–2003, with sixty incidents reported in 2003 – two years after 9/11 and the tightened export controls and surveillance and regulatory efforts.[31]

---

[29] Madeleine Albright and Robin Cook, 'We Must Cut Our Nuclear Arsenals', *Guardian*, 9 June 2004.

[30] Mohamed El-Baradei, 'Nuclear Proliferation and the Potential Threat of Nuclear Terrorism', Keynote Speech at the Asia-Pacific Nuclear Safeguards and Security Conference, Sydney, 8 November 2004; available at www.iaea.org.

[31] Ibid.

The UN can also establish ad hoc bodies specifically targeted at problem states or regions. The most prominent in recent times were the UN
Special Commission (UNSCOM, 1991) and the UN Monitoring, Verification and Inspections Mission (UNMOVIC, 1999), charged with the
disarmament of the weapons of mass destruction in Iraq.[32] Despite all
the cat-and-mouse games, obfuscation, subversion and evasion by Iraq,
UNSCOM and UNMOVIC found and destroyed Iraq's WMD. The story
of UN inspection in Iraq 'is a success studded with weaknesses', one not
fully recognised in US circles, even though UNSCOM and UNMOVIC
cost around $25–30 million per year, compared with the $900 million
cost of inspections for the year since the Iraq War.[33] A newly created
inspectorate could build on their experience, preserve the expertise on
biochemical weapons and ballistic missiles and continue the fruitful
partnership with other agencies like the IAEA and the OPCW, but it
would have to be properly resourced and mandated.

Faced with a challenge to the norms and laws governing the acquisition, production, transfer and use of arms, the five permanent members of the Security Council (P5) may have to resort to measures of
coercion ranging from diplomatic and economic to military. The non-
proliferation norm became potentially enforceable in January 1992 when
the UNSC declared proliferation to be a threat to international peace
and security (which can trigger enforcement action under chapter 7 of
the Charter). But the UNSC record in addressing proliferation threats
is at best ad hoc, fitful and fretful rather than consistent, uniform and
predictable. The case of North Korea was referred to the Council by the
IAEA back in 1993; Pyongyang has yet to face any consequences for
its serial brinksmanship, hiding safely behind P5 disagreement on
any appropriate policy response. Iraq was disarmed by UNSCOM, but
as a defeated nation under direct UNSC action rather than because
its clandestine activities had been discovered by the IAEA. The difficulty
of knowing just how to deal with the case of Iran in 2004–5 demon-
strates the problematic elements of requiring conclusive evidence of

---

[32] See Trevor Findlay, 'The Lessons of UNSCOM and UNMOVIC', in *Verification Yearbook
2004* (London: Verification Research, Training and Information Centre (VERTIC),
2004), pp. 65–86.

[33] Jessica Tuchman Mathews, 'Weapons of Mass Destruction and the United Nations',
Global Governance 10:3 (July–September 2004), pp. 265–7. See also Hans Blix, *Disarming
Iraq* (New York: Pantheon Books, 2004).

non-compliance before the UNSC can *react* to a proliferation threat; a prophylactic role for it seems hard to imagine.

The margins of tolerance by the international community of non-compliance with WMD non-proliferation and disarmament norms and obligations narrowed dramatically after the terrorist attacks of 11 September 2001. UNSC Resolution 1540 (28 April 2004) crossed a conceptual Rubicon in directing sovereign states to enact non-proliferation legislation. Affirming WMD proliferation as a threat to international peace and security and expressing concern over the threat of WMD terrorism and of illicit trafficking in WMD material, weapons and delivery systems, Resolution 1540 called on all states to enact and enforce laws to prohibit non-state actors to develop, acquire, transfer or use WMD; to take and enforce effective domestic control, physical protection, accounting and border control measures to prevent proliferation; and to set up a committee of the whole to oversee implementation of the resolution.

The unprecedented intrusion into national law-making authority can be read as the toughened new determination of the international community to take effective action. But it was not without controversy. A former member of the UN/OAU Expert Group on the Denuclearisation of Africa noted that 'by arrogating to itself wider powers of legislation', the UNSC was departing from its Charter-based mandate, and that excessive recourse to chapter 7 could signal a preference for coercion over cooperation. Framing the resolution within the global war against terrorism was meant to silence dissenting voices. And the Council's effort to seek global adherence to its resolutions was undermined by its unrepresentative composition and the veto power of the P5.[34] Many NGOs, too, criticised the resolution's silence on the role of disarmament in promoting non-proliferation, as well as the UNSC effort to transform itself into a world legislature.[35]

The reality of contemporary threats means that significant gaps exist in the legal and institutional framework to combat them. The flow of enabling technologies, material and expertise in the nuclear power industry can be used, through strategic pre-positioning of materials and personnel, to build a 'virtual' nuclear-weapons portfolio capable of rapid

---

[34] Abdalnahmood Abdalhaleem Mohammad, 'Security Council and Non-proliferation', *Hindu*, 28 May 2004.
[35] Jim Wurst, 'NGOs Criticize Nonproliferation Draft for Ignoring Disarmament', *UN Wire*, www.unwire.org, 1 April 2004.

weaponisation. Within the constraints of the NPT, a non-nuclear country can build the necessary infrastructure to provide it with the requisite
'surge' capacity to upgrade quickly to nuclear weapons. Non-state actors
are outside the jurisdiction and control of multilateral agreements.

Recognising this, a US-led group of like-minded countries has launched a Proliferation Security Initiative (PSI) to interdict illicit air, sea
and land cargo linked to WMD. Its premise is that the proliferation of
such weapons deserves to be criminalised by the civilised community of
nations. The PSI signals a new determination to overcome an unsatisfactory state of affairs through a broad partnership of countries that,
using their own national laws and resources, will coordinate actions to
halt shipments of dangerous technologies and materiel. While the High-
Level Panel encouraged all states to join the PSI,[36] the Secretary-General
simply welcomed the voluntary initiative.[37] Unilateral approaches will
always have greater flexibility in formulating more precise responses to
meet more specific situations than general and diffuse threats, while
multilateral solutions may be more time-consuming but are also likely
to prove more enduring and stable. Of course, even multilateral products
depend on national level implementation.

The High-Level Panel recommended also that the implementation
committee of Resolution 1540 should establish a permanent liaison with
the IAEA, the Nuclear Suppliers Group and the OPCW; the Directors-
General of the OPCW and IAEA should be invited by the UNSC to
report to it twice-yearly on the status of safeguards and verification
processes, and on any serious concerns they have short of actual treaty
breaches; and the UNSC should be prepared to deploy inspection capacities for suspected nuclear and chemical violations, drawing on the
OPCW and IAEA capacities.[38]

Weaknesses in the normative architecture of arms control

There are several major gaps in the arms control and disarmament
regime:[39]

---

[36] *A More Secure World*, para. 132.

[37] Annan, *In Larger Freedom*, para. 100.

[38] *A More Secure World*, paras. 136, 140, 141.

[39] See Natasha Bajema, rapporteur, *Weapons of Mass Destruction and the United Nations: Diverse Threats and Collective Responses* (New York: International Peace Academy, June 2004).

- the continuing existence of stockpiles of nuclear weapons;
- the lack of a nuclear weapons convention outlawing the possession and use of nuclear weapons by all actors;
- the lack of verification machinery and compliance mechanisms for the disarmament obligations (Article 6) of the NPT;
- the lack of NPT universality;
- the lack of a credible and binding inspections regime for non-proliferation;
- the lack of agreed criteria to assess proliferation threats;
- the lack of a basis in international law to enforce non-proliferation norms for states outside the treaty regimes; and
- the inapplicability of norms and regimes to non-state actors.

The NPT's remarkable success notwithstanding, some weaknesses are also apparent with the benefit of hindsight.[40] By failing to include clearly timetabled, legally binding, verifiable and enforceable disarmament commitments, it temporarily legitimised the nuclear arsenals of the P5. By relying on the promise of signatories to use nuclear materials, facilities and technology for peaceful purposes only, it empowered them to operate dangerously close to a nuclear-weapons capability. It proscribed non-nuclear states from acquiring nuclear weapons, but failed to design a strategy for dealing with non-signatory states parties. It permits withdrawals much too easily: North Korea joined the NPT in 1985, but in January 2003 announced its intention to withdraw. While consciousness of the risks of nuclear weapons falling into the hands of terrorists, militant fanatics and other non-state groups has grown enormously, the collective memories of the horrors of Hiroshima and Nagasaki may have begun to fade, lowering the normative barriers to the use of nuclear weapons by some state actors. Because there is no standing agency or secretariat, the NPT depends on five-year review conferences for resolving implementation problems. Even these operate by the consensus rule, which does not make for decisive resolution of contentious issues. Verification and enforcement are one step removed to the extent that the IAEA acts as a buffer between the NPT and the UNSC.

The Iraq experience shows the enormous difficulty of ensuring compliance with international norms and commitments, *even with respect to*

---

[40] For a good, balanced and succinct analysis in advance of the May 2005 NPT Review Conference, see Rebecca Johnson, 'Is the NPT Up to the Challenge of Proliferation?', *Disarmament Forum* 4 (2004), pp. 9–19.

one of the world's most odious regimes pursuing some of the world's most destructive weapons. For the failure to find WMD since the war cannot eradicate the known historical record of Saddam Hussein's past pursuit of them and his will to use them against outsiders as well as Iraqis. Moreover, there is an inherent tension between the IAEA's mandate for promoting peaceful nuclear energy use and the overall strategic goal of non-proliferation. This is best illustrated by the fact that India and Pakistan, outside the NPT regime, are on the IAEA Board of Governors. It is also increasingly a problem because more and more nuclear technology, materials and equipment are dual-use. When the chief distinction between peaceful and offensive use rests on intent, there is a problem.

Strengthening treaty regimes means national legislation and measures on criminalisation of proliferation activities, effective protection of proliferation-sensitive personnel, materials and equipment, control and accounting systems for monitoring materials and stocks, and regulation and surveillance of dual-use transfers. The NPT could be strengthened by making the IAEA Additional Protocol mandatory for all states parties, toughening up or even eliminating the exit clause and making clear that withdrawal from the NPT will be treated as a threat to peace and security. But these cannot be done without also addressing gaps on the disarmament side of the NPT and reform of the composition and procedures of the UNSC.

Some of the NPT's weaknesses are not just intrinsic to it but were intentional. For example the wording of Articles 1 and 2 deliberately permits the NWS to transfer nuclear weapons to other countries (Cold War allies at the time) – that is, engage in geographical proliferation – as long as control of the weapons remained in the hands of the NWS. The subsequent popularity of NWFZ owed much to the desire to plug this loophole.[41] The desire to marry two possibly incompatible goals – President Dwight Eisenhower's vision of 'atoms for peace' and non-proliferation – produced the odd juxtaposition of Articles 3 and 4, and led in time to crises in North Korea and Iran. For nuclear energy for peaceful purposes can be pursued legitimately to the point of being a screwdriver away from a weapons capability.

The problem of non-parties and non-state actors could be taken care of by accepting the suggestion that the fruitless search for universal

---

[41] See Ramesh Thakur, ed., *Nuclear Weapons-Free Zones* (London and New York: Macmillan and St. Martin's Press, 1998).

membership should be replaced by 'universal compliance' with the terms of arms control regimes. The Carnegie Endowment for International Peace lists a set of six obligations to make this a reality: making non-proliferation irreversible; devaluing the political and military currency of nuclear weapons, which would have to include the steady, verified dismantlement of nuclear arsenals; securing all nuclear materials through robust standards for monitoring and accounting for fissile materials in any form; enforceable prohibitions against efforts by individuals, corporations and states to assist others in secretly acquiring the technology, material and know-how for nuclear weapons; a commitment to conflict resolution; and persuading India, Israel and Pakistan to accept the same non-proliferation obligations as the NWS signatories to the NPT.[42]

Non-proliferation and disarmament

The biggest tension in the arms control regimes remains that between non-proliferation and disarmament. The NPT contains a triangular linkage between verified nuclear non-proliferation, cooperation in peaceful uses of nuclear energy and nuclear disarmament. Article 6 of the NPT is the only explicit multilateral disarmament commitment undertaken by all the NWS. Implementing Article 6 of the NPT instead of dusting it off occasionally as a rhetorical concession would dramatically transform the NPT from a non-proliferation into a prohibition regime. That is both its attraction and its fatal flaw. The five NWS and the other non-NWS states parties to the NPT regard the Article 6 disarmament clause as a peripheral and central obligation respectively. Yet 'Without this linkage, there would have been no agreement on an NPT in 1968 – and it is hard to envisage any new international nonproliferation compact that would not inherently contain such a linkage.'[43]

For arms control regimes – the infrastructure of sustainable disarmament[44] – to be vested with legitimacy, they must incorporate a balance of obligations between the present nuclear haves and have-nots. There is

---

[42] George Perkovich, Jessica Tuchman Mathews, Joseph Cirincione, Rose Gottemoeller and Jon Wolfsthal, *Universal Compliance: A Strategy for Nuclear Security* (Washington, DC: Carnegie Endowment for International Peace, March 2005).

[43] Mohamed El Baradei, 'Preserving the Non-Proliferation Treaty', p. 3.

[44] The concept is discussed in Ramesh Thakur, 'Sustainable Disarmament', in Carl Ungerer and Marianne Hanson, eds., *The Politics of Nuclear Non-Proliferation* (Sydney: Allen & Unwin Australia, 2001), pp. 11–30.

profound scepticism about the country with the world's most powerful nuclear weapons using military force to prevent their acquisition by others. The 2004 NPT PrepCom meeting effectively collapsed without any significant agreements.[45] Most of the non-NWS strongly resisted US efforts to back away from the 1995 Review Conference consensus and the agreed thirteen steps from the 2000 review conference. Washington no longer accepts some of these earlier undertakings, including the entry-into-force of the test ban treaty, the 'unequivocal undertaking' to eliminate their nuclear arsenals eventually and the ABM treaty.

The Brahimi Panel noted that in some cases local parties consist not of moral equals but aggressors and victims, and consequently 'peacekeepers may not only be operationally justified in using force but morally compelled to do so.'[46] Can this insight be applied to the nuclear dilemma? It seems counter-intuitive to postulate that in the eyes of most people and countries, nuclear weapons in the hands of Britain and North Korea would pose equal risks to international peace and security. The UN, resting on the principle of sovereign equality of member states, is compelled to assert the danger of nuclear weapons per se arising from their uniquely destructive properties. But if the UN is not capable or willing to distinguish between regimes with respect to the risks they pose and the threats they constitute, then it must either be reformed and reconfigured to enable such determination, or else we must accept the reality that concerned countries will make these tough decisions and act on them outside the UN framework. They are not going to imperil their national security in an idealistic faith in the UN system of collective security resting on demonstrably false assumptions.

Yet another effect of 9/11 may have been to change the focus of concern from universal to differentiated nuclear proliferation. US policy would appear to have shifted de facto from universal non-proliferation based on the NPT to differentiated proliferation based on relations of the regimes in question with Washington. US-friendly countries like Israel never evoked outrage over their nuclear weapons programmes. Since 9/11, even India and Pakistan have been lifted out of countries of concern in favour of concentrated attacks on the axis of evil countries;

---

[45] Rebecca Johnson, 'NPT PrepCom Crashes in Disarray', newsletter circulated by Acronym Institute, 8 May 2004; Jim Wurst, 'Nuclear Nonproliferation Treaty Meeting Ends with Deep Divides', *UN Wire*, www.unwire.org, 7 May 2004.

[46] *Report of the Panel on United Nations Peace Operations*, UN doc., A/55/305-S/2000/809, 21 August 2000, para. 50.

that is, US-hostile proliferators. Without explicitly saying so, the Bush administration in effect seems to have decided to rewrite the rules of the treaty without embarking on the impossible task of renegotiating it. 'In what amounts to a reinterpretation of the [NPT], Bush now argues that there is a new class of nations that simply cannot be trusted with the technology to produce nuclear material, even if the treaty makes no such distinction.'[47]

However, such a dramatic deterioration of the security environment hardens the determination of the 'rogues' to acquire the most lethal weapons precisely in order to check armed attacks they fear will be launched by the USA. Some countries could conclude that only nuclear weapons can deter Washington from unilateral wars of choice. Just as Iraq as a hotbed of terrorism became a consequence more than a cause of war, so proliferation of nuclear weapons may result from the war. Thus as Washington throws off fetters on the unilateral use of force and the universal taboo on nuclear weapons, it strengthens the attraction of nuclear weapons for others while simultaneously weakening the restraining force of global norms and treaties.

As of the end of 2004, Iran remained defiant that it would not abandon its quest for nuclear energy. The security deficits of Iran's geostrategic environment include three de facto nuclear powers (Israel, Pakistan and India) in its own region to the west and east; aggression in recent memory by neighbour Iraq, including the use of chemical weapons delivered by Scud missiles, which was at least tolerated if not condoned by the same Western powers that later turned against the author of the aggression; two NWS (China and Russia) in the Central Asian regional context; and a circle of US bases and forces around it in the context of having been designated a member of the axis of evil. Should one be surprised that Iran's security elite should show an interest in the nuclear weapons option?

Conclusion

Kofi Annan noted that the NPT 'faces a crisis of confidence and compliance born of a growing strain on verification and enforcement'.[48] In an illustration of the third theme of this book, Nina Tannenwald writes:

---

[47] David E. Sanger, 'Bush Seeks to Alter Global Nuclear Pact', *IHT*, 16 March 2005.
[48] Annan, *In Larger Freedom*, para. 97.

The critical issue is how the UN will deal with US power . . . The real
question is whether the UN can remain the arena for negotiated bargains
over WMD or whether it will become – like the former Warsaw Pact –
simply a handmaiden for the hegemon. The UN will need to find a way to
deal constructively with the reality of US hegemony without making itself
irrelevant by simply succumbing to it.[49]

In the words of a former US deputy secretary of defense, 'America is
sleepwalking through history, armed with nuclear weapons. The Cold
War left us with a massive inventory of weapons we no longer need, an
infrastructure we can no longer use or maintain, and no thought of
where our future lies.'[50] The three policy imperatives are to encourage
the reduction of nuclear inventories among the NWS, strengthen controls over nuclear stocks and material among them and minimise the
attraction of the nuclear option to those who do not have these weapons.
There was great merit in relying on an integrated strategy of norms,
treaties and coercion to keep the nuclear threat in check.

Norms cannot successfully regulate the behaviour of those who reject
the legitimacy of the existing order. Their compliance with such norms
will be a function of their incapacity to break out, not of voluntary
obedience. The de facto position of 'nuclear might equals right' is an
inducement to join the club of nuclear enforcers. Hence the need to go
back to regime-based solutions. Relying solely on coercion with little
basis any longer on norms (morality) and treaties (legality) simply
creates fresh problems. The three pillars are mutually reinforcing in
holding up the structure of global arms control. Amy Smithson notes,
in the context of the Chemical Weapons Convention, that the USA 'runs
the twin risks of continuing to alienate its allies, on the one hand, and,
on the other, of enticing proliferators to build arsenals in the face of
inconsistent US support for treaty regimes.'[51] In order to enhance their
credentials as critics and enforcers of the norm, the NWS need to move
more rapidly from deterrence to disarmament. The Canberra Commission had argued that the case for the elimination of nuclear weapons was

[49] Nina Tannenwald, 'The UN and Debates Over Weapons of Mass Destruction', in Richard
      M. Price and Mark W. Zacher, eds., *The United Nations and Global Security* (New York:
      Palgrave Macmillan, 2004), p. 18.
[50] John J. Hamre, 'Toward a Nuclear Strategy', *Washington Post*, 2 May 2005.
[51] Amy E. Smithson, 'The Chemical Weapons Convention', in Stewart Patrick and Shepard
      Forman, eds., *Multilateralism and US Foreign Policy: Ambivalent Engagement* (Boulder:
      Lynne Rienner, 2002), pp. 259–60.

based on three propositions: their destructive power robs them of military utility against other NWS and renders them politically and morally indefensible against non-NWS; it defies credulity that they can be retained in perpetuity and never used either by design or inadvertence; and their possession by some stimulates others to acquire them.[52] The edifice began falling apart in 1998 because ultimately, the logic of non-proliferation is inseparable from the logic of disarmament. Hence the axiom of non-proliferation: as long as any one country has them, others, including terrorist groups, will try their best (or worst) to get them. The pursuit of nuclear non-proliferation is doomed without an accompanying duty to disarm.

The High-Level Panel's prescriptions focus on four layers:

- demand reduction, including restarting nuclear disarmament by the NWS, de-alerting of strategic nuclear weapons, and explicit pledges by the Security Council to take collective action if a non-NWS is attacked by nuclear weapons;
- supply-side restrictions, including recognition of the IAEA's Model Additional Protocol as the international gold standard, the IAEA acting as the guarantor for the supply of fissile material to civilian nuclear users, a voluntary moratorium on the construction of any further enrichment or reprocessing facilities, the conversion of highly enriched uranium research reactors to proliferation-resistant reactors, and the prompt negotiation of a fissile material cut-off treaty;
- enhanced enforcement, including biannual reporting to the UNSC by the directors-general of the IAEA and OPCW; and
- improved public health defences, especially against biochemical warfare.

But, at a time when so much world attention is focused on the subject, the panel failed to grasp the opportunity to upgrade the UN's Department of Disarmament Affairs from a poor relation (in human and financial resources) to one of the major departments in the UN Secretariat. Nor does it make with sufficient force and clarity the link between the possession of nuclear weapons by some and the attractiveness of the nuclear option to others. As the foreign ministers of the New Agenda

---

[52] *Report of the Canberra Commission on the Elimination of Nuclear Weapons* (Canberra: Department of Foreign Affairs and Trade, 1996), pp. 18–22.

Coalition noted, that which does not exist cannot proliferate.[53] This is best illustrated by the conceptual fudge in asking Middle Eastern and South Asian countries to ratify the CTBT and negotiate regional nuclear-weapons-free zones.[54] Should India, Pakistan and Israel do so as nuclear-weapons-states? If so, does this not formalise their nuclear status outside the NPT, and also, why not make the same call to the other five nuclear powers? If not, w(h)ither realism?

The Secretary-General's report is clear in affirming that 'Progress in both disarmament and non-proliferation is essential and neither should be held hostage to the other.' Although some might read the second half of the sentence as an alibi for postponing disarmament, Annan goes on to argue that the unique status of the NWS 'also entails a unique responsibility', and they must do more, including further and irreversible reductions in non-strategic nuclear arsenals, reaffirmation of negative security assurances, swift negotiation of a fissile materials cut-off treaty and the maintenance of the moratorium on nuclear testing until the entry into force of the CTBT. He strongly urged states to agree on these measures at the 2005 NPT Review Conference. On the non-proliferation side, he urged a strengthening of the IAEA verification machinery through universal adoption of the Model Additional Protocol and the creation of incentives for states to forgo uranium enrichment and plutonium separation capacities, with the IAEA to act as a guarantor for the supply of fissile material to civilian nuclear users at market rates.[55]

In the event, the NPT Review Conference in May 2005 ended in complete collapse. The first half of the conference was dogged by procedural wrangling, the second half was equally rancorous, and the exercise ended in acrimony and recriminations over where the primary blame lay for the lost opportunity to bolster the NPT. Washington, which has historically led international efforts to reinforce the NPT regime, faulted the international community, yet again, for failure to confront the reality of the threat of proliferation by countries like Iran and North Korea. It will likely retreat even more strongly into extra-UN multilateral efforts like the PSI in which more than sixty countries are cooperating on monitoring and, if necessary, interdicting the illegal

---

[53] Celso Amorim et al., 'What Does Not Exist Cannot Proliferate', *IHT*, 2 May 2005.
[54] *A More Secure World*, para. 124.
[55] Annan, *In Larger Freedom*, paras. 97–100. See also Mohamed El Baradei, 'Seven Steps to Raise World Security', *Financial Times*, 2 February 2005.

trade in nuclear materials. Arms control advocates countered that the
US delegation had come intent on focusing on the proliferation side of
the equation and was totally intransigent with regard to previously
agreed-to commitments on arms control and disarmament measures
by the existing nuclear powers. In an echo of communist systems, the
information booklet produced by the US government during the conference blanked out milestones no longer popular with the current
administration, including the 1996 CTBT and the 2000 NPT Review
Conference. Joseph Cirincione commented that 'official disdain for
these agreements seems to have turned into denial that they existed'.[56]
It will be interesting to see if the failure of the Review Conference is
offered as vindication of the line that Washington cannot depend for its
security on multilateral approaches and instruments that cannot produce any final document. The September 2005 summit similarly failed to
come to any agreement on non-proliferation and disarmament, a failure
described as 'inexcusable' and 'a disgrace' by Kofi Annan and blamed on
'posturing' getting in the way of results.[57]

Proliferation threats are deeply politicised. The UN's strengths and
assets in arms control and disarmament are research, advocacy, norm-
building and networking. It has established procedures and forums for
sustaining annual debates and discourses, provides a rare channel for
non-nuclear countries to network with one another and exert pressure
on the nuclear holdouts, tries to coordinate global regimes and regional
initiatives, and undertakes analytical, empirical and problem-solving
research. The organisation's weaknesses are antiquated procedures that
are easily captured by holdouts and recalcitrants to block any initiative,
meagre resources devoted to what is said to be among the gravest threats
to international security, and the most powerful enforcers of peace and
security being the worst offenders in terms of military arsenals and sales.
Some senior diplomats blamed the 2005 summit's failure to tackle the
nuclear threat effectively on Washington. The Bush administration's
refusal to countenance any form of disarmament blocked attempts to
adopt measures that would prevent regimes seeking to develop a nuclear

---

[56] 'US "rewrites history" of arms-control deals in conference brochure', *Japan Times*, 26
May 2005.
[57] William M. Reilly, 'Analysis: The UN's Document', United Press International, 14 September 2005, http://about.upi.com/products/upi_scitech/UPI-20050914-052229-8545R.

capability. One diplomat remarked that Washington refused to accept the 'logical premise' that it must engage in disarmament if it wants to discourage a 'new nuclear arms race'. Annan's chief of staff Mark Malloch-Brown noted that more countries are bumping against the nuclear weapons ceiling at the same time as the world energy crisis is encouraging a move to nuclear energy.[58]

---

[58] Mark Townsend, 'Summit Failure Blamed on US', *Observer* (London), 18 September 2005.

8

International terrorism

On 11 September 2001 (9/11), global terrorism struck at the symbolic headquarters of global power and globalisation. This was followed over the next three years by equally horrific terrorist outrages in Bali, Madrid and Beslan. Iraq saw more terrorist attacks than anywhere else in 2004–5, with large-scale car bombings the preferred modus operandi but also the kidnapping and beheading of foreigners. All these examples confirm that terrorism is indeed 'an assault on the principles of law, order, human rights and peaceful settlement of disputes on which the . . . [UN] was founded'.[1]

The problem pre-dates the UN. The League of Nations drafted a Convention for Prevention and Punishment of Terrorism. The twenty-first century was foreshadowed also in efforts by the Czech government to bring national laws into unison in order to cope with 'the use of criminal violence for political ends'.[2] UN interest in terrorism increased in the 1990s with proportionately more attacks being directed at US targets, the rise in the casualty rate per incident, the globalisation of the terrorist networks, the fear of terrorists acquiring and using weapons of mass destruction (WMD) and the role of states as sponsors and support-ers of international terrorism. Sanctions regimes established in response to the rising concern with terrorism were important in stigmatising terrorism as an illegal and criminal activity, highlighting the role of international cooperation in combating the threat and raising the costs to states of supporting terrorism. But they failed to have comparable effects on non-state terrorist actors.[3]

---

[1] United Nations, *Report of the Working Group on the United Nations and Terrorism*, A/57/273 (6 August 2002), Annex 4, para. 11.

[2] Edward C. Luck, 'Another Reluctant Belligerent: The United Nations and the War on Terrorism', in Richard M. Price and Mark W. Zacher, eds., *The United Nations and Global Security* (New York: Palgrave Macmillan, 2004), pp. 96–7.

[3] Chantal de Jonge Oudraat, 'The Role of the Security Council', in Jane Boulden and Thomas G. Weiss, eds., *Terrorism and the UN: Before and After September 11* (Bloomington: Indiana University Press, 2004), pp. 151–8.

Yet studies on the UN and the problem of terrorism are sparse. On the one hand, the problem of terrorism has been peripheral to most UN analysts; on the other, the organisation has been peripheral to most students of terrorism. In this chapter, I will first discuss the emotional impact of 9/11, followed by an outline of the broad framework within which the international community should address the threat of international terrorism, and then look at a mixed-strategy approach that can combine being tough on the terrorists with being tough on the causes of terrorism and in defending the values of human rights, civil liberties and the rule of law. The UN role in these will draw on its functions as font, forum and funnel.

9/11 and the 'war on terror'

The tragedy of 9/11 inflicted on the American body politic a pain that is yet to ease and aroused an anger not easily appeased. In their insular innocence, Americans had embraced the illusion of security behind supposedly impregnable lines of continental defence. The USA, too, had suffered acts of terror even before 9/11 – but not as a daily fear, an everyday reality, a way of life that had become commonplace in so many other countries. No one, anywhere, had suffered terrorist carnage on such a devastating, mind-numbing scale. The world grieved with America, understood its pain, shared its anger and supported the ensuing 'war on terrorism' – at least until the Iraq War. By 2004 the fates of Afghanistan, Iraq and the broader 'war on terror' had become interlocked.[4]

The rhetoric of 'war' is fundamentally misleading. No state is the target of military defeat, there are no uniformed soldiers to fight, no territory to invade and conquer, no clear defining point that will mark victory. Coral Bell draws some interesting parallels between the Cold War and the war on terrorism. Both were hegemonial wars, about the order of power in the world. Both were ideological, about the norms on which societies should be ordered, and transcendental, with the whole world as the battle-space, albeit with some areas being more vital and vulnerable than others. Both had two military campaigns: Korea and Vietnam, and Afghanistan and Iraq. In both cases the first campaign was defensive and necessary, the second wars of choice in which the enemy chose insurgency over set-piece battles. Of course, the Cold War was a conflict

---

[4] See Amin Saikal, 'Struggle for the Global Soul', *The World Today* 60 (August/September 2004), pp. 7–10.

between states ranged against one another in two heavily militarised alliances, while the war on terrorism is between the society of states as a whole and a worldwide but loosely connected group of terrorist cells using the tactic of asymmetric warfare. And the guerrilla warfare in Vietnam was rural, while in Iraq it is urban.[5]

Osama bin Laden's evil genius was to fuse the fervour of religious schools (madrassas), the rallying power of the call to holy war (jihad), the cult of martyrdom through suicide (shahid), the reach of modern technology and the march of globalisation into the new phenomenon of global terrorism.[6] Globalisation has empowered terrorist organisations by democratising information and telecommunications technologies, linking like-hating groups and making it much easier to set up support structures among far-flung diasporas. Al Qaeda is a good example of how globalisation has helped transnational networks of 'uncivil society' to disseminate propaganda, raise and move funds and weapons and recruit and train terrorists with the world as their stage.

What did the terrorists want? To inflict a searing wound on the American psyche, avenge a litany of real and imagined historic wrongs and grievances of the Arab and pan-Islamic community and achieve such specific targets as the ouster of US forces from the sacred soil of Saudi Arabia and of the Jews from Palestine. But those who seek to return Islam to the purity of its fundamental tenets wish also to divide the West from the Arab-Islamic world, provoke disproportionate and ruthless retaliation that will create a new generation of radicalised terrorists and destroy the values of freedom, secularism, tolerance and the rule of law. They want to polarise the world into hard divisions, break harmony into strife and replace the community of civilised countries with the flames of hatred between communities.

Worst-case scenarios see terrorists using nuclear or radiological weapons to kill hundreds of thousands of people.[7] In its annual report to Congress for 2004, the Central Intelligence Agency (CIA) warned that al Qaeda is fully capable of building a radiological 'dirty' bomb targeting

---

[5] Coral Bell, 'Power and World Order', in Ramesh Thakur, Edward Newman and John Tirman, eds., *Multilateralism under Challenge? Power, International Order, and Structural Change* (Tokyo: United Nations University Press, forthcoming).

[6] Not all terrorist groups are global in their orientation and scope; the Liberation Tigers of Tamil Eelam (LTTE) are not al Qaeda.

[7] For an assessment, see Robin Frost, 'Nuclear Terrorism Post-9/11: Assessing the Risks', *Global Society: Journal of Interdisciplinary International Relations* 18:4 (October 2004), pp. 397–422.

the USA and others, and has 'crude procedures' for producing chemical weapons using mustard, sarin, VX and cyanide. The danger of terrorists using chemical, biological, radiological and nuclear materials 'remained high'.[8] Similarly, an Aspen study group concluded that the danger of nuclear terrorism is greater than most people realise, and that the US government has not prepared adequately for it.[9]

We cannot be confident that an attack combining the sophistication and ruthlessness of 9/11 with the use of nuclear weapons will not happen. As far as we know, however, no terrorist group has the competence to build nuclear weapons. An element of scepticism is warranted about the capacity of non-state actors to manufacture nuclear weapons undetected by the intelligence agencies of the advanced countries. Nor is there any evidence so far to suggest that nuclear weapons have been transferred to terrorist organisations. The most realistic concern is that al Qaeda or a related group could detonate a 'dirty bomb' (a conventional explosive wrapped in radioactive material) that could spray radioactive fallout across a major city. While the death and devastation caused by it would be significantly less than that of a nuclear bomb, it would cause some casualties and radiation sickness, producing mass panic, making it a weapon of mass disruption more than destruction.

Bioterrorism may be more likely as pathogens and toxins can be made easily and clandestinely in a small area and can cause widespread death and panic if dispersed in sufficient quantities. The absence of effective verification measures and an organisation to implement the Biological Weapons Convention are serious loopholes. By contrast, the state-of-the-art verification provisions of the Chemical Weapons Convention and the Organisation for the Prohibition of Chemical Weapons (OPCW) at The Hague as the implementing arm of the convention are effective bulwarks against terrorists using chemical weapons.[10]

Fashioning a global response

How can we marry the international legitimacy of the UN to the global reach and power of the USA? The struggle against terrorism is one from

---

[8] *Japan Times*, 25 November 2004.
[9] Nicholas D. Kristof, 'An American Hiroshima is All Too Likely', *International Herald Tribune (IHT)*, 12 August 2004.
[10] See Ramesh Thakur and Ere Haru, eds., *The Chemical Weapons Convention: Implementation Challenges and Opportunities* (Tokyo: United Nations University Press, forthcoming).

which the USA can neither stay disengaged nor win on its own, nor one that can be won without full American engagement. It spans the full range of responses, from social and economic to political and security, and engages every level of government. A combination of factors determines whether terrorist organisations will thrive, be defeated or simply fade away. They include their emotional/political appeal, organisational efficiency, access to resources and the extent of their support base. The wise strategy has to be a multilayered one that addresses grievances and counteracts the causes of individual and group humiliation and indignity. The object is not to destroy the motivation of every individual terrorist but to neutralise support for terrorists in the communities in which they live and generate the will and capacity to act against them by relevant authorities.

The line between global terrorism and organised crime has become increasingly blurred. Terrorism is a problem to be tackled mainly by law-enforcement agencies, in cooperation with military forces; its magnitude can be brought down to 'tolerable' levels, but it can never be totally 'defeated', just as we cannot have an absolutely crime-free society; and it is part of the growing trend towards the lowered salience of the state in the new security agenda that emphasises human as well as national security.

The global coalition to combat threats to international security is already in place. We call it the United Nations. The General Assembly (GA) has played the dual role of developing a normative framework on terrorism and encouraging cooperative action among states. While the UN Security Council (UNSC) might concentrate on preventing acts of terrorism through cooperation between the security, law enforcement and border control authorities, the GA can mould the global response to terrorism through its power of budgetary allocations.[11] The international civil and maritime organisations are addressing threats to the world's air and shipping traffic respectively, the International Atomic Energy Agency (IAEA) and the OPCW seek to ensure compliance with chemical and nuclear weapons treaties, the World Health Organisation (WHO) is preparing defences against terrorist attacks using biochemical weapons, and the Terrorism Prevention Branch of the UN Office on Drugs and Crime provides legislative assistance to many countries in connection

---

[11] See M. J. Petersen, 'Using the General Assembly', in Boulden and Weiss, eds., *Terrorism and the UN*, pp. 173–97.

with the ratification and implementation of anti-terrorism conventions and UNSC resolutions.

There was a fresh opportunity to rededicate the terms of US engagement with the international community in protecting the world from deadly new threats immune to conventional tools of statecraft. That is why the world joined forces with Americans to rid succeeding generations of the scourge of terrorism – not blinded by hatred and a lust for revenge, nor driven by the calculus of geopolitical interests, but ennobled by the vision of a just order and empowered by the majesty of laws. Although the monuments to American power and prosperity were shaken to their foundations on 9/11, the foundation of a civilised discourse among the family of nations must not be destroyed. Responses that are crafted must be carefully thought out and their consequences fully thought through, with a balance between retaliatory countermeasures and long-term resolution. We must also bear in mind the lessons of history, including insurgency movements against colonial empires. The rhetoric and metaphors of frontier justice from the time of the Wild West or the Crusades roused domestic fervour but risked fracturing the fragile international coalition. Fortunately, such language was soon eschewed. An order that is worth protecting and defending must rest on the principles of justice, equity and law that are embedded in universal institutions. The nation of laws must turn its power to the task of building a world ruled by law.[12]

The threat of international terrorism has been addressed internationally both within the framework of international law and specific UN resolutions and measures. In the *Corfu Channel Case* in 1949 the International Court of Justice (ICJ) affirmed 'every State's obligation not to allow knowingly its territory to be used for acts contrary to the rights of other States'.[13] There are thirteen global, seven regional and three related global treaties for combating terrorism.[14] Nevertheless, until the 1970s terrorism in UN circles was viewed largely as a local phenomenon. As the frequency, violence and reach of terrorist incidents began to

---

[12] For a fuller discussion, see Nico Schrijver, 'September 11 and the Challenges to International Law', in Boulden and Weiss, eds., *Terrorism and the UN*, pp. 55–73.

[13] Milan Sahović and William W. Bishop, 'The Authority of the State: Its Range with Respect to Persons and Places', in Max Sørensen, ed., *Manual of Public International Law* (London: Macmillan, 1968), p. 316.

[14] V. S. Mani, 'ISAF in Afghanistan: A Study in Recuperation after a "Humanitarian Surgery"', paper prepared for a UN University and Chuo University workshop, Hakone, 9–11 March 2005.

expand, the GA seemed to be as interested in understanding and ration-
alising terrorism as in suppressing it, while the UNSC was more exercised
by the counter-terrorism tactics of Israel and the USA than by the acts of
terrorism themselves.[15] Many of the traditional support constituencies of
the UN are instinctively suspicious of actions to counter terrorism.
Human rights groups want their pet cause factored in; humanitarian
actors and arms control activists are worried about rollbacks to international humanitarian law and disarmament; and many developmental-
ists want to limit the diversion of resources from development and the
'root causes' of terrorism like poverty and inequality.

The day after 9/11, both the UNSC and the GA adopted resolutions
strongly condemning the acts of terrorism and urging all states to cooperate to bring the perpetrators, organisers and sponsors of 9/11 to justice.
Resolution 1368 (12 September 2001) was the first to incorporate acts
against terrorism into the right of self-defence. In doing so the UNSC
effectively sidelined itself from oversight of the measures taken in response. Resolution 1373 (28 September 2001), adopted under chapter 7
of the Charter, imposed significant requirements on member states within
their domestic jurisdictions and expanded the Council's oversight role in
relation to them. 'This posed a remarkable dichotomy. The Security
Council chooses to exercise no control or oversight on the use of military
force in response to terrorism but is vigilant and arguably intrusive when
it comes to dealing with terrorism through national mechanisms and
controls.' Moreover, because neither 'self-defence' nor 'terrorism' is defined or self-explanatory, the result 'compounds the [unlimited] expan-
siveness of the mandate'.[16] The most egregious example of the subversion
of the UNSC to serve propaganda goals came after the 2004 Madrid
bombings when the Council strongly condemned the attacks 'perpetrated
by the terrorist group ETA' (Resolution 1530, 11 March 2004). Many
suspected at the time of the attack itself that Islamic groups might have
perpetrated the outrage, and this was soon confirmed. The UNSC resolution had nothing to do with fighting terrorism and everything to do
with trying to help an ally win an election.

On 13 April 2005, after seven years of negotiations, the GA unanimously adopted the International Convention for the Suppression
of Acts of Nuclear Terrorism. The thirteenth UN convention against

---

[15] Luck, 'Another Reluctant Belligerent', p. 98.
[16] Jane Boulden and Thomas G. Weiss, 'Whither Terrorism and the United Nations?', in
Boulden and Weiss, eds., *Terrorism and the UN*, pp. 11–12.

terrorism, which opened for signature on 14 September 2005 and will enter into force one month after the twenty-second ratification, makes it a crime to possess or demand any radioactive material or device with the aim of causing death or serious injury or substantial damage to property. It calls on states to adopt national laws to make these acts criminal and to provide for appropriate penalties for those convicted of such acts. Between them, the thirteen global treaties define, proscribe and punish such individual categories of terrorism as hijacking, piracy, hostage taking, bombing civilians, procuring nuclear materials, and financing terrorist activities. But they do not address the totality of terrorist acts within one comprehensive normative or institutional framework.

The *final* line of defence against international terrorism is preventive national measures in countries that are the targets of attack. This includes robust counter-terrorism intelligence and surveillance efforts by the law enforcement, national security and border control, and financial regulatory and surveillance agencies. There is not much scope for UN involvement here, although the political cover of the UN can make programmes of bilateral technical assistance more palatable to the domestic constituency. Security experts will continue to scrutinise and rectify procedural and organisational flaws that permitted the planes to be hijacked on 9/11 and the intelligence failures that enabled it all to be plotted without detection. But in the end there can be no guaranteed security against suicide terrorists who know no limits to their audacity, imagination and inhumanity.[17]

Efforts to build effective defences against international terrorism should focus *first* on countries that harbour or host individuals and groups advocating, financing, arming and otherwise supporting international terrorism. This is where the export of terror can be stopped or contained most cost-effectively. This requires both capacity-building in countries that lack institutional resilience in their security sectors to tackle terrorist cells in their midst; and mustering political will in other countries that have the capacity but lack the determination to root out cells from their midst. Fragile states with frail institutions are the soft underbelly for

---

[17] For some recent books on the phenomenon of suicide bombing, see Joyce M. Davis, *Martyrs: Innocence, Vengeance and Despair in the Middle East* (London: Palgrave Macmillan, 2003); Aharon Farkash, *The Shahids: Islam and Suicide Attacks* (Piscataway, NJ: Transaction, 2004); Christoph Reuter, *My Life is a Weapon: A Modern History of Suicide Bombing* (Princeton: Princeton University Press, 2004); and Barbara Victor, *Army of Roses: Inside the World of Palestinian Suicide Bombers* (New York: Rodale Books, 2003).

global terrorism. Terrorists take advantage of porous borders, weak and corrupt law-enforcement forces and limp judicial systems.

An appropriate mix of carrots and sticks is required. We must build the security capacity of countries fighting to liquidate terrorist cells. This means, in effect, engagement with narrowcast 'nation-building' in which the UN has long experience, institutional expertise and international legitimacy. A related task is to persuade, coax or coerce regimes that are tolerant of terrorist cells to confront the menace instead. There must also be bilateral and multilateral regimes for regulating and controlling the in-border production and storage, and the cross-border transfer, of terrorism-related materials, skills and technology. This would be best accomplished with concerted encouragement and pressure from bilaterally relevant actors *and* the United Nations.

Root causes

'While poverty and denial of human rights may not be said to "cause" civil war, terrorism or organised crime, they all greatly increase the risk of instability and violence.'[18] The controversy over root causes highlights the tension between tackling today's priorities, better done outside the UN framework, and adopting a holistic approach, best done through the UN. To describe terrorism as an *understandable* response does not make it into a *legitimate* response. Explanation is not justification; to try to understand is not to seek to condone, let alone to endorse. But because the root cause argument is deeply connected to the global fault lines on terrorism, it has been summarily dismissed as implying that the USA had provoked or somehow deserved 9/11. In its single-minded focus on retributive justice, Washington lost interest in redistributive justice. The underlying or root causes of terrorism can be grouped into five categories: lack of democratic institutions and practices, political freedoms and civil liberties; group grievance based in collective injustice; intractable conflicts; poverty; and inter-civilisation suspicions.

Democracy

The campaign against terrorism must be anchored in the norms of accountability, the rule of law and non-derogation of core human rights

---

[18] Kofi A. Annan, *In Larger Freedom: Towards Development, Security and Human Rights for All*. Report of the Secretary-General (New York: UN, document A/59/2005, 21 March 2005), para. 16.

and civil liberties, including life, liberty and due process. Democracy legitimises the struggle for power; its denial drives dissent underground.[19] Good governance and the rule of law constrain capricious behaviour and the arbitrary exercise of power by rulers, mediate citizen–state relations and absorb the strains and stresses of political contestation. Terrorism flourishes amidst frustration with repressive, inept, unresponsive and dynastic regimes that spawn angry and twisted young men, and sometimes even women, taking recourse to lethal violence.[20] Sometimes the house of worship has been the only alternative rallying point in autocratic regimes. The gap between the lofty, soaring rhetoric of liberty and freedom in President George W. Bush's second inauguration speech and the reality of his administration's ties to authoritarian regimes in Asia and the Middle East was particularly pronounced. In Pakistan, Washington has reverted to its familiar policy of supporting a general in power as the best bulwark against the growth of Islamic extremism in a nuclear state.[21]

Terrorism has an impact on human rights in three ways. First, it is an extreme denial of the most basic human right, namely to life, and it creates an environment in which people cannot live in freedom from fear and enjoy their other rights. Second, the threat of terrorism can be used by governments to enact laws that strip away many civil liberties and political freedoms. One simple but popular technique is to reverse the burden of proof: those accused of terrorist activities, sympathies or even guilt by association on the basis of accusations by anonymous people are to be presumed to be guilty until they can prove their innocence of unspecified charges. And third, without necessarily amending laws or enacting new ones, governments can use the need to fight terrorism as an alibi to stifle dissent and criticism and imprison or threaten domestic opponents.

The UN has been pursuing a 'whole-of-system' approach to the promotion of democracy, good governance, human rights and the rule of law. It is the single best font for the authoritative promulgation of the international rule of law and the single best forum for building global

---

[19] 'Those who make peaceful revolutions impossible make violent revolutions inevitable'; Mai Yamani, 'Saudi Arabia Pushing Sand against Tide', *Japan Times*, 29 May 2005.

[20] Thus a headline after the May 2005 uprising in Uzbekistan: Jeremy Page, 'Uzbek Corruption and Poverty Help Islamist Message to Spread', *Daily Yomiuri* (reprint from *The Times* of London), 29 May 2005.

[21] See Larry Pressler, 'Dissing Democracy in Asia', *New York Times*, 21 March 2005, and Alfred Stepan and Aqil Shah, 'Pakistan's Real Bulwark', *Washington Post*, 5 May 2004.

respect for democracy and good governance. Kofi Annan affirms the right of peoples 'to choose how they are ruled, and who rules them', notes that the UN gave support to elections in more than twenty countries 'in the last year alone' and laments that 'The United Nations does more than any other single organization to promote and strengthen democratic institutions and practices around the world, but this fact is little known.'[22]

Americans, who rightly reject moral equivalence between their own 'virtuous' power and their 'evil' enemies, should reflect on their own propensity to political ambivalence between perpetrators of terrorism and efforts of legitimate governments to maintain national security and assure public safety. Governments that have been at the receiving end of moral and political judgement about robust responses to violent threats posed to their authority and order from armed dissidents are entitled to a more mature understanding forged in the crucible of shared suffering. But the struggle against terrorism 'must not take place at the expense of the fundamental freedoms and the basic dignity of individuals. Success in defeating terrorism can come only if we remain true to those values which terrorists eschew.'[23] In resorting to the lesser evil of curtailing liberties and using violence in order to defeat terrorism, we must be careful not to succumb to the greater evil of destroying the very values for which democracies stand.[24] Governments must justify all restrictive measures publicly, submit them to judicial review and circumscribe them with sunset clauses to guard against the temporary becoming permanent. Safeguards are especially important because history suggests that most people, even in the mature democracies, privilege the security of the majority over the harm done to minorities who are deprived of their rights in the name of national security.

After 9/11, American priorities shifted to subordinate human rights to victory in the 'war' against terrorism. The president declared that detainees in the war on terror fell outside the Geneva Conventions as a deliberate tactic for reducing chances of successful claims against the government in the courts of the land. The defence department adopted

---

[22] Annan, *In Larger Freedom*, paras. 148–51. For a study of the UN's role, see Edward Newman and Roland Rich, eds., *The UN Role in Promoting Democracy: Between Ideals and Reality* (Tokyo: United Nations University Press, 2004).

[23] Kofi A. Annan, *Report of the Secretary-General on the Work of the Organization* (New York: UN, 2004, document A/59/1), para. 77.

[24] Michael Ignatieff, *The Lesser Evil: Political Ethics in an Age of Terror* (Princeton: Princeton University Press, 2004).

stress and duress techniques that were both in violation of international humanitarian law and questionable in their effects. As the conditions of detention of suspected foreign terrorists in American prisons became widely known in the Muslim world, they contributed to a hardening of the jihad through shahid, for 'death is preferable to Guantánamo Bay'.[25]

Two separate issues became merged in the public debate: the relevant legal regime that should apply to prisoners in this particular war, and abuses in the actual treatment of the prisoners. The designation of prisoners as 'enemy combatants' and their confinement and treatment at Guantánamo Bay in Cuba raised serious questions about the US commitment to fair trials and impartial justice. The abused accounted for a minority of prisoners held by the USA but, like the Gulags in the Soviet system, they were integral to the war: they provided the standard of terror by which the good behaviour of the rest would be judged and enforced.[26] In a validation of Hannah Arendt's thesis of the banality of evil, ordinary Americans went about their daily business while all this was being done in their name. Even many other democracies, including Australia, Canada and the UK, joined the USA in shifting the balance of laws and administrative practices towards state security. And there developed also the distasteful practice of 'rendition to torture', sending prisoners to their home or third countries precisely because the latter are known to practise torture as part of their interrogation routine.

President Bush's response to 9/11 was to elevate terrorism from a tactic or a method into a transcendental conflict that was at once simpler yet more fundamental: an epic struggle of historic proportions between the greatest force for good on earth, responding to a calling from beyond the stars against enemies bent on destroying it. Neutrality was not an option. But this reinterpretation of 9/11 in Manichean terms of good and evil that lumped the jihadists of al Qaeda with the terrorists of Hamas, Hizbullah and Chechnya also allowed many other governments to relabel their domestic difficulties as part of the global war on terror and to justify their own version of 'a might-is-right approach to governance'.[27] One of the worst examples of such an approach took place in Macedonia. In March 2002, the nationalist government, recovering from a five-month insurrection by Muslim Albanians, ordered a police chief to find migrants who could fit the description of Islamic terrorists. A group

---

[25] Nasra Hassan, 'Al-Qaeda's Understudy', *Atlantic Monthly* (June 2004), p. 44.
[26] See Sidney Blumentahl, 'This is the New Gulag', *Guardian*, 6 May 2004.
[27] Roger Cohen, 'A Global War: Many Fronts, Little Unity', *New York Times*, 5 September 2004.

of six Pakistani and one Indian migrants was ambushed, kidnapped, killed by the security forces and photographed with handguns stuck in waistbands, so that the government could claim a victory against Mujahideen terrorists in order to win American sympathy and support. This came to light two years later when a new government charged the former interior minister and six security officers with murder in connection with the incident.[28]

To defeat the terrorists, it is absolutely critical that the symbolism of America – the home of the free and the land of the brave, yes, but also the bastion of liberty, freedom, equality between citizens and rulers, democracy and a nation of laws – be kept alive. 'How can President Bush preach to the world about democracy, about transparency, about the rule of law, and at the same time disregard national and international law at will? What message can Vladimir Putin be hearing? Or the dictators in Beijing? Or the mullahs in Tehran?'[29] The dream of a world ruled by law is a shared vision. As Benjamin Franklin, one of the fathers of American independence, said, those who would sacrifice essential liberty to temporary safety deserve neither liberty nor safety.

The robustness and resilience of the US commitment to human rights norms and values will be judged in the final analysis not by the breaches in the aftermath of 9/11, but by the reversal and attenuation of the breaches through domestic judicial and political processes as well as the pressures of civil society. In July 2004 the US Supreme Court ruled that US courts do have jurisdiction to consider challenges to the legality of the detention of foreign nationals captured abroad and interned at Guantánamo Bay, and that the denial of *habeas corpus* is illegal: the first significant breach of Guantánamo's status as a legal black hole.

Just as America is a nation of laws that find expression in institutions, so Americans should work to construct a world of laws functioning through international institutions. The UN role consists of norm-setting, codification, drafting and monitoring of multilateral agreements and instruments: 'the UN can and does serve as the institutional vehicle through which international norms are codified into international agreements'.[30] UNSC Resolution 1456 (20 January 2003) obligates states to

---

[28] 'Killings "Staged to Win US Support"', *Guardian*, 1 May 2004; 'Macedonian Ex-Minister Charged with Murder', *Daily Yomiuri*, 2 May 2004.
[29] Eugene Robinson, 'Torture Whitewash', *Washington Post*, 3 May 2005.
[30] Christopher C. Joyner, 'The United Nations and Terrorism: Rethinking Legal Tension between National Security, Human Rights, and Civil Liberties', *International Studies Perspectives* 5 (2004), pp. 241–2.

ensure that counter-terrorism measures comply with international human rights, refugees and international humanitarian law obligations. Annan has urged all countries to create special rapporteurs who would report to the Human Rights Commission on the compatibility of counter-terrorism measures with international human rights laws.[31] The UN can provide technical assistance in drafting model legislation. The Office of the High Commissioner for Human Rights has published advice on how the war against terrorism can be balanced with human rights standards and norms.[32]

Group grievance

Second, grievance rooted in collective injustice against ethnic and religious groups generates anger and armed resistance when the weaker resort to their comparative advantages in 'asymmetric warfare'. Often the driving force behind fanatic hatred is individual despair born of collective humiliation. If relations are based purely on power, with no concession to justice and equity, then peace and stability rest on insecure foundations, on the temporary inability of the revisionists to challenge the entrenched status quo, and not on their acceptance of the status quo as the legitimate order. It would be as futile for Indians to deny that the quality of governance in Kashmir has often been strained as for Americans to deny their past propensity to back repressive regimes throughout the world so long as they were 'our bastards': 'the anger of young Muslims results primarily from revulsion at their corrupt leaders, and the subservience of these rulers to the United States'.[33] Victims – Chechnyans, Kashmiris, Palestinians, Tamils – cannot be made to give up their right of resistance.

Security from the fear of terrorism is indivisible. Washington must not fall into the trap of converting terror on America into terror against the world, but terrorist attacks elsewhere are merely local problems to be solved by the countries concerned; condoning or tolerating one lot while isolating and liquidating another. Kishore Mahbubani, Singapore's

---

[31] Annan, *In Larger Freedom*, para. 94.

[32] *Digest of Jurisprudence of the UN and Regional Organizations on the Protection of Human Rights While Countering Terrorism* (Geneva: Office of the High Commissioner for Human Rights, July 2003).

[33] Mai Yamani, 'Alienated Muslims Build Internet Shrine', *Australian Financial Review*, 30 June 2004.

ambassador to the UN during its two-year term on the UNSC, notes that while the New York City Fire Department is obligated to respond to every fire, whether in a Park Avenue penthouse or a public housing complex in the South Bronx, the UNSC picks and chooses which emergencies to respond to on the basis of geopolitics and the national interests of its most important members.[34] How many of today's radical extremists, embracing terror against a host of countries, are yesterday's 'freedom fighters' trained and financed by the West as jihadis against the former enemy? Muslims from all over the world flocked to the Afghan resistance against Soviet occupation, received CIA training in, and arms and explosives for, guerrilla fighting, became battle hardened and acquired pride, power and comradeship in the victorious struggle. After the expulsion of the Soviets, Afghan veterans fanned out to every struggle involving Islamic communities.

The USA is not the only culprit; there are many other examples of 'blowback'. Indira Gandhi paid with her life for having tried to harness Sikh religious nationalism to her politics of divide-and-rule in the Punjab; Rajiv Gandhi was consumed by Tamil terrorism exported from Sri Lanka, outposts of which had been tolerated on Indian soil by his government. President Pervez Musharraf knows the feeling of becoming the target of the very monsters of terrorism that in the past one may have created or tolerated. Rather than feeding the fires of group grievance across one another's borders, nations would be better advised to cooperate in dousing the flames and containing the common threat.

Fanaticism feeds on grievance, and grievance is nurtured by deeply felt injustice. The USA becomes the focus of grievance if its arms and policies are seen to be propping up occupying or brutalising forces.[35] Of all the so-called 'root causes', the most proximate is the sense of humiliation of the collective Arab identity.[36] Through 'ignorance and negligence' in the way it dismissed world opinion before the war and managed the aftermath of the war in Iraq itself, 'Even those Iraqis who saw Americans as liberators during the first heady days after Saddam Hussein was ousted from power now see America as an ignorant, brutal, occupying power.'

[34] At a seminar on terrorism organised by Norway and the International Peace Academy in New York, 22 September 2003; William G. O'Neill, *Fighting Terrorism for Humanity*. Conference Report (New York: IPA), p. 7.

[35] To cite just one example: 'Planner of Attacks was Motivated by US Support for Israel', *Japan Times*, 24 July 2004.

[36] See Jessica Stern, *Terror in the Name of God: Why Religious Militants Kill* (St. Paul: Ecco, 2003).

The occupation by US tanks and soldiers of Baghdad, the capital of the Islamic world during the golden age of their civilisation, is deeply humiliating. For young Muslims, 'it is better to carry arms and defend their religion with pride and dignity than to submit to this humiliation.'[37]

Like the famous photo of the young girl on fire running naked to escape the horror of napalm in the Vietnam War, the trophy photographs emerging from the Abu Ghraib prison (and the subsequent video clip of the marine killing a wounded and unarmed prisoner during the assault on Fallujah) will be the icons defining the Iraq War. They managed to combine everything that is most depraved in victors by inflicting the worst possible humiliations and indignity in the Arab world.[38] America's standing among the Muslim people and its long-term position in Asia suffered deleterious consequences, as attested to by the continuing arc of instability in Afghanistan, Pakistan, Iraq and Saudi Arabia.[39]

Terror is the tactic of choice of those who harbour the sense of having been wronged, are too weak to do anything about it through conventional means and are motivated to seek vengeance by other means. Terrorism is the attempt to use indiscriminate violence to change politics. Therefore the defeat of terrorism can never be simply a law enforcement problem, but must inject the political calculus into the centre of debates over tactics and strategy. A refusal to negotiate with terrorists should not be confused with fear of negotiating. Those resorting to the illegitimate tactic of terrorism can be isolated, but their goals may still be worth supporting and may even be necessary to support for the sake of separating the perpetrators from their sympathisers in the wider community. The British did this successfully in Northern Ireland, the Indians in Punjab. The UN is the ultimate symbol of intergroup relations based on equality, law and justice that temper the raw interplay of power and money. It is the forum of choice for mediating power asymmetries.

Intractable conflicts

Third, long-running conflicts spawn generations of radicalised populations, from Palestine to Kashmir and Sri Lanka. Robert Pape, having

---

[37] Jessica Stern, 'Terrorism's New Mecca', *Globe and Mail* (Toronto), 28 November 2003.

[38] See Mark Danner, 'The Logic of Torture', *New York Review of Books* 51:11 (24 June 2004).

[39] See Ashley J. Tellis, *Assessing America's War on Terror: Confronting Insurgency, Cementing Primacy* (Washington, DC: National Bureau of Asian Research and Carnegie Endowment for International Peace, 2004).

compiled a comprehensive database of every single suicide terrorist attack in the world from 1980 to early 2004, argues that 95 per cent of suicide terrorists aim at compelling military forces to withdraw from the territory that terrorists view as their homeland under foreign occupation.[40] Thus territorial liberation, not religion, is what they have in common, with the leading practitioner of the tactic being the Liberation Tigers of Tamil Eelam (LTTE) in Sri Lanka. Simply allowing conflicts to lie dormant for decades, in the hope that something will come right eventually, is not enough. Al Qaeda is a vast, decentralised and clandestine operation spread across Asia, the Middle East and Africa that has successfully infiltrated and colonised many separatist and independence movements. Its three-part goals, repeated in many messages over several years, are an end to the US military presence in the Middle East, US support for Israeli occupation of Palestinian territories and US support of corrupt and coercive regimes in the Muslim world. The US-led response after 9/11 achieved many successes in efforts to strangle al Qaeda: their bases were destroyed, their finances disrupted and their sponsors isolated from them. Yet from another point of view al Qaeda arguably won the first three years of the war. The Middle East was more violent and less stable, the American military was out of Saudi Arabia, a major new front had been opened in Iraq and the Iraq War had turned out to be a major source of fresh recruitment to the cause.

While the USA will always be the most forceful and sometimes may even be the most welcome mediator and peacemaker, usually the UN forum is more authoritative and more broadly acceptable for conflict resolution efforts. Washington therefore has a vested interest in strengthening both the principle of UN-centred multilateralism and its administrative, technical and financial capacity for conflict resolution.

Poverty

Fourth, terrorism highlights the development–security nexus. No serious analyst postulates a simple and direct causal link between poverty and terrorism. But it can be an incubator of terrorism. A quick and simple review of the countries in which the systematic use of terror by state and non-state groups is commonplace confirms its link with poverty, under-development and lack of democracy. The leaders of terrorist

---

[40] Robert Pape, *Dying to Win: The Strategic Logic of Suicide Terrorism* (New York: Random House, 2005).

actions – like leaders in most walks of life – tend to be affluent and well-educated, but they find ready recruits as foot soldiers among the poor, illiterate and marginalised groups. Alienation, despair and discontent provide fertile grounds to recruit would-be terrorists and maintain a pool of supporters in society at large.

Poverty detracts from the state capacity to provide universal education through the public sector, resulting in thousands of children going to private religious institutions and being schooled in the twin cultures of the Koran and the Kalashnikov. It is hard to imagine Palestine, Pakistan, Afghanistan, Indonesia and the Philippines as long-term major recruiting and training bases and safe havens for terrorism if they were comfortably well-off, middle-class countries. Poverty precludes social insurance and promotes large families as a hedge against hardship in old age. A family with many children without prospects of stable employment and income is tempted to 'donate' one child to the holy cause of the community. Martyrs and their family receive hero worship, honour, social recognition and material assistance, as well as the promise of everlasting glory for the martyr in the next world. In such circumstances, is suicide bombing necessarily such an irrational outcome of a cold and calculating cost-benefit analysis of the relative value of life and death?

Poverty elimination is the UN's biggest goal and challenge. The organisation is dedicated to the task of economic development and the goal of poverty reduction in general and the eradication of extreme poverty in particular. Such a role for the UN is not just accepted by the developing countries: it is demanded by them. The world had signed on to the Millennium Development Goals already before 9/11. The calls to help combat the scourge of poverty have found a more sympathetic and receptive audience after that date. The effort to reach the agreed targets is an inalienable part of the UN's reform agenda.

Clash of or dialogue among civilisations?

Finally, a dialogue among civilisations will help to promote intercultural harmony and defuse hate-based terrorism. Just as there coexist many ways of thinking and many different value systems within the 'West', so are there many who daily honour Islam against the tiny minority who sometimes dishonour it.[41] Individual terrorism should not provoke mass

---

[41] For a poignant cry of anguish from a woman Muslim believer at the hijacking of her faith by extremists responsible for the massacre of schoolchildren in Beslan, Russia, see

intolerance. After 9/11, some sought to resurrect the vacuous and discredited thesis of the clash of civilisations.[42] Islamic terrorists are no
more representative of Islam than any fundamentalist terrorists are of
their broader community: the Irish terrorists of Christianity, or those
who destroyed the Babri Masjid in Ayodhya in 1992 of Hinduism.[43] The
victims of the hijacked planes and the World Trade Center destruction,
along with the rescuers, reflected modern American society in all its
glorious diversity. The best way to honour victims is to recognise our
common humanity and work for peace in and through justice.

The real struggle is likely to be within Islam,[44] not a clash of civilisations between Islam and the rest. And this struggle will be fought most
intensely as a war of ideas. Perceptions of a US or Western crusade
against Islam are likely to alienate many Muslims from the West and
drive them into the arms of the fundamentalists. Instead of viewing
terrorism through the lens of a war between civilisations, we have to
see it as a war *on* civilisation (an assault on values and freedoms we
hold dear), and a war *for* civilisation (the defence of the values and
freedoms that we hold dear). The United Nations is both the symbolic
meeting place of all civilisations and the most readily accepted forum for
promoting and engaging in the dialogue among civilisations.

Conclusion

Defeating international terrorism requires both military and police
action, and nation-building: repairing and stabilising war-torn countries,
establishing the institutions and structures of government and the rule of
law, consolidating civil society, and building markets. The first, spectacular part can be left to the powerful, although even unilateral action needs
an institutional context. The second, less glamorous part underlines the
importance of international agreements, institutions and policing.

Nassrine Azimi, 'Beslan Massacre: The Anguish of a Faithful Muslim', *IHT*, 8 September
2004.

[42] The classic statement of the thesis remains Samuel P. Huntington's *The Clash of Civiliza-
tions and the Remaking of World Order* (New York: Simon and Schuster, 1998).

[43] See Ramesh Thakur, 'Ayodhya and the Politics of India's Secularism: A Double-Standards
Discourse', *Asian Survey* 33 (July 1993), pp. 645–64.

[44] For an analysis of the struggles from within for 'the soul of Islam', as well as relations
between Islam and the West, see Amin Saikal, *Islam and the West: Conflict or Cooperation?*
(London: Palgrave Macmillan, 2003).

The UN role in countering terrorism must necessarily be limited and modest. It is the forum of choice for regime negotiation and norm promotion. It lacks enforcement capacity, but it can promulgate and promote the normative and legal framework of a counter-terrorism regime. It can also be the coordinating forum for counter-terrorism efforts by states, regional organisations and technical agencies like the IAEA. With respect to biological and chemical weapons, the UN could be the central coordinator and clearing house for information, aligning the work of national and functional agencies; and a clearing house for the global stockpiling and distribution of drugs and vaccines in a global crisis.

An urgent task is adopting a universally accepted definition. The Secretary-General's High-Level Panel defined terrorism as 'any action . . . that is intended to cause death or serious bodily harm to civilians or non-combatants, when the purpose of such an act, by its nature or context, is to intimidate a population, or to compel a Government or an international organisation to do or to abstain from doing any act'.[45] The focus on the nature of the acts breaks the unhelpful link with causes and motivations. It affirms that 'terrorism is never an acceptable tactic, even for the most defensible of causes' and therefore 'must be condemned clearly and unequivocally by all'.[46] That the Palestinian people have a just cause and a justified grievance does not mean that blowing up a busload of school children is just: it is an act of terrorism, not a battle in an armed liberation struggle. If the Palestinians resorted to a 'clean' war, given overwhelming Israeli superiority, the Palestinians would lose. But it is equally true that the violation of the civilian immunity principle by suicide bombers has been a political catastrophe for their cause. The proposed definition brings clarity and rigour, removes the ideological edge from the debate and mutes the charges of inconsistency and double standards. Because terrorism is a tactic of deliberately targeting civilians in order to achieve political goals, it always represents a conscious choice of one tactic over others.

Resolution 1373's legislative and reporting requirements imposed uniform obligations on all countries to end any form of support for terrorism and established the Counter-Terrorism Committee (CTC)

---

[45] High-Level Panel on Threats, Challenges and Change, *A More Secure World: Our Shared Responsibility* (New York: UN, A/59/565, December 2004), para. 164.d. What does this definition imply for the doctrines and practice of nuclear deterrence?

[46] Ibid., paras. 157, 161.

made up of all fifteen members of the UNSC to monitor implementation and increase state capacity to combat terrorism.[47] The scope of Resolution 1373 is quite broad, encompassing domestic legislation, national executive machinery and international cooperation. An untold UN success since 9/11, the CTC calls on the advice of experts in the fields of legislative drafting; financial, customs, immigration and extradition law and practice; police and law enforcement; and illegal arms trafficking. Some states will lack the capacity to implement the domestic requirements imposed by UNSC resolutions, others will want in inclination. Both will be the very states that attract the interest of terrorist cells. The CTC also helps with the capacity-building of member states through dissemination of best practices, provision of technical, financial, regulatory and legislative expertise, and facilitating cooperation between national, regional and international organisations. But it does not have the resources and capacity to monitor state compliance with Council-imposed obligations. While human rights per se is beyond the CTC's mandate, it has been in active dialogue with the Office of the High Commissioner for Human Rights with respect to guidelines for states on their human rights obligations in the context of counter-terrorism.

On 8 October 2004, the UNSC adopted Resolution 1566, setting up a working group, consisting of all UNSC members, to create a global blacklist of groups considered to be terrorist organisations and recommend more effective ways to curb terrorist activities, including prosecution and extradition, freezing assets, banning travel and prohibiting arms sales. The 2005 convention on nuclear terrorism is a good illustration of how the General Assembly, when it has the political will, can play an important role in the global fight against terrorism.

Recalling that existing normative instruments for the use of force by states are well-developed and robust, the High-Level Panel calls for similar strength concerning non-state actors.[48] The last remains a contentious and contestable claim. Tom Farer points out that for decades, it has been common to use the word 'terrorist' to describe regimes 'that kill, torture and make people disappear in order to terrify the rest of the population'. The HLP and the SG are trying to alter this powerful moral discourse for the worse, especially as the moral effects of shaming 'are

[47] Information on the CTC is available at www.un.org/Docs/sc/scommittees/1373.
[48] High-Level Panel, *A More Secure World*, para. 159.

likely to be greater where state officials fall within the definition of terrorist than when private actors do'.[49]

In his response the Secretary-General reaffirms the definition, notes that terrorism is 'neither an acceptable nor an effective way to advance' a cause, and calls for it to be included in a comprehensive convention.[50] He outlines five pillars of a counter-terrorism strategy, all of which are included in the above analysis: dissuasion of people from resorting to or supporting terrorism; denial of access to funds and materials to terrorists; deterrence of states from sponsoring terrorism; capacity development so states can defeat terrorism; and defence of human rights.[51] The strong condemnation of terrorism 'in all its forms and manifestations', no matter what the cause, was reiterated in the draft outcome document at the 2005 summit, and the call for a comprehensive convention and the Secretary-General's counter-terrorism strategy were endorsed.[52] But the assembled leaders failed to agree on a definition.

The UN and the USA share an interest in isolating and defeating terrorism, not each other, and in containing the threat of weapons of mass destruction falling into the hands of state or non-state terrorists. The fight against terrorism is a war with no frontiers, against enemies who know no borders and have no scruples. If we abandon our scruples, we descend to their level. The dialogue of civilisations is a discourse across all frontiers, embracing communities who profess and practise different faiths, but have scruples about imposing their values on others. We must talk to and welcome into the concert of civilised communities believers in moral values from all continents, cultures and faiths. The need of the hour is for discourse among the civilised, not a dialogue of the uncivilised deafened by the drumbeats of war.

---

[49] Tom Farer, 'The UN Reports: Addressing the Gnarled Issues of Our Time', *International Spectator* 2 (2005), p. 12.

[50] Annan, *In Larger Freedom*, paras. 84, 88, 91.

[51] Ibid., para. 88.

[52] Draft Outcome Document, 13 September 2005, paras. 81–3.

9

Kosovo 1999

If the Gulf War (1990–1) marked the birth of the new world order, Somalia (1992–4) was the slide into the new world disorder and Rwanda (1994) and Srebrenica (1995) marked the loss of innocence after the end of the Cold War. This background and sequence of events and developments help to explain the forging of a normally elusive political will among the major actors of the Euro-Atlantic alliance when, faced with a compelling humanitarian tragedy in Kosovo, the North Atlantic Treaty Organisation (NATO) launched a 'humanitarian war' without UN authorisation. As discussed already in chapter 2, by 1999 Yugoslav President Slobodan Milošević had exhausted their patience. They were determined to confront him if necessary, instead of allowing him to get away with his murderous practices yet again. But the action raised many troubling questions about what we can and should do when faced with a humanitarian tragedy. The triple policy dilemma can be summarised thus:

- to respect sovereignty all the time is to be complicit in humanitarian tragedies sometimes;
- to argue that the UN Security Council (UNSC) must give its consent to international intervention for humanitarian purposes is to risk policy paralysis by handing over the agenda either to the passivity and apathy of the Council as a whole, or to the most obstructionist member of the Council, including any one of the five permanent members (P5) determined to use the veto clause;
- to use force without UN authorisation is to violate international law and undermine world order.

The three propositions together highlight a critical gap between the needs and distress felt in the real world and the codified instruments and modalities for managing world order. In their addresses to the opening of the annual session of the General Assembly in September 1999, both US President Bill Clinton and UN Secretary-General Kofi Annan referred to the need for 'humanitarian intervention'[1] to avert or stop mass killings. The challenge, twin to the dilemma, is this: faced with another Holocaust or Rwanda-type genocide on the one hand and a Security Council veto on the other, what would we do? Because there is no clear answer to this poignant question within the existing international consensus as embodied in the UN Charter, a new consensus is urgently needed.

The Kosovo War had a threefold significance for the central theme of this book on the UN and the international use of military force. The first is the manner in which it encapsulated the evolving UN–NATO relationship: largely complementary and mutually reinforcing, but at times also ambivalent. The second is the way in which it unleashed a wave of policy and scholarly reflections on the 'challenge of humanitarian intervention'.[2] And the third is the extent to which it may have paved the path to the Iraq War in 2003.

NATO and the United Nations

Illegal and dangerous precedent

There are five possible responses to the implications of Kosovo for the UN–NATO relationship. First, NATO may have acted illegally in terms of

---

[1] 'Humanitarian intervention' is put in quotation marks because its usage has been seriously questioned by the International Commission on Intervention and State Sovereignty (ICISS), as we shall see in chapter 11.

[2] For a sample of the books on the subject, see William J. Buckley, *Kosovo: Contending Voices on Balkan Interventions* (Grand Rapids: William B. Eerdmans, 2000); Deen K. Chatterjee, Don E. Scheid and Douglas MacLean, eds., *Ethics and Foreign Intervention* (Cambridge: Cambridge University Press, 2003); Robert C. Diprizio, *Armed Humanitarians: US Interventions from Northern Iraq to Kosovo* (Baltimore: Johns Hopkins University Press, 2002); Michael J. Glennon, *Limits of Law, Prerogatives of Power: Interventionism after Kosovo* (New York: Palgrave Macmillan, 2001); Richard N. Haass, *Intervention: The Use of American Military Force in the Post-Cold War World* (Washington, DC: Carnegie Endowment for International Peace, 1999); Karin von Hippel, *Democracy by Force: US Military Intervention in the post-Cold War World* (Cambridge: Cambridge University Press, 1999); J. L. Holzgrefe and Robert O. Keohane, eds., *Humanitarian Intervention: Ethical, Legal and Political Dilemmas* (Cambridge: Cambridge University Press, 2003); Aleksandar Jokic, ed., *Lessons of Kosovo: The Dangers of Humanitarian Intervention* (Peterborough, Ontario: Broadview Press, 2003); Albrecht Schnabel and Ramesh Thakur, eds., *Kosovo and the Challenge of Humanitarian Intervention: Selective Indignation, Collective Action, and International Citizenship* (Tokyo: United Nations University Press, 2000); and Raju G. C. Thomas, ed., *Yugoslavia Unraveled: Sovereignty, Self-determination, Intervention* (Lanham: Lexington Books, 2003).

its own constitution, the UN Charter and state practice. This position was articulated most forcefully by China, Russia and India (as well as Serbia). Under the UN Charter, states are committed to settling their disputes by peaceful means (Article 2.3) and refraining from the threat or use of force against the territorial integrity or political independence of any state (Article 2.4). Article 53(1) empowers the UNSC to 'utilise . . . regional arrangements or agencies for enforcement action *under its authority. But no enforcement action shall be taken under regional arrange-ments or by regional agencies without the authorisation of the Security Council*' (emphasis added).

Neither the UN Charter nor the corpus of modern international law incorporates the right to 'humanitarian intervention'. State practice in the past two centuries, and especially since 1945, provides few genuine cases of such intervention. According to the weight of legal opinion and authority, the prohibition on the use of force has become a peremptory norm of international law from which no derogation is permitted and NATO was not permitted to contract out at a regional level. On pruden-tial grounds, the scope for abusing any right of intervention is so great as to argue strongly against its creation.

The precedent was dangerous both because it could encourage others to ignore the existing normative and legal prohibitions on the use of force, and because those fearing outside interventions could embark on military rearmament to forestall such action. Kosovo was a setback to the cause of slowly but steadily outlawing the use of force in solving disputes except under UN authorisation. The argument that NATO had no intention to set a precedent is less relevant than that its actions were interpreted by others as having done so. Would Westerners be comfort-able with a parallel situation where the Arab League claimed the com-mensurate right to determine on its own that Israel was guilty of gross human rights atrocities against Palestinians and the Arab League inter-vened with military force in their defence? To say that they lack the power or military capacity to do so is to say that might is right. Similarly, would we accept former or present Israeli leaders being put on trial for crimes against humanity by a tribunal that was set up essentially by the Arab League, funded by them and dependent on them both for collecting crucial evidence through national intelligence assets and for enforcement of arrest warrants?

For most Westerners, NATO is an alliance of democracies and as such a standing validation of the democratic peace thesis. For former colonies, one of the more notable features of NATO is that it is a military alliance of former colonial powers: every European colonial power is a member of NATO.

The worst-case scenario would be to encourage states to acquire nuclear weapons: 'The affair provided a lesson in the utility of nuclear deterrence. Had Slobodan Milošević possessed a nuclear deterrent, NATO would not have bombed his country.'[3] Sha Zukang, China's chief arms control negotiator, used Kosovo as the alibi for missiles exports.[4] At the Third Preparatory Committee (PrepCom) meeting of the NPT 2000 Review Conference in New York in May 1999, 'though the Chinese were the only ones publicly to wonder if NATO would have bombed Belgrade if Yugoslavia had also been nuclear armed, there were many in the corridors who made the obvious connection'.[5] In India, the same point was made by a former foreign secretary[6] and a leading newspaper.[7] In Russia, Alexei Arbatov, deputy chair of the Russian State Duma (Parliament) Defence Committee, argued that NATO's attack on Serbia suddenly removed a Russian taboo against the use of military force in Chechnya:

> Russia has learned many lessons from Kosovo. Above all, the end justifies the means. The use of force is the most efficient problem solver, if applied decisively and massively. Negotiations are of dubious value and should be used as a cover for military action. International law and human suffering are of secondary significance in achieving the goal. Massive devastation and collateral fatalities among the civilian population are acceptable in order to limit one's own casualties.[8]

The Kosovo war was almost certainly a factor in the more prominent role given to nuclear weapons in Russia's new security doctrine signed by Acting President Vladimir Putin in January 2000.[9]

---

[3] William Pfaff, 'No Nonproliferation Without Nuclear Reduction', *International Herald Tribune (IHT)*, 23 August 1999.

[4] Jim Mann, 'Quietly, US and China Negotiate Arms Control,' *IHT*, 6 October 2000, and Michael R. Gordon, 'China Looks to Foil Missile Defense', *IHT*, 30 April 2001.

[5] Rebecca Johnson, 'NPT Report', *Disarmament Diplomacy* 37 (May 1999), p. 16.

[6] Muchkund Dubey, 'The NATO Juggernaut: Logic of an Indian Defence Deterrent', *Times of India* (Delhi), 8 April 1999.

[7] *Times of India*, 2 April 1999.

[8] Alexei G. Arbatov, *The Transformation of Russian Military Doctrine: Lessons Learned from Kosovo and Chechnya* (Washington, DC: The George C. Marshall Center Papers, No. 2, 20 July 2000), 'Executive Summary', p. v.

[9] Michael Wines, 'Moscow Issues New Policy Emphasizing Nuclear Arms', *New York Times*, 15 January 2000. The link to NATO's bombing campaign in Kosovo was made explicitly in this report.

Implicit UN authorisation

NATO action was neither explicitly authorised nor prohibited by any UN resolution. NATO leaders argued that military action outside the UN framework was not their preferred option of choice. Rather, NATO's resort to force was a critical comment on the institutional hurdles to effective and timely action by the United Nations. The campaign against Serbia took place in the context of a history of defiance of UN resolutions by Milošević. Over the years, the UNSC had become increasingly more specific in focusing on human rights violations by the Milošević regime, not by both sides; and increasingly coercive in the use of language threatening unspecified response by the international community. Moreover, the UNSC had relied progressively on NATO as its enforcement arm in the Balkans over the 1990s. NATO actions in Kosovo were thus a logical extension and evolution of a role already sanctified by the Security Council.

The Milošević challenge to UN ideals

A third response is that Serbian atrocities in Kosovo challenged some of the cherished UN values. The days when a tyrant could shelter behind the norm of non-intervention from the outside in order to use maximum brutal force inside territorial borders are past. The UN Charter is a dynamic compromise between state interests and human rights. Had Milošević been allowed to get away with his murderous campaign of ethnic cleansing, the net result would have been a fundamental erosion of the idealistic base on which the UN structure rests. Czech President Václav Havel famously described the Kosovo war as one fought over 'principles and values' rather than over national interests and as showing, not disrespect for international law, but respect for the higher law of human rights over state sovereignty.[10] NATO action was not a regression to old-style balance-of-power politics but a progression to new-age community of power. NATO Secretary-General Javier Solana proclaimed that for the first time, 'an alliance of sovereign states fought not to

---

[10] In a speech originally delivered to a joint sitting of Canada's houses of parliament in Ottawa on 29 April 1999, subsequently reprinted as Václav Havel, 'Kosovo and the End of the Nation-State', *New York Review of Books*, 46:10 (10 June 1999), p. 6; quoted in Robert M. Hayden, 'Biased Justice: "Humanrightism" and the International Criminal Tribunal for the Former Yugoslavia', in Thomas, ed., *Yugoslavia Unraveled*, p. 279.

conquer or preserve territory but to protect the values on which the alliance was founded'.[11]

Support for this line of argument can be found in the UN's official report, published after the Kosovo War ended, on the fall of Srebrenica in 1995. Acknowledging at least partial responsibility for the tragedy, the report in effect concludes that the UN peacekeeping philosophy of neutrality and non-violence was unsuited to the conflict in Bosnia. The approach of the international community was wholly inadequate to the Serb campaign of ethnic cleansing and mass murder which culminated in Srebrenica. Evil must be recognised as such and confronted by the international community; the UN's commitment to ending conflicts, far from precluding moral judgement, makes it all the more necessary.[12]

NATO = war, UN = peace

The fourth strand is that while NATO made war, it still needed the UN to help secure the peace. A UN-led peacekeeping mission established a de facto protectorate in Kosovo, supported by a military presence (KFOR) with a large NATO component but also a Russian element. Far from discrediting the UN permanently, therefore, Kosovo in 1999 showed that a UN role remains indispensable even for the most powerful military alliance in history. In contrast to the way in which the UN was pushed aside when NATO went to war with Serbia over Kosovo, developments in the province since the war in 1999 mark a sensible division of labour between NATO and the UN.

G8 = real UNSC

Fifth, and finally, one could argue that the sequence of events shows that the real centre of international political and economic gravity has shifted from the UNSC to the G8 (the group of seven industrialised states plus Russia) and China.[13] That was the forum in which the critical negotiations were held and the crucial compromises and decisions made. With the assistance of Russia and through the involvement of the G8, whose

---

[11] Javier Solana, 'NATO's Success in Kosovo', *Foreign Affairs* 78:6 (November/December 1999), p. 114.

[12] *Report of the Secretary-General Pursuant to General Assembly Resolution 53/35 (1998)* (New York: UN Secretariat, November 1999), para. 502.

[13] See Winrich Kuhne, *The Security Council and the G8 in the New Millennium: Who is in Charge of International Peace and Security?* Report prepared for the Stiftung Wissenschaft und Politik (Berlin: SWP, 2000).

mediation was accepted by Belgrade, the war was eventually brought to an end and Yugoslav troops were withdrawn from Kosovo. This reflects the failure to reform the UNSC in composition and procedure, as a result of which it no longer mirrors the world as it really is. In essence, therefore, the 'G8 plus' is the UNSC as it ought to be. The counter to this, however, is the belief that the net result of the Kosovo war was that 'a US-led NATO, with a pliant United Nations in tow . . . set itself up for an active role in world affairs'.[14]

Did Kosovo in 1999 light the path to Iraq in 2003?

Thus Kosovo foreshadowed Iraq in the attack on the United Nations for becoming an after-sales service provider to US-led military interventions. The defeat of Milošević removed the principal threat to Balkan and hence European stability, loosened his grip on the popular hold sufficiently for his own people to vote him out of office in 2000 and the new government to hand him over for international criminal trial at The Hague. The credibility of NATO was preserved; the transformation of its role, from collective defence of members against attack from the outside into the more diffuse role of peace enforcement throughout Europe, was validated; and Washington was kept anchored to Europe. But mobilising domestic support for a short, swift and sweet war against an enemy who has been successfully demonised does not automatically translate into building a new regime for interventions that has general acceptance in the international community. As Michael Glennon notes, 'Justice . . . requires legitimacy; without widespread acceptance of intervention as part of a formal justice system, the new interventionism will appear to be built on neither law nor justice, but on power alone.'[15]

The template of robust 'humanitarian intervention' and foreign-led 'regime change' proved too rusty to the task in Iraq in 2003. One of the curious features of the Iraq War was the serious split across the Atlantic. What seemed to puzzle and infuriate Americans was why the major European powers, having signed on to war without UN authorisation against Milošević, 'the butcher of Belgrade', refused to do so against Saddam Hussein, 'the butcher of Baghdad'. Was the road to Baghdad

---

[14] Raju G. C. Thomas, 'Sovereignty, Self-Determination, and Secession: Principles and Practice', in Thomas, ed., *Yugoslavia Unraveled*, p. 17.

[15] Michael J. Glennon, 'The New Interventionism: The Search for a Just International Law', *Foreign Affairs* 78:3 (May/June 1999), p. 7.

in 2003 paved with good intentions via Belgrade in 1999? Was the choice between action and no action – and responsibility for the consequences of the choices made – the same in both cases? On balance the Americans would appear to have just cause for their complaint of European double standards. To be sure, there are important differences. But in some respects the differences are exaggerated and in other respects there are also important similarities and continuities that overshadow the differences.

The differences were that the ethnic cleansing by Milošević was much closer in time to the 1999 war, not fifteen years in the past; no NATO power had been complicit through diplomatic and material assistance to Serbia in the perpetration of those atrocities at the time that they were committed; instead the Europeans were sick and tired of Milošević's deceit, evasions and atrocities being committed on European territory itself. As there was no oil, the humanitarian motive stood out far more clearly as the main driver of the intervention for most countries that went to war. Because of this, the major Western allies, both people and governments, stood solidly united in 1999, whereas the democratic alliance was deeply fractured over Iraq.

Raju Thomas attributes the 'self-righteous and one-sided perspectives and policies' animating NATO in Kosovo to the end of the Cold War, the collapse of countervailing power and the ascendancy of 'a new moral liberalism which emphasized global humanitarianism'.[16] The lines of continuity from Kosovo in 1999 to Iraq in 2003 can be traced along this explanation. And it foreshadowed Iraq by four years also in the argument that was being made already in 1999, that the Balkans had provided the USA with an excuse to redesign the world order in its own image, and that Washington under the Clinton administration was already desperate to free itself of the discipline of UNSC-centred multilateralism in the use of military force overseas because this put far too much institutional power in the hands of rivals like China and Russia.[17]

Sidelining the UN

It used to be said during the Cold War that the purpose of NATO was to keep the Americans in, the Germans down and the Russians out. Did

---

[16] Raju G. C. Thomas, 'Prologue: Making War, Peace and History', in Thomas, ed., *Yugoslavia Unraveled*, p. xi.

[17] Michael Mandel, 'Illegal Wars, Collateral Damage, and International Criminal Law', in Thomas, ed., *Yugoslavia Unraveled*, pp. 294–5.

Kosovo mark a turning point, changing NATO into a tool for keeping the Americans in, the Russians down and the United Nations out? In rejecting UN constraints, NATO chose not to play by the rules of the game when the result was not to its liking. More worrying, no system was put in place instead of the UN. Does this mean that any regional hegemon can impose its morality on states in its neighbourhood? Can it do so outside its region? Who decides, and on what basis? Does India have the right to tell Sri Lanka the terms of a peace deal with the Tamils, or else? Or is it only the enlightened USA and the West who can be trusted to judge and act on behalf of the 'international community'? Western criticisms of the Russian use of massive force against Chechnya later in 1999 drew angry reminders of NATO action in Kosovo:[18] an international war, as opposed to Russia's actions within its borders, noted Russian commentators.

Intervening in defence of the rights of minorities is all very well, but where is the protection for the weak against the dominant and assertive international moral majority? A preponderance of power does not encourage negotiation, compromise, political accommodation and settlement. The belief in exceptionalism is contagious. In East Timor, the new interventionist charge was led by Australia. As prone to lecture people in its own Asia-Pacific region on universal values and international norms as the USA is to lecture the world, Australia found itself unexpectedly on the defensive when a UN committee turned the torchlight of an international investigation on the conditions of Aborigines in Australia. In a fit of pique,[19] the Australian government decided to limit all future cooperation with UN bodies investigating Australian human rights conditions.[20]

Being the indispensable power can tempt one into being indisposed to accept the constraints of multilateral diplomacy. But being indispensable does not confer the authority to dispense with the legitimacy of the UN

---

[18] Compare: 'we argued at the time that NATO's "humanitarian intervention" in Serbia would be interpreted as giving the green light to governments around the world, including Russia's, to deal in a similar manner with those whom they saw as terrorists and violators of human rights' Dimitri K. Simes and Paul J. Saunders, 'Russia's Case in Chechnya', *Japan Times*, 20 December 1999.

[19] A critical editorial in the *Japan Times* (3 September 2000) was entitled 'Canberra's Unsightly Pique'.

[20] See the news report by Barbara Crossette, 'Australia Balks at UN Rights Scrutiny', *IHT*, 1 September 2000, and the op-ed article by Amin Saikal, 'Australia Wants No Gruff from the United Nations', *IHT*, 5 September 2000.

as the only entity that can speak in the name of the international community. John Ikenberry notes the irony of the USA being the great champion of enlightened self-interest and humanitarian intervention at the same time as its pre-eminence is an obstacle to the development of capacities and institutions that consolidate the emerging global humanitarian norms and human rights standards. While much of the world worries about unrestrained US power, he adds, within the USA there is a weakening of support for global engagement.[21]

Nuanced morality vs. moral clarity

The case for NATO strikes on Serbia was not made with persuasive enough force to overcome the presumption of doubt – the humanitarian case was asserted, not argued. The inconsistencies with regard to striking Belgrade for its Kosovo policy were substantial and numerous. There were graver and more unprovoked attacks against other minorities in many parts of the world.[22] Some of these were of long standing, and some indeed involved regimes with continuing military links to Western nations. 'Yet the UN and the western powers found little difficulty in restraining themselves when mass murder was perpetrated in Cambodia in the 1970s and in Rwanda in the 1990s . . . Whatever might be said about the most extreme cases of mass murder, the ethnic conflicts in the Balkans were not on this scale.'[23]

Just as anyone who attempted to question the humanitarian warriors over the case for Iraq risked being branded an apologist for Saddam in 2003, so with Milošević in 1999. The scale of killing by Serbian forces was grossly exaggerated and the humanitarian and other costs of war greatly downplayed. Just as the claims of Iraqi weapons of mass destruction (WMD) have been shown to have been greatly exaggerated and amplified

---

[21] G. John Ikenberry, 'The Costs of Victory: American Power and the Use of Force in the Contemporary Order', in Schnabel and Thakur, eds., *Kosovo and the Challenge of Humanitarian Intervention*, pp. 85–100.

[22] In August 1998, for example, between 5,000 and 8,000 people were killed over three to four days because of their ethnic identity by the Taliban in the northern Afghan city of Mazar-i-Sharif. To all intents and purposes, that massacre slipped through 'the floorboards of history'; Rupert C. Colville, 'One Massacre That Didn't Grab the World's Attention', *IHT*, 7–8 August 1999.

[23] Jeremy Rabkin, 'Humanitarian Intervention in the New World Order: Why the Old Rules Were Better', paper presented at the conference on 'Humanitarian Intervention and International Relations', China Institute of International Studies, Beijing, 21–22 August 2000, pp. 27–8.

through a surprisingly gullible media, so were the claims of mass murders of up to 200,000 people in Kosovo. 'Humanitarianism' was married to 'war' in a clever and successful ploy to label opponents of the war as anti-humanitarian. The moral urgency underpinning NATO actions, and the military success of those actions, would in due course shape legal justification to match the course of action.[24]

By fighting and defeating Serbia, NATO became the tool for the Kosovo Liberation Army's (KLA) policy of inciting Serb reprisals through terrorist attacks in order to provoke NATO intervention.[25] 'Led by Germany, European and American recognition of the former Yugoslav republics was accomplished in disregard of international law doctrine forbidding recognition of secessionist units whose establishment is being resisted forcibly by a central government.'[26] The role of outside intervention in promoting territorial disintegration rather than preventing genocide was downplayed. Kofi Annan acknowledges that his call for a debate on the challenge of humanitarian intervention led to fears that the concept 'might encourage secessionist movements deliberately to provoke governments into committing gross violations of human rights in order to trigger external interventions that would aid their cause'.[27]

The basis for discriminating between the Serbs and Kosovars ignored the centuries of conflict and the alternating cycle of oppression and

---

[24] For development of this line of argumentation, see in particular Louis Henkin, 'Kosovo and the Law of "Humanitarian Intervention"', *American Journal of International Law* 93:4 (October 1999), pp. 824–8, and Ruth Wedgwood, 'NATO's Campaign in Yugoslavia', *American Journal of International Law* 93:4 (October 1999), pp. 828–34. For the structural link of Wedgwood's argument to Iraq, see her 'Iraq: Legal and Legitimate', in Ramesh Thakur and W. P. S. Sidhu, eds., *The Iraq Crisis and World Order: Structural, Institutional and Normative Challenges* (Tokyo: United Nations University Press, forthcoming).

[25] 'The KLA's success between 1997 and 1999 was a vintage demonstration of how to exploit the human rights conscience of the West in order to incite an intervention that resulted eventually in guerrilla victory'; Michael Ignatieff, *Human Rights as Politics and Idolatry*, edited and introduced by Amy Gutmann (Princeton: Princeton University Press, 2001), p. 45. For a succinct account of the KLA strategy as well as a discourse on the many 'subtexts' underlying the NATO campaign, see Michael McGwire, 'Why Did We Bomb Belgrade?' *International Affairs* 76:1 (January 2000), pp. 1–24. In answering his question, McGwire is sceptical of the claim that humanitarianism had displaced geopolitical interests as the principal motive.

[26] Donald L. Horowitz, quoted in Raju G. C. Thomas, 'Sovereignty, Self-Determination, and Secession: Principles and Practice', in Thomas, ed., *Yugoslavia Unraveled*, p. 3.

[27] Kofi A. Annan, *We the Peoples: The Role of the United Nations in the 21st Century* (New York: UN Department of Public Information, 2000), p. 48.

repression between the two groups. The Kosovars cannot appropriate the mantle of innocent 'victimhood' of the Jews under the Nazis.[28] Relying on threats as a bluff transformed a humanitarian crisis in Kosovo into a humanitarian catastrophe when the bluff was called. The 'inhuman methods' used in the cause of 'humanitarian intervention' are also common to both Kosovo and Iraq.[29] Air strikes did not prevent widespread atrocities against civilians on the ground in Kosovo nor the mass exodus of refugees into neighbouring countries. High altitude, zero-casualty air war shifted 'the entire burden of risk and harm' to life and limb completely to the target society, 'including the supposed beneficiaries and innocent civilians'.[30] Expanding the list of bombing targets, such as water and electricity infrastructure and broadcasting stations, reversed progressive trends in the laws of war over the course of the twentieth century. And bombing mistakes, the increased risk of which was deliberately accepted by political leaders in order to minimise risks to their own soldiers, 'caused the finger of criminality to be pointed in NATO's direction'.[31]

The use of force requires moral clarity between the good and bad, not shades of ambiguity. The colour of truth in complex emergencies is grey,[32] and good intentions do not infuse bad outcomes with virtuous morality. This proved too much for most of the Western media who reduced the conflict to a simple story of good (Kosovo) against evil (Serbia);[33] even much of the Western academic writing on the crisis fell victim to 'advocacy scholarship'.[34] The same one-sided perspective permeates Richard Holbrooke's memoirs in which the USA ended a brutal war of genocide and rape by the Serbs.[35] No regional organisation,

---

[28] Apropos of Serbia's ethnic cleansing via expulsions, Julie Birchill remarked that the Nazis did not put Jews on trains to Israel; Julie Birchill, '40 Reasons Why the Serbs are Not the New Nazis and the Kosovars are Not the New Jews', *Guardian* (London), 10 April 1999.

[29] Robert W. Tucker and David C. Hendrickson, 'The Sources of American Legitimacy', *Foreign Affairs*, 83:6 (November/December 2004), p. 31.

[30] Richard Falk, 'Reflections on the Kosovo War', *Global Dialogue* 1:2 (Autumn 1999), p. 93.

[31] Ibid., p. 94.

[32] Compare: 'Good motives give assurance against deliberately bad policies; they do not guarantee the moral goodness and political success of the policies they inspire'; Hans J. Morgenthau, *Politics among Nations: The Struggle for Power and Peace*, 4th edn (New York: Alfred A. Knopf, 1967), p. 6.

[33] See Ed Hermann and Philip Hammond, *Degraded Capability: The Media and the Kosovo Crisis* (London: Pluto Press, 2000).

[34] Thomas, 'Prologue', p. xiii.

[35] Richard Holbrooke, *To End a War* (New York: Random House, 1998).

and in fact not even the UN, has the right to impose the terms of political settlement between the central and provincial governments of sovereign countries – which was the trigger to the NATO attacks on Serbia after the Rambouillet ultimatum.

The costs of the war in Kosovo drained development funds away from needy populations in Africa and Asia, just as the requirements for Iraqi reconstruction distorted foreign aid programmes in 2003–5. The poor of Africa and Asia had to pay through opportunity costs for the white man's war in Europe. Nigeria's ambassador to the UN called it 'morally repugnant' that the international community spent $1.50 per day per refugee in Kosovo, but only $0.11 in Rwanda and Sierra Leone.[36]

Legality vs. legitimacy

The Independent International Commission on Kosovo, chaired by Richard Goldstone and Carl Tham, concluded that NATO's intervention was illegal but legitimate.[37] Goldstone is also quite clear in his mind that legitimacy is on a higher plane than legality: thus opposition to the perfectly legal apartheid regime in South Africa (of which he was a notable opponent from within the legal profession and the white establishment in the country) was fully justified.[38] The legality–legitimacy distinction was to resurface four years later over Iraq.

There is a problem, nevertheless. Suppose I have witnessed a murder by a rich celebrity. Suppose further that for reasons to do with courtroom techniques of expensive trial lawyers who exploit every technicality, the murderer is acquitted. Can I claim legitimacy in inflicting vigilante justice on the murderer?[39] A normative commitment to the

---

[36] Statement by the Permanent Representative of Nigeria, HE Ibrahim Gambari, to the United Nations Security Council, 30 September 1999. In 2005 Gambari was appointed the UN Under-Secretary-General for Political Affairs.

[37] *Kosovo Report: Conflict, International Response, Lessons Learned* (Oxford: Oxford University Press for the Independent International Commission on Kosovo, 2000). For discussions of the lawfulness and legitimacy of the war, see Christine M. Chinkin, 'Kosovo: A "Good" or "Bad" War?', *American Journal of International Law* 93:4 (October 1999), pp. 841–7; Michael J. Glennon, *Limits of Law, Prerogatives of Power: Interventionism After Kosovo* (New York: Palgrave Macmillan, 2001); Henkin, 'Kosovo and the Law of "Humanitarian Intervention"'; and Wedgwood, 'NATO's Campaign in Yugoslavia'.

[38] Personal discussion, Maputo, 10 March 2001.

[39] The analogy of vigilante justice was used explicitly by the co-chairs of the Commission on Global Governance, one of whom is a former prime minister of Sweden and the other the former secretary-general of the Commonwealth. Writing of NATO bombing shortly

rule of law implies a commitment to the principle of relations being governed by law, not power. It also implies a willingness to accept the limitations and constraints of working within the law, in specific instances if necessary against individual notions of just or illegitimate outcome. The best that can be said of the NATO actions was that it fell into, indeed enlarged, a 'grey area' between lawfulness and legitimacy, where the use of force is neither condemned nor condoned, but tolerated.

The legality–legitimacy distinction rests on an implicit hierarchy of norms which also poses a fundamental challenge to the existing basis of state order.[40] The international order, being a society of sovereign states, has only a horizontal system of rules derived logically from the principle of sovereign equality. If the UN Charter's proscriptions on the threat and use of force can be set aside, the justification for this must necessarily rest on the existence of a higher order of norms which override Charter clauses. The use of force may be lawful or unlawful; the decision to use force is a political act; almost the only channel between legal authority and political legitimacy with regard to the international use of force is the United Nations. Conceding to any regional organisation the authority to decide when political legitimacy may override legal technicality would make a mockery of the entire basis of strictly limited, and in recent times increasingly constricted, recourse to force for settling international disputes. Conversely, restricting the right solely to NATO is 'an open argument for law-making by an elite group of Western powers sitting in judgement over their own actions'.[41]

It could be argued that the case against Iraq was not framed in terms of the humanitarian argument, but in terms of WMD that has fallen apart completely. Saddam Hussein's alleged links to international terrorism and al Qaeda have also turned out to be based on deceptions and

after it started, they commented that 'This temptation to assume police powers on the basis of righteousness and military strength is dangerous for world order and world peace; what results is a world ordered by vigilante action'; Ingvar Carlson and Shridath Ramphal, 'Air Strikes: Incalculable Damage to Peace under Law', http://www.cgg.ch/kosovo.htm; edited versions were also published in the *IHT*, 1 April 1999 and *Guardian*, 2 April 1999.

[40] Hideaki Shinoda, 'The Politics of Legitimacy in International Relations: A Critical Examination of NATO's Intervention in Kosovo', *Alternatives* 25:4 (October–December 2000), pp. 528–31.

[41] David Chandler, *From Kosovo to Kabul: Human Rights and International Intervention* (London: Pluto, 2002), p. 135.

flawed conclusions drawn from heavily qualified, faith-based intelligence. Instead of policy being influenced by intelligence, a predetermined policy shaped the collection, analysis, interpretation and public presentation of intelligence.

True, but the case against Serbia in 1999 was not framed in humanitarian language either. People overlooked then that NATO's case was equally dubious: they went to war because Milošević rejected the Rambouillet ultimatum. Cause and effect were mixed: the war turned what had been targeted attacks on KLA cadres into a more generalised Serbian assault on Kosovars. Had the Rambouillet diktat been given as close a scrutiny in 1999 as the WMD argument in 2003, it would likely have met with matching scepticism. Leaked documents during the British election campaign in May 2005 confirmed what could be deduced from the known facts in any case. In 2002, British analysts had concluded that war against Iraq was inevitable and so intelligence and facts were being fixed around the policy. But Foreign Secretary Jack Straw noted that the case for war was thin because Saddam Hussein was not threatening his neighbours and his WMD capability was less than that of Iran, Libya or North Korea. He proposed, therefore, giving Saddam an ultimatum to allow the UN inspectors back into the country with a toughened mandate. A refusal by Baghdad would 'help with the legal justification for the use of force', he argued.[42] The tactic – the modus operandi (MO), in popular detective fiction parlance – had been tried, tested and not found wanting three years earlier. NATO succeeded in 1999 in diverting attention from Rambouillet to the humanitarian liberation argument; Blair and Bush have had more difficulty trying to shift the chief justification from WMD to humanitarian outcomes in the case of Iraq.

How much closer scrutiny would have been given by NATO to the links between al Qaeda and the KLA, Serbia's main military opponents in Kosovo, after 9/11? Efforts to demonise Milošević deflected attention from those who until recently were branded terrorists by Western governments[43] and by the UNSC,[44] but in 1999 became the principal

---

[42] 'US and UK Discussed Early Plan to Topple Hussein: Blair', *Japan Times*, 2 May 2005.

[43] Thus a former US ambassador to Yugoslavia (1977–81) and then secretary of state (1992–3), in an article not exactly friendly to Milošević: 'The Kosovo Liberation Army *earned* its reputation as a terrorist group'; Lawrence S. Eagleburger, 'Taking a Stand Against the Miloševićs of the Future', *IHT*, 5 April 1999 (emphasis added).

[44] Security Council Resolution 1160 (31 March 1998). Its preamble condemned 'the use of excessive force by Serbian police forces against civilian and peaceful demonstrators in Kosovo, as well as acts of terrorism by the Kosovo Liberation Army'; para. 2 called on the

beneficiaries of the bombing. For example, the KLA's director of elite services was allegedly al Qaeda's top operative in the Balkans, Mohammed al-Zawahiri, brother of Osama bin Laden's military chief of staff Ayman al-Zawahiri, according to Interpol and bin Laden's biographer Yossef Bodansky.[45]

Relegitimising the use of force

Kosovo was the terrain on which the rules of post-Cold War intervention and the terms of Russo-US engagement were rewritten. It had the potential to mark a watershed in Russia's transition from strategic partner to dormant, bankrupt but still nuclear-armed rival.[46] NATO, portrayed as a purely defensive alliance, bombed Serbia even though the latter had not attacked any member of the alliance. Many Russians concluded that perhaps all these years the Warsaw Pact had held NATO in check and not the other way round. China was traumatised by the US bombing of its embassy in Belgrade and did not accepted repeated assurances that the attack was an accident. Both China and Russia were shaken by the ease with which NATO evaded the requirement of UN authorisation for the international use of force, and both challenged any emerging doctrine of humanitarian intervention.[47]

NATO's war over Kosovo, however understandable, was wrong from the point of view of discouraging and restricting the use of force in world affairs. To him who has a hammer, it is said, the world looks like a nail. Bombing was the option of choice by an alliance overly confident of its overwhelming military superiority. The overriding message is not that force was put to the service of law, but that might is right. The symbolism of the United Nations as the institution for moderating the use of

---

KLA to condemn all terrorist action; and para. 3 emphasised that the way to defeat terrorism in Kosovo was for the Belgrade authorities to offer the Kosovars 'a genuine political process'.

[45] George Bogdanich, 'UN, NATO Policies Fail: Oppressed Now the Oppressors', *Chicago Tribune*, as reprinted in the *Daily Yomiuri*, 17 July 2004. There is also the curious case of the young Australian David Hicks who fought with the KLA in the Balkans before graduating to join the Taliban directly in Afghanistan, where he was captured by US forces and then detained in Guantánamo Bay.

[46] See Oksana Antonenko, 'Russia, NATO and European Security after Kosovo', *Survival* 41:4 (Winter 1999–2000), pp. 124–44.

[47] See Vladimir Baranovsky, 'Russia: Reassessing National Interests', and Zhang Yunling, 'China: Whither the World Order after Kosovo?', in Schnabel and Thakur, eds., *Kosovo and the Challenge of Humanitarian Intervention.*, pp. 101–16 and 117–27 respectively.

force to settle international quarrels was dealt a blow from which it had barely recovered before being hit by a worse blow in Iraq.

Military victory vs. nation-building

Kosovo anticipated Iraq also in the painfully difficult task of nation-building after military victory in the war. To supporters, NATO cured Europe of the Milošević-born disease of ethnic cleansing. The poignant images of long lines of refugees fleeing from their homes and of gaunt and seriously malnourished families documented only too graphically how the spectre of racial genocide had come back to haunt Europe from the dark days of the Second World War. The challenge to the humane values of European civilisation had to be met, and met decisively. To critics, however, 'the NATO cure greatly worsened the Milošević disease'.[48] The trickle of refugees before the war turned into a flood during it,[49] and afterwards the Serbs were ethnically cleansed by the Albanians in revenge attacks.[50] As the Serbs pulled out of Kosovo and the structures of state administration collapsed, the power vacuum was filled by a mixture of KLA cadres and criminal organisations. In this chaotic environment, Kosovo became a major destination country for women and girls forced into prostitution since the July 1999 deployment of KFOR and the establishment of the UN Mission in Kosovo (UNMIK) as the civilian administration.[51]

Communities bitterly divided for centuries cannot be forced by outsiders to live together peacefully. Five years after the war, NATO forces and the UN administration had 'utterly failed to protect the most vulnerable inhabitants, the non-ethnic Albanian minority'.[52] Some 250,000 Serbs and 100,000 Muslims, Gypsies, Turks and Jews – two-thirds of the original population – had been driven out by more than 4,000 recorded attacks by extremists. More Serbian churches were destroyed during NATO's first year of occupation than in 500 years of Ottoman

---

[48] Falk, 'Reflections on the Kosovo War,' p. 93.
[49] See Steven Erlanger, 'NATO Bombing Sparked Butchery, Survivors Say', *IHT*, 21 June 1999.
[50] 'The Future of Kosovo: An Indefinite NATO Presence', *IISS Strategic Comments* 6:1 (January 2000), p. 1.
[51] *Protecting the Human Rights of Women and Girls Trafficked for Forced Prostitution in Kosovo* (London: AI, document EUR 70/010/2004, 2004), pp. 7–9. UNMIK denied the accusations; *UN Wire* (www.unwire.org), 7 May 2004.
[52] Bogdanich, 'UN, NATO Policies Fail: Oppressed Now the Oppressors'.

rule.[53] The UN Special Rapporteur for Human Rights, Jiri Dienstbier, concluded that Kosovo was a more dangerous place in 2004 than before 24 March 1999 when NATO intervened. Ethnic violence rocked Kosovo in March 2004 with the Serb minority as the victims.[54] Will NATO be the perpetual guarantor of an independent Kosovo protectorate or the indefinite guardian of a sullen and defeated Serbian ward?

The International Crisis Group concluded that five years of failed policy-making and peacekeeping had left Kosovo in danger of becoming Europe's West Bank.[55] While KFOR's humanitarian work had been creditable, its military response had created a credibility deficit.[56] Criticising both the ethnic Albanian leadership of Kosovo and the Serb government, the report called for a new structure and mandate for UNMIK, arguing that the policy of 'standards before status'[57] – whereby certain standards on self-governance, refugees and returnees etc. had to be met before the future status of Serbia and Montenegro could be decided – needed revision. Effectively there are three options for Kosovo: independence, partition or a Serb province. 'The status quo will not hold . . . Either 2005 sees major progress on a future status solution that consolidates peace and development, or the danger is that Kosovo will return to conflict and generate regional instability.'[58] It is hard to think of an ultimate outcome other than independence with guarantees for the endangered Serb minority and the carrot of EU membership for Serb acquiescence to this sundering of their historic heartland.

---

[53] Ibid.

[54] Human Rights Watch, *Failure to Protect: Anti-Minority Violence in Kosovo, March 2004* (New York: Human Rights Watch, Vol. 16, No. 6(D), July 2004).

[55] International Crisis Group, *Collapse in Kosovo* (Brussels: ICG, Europe Report No. 155, 22 April 2004).

[56] Echoing this three months later, Human Rights Watch reported that 'ethnic Albanian extremists now know that they can effectively challenge the international security structures, having demolished the notion of KFOR and UNMIK invincibility; and ethnic minorities have lost almost all of the remaining trust they had left in the international community'; *Failure to Protect*, p. 3.

[57] Richard Holbrooke described this as 'a phrase that disguised bureaucratic inaction inside dilomatic mumbo-jumbo'; Richard Holbrooke, 'New Course for Kosovo', *Washington Post*, 20 April 2005.

[58] International Crisis Group, *Kosovo: Toward Final Status* (Brussels: ICG, Europe Report No. 161, 24 January 2005), p. i.

Conclusion

The majority of developing countries were strongly opposed to NATO intervention in Kosovo. Their strongest opposition was grounded in the violation of the norm of non-intervention without UN authorisation. Most NATO countries insisted that their action did not set a precedent. The Iraq War proves that claim to have been false: the attempt 'to limit the reach of the Kosovo precedent did not prevent the advocates of the Iraq war from invoking it to justify toppling Saddam'.[59] According to Ian Johnstone:

> the different reactions to the Kosovo and Iraq interventions can be explained in part by the differing normative contexts. NATO's actions in Kosovo, though widely viewed as unlawful, built on an evolving legal framework and may well have contributed to an emerging consensus on humanitarian intervention. The Iraq intervention, on the other hand, was perceived as a sharp break from the existing normative and institutional framework, for which the US has paid a price, economically, politically and in other ways.[60]

Humanitarianism provides us with a vocabulary and institutional machinery of emancipation. But it must be judged also against the pragmatism of intentions and consequences. For example, 'Far from being a defense of the individual against the state, human rights has become a standard part of the justification for the external use of force by the state against other states and individuals.'[61] In making up the rules of intervention 'on the fly',[62] the NATO countries put at peril the requirements for a lasting system of world order grounded in the rule of international law. They did so because the long-term and systemic consequences of intervention in Kosovo lacked a political constituency in NATO decision-making circles. It took Iraq four years later to drive home that the sense of moral outrage provoked by humanitarian atrocities must be tempered by an appreciation of the limits of power, a concern for international institution-building and sensitivity to the law of perverse consequences.

---

[59] Tucker and Hendrickson, 'Sources of American Legitimacy', p. 31.

[60] Ian Johnstone, 'Deliberative Legitimacy in International Decision-making', in Hilary Charlesworth and Jean-Marc Coicaud, eds., *The Faultlines of Legitimacy* (Tokyo: United Nations University Press, forthcoming).

[61] David Kennedy, *The Dark Sides of Virtue: Reassessing International Humanitarianism* (Princeton: Princeton University Press, 2004), p. 25.

[62] Glennon, 'The New Interventionism', p. 6.

10

Iraq's challenge to world order

'We're an empire now, and when we act we create our own reality.'[1]

'. . . truth can be created by assertion, principle can be established by deception and democracy can be imposed through aggression.'[2]

Wars are cataclysmic events. Out of the destruction of major wars emerge new fault lines of international politics. This is why the Iraq war has the potential to reshape the bases of world order in fundamental, profound and long-lasting ways. The war proper proved to be swift and decisive. The most pressing task in 'post-war' Iraq became to stabilise the security situation, establish a transitional political authority, initiate the necessary steps for post-war reconstruction, peacebuilding and reconciliation, and embed these in durable institutions and structures sufficiently resilient to survive the withdrawal of a foreign presence in due course. The larger goal in the region was to assuage the humiliation inflicted on the collective Arab identity, deal with legitimate Palestinian grievances with the same mix of boldness and firmness shown in Iraq, and impress upon the Arab world in general the need for deep political, social and economic reforms.

In this chapter I propose to examine the impact of Iraq through three 'cuts': the impassioned debate before the war; the relationship between the goals pursued and the means employed; and the need for the international organisation and the hyperpower to come together in the common cause of peacebuilding after the war. I conclude by reviewing the argument that the world is better off with the ouster of Saddam Hussein.

---

[1] Unnamed Bush administration official, quoted in Bob Herbert, 'Bush's Blinkers', *New York Times*, 22 October 2004, p. A23.

[2] Gary Younge, 'In a Warped Reality', *Guardian* (London), 21 March 2005.

The UN and Iraq: irrelevant, central, or complicit?

Reasons for the failure of the world community to support the Iraq War included deep doubts over the justification for going to war; anxiety about the human toll, uncontrollable course and incalculable consequences of war in a volatile and already inflamed region; and profound scepticism about the US capacity to stay engaged – politically, economically and militarily – for the years of reconstruction required after a war. The war's legality, legitimacy and impact on UN–US relations will be debated for years to come. This matters because the fabric of orderly relations between nations, the health of the human rights norm and the struggle for a better world are built on respect for international law. The belligerent countries insisted that the war was both legal and legitimate, based on a series of prior UN resolutions and the long and frustrating history of belligerent-cum-deceitful defiance of the UN by Saddam Hussein. Others conceded that it may have been illegal, but they were still prepared to support it because it was nevertheless legitimate, as with the Kosovo War in 1999, in its largely humanitarian outcome. This therefore amounts to an unflattering judgement on the adequacy of existing international law. Yet a third group insisted that the war was both illegal and illegitimate, and hence their strong opposition to it.[3]

In a matching vein, there were three views on the significance of the war for the UN–US relationship: that it had demonstrated the irrelevance, centrality or potential complicity of the UN.

UN irrelevance

President George W. Bush famously declared that by refusing to support the war, the UN would become irrelevant. Driven by moral clarity, the administration was determined to distinguish good from evil in order to promote one and destroy the other. For many people, if the UN did not exist, it would surely need to be invented. For American neo-conservative intellectuals, because it exists, the UN deserves to be disinvented. Consider the following prematurely triumphalist passage from one of their leading lights:

---

[3] The three points of view are articulated in separate chapters by Ruth Wedgwood (legal and legitimate), Charlotte Ku (illegal but legitimate) and David Kreiger (illegal and illegitimate), in Ramesh Thakur and W. P. S. Sidhu, eds., *The Iraq Crisis and World Order: Structural, Institutional and Normative Challenges* (Tokyo: United Nations University Press, forthcoming).

Saddam Hussein's reign of terror is about to end. He will go quickly, but not alone: in a parting irony, he will take the UN down with him. Well, not the whole UN. The 'good works' part will survive, the low-risk peacekeeping bureaucracies will remain, the chatterbox on the Hudson will continue to bleat. What will die is the fantasy of the UN as the foundation of a new world order. As we sift the debris, it will be important to preserve, the better to understand, the intellectual wreckage of the liberal conceit of safety through international law administered by international institutions.[4]

For Washington the issues could hardly have been more serious. Could one of the world's most brutal regimes be permitted to remain in power until it succeeded in acquiring the world's most destructive weapons? America's threat of war, unilaterally if necessary, galvanised the UN into putting teeth into the inspection machinery and produced unprecedented cooperation from the Iraqis. That would not have lasted forever. Based on all previous experience, with the passage of time, international pressure would have slackened and Saddam would have returned to his familiar game of cheat, deny, defy, retreat and live to cheat another day. His survival after full US military mobilisation would have gravely dented US global credibility. In that case, the UN, with no independent military capability, would have lost its most potent enforcement agent (the USA) even as other would-be tyrants would have been emboldened. The resulting political backlash in the USA would have imperilled continued American membership and the UN would have become this century's League of Nations. Conversely, if the war leads to a hundred flowers of freedom blooming in the politically arid Arab nation, it will ultimately damage the credibility and authority of the UN and enhance the prestige and mana of the USA.

UN centrality

The second point of view acknowledged the need to confront Saddam but ruled out acting without UN authorisation. From a test of UN relevance, the agenda shifted to being a test of the legitimacy of US action. Imperceptibly and subtly, the issue had metamorphosed into the question of what sort of world we wish to live in, who we wish to be ruled by, and if we wish to live by rules and laws or by the force of arms.

---

[4] Richard Perle, 'Thank God for the Death of the UN', *Guardian*, 21 March 2003.

The UN found itself front and centre in the debate, the focus of hopes, fears and the media's most pressing attention.

Few outsiders were convinced of the case for war. Little evidence linked Saddam Hussein to Osama bin Laden. Saddam had been successfully contained and disarmed and did not pose a clear and present danger to regional, world or US security.[5] Washington scarcely concealed its real agenda of regime change. Cynicism about US motives ran deep because of its history of past material and diplomatic support for Saddam during the days when his behaviour was at its worst, including the use of chemical weapons against his own people in Halabja and the attack on Iran. There was confusion about the mix of personal,[6] religious,[7] oil, geopolitical and military-technological motives for going to war. Two things were widely believed to follow from the contrasting US policies towards Iraq and North Korea: Iraq did not have usable nuclear weapons, North Korea does not have oil.

Time was when those threatening to go to war had to prove their case beyond reasonable doubt. Today we are asked to prove to the powerful, to their satisfaction, why they should not go to war. The determined rush to war ignited a worldwide debate on the legitimacy of war, the likes of which we have not seen before. The UN Security Council (UNSC) played precisely the role envisaged for it by the founders of the UN; it did so for six long months; and it was more of a central player in this crisis than

---

[5] Ironically, not only did the coalition forces fail to find any WMD after invasion; they managed to lose almost 350 tonnes of high explosives stored under IAEA seal at Iraq's Al-Qaqaa military installation, and this despite IAEA warnings to the USA; 'IAEA says it Warned US about Explosives', *USA Today*, 29 October 2004; 'IAEA Warned US about Arms Dump', *Daily Yomiuri*, 30 October 2004. The timing of the news item – in the final week of the US presidential campaign – led to charges that the IAEA and the UN might have leaked the story in revenge at the Bush administration; see Clifford D. May, 'UN Manipulation?', *Washington Times*, 31 October 2004. Mohamed El Baradei, director-general of the IAEA, described such charges as 'total junk', noting that while the timing may have been unfortunate, it arose from external pressures and events: 'there is a world out there other than the American election'; 'El Baradei Dismisses Revenge Claim', *BBC News* (http://news.bbc.co.uk), 31 October 2004.

[6] Many of the key policy-makers in the administration of George W. Bush are veterans from the administration of the Gulf War under his father and viewed Saddam as an unfinished agenda from a decade ago. In addition, Saddam had tried to assassinate Bush Sr., a point not forgotten by the son.

[7] See John B. Judis, 'The Chosen Nation: The Influence of Religion on US Foreign Policy', *Policy Brief* No. 37 (Washington DC: Carnegie Endowment for International Peace, March 2005); and Adam Nicolson, 'Heading Towards the Apocalypse', *Age* (Melbourne), 23 October 2004.

at any other time in its history. From being an optional add-on in
September 2002, by March 2003 the Council had become the forum of
choice for making the case for the use of military force, for debating –
openly, publicly, globally – the merits, wisdom, legality and legitimacy
of war. This was a critical and historic dialogue that the world had to
have. For the first time ever in human history, 'we the peoples of the
world' united to wage peace before a war starts.[8] Call it the people's pre-
emption. Winning the war without UN blessing was the easy part.
Securing the peace without UN endorsement and involvement proved
to be the tougher challenge – and victory in battle is pointless without
a resulting secure peace afterwards. 'Operation Desert Storm' of Gulf
War I became 'Operation Storm in a Teacup' in Gulf War II – with other
contenders for the name of the war including 'Mission Implausible:
A Job Well Spun' and 'Operation Rolling Blunder'.[9]

UN complicity

The third argument accepted UN authorisation as necessary, but not
sufficient, and preferred UN irrelevance to complicity. For all its moral
authority, many feared, the UN lacks moral clarity. The UNSC record
is not especially notable for a sense of moral compass and courage of
international convictions. There was a growing sentiment that if the UN
was bribed and bullied into submission and sanctioned war, instead of
UN legitimacy being stamped on military action against Iraq, that
legitimacy itself would have been eroded.

During the mini-crisis in the UNSC in July 2002 over the ICC,[10]
Washington had already demonstrated that it views the UN as a forum
for augmenting policy options, not limiting them. The Bush statement
in the General Assembly in September 2002 was not an American concession to UN multilateralism, but a demand for international capitula-
tion to the US threat to go to war. But in doing so Bush presented the
UN with an impossible choice between effectiveness and integrity. And
while demanding Iraqi compliance with the resulting Security Council

---

[8] See David Cortright, *A Peaceful Superpower: The Movement against War in Iraq* (Goshen,
Indiana: Fourth Freedom Forum, 2004).

[9] For an inventive inventory of possible names suggested by readers, see Nicholas
D. Kristof, 'The Name of the War', *International Herald Tribune* (IHT), 1 December 2003.

[10] See Ramesh Thakur, 'The International Criminal Court: Politics vs. Justice at The Hague',
IHT, 16 August 2002.

Resolution 1441, Washington insisted on retaining the freedom to strike at Iraq without a follow-up resolution if necessary – in effect proclaiming exemption for itself from the same resolution.[11] The choice between irrelevance and complicity would be a fatal one for the organisation. For it comes down to a choice between knowing and accepting its place as a mere speedbump or becoming a roadkill on the highway of power politics.

Washington found it especially difficult to answer two crucial questions: Why Iraq? Why now? It did not help its cause by a continually shifting justification. Containment and deterrence worked against the far more formidable Soviet enemy during the Cold War; why did they have to be replaced by the destabilising doctrine of prevention? In effect, Iraq became the testing ground for the doctrine and weapons of preventive war. Washington was seen as determined to wage war not because it had to, but because it wanted to and could; not because Iraq was strong and as such posed a threat, but because it was weak and could be attacked without fear of catastrophe. Saddam was on this administration's agenda when it came into office: 9/11 provided the alibi, not the reason.[12] Deputy Defense Secretary Paul Wolfowitz was reported as having conceded subsequently that the WMD issue was chosen in the end for good 'bureaucratic' reasons, in that that was the only issue on which all the different sectors of the vast US bureaucracy could come to an agreement as an acceptable justification for going to war.[13] Maureen Dowd notes that 'The Iraq WMD's and ties to al Qaeda were merely MacGuffins, as Alfred Hitchcock called devices that drove the plot but were otherwise inconsequential.'[14] The UN inspectors could indeed have been given more time to complete their job.

---

[11] See Michael J. Glennon, 'How War Left the Law Behind', *New York Times*, 21 November 2002.

[12] See Richard A. Clarke, *Against All Enemies: Inside America's War on Terror* (New York: Free Press, 2004); Ron Suskind, *The Price of Loyalty: George W. Bush, the White House, and the Education of Paul O'Neill* (New York: Simon and Schuster, 2004); and Bob Woodward, *Plan of Attack* (New York: Simon and Schuster, 2004). The most authoritative existing account in public of the many dimensions of 9/11 is the report of the 9/11 Commission: *The 9/11 Commission Report: Final Report of the National Commission on Terrorist Attacks Upon the United States* (New York: W. W. Norton, 2004).

[13] In an interview with *Vanity Fair* in July 2003; quoted in 'WMDs Only "Bureaucratic Reason" for War: Wolfowitz', *Sydney Morning Herald*, 29 May 2003.

[14] Maureen Dowd, 'Iran, al Qaeda and Weapons of Mass Destruction', *IHT*, 26 May 2003.

Imagine if the government of any country insisted that someone was guilty and must be hanged. The evidence of his guilt would be produced only after his execution, and the nature of his offence (murder, rape, treason) identified only after the evidence had been collected posthumously. In the same way, Washington reversed the usual sequence of trial, conviction and punishment. The outcome was predetermined: a swift and heavy military defeat leading to regime change in Baghdad. The justification (WMD, involvement with international terrorism, humanitarian atrocities) came after the fact and was changed from WMD to liberation theology.

Arguably, the United Nations had already allowed itself to become complicit in the Anglo-US strategy to try to provoke Iraqi defiance as a pretext for war. This is indicated in the now-famous Downing Street Memorandum.[15] It refers to a memorandum written by British foreign policy aide Matthew Rycroft on 23 July 2002 (sic) summarising a briefing by Richard Dearlove, head of MI6 (Britain's overseas intelligence agency). The memorandum makes clear that the US administration was determined to go to war and military action was thus seen as inevitable, but that British officials did not believe there was sufficient legal justification since there was no recent evidence of Iraqi complicity with international terrorism, Saddam's WMD capability was less than that of Libya, North Korea or Iran, and he was not a threat to his neighbours. But because it was necessary to create the conditions that would make an invasion legal, 'the intelligence and facts were being fixed around the policy'. The USA 'had already begun "spikes of activity" to put pressure on the regime', and an ultimatum for the return of UN weapons inspectors to Iraq might help to create the conditions necessary to justify military action.

As we know, the UN did coerce Saddam along these lines, but he acquiesced to the UN demand, thereby thwarting the search for a pretext to justify the invasion. Precisely because the WMD rhetoric was seen as a transparent ruse, the recourse to the UNSC was seen simply as an effort to harness UN legitimacy to a predetermined US agenda. Hence the following from one US critic as the tumultuous year drew to a close:

---

[15] The memorandum was originally published as 'The Secret Downing Street Memo' in the *Sunday Times* (London), 1 May 2005. It quickly acquired a dedicated website of its own: www.downingstreetmemo.com. All the quotes in this paragraph are from the *Sunday Times* article.

[T]he United Nations [is] now more than ever reduced to the servile function of after-sales service provider for the United States, on permanent call
as the mop-up brigade. It would be a great step forward if several big Third
World countries were to quit the UN, declaring that it has no function
beyond ratifying the world's present distasteful political arrangements . . .
So please . . . no more earnest calls for 'a UN role', at least not until the outfit
is radically reconstituted along genuinely democratic lines.[16]

Goals contradicted by means

Washington had five great claims for the war on Iraq: the threat posed by
WMD proliferation; the threat of international terrorism; the need to
establish a beachhead of democratic freedoms and the rule of law in the
Middle East; the need to bring Saddam Hussein to justice for the
atrocities committed by his regime; and the duty to be the international
community's enforcer. The UN is strongly committed to every one of
the five goals. But each goal was badly undermined by the means chosen
and their collective damage to the Empire Lite enterprise is greater than
the sum of their separate parts.[17]

In October 2004, the CIA's Iraq Survey Group headed by Charles
Duelfer reported with finality that while Saddam Hussein had harboured
ambitions to get WMD, the Iraqi programmes to build them had decayed
completely. UN sanctions had helped to dismantle them and UN inspections had given an accurate assessment of Saddam's WMD capability.[18]
Iraq's arsenal of chemical and biological weapons was negligible, its
nuclear weapons programme was virtually non-existent and it had little
ability to revive the weapons programmes.[19] Subsequent studies have

---

[16] Alexander Cockburn, 'It Should Be Late, It Was Never Great', *The Nation*, 22 December
2003, p. 9.

[17] For elaboration, see Ramesh Thakur, 'Iraq War and World Order', in C. Uday Bhaskar,
Uttam K. Sinha, K. Santhanam and Tasneem Meenai, eds., *United Nations: Multilateralism and International Security* (New Delhi: Institute for Defence Studies and Analyses,
2005), pp. 89–113. There were still other contradictions not covered in my analysis. For
example, 'The Russians were mocked [by Americans] for protecting their economic self-
interest, while Halliburton positioned itself at the center of Iraqi reconstruction'; Paul
Heinbecker (Canada's ambassador to the UN at the time), 'Washington's Exceptionalism
and the United Nations', *Global Governance* 10:3 (July–September 2004), p. 277.

[18] For the story by the chief weapons inspector himself, see Hans Blix, *Disarming Iraq* (New
York: Pantheon, 2004).

[19] The report can be downloaded at: http://www.cia.gov/cia/reports/iraq_wmd_2004. For
a summary analysis, see Kevin Whitelaw, 'The Vanishing Case for War', *Daily Yomiuri*,
15 October 2004 (reprinted from *US News & World Report*).

confirmed that US intelligence analysts were internally questioning almost all pre-war claims about Iraq's WMD: that it tried to buy uranium in Africa for its nuclear programme, was producing biological weapons in mobile labs, had an active chemical weapons programme, and had acquired unmanned aircraft for delivery of WMD. Moreover, as recognised by Senator Robert Byrd, 'we may have sparked a new international arms race as countries move ahead to develop WMD as a last ditch attempt to ward off a possible preemptive strike from a newly belligerent US which claims the right to hit where it wants'.[20]

Second, how is it possible to achieve victory in the war on international terrorism against American targets by inciting a still deeper hatred of US foreign policy? Most informed observers predicted that the sight of American forces occupying Baghdad would spur more terrorism, not less, especially while the open Palestinian wound still festers on the collective Arab-Islamic body politic.[21] Iraq became a hotbed of terrorism as a result of the war. Diverse strands of evidence corroborate the thesis that the radicals were dispirited and at a loss in 2002 after the rapid defeat of the Taliban in Afghanistan, but became exuberant with the USA being tied down in Iraq in 2003–5. They were able to 'expose' the real nature of the USA as a global enemy of Islam bent on stealing the Arab oil patrimony.[22] The inconsistency in US policy is exploited by al Qaeda recruiters as the perpetual and systematic hypocrisy of American foreign policy. 'There was no al-Qaida in Iraq before the arrival of US and British troops. Now fundamentalists are descending like spores of anthrax on the gaping wounds torn open by the war.'[23] Nor was the spur to terrorism confined to Iraq or the Middle East. US officials in Southeast Asia conceded that recruitment and fund-raising for the terrorist organisation Jemaah Islamiyah had become easier because of the widespread opposition in the region to the war on Iraq.[24] And the British public simply refused to accept the government's denial of any link between the Iraq War and the London bombings on 7 July 2005.[25]

---

[20] Robert C. Byrd, 'The Truth Will Emerge', 21 May 2003, available at http://byrd.senate.gov.
[21] See Jessica Stern, 'Terrorism's New Mecca', *Globe and Mail* (Toronto), 28 November 2003.
[22] Daniel Benjamin and Gabriel Weimann, 'Terrorist Talk Shows Just How Wrong Bush Is', *IHT*, 28 October 2004.
[23] George Galloway, 'These are Blair's Last Days', *Guardian*, 3 May 2005.
[24] Raymond Bonner, 'New Attacks Expected to hit Southeast Asia', *IHT*, 25 November 2003.
[25] See, in particular, Seumas Milne, 'It is an Insult to the Dead to Deny the Link with Iraq', and Andrew Murray, 'Cause and Consequence', *Guardian*, 14 and 27 July 2005.

The most problematic contradiction is in relation to the professed goal of establishing democracy in Iraq and using it as a beacon to promote political freedoms across the Arab world. How does one instil democracy in an inhospitable terrain by punishing friends and allies – in the home continent of the founding values of Western civilisation – who dared to exercise their democratic right to dissent from a war whose justification still remains contentious,[26] while rewarding dictators who lent ready support?[27] Then there is the little matter of normative inconsistency, when the goal of democracy in Iraq is imposed by bombers, helicopter gunships and tanks but other regimes with equally questionable democratic credentials are not just tolerated, but in many cases remain solid US allies. The global expansion of democracy has not been a pillar of American foreign policy; the rhetoric of democracy is an expedient justification in support of other more traditional goals.

Liberal democracy rests on the rule of law. The legal basis for going to war continued to haunt the British government during the 2005 election campaign.[28] The Attorney-General, Lord Goldsmith, had serious reservations about the legality based on six arguments: it was for the UN, not individual states, to decide if Iraq was in breach of UN resolutions; Resolution 1441 was an unreliable ground for war because it did not use the key phrase 'all necessary means' to enforce it; hence the need for a second UN resolution; earlier UN resolutions going back to the first Gulf War could not easily be revived to suit the exigencies of 2003; reports from Hans Blix that UN inspectors were still doing their job and Iraq was being compliant; and the US position on legality did not apply to Britain because

---

[26] Thus Senator Byrd: 'It is astonishing that our government is berating the Turkish government for conducting its affairs in accordance with its own Constitution and its democratic institutions'; Byrd, 'The Truth Will Emerge'. See also Husain Haqqani, 'Why Muslims Always Blame the West', *IHT*, 16 October 2004.

[27] For just a few contemporary examples, see Paul Foot, 'Our Kind of Dictators', *Guardian*, 9 June 2004; Rajan Menon, 'America's Dictator Problem in Uzbekistan', *IHT*, 13 August 2004; Nick Paton Walsh, 'US Sidles Up to Well-oiled Autocracy', *Guardian*, 2 July 2004. After General Pervez Musharraf reneged on his promise to give up his military post as army chief, the *Washington Post* commented in an editorial that 'the general has become a classic example of the sort of US ally Mr. Bush has repeatedly vowed to repudiate: an authoritarian ruler who offers tactical security cooperation with the United States while storing up trouble for the future'; 'Another Pass for Pakistan', 31 December 2004. See also the trenchant analysis by a leading Pakistani journalist Farhan Bokhari, 'Musharraf's Penchant to Stay in Charge', *Japan Times*, 7 January 2005.

[28] See Robin Cook, who resigned as foreign minister rather than support the war, 'Not Even in His Worst Nightmares', *Guardian*, 25 March 2005.

Congress had granted special war-making powers to President Bush.[29] He was persuaded to change his mind just before the war began.[30] In her resignation letter submitted on the eve of the Iraq War, Elizabeth Wilmshurst, the deputy legal adviser to the Foreign Office, described military action in Iraq as 'an unlawful use of force' that 'amounts to the crime of aggression'.[31]

What answer to those who claim that aggression abroad was matched by repression at home, with serious cutbacks to many liberties that US citizens, residents and visitors alike had come to take for granted for decades?[32] The Bush administration 'treated criticism and dissent as treason, ethnicity as grounds for suspicion and Congressional and judicial oversight as inconvenient obstacles'.[33] The most perverse policy was the charade of justice in Guantánamo Bay, which even a British law justice called a 'legal black hole' that was 'a stain on United States justice'.[34] In effect Washington asserted the right to be able to 'pick up foreign citizens anywhere in the world, spirit them off to Guantánamo and lock them up forever, with no court questioning its actions, and therefore without any legal limits'. The US military can 'hold people indefinitely without trial in an undeclared and permanent war against unidentified foes'.[35]

Nor is it possible to promote the rule of law and the role of international law in world affairs, to act as the world's policeman, by hollowing out some of the most important parts of international law that restrict

---

[29] Gaby Hinsliff, 'Blair Blow as Secret War Doubts Revealed', *Observer*, 24 April 2005 and Michael White, 'Opposition Goes on Iraq Offensive', *Guardian*, 25 April 2005. See also John Ware, 'MI6, Jack Straw, Defence Staff: Blair Ignored Them All', *Guardian*, 26 March 2005.

[30] For a critique of how Washington has ridden roughshod over international law and the failure of the Blair government to exercise any restraining influence, see Philippe Sands, *Lawless World: America and the Making and Breaking of Global Rules* (London: Allen Lane, 2005).

[31] 'Iraq War "Crime of Aggression"', *BBC News*, 24 March 2005 (http://news.bbc.co.uk/2/hi/uk_news/politics/4377469.stm).

[32] There is also the surreal, Kafkaesque situation of Dr Amer al-Saadi, the Iraqi scientist who insisted all along that Iraq's WMD had been destroyed yet who, a year after the war, was still held in solitary confinement. See Jonathan Steele, 'Why Being Right on WMD is No Consolation to Iraqi Scientist Labelled Enemy of America', *Guardian*, 5 May 2004.

[33] Editorial, *The Nation* (29 November 2004), p. 3.

[34] Clare Dyer, 'Law Lord Castigates US Justice', *Guardian*, 26 November 2003. Extracts of his speech were published as Johan Steyn, 'A Monstrous Failure of Justice', *IHT*, 28 November 2003.

[35] David Cole, 'Korematsu II?', *The Nation* (Boston), 8 December 2003, p. 6.

the right to go to war except in self-defence or when authorised by the UN. In order to oust a regime based solely on might with few redeeming features to make it right, established institutions and conventions for ensuring that force is legitimately exercised were set aside by a power supremely confident of its might. If the normative restraints of the legal code of behaviour are overthrown by the eagle-eyed predators of the international jungle, will not others, guided by the age-old instinct of self-preservation, seek recourse to whatever weapons of deterrence they can acquire by hook or by crook? Former US Secretary of State (1997–2001) Madeleine Albright writes that 'The administration, openly allergic to treaties and arms control, has made no effort to promote restraint in developing arms as a normative ethic to which all nations have an interest in abiding.'[36]

Fourth, the troubling question of normative inconsistency crops up again with particular cogency after Saddam's capture in relation to the occupying powers in Iraq establishing an ad hoc criminal tribunal to try him and his henchmen. For, against the backdrop of US rejection of the International Criminal Court and active efforts to undermine it, the denial of basic justice to prisoners at Guantánamo Bay and the history of supporting and arming repressive regimes in the Middle East and elsewhere,[37] justice dispensed by such an occupying power will be 'of dubious legality and questionable legitimacy'.[38]

Finally, it is difficult to see how one country can enforce UN resolutions by defying the authority of the world body, denigrating it as irrelevant and belittling its role in reconstruction efforts after the war.

Liberation as a collateral benefit

Saddam Hussein is gone, and the people of Iraq are freed of his tyranny – that is a decided benefit. There is still the potential to remake the regional order around Iraq's neighbourhood. The war has also given real urgency to the debates on reforming the system of multilateral governance so

---

[36] Madeleine Albright, 'US Faces Intractable Dilemmas with Depleted Capital', *Japan Times* (reprinting article from the *Washington Post*), 23 July 2003.

[37] See Gwynne Dyer, 'Ailing Middle East Created by a Contemptuous West', *Canberra Times*, 22 July 2004; Stephen J. Hedges, 'US Must Do a Better Job of Picking its Friends', *Yomiuri* (reprinted from the *Chicago Tribune*), 7 August 2004. For a humorous roster of some US friends and allies past and present, see Scott Burchill, 'The Bad Guys We Once Thought Good', *Age*, 27 December 2003.

[38] Hanny Megally and Paul van Zyl, 'US Justice with an Iraqi Face?', *IHT*, 4 December 2003.

that we focus on today's real threats, and how best to tackle those threats through collective efforts.

These are all real, significant and weighty gains, not to be lightly dismissed. But even so, they do not trump all other considerations. Saddam's removal is a collateral benefit amid the carnage of destruction to the agreed principles and established institutions of world order. It is difficult to be joyous at the descent from the ideal of a world based on the rule of law to that of the law of the jungle – though one can see why the lion would welcome such a change.

Victory in Iraq came at the price of relegitimising wars of choice as an instrument of unilateral state policy.[39] How are we going to prevent the proliferation of the unlawful and unjustified use of force, of going to war as an instrument of state policy by other countries? To argue that military victory bestows legitimacy is to say that might is right, and that means justify the ends: two long-standing *Western* taboos. It also begs the question: Will others politely accept the new US imperial order, or will they begin to arm and align themselves so as not to become tomorrow's Iraq? Few will accept the doctrine that the administration of the day in Washington can decide who is to be which country's leader, and who is to be toppled. Nor has Washington been known to urge the abolition of the veto power of the five permanent members because it is an obstacle to effective decision-making by the UN. The veto may be an outmoded relic of the Cold War – but the USA is in no position to criticise others. Since the end of the Cold War Washington has wielded the veto most frequently (see table 13.1).

Not only do claims advanced to justify the war not stand up; the balance sheet has also to include the many and substantial damaging effects of the war. First, of course, the casualties. By Autumn 2005 almost 2,000 US soldiers had been killed. People usually frame an argument in terms of the risks to the lives of their own soldiers. Yet arguably an even greater moral cost is asking one's young soldiers to kill large numbers of others on the basis of suspect claims. A US medical team calculated the civilian casualties based on a scientific household survey and came up with the stunning figure of 98,000 deaths, *without counting Fallujah* (because it has been the scene of the fiercest and most prolonged

---

[39] In the words of Robin Cook, 'What makes this [neo-conservative] web of reactionary ideologues a menace to the world is that they believe complex, historic problems have simple, instant, military solutions'; Robin Cook, 'Bush Will Now Celebrate by Putting Falluja to the Torch', *Guardian*, 5 November 2004.

fighting, Fallujah was categorised as an outlier), in the eighteen months after the war. Moreover, 84 per cent of the casualties were attributable to coalition air strikes, not rebels, and women and children made up more than half the total killed.[40] While the public database Iraqi Body Count estimated the Iraqi civilian toll at around 25,000 deaths, the Graduate Institute of International Studies in Geneva re-examined the *Lancet* study to conclude that the more accurate estimate should be around 40,000 deaths.[41]

[40] Les Roberts, Riyadh Lafta, Richard Garfield, Jamal Khudhairi and Gilbert Burhnam, 'Mortality Before and After the 2003 Invasion of Iraq: Cluster Sample Survey', *Lancet* 364:9445 (30 October 2004). The team was from Johns Hopkins University's Bloomberg School of Public Health and was assisted by doctors from al-Mustansiriya University Medical School in Baghdad. Coalition governments disputed the findings, but failed to provide numbers of civilian casualties themselves whose accuracy can be assessed against the *Lancet* article's. Because the study attracted great international coverage but was criticised for its methodology in many US circles, it is worth a comment. The methodology employed is called clustered sampling, which is the rule in public health studies, for example of epidemics. The alternative technique, called passive-surveillance systems, relies on waiting for reports of deaths to come in, rather than reporters going out randomly into the field to see if anyone has been killed in a violent attack. For this reason, it tends seriously to undercount mortality, in epidemics as in violence. The Iraq study team picked out thirty-three towns in Iraq at random, then within each town, picked out thirty-three neighbourhoods – clusters – at random, and then visited the nearest thirty households. A total of 7,868 people in 988 households were interviewed in all about births and deaths that had occurred since 1 January 2002. Based on these interviews, the team calculated the number of deaths caused by the war by comparing the aggregate death rates before and after 18 March 2003, and attributing some 60 per cent of the excess deaths directly to the violence (from both sides), with the remaining being due to accidents, disease and infant mortality. Because of the variable distribution of deaths in a war, violence can be highly localised. From that point of view, thirty-three clusters is a relatively small sample size, perhaps too small to be representative. In fact the decision to exclude Fallujah reflected precisely the study team's concerns that its violence was far too unrepresentative. The rather large range of *possible* death numbers, from 8,000 to 194,000, reflects the small sample size for a study of this type. Nevertheless, the figure of 98,000 is *the most likely number* in that huge range. This does not mean, therefore, that any number in that range is just as probable as any other number. The further away we move from 98,000, *in either direction*, the lower the probability of that number, so that the lowest estimate of 8,000 is just as (un)likely as the highest estimate of 194,000. Experts consulted by the *Economist* – not one's average left-wing anti-war propaganda tract – confirmed that the study had been carried out to the standard professional level; 'Counting the Casualties', *Economist*, 6 November 2004, pp. 80–1.

[41] Irwin Arieff, 'New Study Raises Iraq Death Toll', *Age*, 13 July 2005. On the other hand, epidemiologists and public health experts I have spoken to confirm that the methodology used for the *Lancet* study is standard practice in the profession and was correctly followed by the Johns Hopkins team.

The United Nations itself stands doubly damaged. Many say it failed the test of standing up to a tyrant who had brutalised his own people, terrorised his neighbours and thumbed his nose at the UN for twelve years. Many more say it failed to stand up to the superpower in defence of a country that posed no threat to any outsider any more.

The relationship between the UN and the USA is badly frayed. Yet they need each other, not just in Iraq, but also in Afghanistan, Haiti and elsewhere. Besides, a completely pliant UN would indeed become irrelevant, even to the USA.

Transatlantic relations have been damaged. When the major European nations objected that the case for war had not been proven beyond reasonable doubt, instead of dialogue they got bad-tempered insults. The neo-conservative ideologues 'regard allies not as proof of diplomatic strength but as evidence of military weakness'.[42] If friends and allies are to be useful, they must avoid both slavish obedience and instinctive opposition; be prepared to support Washington when they are right despite intense international unpopularity; but be willing to say no to Washington when they are wrong, despite the risk of intense American irritation.

European unity itself was shattered, and the fragile single European project badly shaken. The characterisation of old and new Europe was, in fact, quite mistaken. Considering the past few centuries of European history, France and Germany standing together in resisting war is the new Europe of secular democracies and welfare states, built on peaceful relations embedded in continental institutions. The former Soviet satellites that sided with the USA represent the continuity from the old Europe built on balance of power policies that had led to the world wars.

The USA has been deeply divided from world opinion. There has been a startlingly precipitous worldwide decline in US global leadership.[43] A ten-nation poll conducted for the *Guardian* documented a general rejection of the Iraq invasion, rising hostility to US foreign policy under the Bush administration, but favourable opinions of Americans (table 10.1).[44] Rarely has an American administration faced such

---

[42] Cook, 'Bush Will Now Celebrate by Putting Falluja to the Torch'.

[43] 'Instead of isolating Saddam Hussein, we seem to have isolated ourselves. We proclaim a new doctrine of preemption which is understood by few and feared by many'; Robert C. Byrd, 'The Arrogance of Power', 19 March 2003, available at http://byrd.senate.gov.

[44] The annual survey of global attitudes towards the USA by the Pew Research Center, published earlier in March, had shown similar loss of faith in US foreign policy; *A Year*

Table 10.1. *A cross-national survey of world-views on the USA, 2004*

	1		2		3		4		5		6	
	F	U	I	W	Right	Wrong	I	N	Yes	No	Yes	No
Canada	73	23	15	64	24	67	68	28	51	45	46	52
France	72	24	14	70	18	77	49	48	17	80	–	–
UK	62	21	15	45	–	–	–	–	51	40	–	–
Spain	47	32	5	60	13	80	44	45	17	73	–	–
Russia	86	13	–	–	39	54	48	46	–	–	48	46
Japan	74	17	17	74	16	71	71	25	42	54	44	53
Australia	72	21	28	54	–	–	73	23	–	–	–	–
Mexico	51	43	25	56	10	83	76	18	22	74	63	33
Israel	81	10	40	26	68	26	68	26	–	–	61	36
South Korea	65	30	25	67	11	85	67	31	48	48	47	49
Average	68	23	20	57	25	68	63	32	35	59	52	45

1. Overall, do you have a favourable (F) or unfavourable (U) opinion of Americans?
2. Over the past 2 or 3 years, has your opinion of the USA improved (I) or worsened (W)?
3. Was the USA right or wrong in invading Iraq?
4. Is it important (I) or not (N) that the USA plays a leadership role on the world stage?
5. Does the war waged by the USA and its allies in Iraq contribute to the war against terrorism?
6. By its actions, does the USA contribute to world peace?
Source: An ICM research poll conducted for the *Guardian*; *Guardian*, 15 October 2004.

isolation and loss of public support among its closest allies from essentially pro-American people.[45] All cross-national public opinion polls

---

after Iraq War: Mistrust of America in Europe Ever Higher, Muslim Anger Persists, Pew Global Attitudes Project, Pew Research Center for the People and the Press, 16 March 2004. Former secretary of state Madeleine Albright commented dryly: 'It's nice to be feared by your enemies, but it's not nice to be feared by your friends'; *BBC News* (http://news.bbc.co.uk), 17 March 2004.

[45] Even President Jacques Chirac of France, the bête noir of US conservative commentators, gave a wonderfully evocative speech to mark the D-Day anniversary in Normandy on

continue to show plummeting confidence in US credibility and leadership. One commissioned by the BBC World Service showed that with Bush's re-election, the high negative feelings towards the president were translating into dislike of Americans in general. In the poll of 22,000 people in twenty-one countries, 58 per cent believed his re-election would worsen world peace and security, while only 26 per cent thought the contrary.[46] One of the more poignant comments came from outgoing Deputy Secretary of State Richard Armitage in an interview with an Australian newspaper. His biggest regrets, he said, were that they did not stop 9/11 and afterwards, 'instead of redoubling what is our traditional export of hope and optimism we exported our fear and anger. And presented a very intense and angry face to the world.'[47]

The problem of US credibility with the Islamic world is still more acute. Muslims are embittered, sullen and resentful of a perceived assault on Islam.[48] Their sense of grievance is inflamed by perceptions of collective humiliation and rank double standards. In November 2004, even the Defense Science Board, an advisory panel to the Pentagon, concluded that Washington was losing the war of ideas among the Muslims of the world who were dismissive of US intentions and self-serving hypocrisy. 'Muslims do not hate our freedom, but rather they hate our policies', in particular the one-sided support of Israel and of tyrannies in the Islamic world like Egypt, Saudi Arabia, Jordan, Pakistan and the Gulf states, the report said.[49]

US credibility suffered a calamitous collapse with the publication of abuse photographs from the Abu Ghraib prison, graphically depicting the extent to which the war had brutalised the US military. The abuses

---

Sunday, 6 June 2004 which paid tribute simultaneously to the bonds uniting France and the USA and the idealism that underpins the UN: 'From the plains of Yorktown to the beaches of Normandy, in the suffering of those global conflicts that have rent the past century, our two countries, our two peoples have stood shoulder to shoulder in the brotherhood of blood spilled, in defence of a certain ideal of mankind, of a certain vision of the world – the vision that lies at the heart of the United Nations Charter.' Quoted in Claude Salhani, 'Analysis: Chirac's "Finest Hour"', United Press International, 7 June 2004 (www.upi.com/view.cfm/StoryID> 20040607-122434-1149r).

[46] 'Global Polls Slam Bush Leadership', *BBC News* (http://news.bbc.co.uk), 19 January 2005; Ewen MacAskill, 'World Fears New Bush Era', *Guardian*, 20 January 2005.

[47] Greg Sheridan, 'Reflections of a Straight Shooter', *Australian*, 20 January 2005.

[48] See Philip Kennicott, 'America's Image Plumbs New Depths among Arabs', *Japan Times* (reprinted from the *Washington Post*), 30 August 2004.

[49] 'US "Alienating" World's Muslims', *BBC News* (http://news.bbc.co.uk), 25 November 2004; 'US Losing "War of Ideas" among Muslims', *Japan Times*, 26 November 2004.

were not isolated incidents,[50] but reflected a systemic malaise.[51] Indeed they flowed from the backdrop and manner of going to war. The restraints of international law on waging war were pushed aside as mere inconveniences.[52] When leaders exempt themselves from the norms of international behaviour, a few foot soldiers will free themselves from the norms of civilised conduct. Thus Rob Corddry of the satirical *Daily Show*: 'Remember, it's not important that we did torture these people. What's important is that we are not the kind of people who would torture these people.'[53] But the self-correcting mechanisms of a great and enduring democracy were also on public display. Americans led the world in publishing the pictures, reacting to them as a society with revulsion and deep disgust, conducting an anguished public debate promising a due accounting and justice for the perpetrators, and issuing apologies from the president down. As Senator Byrd put it, 'America's true power lies not in its will to intimidate, but in its ability to inspire.'[54]

US soft power has been eroded. Joseph Nye believes that public opinion polls show that 'in most parts of the world the attractiveness of the United States has declined quite dramatically over the past four years, particularly in the Muslim world', and that the drop in the number of foreign students also erodes US soft power.[55]

The US people are domestically divided with an edge to their opinions that is quite disheartening for all well-wishers of the country and all who recognise that the American role in world affairs as a great and virtuous power has been historically unique, essentially beneficial and generous to a fault, and both vital and necessary. The deep internal frictions are especially troubling because of the impressive national unity shown in the aftermath of 9/11.[56]

---

[50] The US army subsequently established that twenty-seven detainees had been killed in Afghanistan and Iraq between August 2002 and November 2004 in suspected or con-firmed homicide cases; '27 Killed Under US Custody in Iraq, Afghanistan', *Japan Times*, 27 March 2005.

[51] See in particular Seymour M. Hersh, *Chain of Command: The Road from 9/11 to Abu Ghraib* (New York: Harper-Collins, 2004).

[52] See Jonathan Schell, 'Healing the Law', *The Nation*, 2 August 2004, pp. 12, 42.

[53] Quoted by Eric Alterman, 'Hawks Eating Crow', *The Nation*, 7 June 2004, p. 10.

[54] Byrd, 'The Arrogance of Power'.

[55] In an interview with a major Japanese newspaper, 'Lessons to be Learned from Mideast Errors', *Daily Yomiuri*, 18 January 2005.

[56] And not just the USA. In the UK, fifty-two distinguished former diplomats published an open letter to Prime Minister Tony Blair on 27 April 2004 urging a major rethink of policy towards the Middle East; in the USA, fifty-three former American diplomats did the same on 4 May 2004; and in Australia, a group of forty-three former service chiefs and

The credibility of the British and US media has also suffered a slow but steady erosion on their coverage and analyses of the Iraq War.[57] A former Australian diplomat notes that 'Of Rupert Murdoch's 174 newspapers worldwide, not one editorially opposed the war; and, once the invasion began, many of their commentaries became hysterically supportive.'[58] This was a remarkable coincidence of identical editorial views in the press magnate's stable, especially when set against the strong, broad and deep sentiment against the war across the world. While some media outlets engaged in self-censorship, some others were subjected to governmental attacks. In effect, patriotism supplanted journalism through such questionable techniques as 'embedded' reporters. Sections of the media became cheerleaders for the humanitarian warriors.[59] Media critics were held accountable for minor flaws and gaps in stories, but officials whose lies and incompetence caused large-scale deaths and killings in an unnecessary war got medals of freedom.[60]

Iraq contributed to a dramatic narrowing of the humanitarian space for non-governmental actors. In areas where governments have vital interests at stake, they lay down the terms under which NGOs may operate. When governments overstep the line or are viewed locally as foreign occupiers, NGOs share the opprobrium.[61]

Finally, the net result of all this has been a distraction from the war on terror. The administration indulged its idée fixe on Saddam Hussein at the cost of letting many of the real culprits behind 9/11 get away.[62] For

---

ambassadors published an open letter on 8 August critical of the government's deceptions in the lead-up to the war. All were without precedent in their respective countries.

[57] See Mike Gilligan, 'On Iraq, We've Been Ill-served by Our So-called Experts', *Canberra Times*, 8 April 2004; Michael Massing, 'Unfit to Print?', *New York Review of Books* 51:11 (24 June 2004), and George Monbiot, 'Our Lies Led Us Into War', *Guardian*, 20 July 2004. For the mea culpa by the *New York Times*, see 'The Times and Iraq', *New York Times*, 26 May 2004.

[58] Alison Broinowski, *Howard's War* (Melbourne: Scribe, 2003), p. 27.

[59] In a related vein, the media tend to use labels in a less than neutral manner. According to 'controversial cartoonist' Ted Rall, a Google News search for 'Muqtada al-Sadr' and 'radical cleric' yielded 616 results, for 'Ayad Allawi' (prime minister under the US-led occupation) and 'collaborationist' yielded zero; failed Democratic presidential candidate Howard Dean was often described as an anti-war firebrand, but Bush was not similarly described as a warmonger; and the Afghan resistance to the Soviet occupation was referred to as 'freedom fighters', while the Iraqi resistance to US occupation is labelled 'insurgents'; Ted Rall, 'Media Labels: Another Form of Propaganda', *Japan Times*, 17 April 2005.

[60] Richard Cohen, 'Hollow Accountability', *Washington Post*, 13 January 2005.

[61] See John S. Burnett, 'In the Line of Fire', *New York Times*, 4 August 2004; Isabel Hilton, 'When Does Aid Become a Weapon of War?', *Age* (reprinted from the *Guardian*), 14 July 2004.

[62] 'When it comes to going after the men who were behind 9/11 and who continue to wage a jihad against the US, Bush has repeatedly turned a blind eye to the forces behind

months, with the focus sharply and almost solely on Iraq's Saddam Hussein, Osama bin Laden in effect became Osama bin Forgotten, while Washington was drawn into fighting a war on the terrorists' terms.[63]

Conclusion

The Iraq experience confirms that, as with terrorism, a war of aggression is an unacceptable tactic no matter how just the cause. The fall from grace of an America that was the object of everyone's sympathy and support after 9/11 is nothing short of astonishing. That support understood and backed the war against the Taliban government of Afghanistan. It fractured when Washington turned its attention to Iraq whose links to 9/11 were tenuous at best. Robert Tucker and David Hendrickson argue that the Bush administration pulled down the four pillars of post-1945 US foreign policy: a commitment to international law; consensual decision-making; moderation; and the preservation of peace.[64] Instead, the radical agenda amounted to a revolutionary attempt to overthrow the post-1945 order.

The ouster of Saddam Hussein flowed from strategic not ethical calculations of foreign policy. The USA is a great power, and a great power has strategic imperatives, not moral ones. To accuse it of double standards and hypocrisy thus misses the point. The State Department and Pentagon are not branches of Human Rights Watch or Amnesty International. Washington is motivated to act internationally not because it cares about foreign people, but because it cares about its own interests. The USA is consistent in its foreign policy, remarkably so: but strategically consistent, not morally so.[65]

The three optimistic assumptions behind Washington's Iraq folly can be summed up as: the people of Iraq will welcome and love the Americans as liberators with the ouster of Saddam Hussein; the UN will

---

terrorism, shielded the people who funded al-Qaida, obstructed investigations and diverted resources from the battle against it'; Craig Unger, '"War President" Bush has Always Been Soft on Terror', *Guardian*, 11 September 2004. See also Craig Unger, *House of Bush, House of Saud: The Secret Relationship between the World's Two Most Powerful Dynasties* (New York: Scribner, 2004); Michael Meacher, 'The Pakistan Connection', *Guardian*, 22 July 2004; Carlotta Gall, 'Pakistan Allows Taliban to Train, a Detained Fighter Says', *New York Times*, 4 August 2004.

[63] See Mark Danner, 'US Fighting the War the Terrorists Sought', *IHT*, 9 September 2005.

[64] Robert W. Tucker and David C. Hendrickson, 'Iraq and US Legitimacy', *Foreign Affairs* 83:6 (Nov./Dec. 2004), pp. 18–32.

[65] See George Monbiot, 'The Moral Myth', *Guardian*, 25 November 2003.

fall flat on its face and the countries of the world will flock to join the coalition as soon as we find and display the weapons of mass destruction in Iraq; and Iraq will virtually rebuild itself with petrodollars. All three proved to be wrong. In late 2004, the administration quietly ended the search for WMD in Iraq. As the *New York Times* commented, 'What all our loss and pain and expense in the Iraqi invasion has actually proved is that the weapons inspection worked, that international sanctions – deeply, deeply messy as they turned out to be – worked, and that in the case of Saddam Hussein, the United Nations worked.'[66] What was meant to have been an awesome demonstration of limitless American firepower and willpower turned out to prove the limits of American power in defeating even a small band of insurgents fighting urban warfare with their own bodies as their primary weapon delivery system.

By the end of 2004, the general international sentiment was that Iraqi transition, reconstruction and nation-building cannot be allowed to fail, not after everything that has happened. The UN has expertise, credibility and legitimacy in reintegration of former combatants, reconciliation of former enemies and reconstruction of war-torn societies. Unlike the reflexive hostility of the Pentagon and the Bush administration to 'nation-building', the UN has considerable experience and expertise in this area. The US army is simply not suited to a quasi-imperial vision. Built for high-intensity war-fighting, it has resisted investing and engaging in peace operations and, once abroad, it lacks both staying power and nation-building skills. The crucial question by 2005 was whether, because of the series of mis-steps and errors of judgement, the USA had become so much a part of the problem that its forces must withdraw from Iraq as a precondition for stabilising the country.[67] Their presence had become a focus of grievance and a lightning rod for terrorists and jihadists. This presented an acute dilemma: should they withdraw and risk an immediate descent into chaos, anarchy and civil war, or would their continued presence ensure a slow but steady slide into an insurgency-fuelled chaos and anarchy?[68]

---

[66] 'Bulletin: No WMD Found', editorial, *New York Times*, 13 January 2005.

[67] 'Washington's missteps are now largely viewed as intentional, its statements as hypocritical, and its perceived undeclared agenda – of long-term domination of Iraq – as responsible for the armed opposition's violence'; Robert Malley and Peter Harling, 'How the US Can Salvage Iraq', IHT, 11 January 2005.

[68] See Phyllis Bennis and Erik Leaver, *The Iraq Quagmire: The Mounting Costs of War and the Case for Bringing Home the Troops* (Washington, DC: Institute for Policy Studies and Foreign Policy in Focus, 31 August 2005), available at www.ips-dc.org/iraq/quagmire.

The UN had had to tread the fine line between (a) being seen as legitimising an illegal and unjust war by collaborating with the occupiers 'who wanted a UN presence in occupied Iraq as a legitimizing factor – not as a partner with a vast reservoir of post-conflict peace-building experience'[69] – it has already lost its image of neutrality across the Middle East;[70] and (b) abandoning the people of Iraq who are the true victims thrice over (of Saddam's brutality, UN sanctions, and US war). The UN was criticised by one side for not doing enough to help the Iraqis prepare for the January elections, and by the other side for being too ready and willing to provide the veneer of legitimacy to occupying forces and their puppets.[71] Those who wish to degrade the UN should be careful of what they wish, for the organisation is often useful in picking up the pieces after others have shattered the fragile edifice of world order. Its capacity to mobilise political will in reluctant governments and rally the faithful to the internationalist dream whose death has been prematurely predicted can neither be matched nor substituted by anyone else.

---

[69] Salim Lone (the former director of communications for the UN mission in Iraq and among the injured in the 19 August 2003 bombing of the UN compound), who adds that 'the UN effectively sanctioned the invasion after the fact with resolutions that accepted US occupation goals in Iraq': 'One More Casualty of the War on Terrorism', *Washington Post*, 29 August 2004. See also the full-page ad from a private South African citizen who asserted that in the unanimously approved Security Council Resolution 1546 (8 June 2004), the UN recognised the occupation of Iraq, 'retrospectively approved the Iraq War', and so 'committed political suicide. With this decision the UN Security Council destroyed its own code of international law, the UN Charter and thereby, the very basis for the UN's existence'; Matthias Rath, 'The United Nations Committed Suicide!' (advertisement), *IHT*, 3–4 July 2004. The point is not to debate the merits of this perception, but to record it as reflecting a fairly widespread perception in many parts of the world that I have had to respond to during my travels and talks. Indeed even pro-war enthusiasts interpreted Resolution 1546 in these terms, saying it gave legitimacy to the war; see Tony Parkinson, 'Better Late than Never', *Age*, 10 June 2004.

[70] Even some UN officials seem to believe that the organisation has tilted towards rather than away from the USA, and that this perception has intensified the attacks against it. Salim Lone states that the Iraq mission had been trying 'to hammer out a plan to counter the intensifying perception among Iraqis that our mission was simply an adjunct of the US occupation'. Since then, 'on the question of the need for a democratically elected interim government and, more recently, the composition of the interim government, it has looked as if the UN has buckled to US pressure again'; Salim Lone, 'I Lived to Tell the Tale', *Guardian*, 19 August 2004.

[71] See Thalif Deen, 'UN, Iraq Clash Over Elections', Inter Press News Agency (www.ipsnews. net), 21 October 2004.

11

The responsibility to protect

The worst act of domestic criminal behaviour by a government is large-scale killings of its own people; among the worst acts of international criminal behaviour, to attack and invade another country. The history of the twentieth century is in part the story of a twin-track approach to tame, through a series of normative, legislative and institutional fetters, both these impulses to armed criminality by states. Cumulatively and in combination, these attempted to translate an increasingly international-ised human conscience and a growing sense of an international commu-nity into a new normative architecture of world order. There is growing recognition of the authority of international consensus over individual state consent as the foundation of legal obligation. The notion of 'excess state violence' has evolved to challenge the use of violence by any state in its internal and international behaviour beyond the level that international political actors consider to be legitimate.[1]

Saddam Hussein's record of brutality was a taunting reminder of the distance yet to be traversed before we reach the first goal of eradicating domestic state criminality; his ouster and capture by unilateral force of arms is a daunting challenge to the effort to outlaw and criminalise war as an instrument of state policy in international affairs. But what if the second failure is a response to the first, if one country is attacked and invaded in order to halt or prevent atrocities inside its sovereign territory by the 'legitimate' government (which already indicates a troubling appropriation and corruption of the word 'legitimate')? Who bears the responsibility to protect innocent victims of humanitarian atrocities?

As genocide unfolded in Rwanda in 1994 and 800,000 people were butchered in a mere three months, the world bore silent and distant – very distant – witness to its own apathy. That indifference and inaction by the international community remains one of the most shameful episodes

---

[1] See Bruce Cronin, 'International Legal Consensus and the Control of Excess State Violence', *Global Governance* 11:3 (July–September 2005), pp. 311–30.

since the Holocaust. This was not a matter of lack of knowledge and awareness, or even lack of capacity. Rather, it was a failure of collective conscience,
of civic courage at the highest and most solemn levels of responsibility.
What if a 'coalition of the willing' had been prepared to move in with
military force, but the UN Security Council (UNSC) was deadlocked?

The UN is dedicated to the territorial integrity of its member states
and the maintenance of international peace and security on that basis.
But the overwhelming majority of contemporary armed conflicts are
internal, not interstate, and civilians comprise the dominant portion of
casualties. This presents the UN with a great difficulty: how to reconcile
its foundational principle of member states' sovereignty with the primary
mandate to maintain international peace and security.

The terrain on which the conceptual and policy contest over 'humanitarian intervention' has been fought is essentially normative. It
takes the form of norm displacement, from the established norm of
non-intervention to a claimed emerging new norm of 'humanitarian
intervention'. The United Nations lies at the centre of this contest both
metaphorically and literally. The UN Charter, more than any other
document, encapsulates and articulates the agreed consensus on the
prevailing norms that give structure and meaning to the foundations
of world order. Second, the international community comes together
physically primarily within the UN's hallowed halls. It is not surprising,
therefore, that the organisation should be the epicentre of the interplay
between changing norms and shifting state practice.

This chapter is about a commission that searched for answers to these
painful dilemmas and its report entitled *The Responsibility to Protect*
(R2P).[2] R2P provides a fresh conceptual template for reconciling both
the tension in principle between sovereignty and intervention, and the
divergent interests and perspectives in political practice. The chapter
brings together many of the global trends, evolving norms and state
practice with respect to peace and security – the relationship between
force and diplomacy, human rights and international security, national
security and human security, the UN and the USA – and also fore-
shadows the chapter that follows on UN reforms. The roots of R2P lay
in statements by Secretary-General Kofi Annan; R2P itself is directed

---

[2] *The Responsibility to Protect.* Report of the International Commission on Intervention and
State Sovereignty (Ottawa: International Development Research Centre for ICISS, 2001).
The Report is available on the internet at www.iciss.gc.ca. The members and secretariat of
ICISS use R2P as a standard acronym.

primarily at the UN policy community in New York; it gives pride of place to the UN if the international community is to honour its international responsibility to protect; and, if R2P is to be the basis of a new international consensus, this can only come about in the UN forum. Given the changing nature and victims of armed conflict, the need for clarity, consistency and reliability in the use of armed force for civilian protection now lies at the heart of the UN's credibility in the maintenance of peace and security. Absent a new consensus and clarity, the UN's performance will be measured against contradictory standards, exposing it to charges of ineffectiveness from some and irrelevance from others, increasing the probability of unauthorised interventions and further eroding the UN's primacy in the realm of peace and security.

The chapter is divided into five parts. First I provide the background to the added value of the independent international commission. Relatively greater attention is paid after that to elaborating the concepts of the responsibility to protect and sovereignty as responsibility. The fourth section alludes briefly to other parts of the Commission's report, while the final section considers the tension between UN and great power responsibility to protect deriving from lawful authority and military capacity.

Background to ICISS

The debate on intervention was ignited in the closing years of the last century by humanitarian crises in Somalia, Rwanda, Srebrenica and East Timor which revealed a dangerous gap between the codified best practice of international behaviour as articulated in the UN Charter and actual state practice as it has evolved in the six decades since the Charter was signed. The 1990s were a challenging decade for the international community with regard to conscience-shocking atrocities in many parts of the world. We generally failed to rise to the challenge, and the price of our failure was paid by large numbers of innocent men, women and children. As noted earlier, Kosovo underlined the triple policy dilemma of complicity, paralysis or illegality.

Under the impact of contrasting experiences in Rwanda and Kosovo, Annan urged member states to come up with a new consensus on the competing visions of national and popular sovereignty and the resulting 'challenge of humanitarian intervention'.[3] Responding to the challenge,

---

[3] Kofi A. Annan, *Facing the Humanitarian Challenge: Towards a Culture of Prevention* (New York: United Nations Department of Public Information, 1999).

Canadian Foreign Minister Lloyd Axworthy set up the International Commission on Intervention and State Sovereignty (ICISS) to wrestle with the whole gamut of difficult and complex issues involved in the debate.[4] ICISS members were carefully chosen to reflect a range of geographical, political and professional backgrounds. The work over the year also took us to all continents and most major capitals in an extensive outreach exercise, in order to hear and reflect different streams of international opinion on the subject.

R2P seeks to do three principal things: change the conceptual language from 'humanitarian intervention' to 'responsibility to protect', pin the responsibility on state authorities at the national and the UNSC at the international level, and ensure that interventions, when they do take place, are done properly. Because R2P is not an interveners' charter (any more than the UN Charter is a shield behind which tyrants may torture and kill their own people with impunity), it does not provide a checklist against which decisions can be made with precision. Political contingencies cannot be fully anticipated in all their glorious complexity and, in the real world, policy choices will always be made on a case-by-case basis. With that in mind, we set out to identify those conscience-shocking situations where the case for international intervention was compelling and to enhance the prospects of such interventions. In turn this meant that the circumstances have to be narrow, the bar for intervention high and the procedural and operational safeguards tight, for the probability of international consensus is higher under conditions of due process, due authority and due diligence.

As there is already a vast literature on the subject,[5] why bother with another study? ICISS had six distinguishing features: balance, outreach, independence, comprehensiveness, innovativeness and political realism.

---

[4] As I was an ICISS Commissioner and one of the principal authors of *The Responsibility to Protect*, this chapter is more of an insider account of the Commission's workings and thinking and a work of advocacy rather than an independent and critical assessment of its Report.

[5] The Commission's own supplementary volume provides sixteen pages of bibliographic entries under 'Humanitarian Intervention' and 'Sovereignty and Intervention', plus many more entries under specific case studies including Kosovo and East Timor. *The Responsibility to Protect: Research, Bibliography, Background*. Supplementary Volume to the Report of the International Commission on Intervention and State Sovereignty (Ottawa: International Development Research Centre for ICISS, 2001). This too is available at www.iciss.gc.ca.

The Commission was balanced in composition, starting with the co-chairs, with regard to professional backgrounds (former heads of state and foreign ministers, UN officials, generals, scholars, journalists), continents-cum-civilisations, industrialised–developing country perspectives, and initial starting positions on the intervention–sovereignty debate.[6] The personal chemistry between the commissioners, combined with their willingness to listen to one another and adapt and evolve their thinking, without necessarily giving up bottom lines, enabled us to write a unanimous report that is more than a collection of clichés and platitudes. If just twelve reasonable, experienced and intelligent people had failed to come to an agreed report, the prospects of the international community forging a new consensus on the contentious subject of military interventions would have been bleak indeed.

The willingness to listen and adapt was put to the test in an extensive outreach exercise that was one of the most valuable parts of the ICISS process. Commission meetings and round tables were held in all continents and most major capitals, involving continent-wide representatives, over 200 in total, from all sectors and a cross-section of views.[7] The Report reflects a genuine effort to incorporate many of the views that were expressed in Cairo, New Delhi and Santiago as well as Beijing, London, Paris and Washington. The views presented during the outreach exercise were sometimes used as tie-breakers during deadlocked discussions in the Commission.

There would not have been much point to the regional consultations if the Commission was working to a secret agenda. If the Canadian government had a hidden agenda and a predetermined outcome for ICISS, they neglected to tell us. ICISS was notable for its lack of 'shrinking violets', and this reinforced the independent nature of the Commission. The Report reflects our combined and collective thinking as it evolved over the year's deliberations.

---

[6] The co-chairs were Gareth Evans and Mohamed Sahnoun, the remaining ten commissioners being Gisele Côté-Harper, Lee Hamilton, Michael Ignatieff, Vladimir Lukin, Klaus Naumann, Cyril Ramaphosa, Fidel Ramos, Cornelio Sommaruga, Eduardo Stein and Ramesh Thakur. Their biodata can be found in the Report or on the Commission's website at www.iciss.gc.ca.

[7] Commission meetings were held in Ottawa (November 2000), Maputo (March 2001), New Delhi (June 2001), Wakefield, Canada (August 2000) and Brussels (September 2001). Round tables and consultative meetings were held, in chronological order, in Ottawa, Geneva, London, Maputo, Washington, DC, Santiago, Cairo, Paris, New Delhi, Beijing and St Petersburg.

The Report is comprehensive in three senses. First, it includes separate chapters on prevention, intervention, reconstruction, lawful authority and the operational dimension of military interventions. It provides conceptual, normative and operational linkages between assistance, intervention and reconstruction. The inputs from the round table discussions contributed greatly to the comprehensiveness of the Commission's final product, which consists of a supplementary research volume in addition to the main Report.[8] The Commission was assisted by a Secretariat provided by Canada's foreign ministry, plus a research team which in turn was helped by several especially commissioned essays plus submissions and contributions from over fifty specialists. The research volume is supported by an extensive and annotated bibliography that contains more than 2,200 entries, and the entire Report and volume is available in a CD-ROM that is key-worded and indexed to facilitate ease of research.

The 'Responsibility to Protect' formulation is genuinely innovative, as was the 'sustainable development' of the Bruntdland Commission whose success in reconciling the previously opposed concepts of development (which is exploitative) and conservation had formed an inspiring model for us from the start of our deliberations. (ICISS co-chair Mohamed Sahnoun was a member of the Brundtland Commission.)

The ICISS discussions and Report were always grounded in political realism. The Commission was set up to get the international community out of the deep trenches into which the two opposing sides had dug themselves. Our mandate was to bridge the polemical divide and to come up with problem-solving formulations for the future. We adopted the position that any attempt to examine the merits, law, legitimacy and political wisdom of past interventions would be backward-looking, possibly finger-pointing, judgmental and far from helpful to our task.

Nor were we interested in solving all the world's problems, but stuck narrowly to our mandate. Thus we resisted the temptation to recast our Report in the light of the terrorist attacks of 11 September 2001, concluding that horrific and urgent as the latter were, self-defence is conceptually and operationally distinct from the protection of at-risk foreign populations. Similarly, we resisted the temptation to urge amendments to the Charter, for example with respect to the composition and functioning of the UNSC.

---

[8] *The Responsibility to Protect: Research, Bibliography, Background.*

In retrospect, the one-year timeframe was probably a very useful discipline. This meant the momentum never flagged, we worked to a tight deadline and we remembered where we had got to at the last meeting and the progress that had already been made. The tight timeframe was a further check on any temptation to wander beyond our critical but narrow mandate. There are many other things we could have written about. But one of the great merits of this Report was the tightness of the focus on the core objective to the exclusion of other debates, no matter how important or interesting, that were extraneous to the central task.

Finally, ICISS was unusual among blue-ribbon international commissions in that its Report was written by a subgroup of commissioners themselves,[9] including yours truly.

From 'humanitarian intervention' to 'responsibility to protect'

The key to the attempt to move the existing consensus forward is a change in the conceptual vocabulary, from the right and duty of 'humanitarian intervention', which is what humanitarian agencies like the International Committee of the Red Cross (ICRC) and the UN High Commissioner for Refugees (UNHCR) do, to the responsibility to protect. They object to the phrase being appropriated by states engaged in military intervention, arguing that far from being an instance, this is a debasement of humanitarian intervention. The discourse on NATO's intervention in Kosovo in 1999 was framed largely in the language of humanitarian intervention – when in fact that intervention consisted of three months of bombing. If that was humanitarian intervention, then it must necessarily also have been humanitarian bombing.[10]

It is easy to dub a war a 'humanitarian intervention' and so label critics as 'anti-humanitarian'. 'Humanitarian intervention' conveys to most Western minds the idea that the principle underlying the intervention is not self-interested power politics but the disinterested one of protecting human life. It conjures up in many non-Western minds

---

[9] For the first comparative study of international commissions, see Ramesh Thakur, Andrew F. Cooper and John English, eds., *International Commissions and the Power of Ideas* (Tokyo: United Nations University Press, 2005).

[10] In a similar vein, on 27 May 2004 the European Union called on coalition troops in Afghanistan to stop the practice of operating in civilian vehicles and clothing because this was raising local hostility towards and endangering the lives of the genuine humanitarian workers. 'EU: Coalition Troops Endangering Afghan Aid Effort', AP news story, *Daily Yomiuri* (Tokyo), 29 May 2004.

historical memories of the strong imposing their will on the weak in the name of the prevailing universal principles of the day, from the civilising mission of spreading Christianity to the cultivation and promotion of human rights. The phrase 'humanitarian intervention' is used to trump sovereignty with intervention at the outset of the debate: it loads the dice in favour of intervention before the argument has even begun, by labelling and delegitimising dissent as anti-humanitarian. It is a mobilising device to mask commercial and geopolitical motives in the call to arms for rallying citizens to the cause of an otherwise unnecessary war.

Where humanitarian intervention raises fears of domination based on the international power hierarchy, R2P encapsulates the element of international solidarity. Moreover, it implies an evaluation of the issues from the point of view of those seeking or needing support, rather than those who may be considering intervention. It refocuses the international searchlight back on the duty to protect the villager from murder, the woman from rape, and the child from starvation and being orphaned.

Sovereignty as responsibility

Intervention for human protection purposes occurs so that those condemned to die in fear may live in hope instead. It is based in the double belief that the sovereignty of a state has an accompanying responsibility on the part of that state; and that if the state defaults on the responsibility to protect its citizens, the fall-back responsibility to do so must be assumed and honoured by the international community. We found it useful to reconceptualise sovereignty, viewing it not as an absolute term of authority but as a kind of responsibility. In part, this expressed what we heard from a cross-section of African interlocutors. State authorities are responsible for the functions of protecting the safety and lives of citizens and accountable for their acts of commission and omission in international as well as national forums.

Crucially, R2P acknowledges that responsibility rests primarily with the state concerned. Only if the state is unable or unwilling to fulfil this responsibility, or is itself the perpetrator, does it become the responsibility of others to act in its place. In many cases, the state seeks to acquit its responsibility in full and active partnership with representatives of the international community. Thus R2P is more of a linking concept that bridges the divide between the international community and the sovereign state, whereas the language of the right or duty to intervene is inherently more confrontational between the two levels of analysis and policy.

Westphalian sovereignty originated in the sixteenth–seventeenth centuries in the European search for a secular basis of state authority. Internally, it refers to the exclusive competence of the state to make authoritative decisions of government with regard to all people and resources within its territory. Externally, it means the legal identity of the state in international law, an equality of status with all other states, and the claim to be the sole official agent acting in international relations on behalf of a society. 'Sovereignty is thus one mode of international governance without international government.'[11] It imparts order, stability and predictability to what otherwise would be international anarchy.

Subsequently, sovereignty was redefined in terms of a social contract between citizens and rulers. Violations of the contract by the rulers voided the duty of the citizens to obey the commands of the sovereign. By the end of the nineteenth century a distinction was being drawn between legal sovereignty as vested in parliament and political sovereignty as vested in the electorate. In the twentieth century the trend was taken further with the notion of popular sovereignty.

The doctrines of sovereign equality and non-interference are thus distinctively European in origin and construct. But the USA is second to none in the jealous defence of national sovereignty against international encroachments. Its 'sovereigntists' have launched three lines of attack: the emerging international legal order is vague and illegitimately intrusive on domestic affairs; the international law-making process is unaccountable and the resulting law unenforceable; and Washington can opt out of international regimes as a matter of power, legal right and constitutional duty.[12]

National sovereignty locates the state as the ultimate seat of power and authority, unconstrained by internal or external checks; constitutional sovereignty holds that the power and authority of the state are not absolute but contingent and constrained.[13] Domestically, power sharing between the executive, legislature and judiciary, at federal and provincial levels, is regulated by constitutional arrangements and practices. Internationally, states are constrained by globally legitimated institutions and practices.

---

[11] Ian Hurd, 'Legitimacy and Authority in International Politics', *International Organization* 53:2 (Spring 1999), p. 404.

[12] Peter J. Spiro, 'The New Sovereigntists', *Foreign Affairs* 79:6 (November/December 2000), pp. 9–15.

[13] See Hideaki Shinoda, *Re-examining Sovereignty: From Classical Theory to the Global Age* (New York: St. Martin's Press, 2000).

The principle of state sovereignty has little to do with the merits and morality of governments in power. Rather, not unlike Churchill's aphorism on democracy, sovereignty is the least bad system of organising international relations. And the UN is the chief agent of this system of states for exercising international authority in their name. UN membership was the final symbol of sovereign statehood for freshly independent countries and their seal of acceptance into the community of nations. The UN also became the principal international forum for collaborative action in the shared pursuit of the three goals of state-building, nation-building and economic development. The UN was therefore the main arena for the jealous protection of state sovereignty, not its casual abrogation.

A condition of any one state's sovereignty is the corresponding obligation to respect every other state's sovereignty. If that duty is violated, the victim state has the further right to defend its territorial integrity and political independence. Yet even during the Cold War state practice reflected the unwillingness of many countries – not just the two power blocs, but also some former colonies like India and Tanzania – to give up intervention as an instrument of policy. Communist leaders sometimes argued that relations within the socialist community could not be subject to a legal order reflecting capitalist class relations and that fraternal assistance to a fellow-socialist regime was not intervention. Others argued that counter-intervention, meant to assist victims of intervention, was lawful. Some justified armed incursions across borders on the principle of hot pursuit, while others claimed the right to pre-emptive self-defence against imminent or apprehended attack. 'Self-defence' was sometimes extended to include the right to launch punitive raids into neighbouring countries that had shown themselves unwilling or unable to stop their territory from being used as a launching pad for cross-border armed raids or terrorist attacks. Many interveners insisted that they had taken action only in response to requests from the governments of the countries concerned. Few were prepared to rule out a priori the use of force in another country in order to rescue nationals who were trapped and threatened there.

Thus the norm of non-intervention was never absolute in practice. But generally the justifications did not challenge the norm itself, pointing instead to exceptional or extenuating circumstances that compelled the intervener to act as it did. Often the breaches provoked such fierce controversy and so much nationalistic passion that their net effect was to reinforce, not negate, the norm of non-intervention.

UN-authorised intervention entails the presumption of legitimacy, that which is not so authorised bears the presumption of illegitimacy. But there are exceptions to both parts of the proposition. UN authorisation is neither a necessary nor a sufficient condition of international legitimacy.

Venerable commentators assert that 'Intervention has become the new norm' in 'a climate in which nonintervention appears as a dereliction of duty, requiring explanation, excuse or apology'.[14] The assertion can be challenged on empirical and doctrinal grounds. The norm of non-intervention may be dented slightly, but is still intact. The number of cases where outsiders could have intervened but did not – the Democratic Republic of the Congo, Sierra Leone, Darfur, Myanmar and Chechnya, to name just a few – is more than the few cases of intervention. The claim, therefore, that the norm of non-intervention is being replaced by that of intervention is empirically false. It also invites questions about how, and by whose interpretation, norms emerge, are consolidated and accepted by a broad enough constituency to justify being labelled a global norm. Elevating the new interventionism to the moral plane is more useful for mobilising domestic constituencies than appeasing international concerns, for it ignores the equally strong sense of moral outrage among others at the violation of the global norm of non-intervention. The West does not own the copyright on moral outrage.

The doctrine of national sovereignty in its absolute and unqualified form, which gave rulers protection against attack from without while engaged in the most brutal oppression within, has gone with the wind. But we cannot accept the doctrine that any one state or coalition can decide when to intervene with force in the internal affairs of other countries, for down that path lies total chaos. War is itself a major humanitarian tragedy: hence the paradox of 'humanitarian intervention' that can unleash still more all-round destruction. The use of force to attack a sovereign state is an extreme measure that can be justified only under the most compelling circumstances regarding the provocation, the likelihood of success – bearing in mind that goals are metamorphosed in the crucible of war once started – and the consequences that may

---

[14] Inis L. Claude, 'The Evolution of Concepts of Global Governance and the State in the Twentieth Century', paper delivered at the annual conference of the Academic Council on the United Nations System (ACUNS), Oslo, 16–18 June 2000. Claude does note, however, that the new norm 'has been no less challenged in principle and dishonoured in practice than was the old norm of nonintervention'.

reasonably be predicted. Moreover, the burden of proof rests on the proponents of force, not on the dissenters. Even in Kosovo, NATO produced no formal white paper providing the doctrinal justification for their action.

R2P's core principle is that state sovereignty implies responsibility,[15] and the primary responsibility for the protection of its people lies with the state itself. But if it should default, the residual responsibility lies with the broader community of states. Where a population is suffering serious harm, as a result of internal war, insurgency, repression or state failure, and the government in question is unwilling or unable to halt or avert it, the principle of non-intervention yields to the international responsibility to protect. The foundations of the international responsibility to protect lie in obligations inherent in the concept of sovereignty; the responsibility of the UNSC, under Article 24 of the UN Charter, for the maintenance of international peace and security; specific legal obligations under human rights and human protection declarations, covenants and treaties, international humanitarian law and national law; and the developing practice of states, regional organisations and the UNSC itself.

The international order is based on a system of sovereign states because this is seen as the most efficient means of organising the world in order to discharge the responsibility to the people of protecting their lives and livelihoods and promoting their well-being and freedoms. If sovereignty becomes an obstacle to the realisation of freedom, then it can, should and must be discarded. In today's seamless world, political frontiers have become less salient both for international organisations, whose rights and duties can extend beyond borders, and for member states, whose responsibilities within borders can be held to international scrutiny. The steady erosion of the once sacrosanct principle of national sovereignty is rooted in the reality of global interdependence: no country is an island unto itself anymore.

For these reasons, and based on changes in the real world and evolving best-practice international behaviour, the Commission concluded that it is necessary and useful to reconceptualise sovereignty as responsibility. This has a threefold significance. First, it implies that the state

---

[15] On this we owe an intellectual debt to Francis M. Deng et al., *Sovereignty as Responsibility: Conflict Management in Africa* (Washington, DC: Brookings, 1996), and Francis M. Deng, 'Frontiers of Sovereignty', *Leiden Journal of International Law* 8:2 (June 1995), pp. 249–86.

authorities are responsible for the functions of protecting the safety and lives of citizens and promotion of their welfare. Second, it suggests that the national political authorities are responsible to the citizens internally and to the international community through the UN. And third, it means that the agents of the state are responsible for their actions, that is to say, they are accountable for their acts of commission and omission.

The substance of the responsibility to protect is the provision of life-supporting protection and assistance to populations at risk. The goal of intervention for human protection purposes is not to wage war on a state in order to destroy it and eliminate its statehood, but to protect victims of atrocities inside the state, to embed the protection in reconstituted institutions after the intervention and then to withdraw all foreign troops. Thus military intervention for human protection purposes takes away the rights flowing from the status of sovereignty, but does not in itself challenge the status as such. It does supplant the rights of the state to exercise protective functions if the state has proven incapable or unwilling to do so with respect to genocidal killings, humanitarian atrocities and ethnic cleansing; or to suspend the right of the state to conduct itself free of external interference if such conduct is the cause of the above atrocities. The prevention of the exercise of sovereign rights under intervention for human protection purposes is always limited in time to a temporary period, until the capacity of the state itself to resume its protective functions can be restored and institutionalised. Intervention may be limited in two further respects. It may be confined to a particular portion of the target state's territory, where the abuses are actually occurring, rather than all of it; or it may be limited with respect to a particular group that is the target of abuse, rather than apply to all citizens.

The UN Charter is itself an example of an international obligation voluntarily accepted by member states. On the one hand, in granting membership to the UN, the international community welcomes the signatory state as a responsible member of the community of nations. On the other hand, the state itself, in signing the Charter, accepts the responsibilities of membership flowing from that signature. There is no transfer or dilution of state sovereignty. But there is a redefinition from sovereignty as right of exclusivity to sovereignty as responsibility in both internal functions and external duties. The United Nations is the symbol and the arena for the shared management of pooled sovereignty.

The continuing validity of the non-intervention norm needed re-statement and gets it in R2P. In most cases, protecting the lives and promoting the welfare of citizens is better done by strengthening state capacity and resilience: the best guarantee of human rights is a world of competent, responsible and legitimate sovereign states.[16] Conversely, the human security of people is put in grave danger in conditions of fragile or failed states.

Doing it right, doing it well

Conflict prevention and peace-building

Action in support of the responsibility to protect necessarily involves and calls for a broad range and wide variety of measures and responses in fulfilment of the accompanying duty to assist. These may include devel-opment assistance to help prevent conflict from occurring, intensifying, spreading or persisting; rebuilding support to help prevent conflict from recurring; and, in extraordinary cases, military intervention to protect at-risk civilians from harm.

Prevention is the single most important dimension of the responsi-bility to protect, so prevention options should always be exhausted before intervention is contemplated. Moreover, the exercise of the responsibility to prevent and react should always involve less intrusive and coercive measures being considered (although not necessarily attempted) before more coercive and intrusive ones are applied. The responsibility to pre-vent requires addressing both the root causes and direct causes of internal conflict and other man-made crises putting populations at risk. The responsibility to react requires us to respond to situations of compelling human need with appropriate measures, which may include coercive measures like sanctions and international prosecution and, in extreme cases, military intervention. The responsibility to rebuild requires us to provide, particularly after a military intervention, full assistance with recovery, reconstruction and reconciliation, addressing the causes of the harm the intervention was designed to halt or avert.

---

[16] See Simon Chesterman, Michael Ignatieff and Ramesh Thakur, eds., *Making States Work: State Failure and the Crisis of Governance* (Tokyo: United Nations University Press, 2005). Ignatieff and Thakur were two of the ICISS commissioners, and this project grew out of their ICISS experience.

Threshold criteria and cautionary principles

Military intervention for human protection purposes is an exceptional and extraordinary measure. To be warranted, there must be serious and irreparable harm occurring to human beings, or imminently likely to occur, of the following kind:

- large-scale loss of life due to deliberate state action, neglect or inability to act, or a failed state situation; or
- large-scale ethnic cleansing, actual or apprehended, whether carried out by killing, forced expulsion, acts of terror or rape.

We concluded that it would be futile to try to anticipate every contingency and provide a uniform checklist for intervention. Rather, the decision on intervention would have to be a matter of careful judgement on a case-by-case basis. Even when the just cause threshold is crossed by conscience-shocking loss of life or ethnic cleansing, intervention must be guided by the cautionary principles of right intention, last resort, proportional means and reasonable prospects.[17] The primary purpose of the intervention, whatever other motives intervening states may have,[18] must be to halt or avert human suffering. Right intention is better assured with multilateral operations, clearly supported by regional opinion and the victims concerned. Military intervention can only be justified when every non-military option for the prevention or peaceful resolution of the crisis has been explored, with reasonable grounds for believing that lesser measures would not have succeeded. The scale, duration and intensity of the planned military intervention should be the minimum necessary to secure the defined human protection objective. And there must be a reasonable chance of success in halting or averting the suffering which has justified the intervention, with the consequences of action not likely to be worse than the consequences of inaction. For example, under no conceivable circumstances would humanitarian goals be advanced by launching an external military intervention against Russia in order to protect, say, the people of Chechnya. Finally, the Report also seeks to identity the operational principles to guide interventions.

---

[17] These are clearly derived from the just war doctrine. But because the doctrine is rooted in the Christian tradition, acknowledging its religious roots would not necessarily have been the wisest political decision. This is just one example, albeit an interesting one, of the clash of academic and policy cultures.

[18] For an intervention to be sustained, at least one state with the requisite military capacity must also have a stake in stabilising the situation, as with Australia in East Timor.

Right authority and due process

Military intervention, even for humanitarian purposes, is just a nicer way of referring to the use of deadly force on a massive scale. Given the enormous normative presumption against the use of deadly force to settle international quarrels, who has the right to authorise such force? On what basis, for what purpose, and subject to what safeguards and limitations? In other words, even if we agree that military intervention may sometimes be necessary and unavoidable in order to protect innocent people from life-threatening danger by interposing an outside force between actual and apprehended victims and perpetrators, key questions remain about agency, lawfulness and legitimacy: that is, about international authority that can override national authority.

R2P came down firmly on the side of the central role of the UN as the indispensable font of international authority and the irreplaceable forum for authorising international military enforcement. The chief contemporary institution for building, consolidating and using the authority of the international community is the UN. There is no better nor more appropriate body than the UNSC to authorise military intervention for human protection purposes. The task, therefore, is not to find alternatives to the UNSC as a source of authority but to make it work better.

The formal authority for maintaining international peace and security is thus vested in the UNSC. But the burden of responsibility, from having the power to make the most difference, often falls on the USA and other leading powers. The conceptual connecting rod that links power to authority is legitimacy. Absent the special arrangements for the allocation of armed forces by member states to the UN (discussed in chapter 1 above), the obligation to execute an activist command by the UN may be open to debate; the obligation to acknowledge UN authority to restrict unilateral great power activism is not. In this sense the United Nations is the symbol of what even major powers *must not do.*[19] In the field of state–citizen relations within territorial borders, the totality of Charter clauses and instruments like the Universal Declaration of Human Rights restrict the authority of states to cause harm to their own people. In the sphere of military action across borders, UN membership imposes the

---

[19] Inis L. Claude, 'The Symbolic Significance of the United Nations', in F. A. Sondermann et al., eds., *The Theory and Practice of International Relations*, 5th edn (Englewood Cliffs: Prentice-Hall, 1979), p. 233.

obligation on the major powers to abjure unilateral intervention in favour of collectively authorised international intervention.

Intervention criteria?

The legal debate on a clear, consistent and workable set of codified criteria for intervention is largely sterile. The political debate quickly degenerates from rational discussion to highly charged polemics. Morally, many fear that any codification of the rules of intervention would relegitimise the use of force in international relations. This would be a major step backward. The response from those with little patience for claims of UN primacy or monopoly on the legitimate use of international force is that the UN system of collective security was fatally flawed from the start. Peace was preserved and justice advanced by the operation of institutions and the pursuit of values by coalitions of the right-minded, able and willing to defend the international order against all challenges.

The real debate is between those who support the development of guidelines for use by the UNSC in authorising international intervention but remain firmly opposed to criteria for circumventing the UN, and those who wish to retain the right to unilateral intervention. The first group is fearful that the norm of non-intervention could become a roadkill on the highway of international power politics, taking us back to the nineteenth-century system of a concert of great powers. Among those who wish to retain the flexibility to launch military intervention without UN authorisation if necessary, there is a further division of opinion between those who would like a 'doctrine' approach and others who want merely an 'exception' approach[20] – a signposted emergency exit from the existing norms as embedded in the UN Charter.

Yet another variation would be to distinguish a 'red light' from the entrenched 'green light' approach.[21] Under the latter, intervention may not proceed until and unless it has been duly authorised by the UNSC.

---

[20] For a review of this debate, see in particular Simon Chesterman, *Just War or Just Peace? Humanitarian Intervention and International Law* (Oxford: Oxford University Press, 2001), pp. 226–32, and Nicholas Wheeler, *Saving Strangers: Humanitarian Intervention in International Society* (Oxford: Oxford University Press, 2000), pp. 33–51.

[21] In some respects, this is similar to the debate in 2003 on whether the US–UK war on Iraq could be sufficiently grounded in Resolution 1441 or needed a second resolution specifically authorising all necessary means to enforce compliance.

Under the former, interventions can take place unless and until specifically prohibited by the Council.[22] The difficulty with this is not just that
it subverts the Charter and turns the principle of authorisation on its
head. In addition, the veto clause would still come into play. Even if the
vote in support of a 'red light' resolution was 14–1, the resolution would
fail, and the red light therefore could not be flashed, if that one solitary
negative vote was that of a permanent member. Equally, when the vital
interests of global or regional major powers are engaged, interventionary
forces may go crashing through an entire forest of flashing red lights
without paying any heed to them.

The UNSC should deal promptly with any request for authority to
intervene where there are allegations of large-scale loss of human life
or ethnic cleansing. R2P recommends that the P5 should agree not to
apply their veto power in matters where their vital state interests are
not involved, so as not to obstruct the passage of resolutions authorising
military intervention for human protection purposes for which there is
otherwise majority support. Action in selected cases outside a veto-
paralysed UNSC framework is less defensible by those who refuse to
accept any dilution of their own veto power.[23]

If the UNSC rejects a proposal or fails to deal with it in a reasonable
time, alternative options are: consideration of the matter by the General
Assembly in Emergency Special Session under the 'Uniting for Peace'
procedure; and action within area of jurisdiction by regional or sub-
regional organisations, subject to their seeking subsequent authorisation
from the UNSC.

The Security Council should take into account in all its deliberations
that, if it dishonours its responsibility to protect in conscience-shocking
situations crying out for action, concerned states may not rule out other

[22] This is reminiscent of the professor of comparative jurisprudence who argued that there
were four basic roots in the various systems of jurisprudence. In the UK, everything is
permitted unless specifically proscribed in law; in Germany, everything is prohibited
unless specifically permitted in law; in the former Soviet Union, everything was permitted in theory but prohibited in practice; and in France, everything is banned in law but
permitted in practice.

[23] This normative inconsistency is fatal to the moral majority proponents of coalitions of
the willing. Yet it is an obvious flaw – so much so that one may question whether failure
to address it reflects intellectual laziness or moral duplicity. Can an intellectually coherent
or morally consistent argument be advanced for any one or several of the P5 to lead such
coalitions when faced with an actual or apprehended Security Council veto, if they are
not prepared to give up the veto right?

means to meet the gravity and urgency of that situation. This carries a double risk. Their actions may not be guided by the just cause and cautionary principles identified in the ICISS Report and so their interventions may not be done well, with due authority, diligence and process. Alternatively, they may do it very well and the people of the world may conclude that their actions were necessary, just and proper, in which case the UN's stature and credibility may suffer still further erosion.

Conclusion

Ill-considered rhetoric of pre-emptive strikes and Iraq as an example of 'humanitarian intervention'[24] risk draining support from R2P rather than adding to the legitimacy of such enterprises. Unfortunately, in the real world of politics based on perceptions and emotive rhetoric, such loose talk may serve to complicate the task of mobilising the requisite political will for those occasions where the responsibility to protect must be discharged by the international community.

When we convened a special ICISS meeting to discuss the implications of 9/11, none of us present needed persuading about the legitimacy of a military response within the accepted understanding of individual and collective self-defence (us against them). But we also concluded that the campaign was conceptually and operationally distinct from intervention for human protection purposes (us between them: victims and perpetrators). Thus Richard Haass, director of the Policy Planning Unit of the US State Department, spoke of sovereignty as responsibility and argued that when states fail to discharge their responsibility to fight terrorism, 'America will act – ideally with partners, but alone if necessary – to hold them accountable.'[25] To the extent that he restricts his comment to self-defence against cross-border terrorism, it is fine. But if his statement is extended to military intervention for human protection purposes, it poses a problem.

---

[24] See, for example, Jim Hoagland, 'Time for Bush to Cast War Aims in Iron', *Japan Times*, 28 October 2002, reprinting an article from the *Washington Post*. The inapplicability of R2P to Iraq is argued in Ramesh Thakur, 'Iraq and the Responsibility to Protect', *Behind the Headlines* 62:1 (Toronto: Canadian Institute of International Affairs, October 2004).

[25] Richard Haass, 'When Nations Forfeit their Sovereign Privileges', *International Herald Tribune*, 7 February 2003.

The fact that a dozen people of diverse backgrounds and varied starting positions were able to agree on a challenging, substantial and wide-ranging report encouraged us to believe that an international consensus can indeed be forged around these ideas and principles. Too often in the past UN peace operations have fallen victim to coalitions of the unwilling, unable and unlike-minded. It is time to put collective might to the service of individual and international right.

12

Developing countries and the eroding
non-intervention norm

> General Bonaparte, following the footsteps of Alexander would have
> entered India not as a devastating conqueror . . . but as a liberator. He
> would have expelled the English forever from India so that not one of them
> would have remained and . . . would have restored independence, peace,
> and happiness to Asia, Europe, and to the whole world . . . All the Princes
> in India were longing for French intervention.[1]

There is an evident divide between the global North and South. The
Non-aligned Movement – with 113 members, the most representative
group of countries outside the United Nations itself – three times rejected 'the so-called "right of humanitarian intervention"' after the Kosovo
War in 1999 and the subsequent statements from UN Secretary-General
Kofi Annan.[2] Many developing countries assert a claim to the privilege of
managing world order on a shared basis but exhibit a strong reluctance
to accept the responsibility flowing from such privilege, for example with
respect to protecting the victims of humanitarian atrocities. Some of the
big and powerful countries insist on claiming the benefits flowing from
collective decision-making, in the form of greater legitimacy and authority, but resist the constraints on policy options that would result from
a genuinely shared process of international policy-making. Curiously,

---

[1] Louis Bourquien, in an article published in 1923 on the failed effort by Napoleon
Bonaparte to take India from the British towards the end of the eighteenth century;
quoted in William Dalrymple, *The White Mughals: Love and Betrayal in Eighteenth
Century India* (New Delhi: Viking, 2002), pp. 147–8.
[2] *The Responsibility to Protect: Research, Bibliography, and Background.* Supplementary
Volume to the Report of the International Commission on Intervention and State
Sovereignty. (Ottawa: International Development Research Centre, 2001), pp. 162, 357.
See also Philip Nel, 'South Africa: The Demand for Legitimate Multilateralism', in
Albrecht Schnabel and Ramesh Thakur, eds., *Kosovo and the Challenge of Humanitarian
Intervention: Selective Indignation, Collective Action, and International Citizenship* (Tokyo:
United Nations University Press, 2000), pp. 245–59.

the two feed on each other. The South points to the North's monopoly of power and privilege to excuse its own lack of a sense of international responsibility; the North points to the many instances of the South's failure to honour the international responsibility to protect to justify its refusal to restrict international policy-making to the collective UN forum.

Ironically, while aspects of sovereignty are being progressively pooled and superseded in Europe, where they originated, in the construction of a borderless continent, some of its most passionate defenders are to be found among developing countries. Western countries are likely to be the subjects not objects of intervention, and their world-view is coloured by this simple fact. Nevertheless, the West is no more homogeneous as a cultural entity than the developing world, and neither industrial nor developing countries are united and cohesive on the tension between intervention and sovereignty. Significant differences exist between and within Africa, Latin America, Asia and the Arab world.[3] This chapter examines the normative contestation between North and South with respect to the so-called challenge of humanitarian intervention. It begins with a survey of views and opinions across the major developing regions. It then addresses issues of normative incoherence, inconsistency and contestation. The final part examines the rise and fall of developing countries as norm setters.

The divisiveness of 'humanitarian intervention'

We no longer have wars, only 'humanitarian interventions' that rest on assumptions of moral superiority. The privileging of some crises that are securitised over others that are not reflects the interests and perspectives of the powerful and the rich at the expense of the weak and the poor. The voiceless in the human rights 'discourse' are the marginalised and powerless in the global power equation. In Europe, centralising states sought to bring order to their societies by claiming a monopoly on the legitimate use of force. Developing countries fear that in some sections of the West today, the view has gained ground that anyone *but* the legitimate authorities can use force.

---

[3] See the summaries of the various round-the-world regional discussions provided in *The Responsibility to Protect: Research, Bibliography, and Background*, III.3, pp. 349–98.

In the era of decolonisation, the sovereign equality of states and the correlative norm of non-intervention received their most emphatic affirmation from the newly independent states. At one level, the developing countries' attachment to sovereignty is deeply emotional. The most important clue to understanding their concerns is the history of Europe's encounter with Arabs, Africans and Asians. The relentless march of colonialism and imperialism is never based on anything so vulgar as commercial and geopolitical calculations: land and wealth grabs. No, it is always driven by a lofty purpose.

The deployment of moral arguments to justify imperialist actions in Iraq in 2003 has a direct structural counterpart in the British annexation of the Indian kingdom of Awadh (Oudh in its anglicised version) in the first half of the nineteenth century. The structure of justification makes use of a specific set of techniques for the mobilisation of democratic consent and international support – through political representatives, the press and the interested and attentive public – of decisions taken in pursuit of national interest by an elite group of policy-makers. Tracing its origins to John Locke and John Stuart Mill, Chatterjee locates it in the paternalistic belief that people and nations who are morally handicapped or in a state of moral infancy deserve a benevolent despot who will protect and look after them.[4]

> What is remarkable is how many of the same arguments, including the evangelical fervour, the axiomatic assumption of the mantle of civilisation, the fig-leaf of legalism, the intelligence reports, the forgeries and subterfuges and the hard-headed calculations of national interest, remain exactly the same at the beginning of the 21st century... the liberal evangelical creed of taking democracy and human rights to backward cultures is still a potent ideological drive, and . . . the instrumental use of that ideological rhetoric for realist imperialist ends is entirely available, as we have seen in Iraq.[5]

Afro-Asian countries achieved independence on the back of extensive and protracted nationalist struggles. The parties and leaders at the forefront of the fight for independence helped to establish the new states and shape and guide the founding principles of their foreign policies. The anti-colonial impulse in their world-view was instilled in the countries' foreign policies and survives as a powerful sentiment in the

---

[4] Partha Chatterjee, 'Empire after Globalisation', *Economic and Political Weekly*, 39:37 (11 September 2004), p. 4158.
[5] Ibid., p. 4163.

corporate memory of the elites. All too often, developing-country views either fail to get a respectful hearing at all in Western policy and scholarly discourse, or are patronisingly dismissed. If I was to try to communicate and provide an explanation for the sense of passionate conviction behind some of the developing countries' positions on the major contemporary controversies regarding the use of force overseas by the major Western powers, I would use strong and forceful language along the following lines.

'They' (the European colonisers) came to liberate 'us' (the colonised natives) from our local tyrants and stayed to rule as benevolent despots. In the name of enlightenment, they defiled our lands, plundered our resources and expanded their empires. Some, like the Belgians in the Congo, left only ruin, devastation and chaos whose dark shadows continue to blight. Others, like the British in India, left behind ideas, ideals and structures of good governance and the infrastructure of economic development alongside memories of national humiliation. Should they be surprised that their fine talk of humanitarian intervention translates in our consciousness into efforts to resurrect and perpetuate rule by foreigners? That we look for the ugly reality of geostrategic and commercial calculations camouflaged in lofty rhetoric? Should we be mute accomplices when they substitute their mythology of humanitarian intervention for our narratives of colonial oppression? Do they think we do not remember or do not care, or is it simply that they themselves do not care?

At another level, the commitment to sovereignty is functional. State sovereignty is the bedrock principle of the contemporary international system that provides order and stability. The most important task on the agenda of the international community, therefore, should be not to weaken states nor to undermine the doctrine of state sovereignty, but to strengthen the institutions of state and make them legitimate and empowering of people, respectful and protective of their rights.[6] In the words of the Secretary-General, 'one of the great challenges of the new millennium is to ensure that all States are strong enough to meet the many challenges they face'.[7]

---

[6] See Simon Chesterman, Michael Ignatieff and Ramesh Thakur, eds., *Making States Work: State Failure and the Crisis of Governance* (Tokyo: United Nations University Press, 2005).

[7] Kofi A. Annan, *In Larger Freedom: Towards Development, Security and Human Rights for All.* Report of the Secretary-General (New York: UN, document A/59/2005, 21 March 2005), para. 19.

Asia

On balance, 'the idea of humanitarian intervention has received a generally hostile response in Asia'. The reformulation of 'humanitarian intervention' as the 'responsibility to protect' does not 'entirely override the developing world's concerns about sovereignty', and it 'does not entirely succeed in separating the humanitarian imperative from the political and geopolitical constraints of a UN system that will remain dominated by the P-5'.[8] Yet Asia could face demands from several potential cases of intervention for human protection purposes: *state breakup, breakdown, incapacity, complicity/perpetration*. The Asia-Pacific also contains at least four countries with the military capacity to launch interventions: China, India, Australia and Japan.[9]

The hardest line against intervention and in defence of sovereignty was taken at the Round Table Discussion in Beijing on 14 June 2001.[10] The Chinese argued that humanitarianism is good, interventionism is bad, and 'humanitarian intervention' is 'tantamount to marrying evil to good'. In such a shotgun marriage, far from humanitarianism burnishing meddlesome interventions, it will itself be tarnished by interventionism.

A number of reasons were advanced for rejecting 'the doctrine of humanitarian intervention'. First, it was claimed that there is no basis for it in the UN Charter which recognises only self-defence and the maintenance and restoration of international peace and security as legitimate grounds for the use of force.

Second, the use of force for moral reasons is dangerous and counterproductive in its practical effects. On the one hand, it can encourage warring parties inside a country to be rigid and irresponsible in the hope of internationalising the conflict. On the other hand, it can facilitate interventions by those exploiting the cloak of legality for their own purposes. Both can prolong or result in large-scale killings.

Third, there is an inherent conceptual incoherence. The individualistic conception of human rights in Western discourse is somehow mystically transformed into collective rights (the protection of groups of people)

---

[8] Amitav Acharya, 'Redefining the Dilemmas of Humanitarian Intervention', *Australian Journal of International Affairs* 56:3 (2002), pp. 377, 378 and 380.

[9] See Ramesh Thakur, 'Intervention Could Bring Safeguards in Asia', *Daily Yomiuri*, 3 January 2003.

[10] Unattributed, 'Rapporteur's Report, ICISS Round Table Consultation, Beijing, 14 June 2001'. The reports from all the ICISS regional discussions are available on the Commission's website at www.iciss.gc.ca.

at the same time as the collective rights of the entire nation are still denied legitimacy.

Fourth, the inconsistent practice, the double standards and the sporadic nature of Western powers' interest in human rights protection, from the Middle East, Africa, Latin America and Asia to Europe, shows that noble principles are convenient cloaks for hegemonic interests.

The Chinese raised other questions which too were recurring refrains in all our consultations. The most important was the question of agency or lawful authorisation, and there was surprising consensus around the world on the central role of the UN. For China as one of the five permanent members, self-interest restricts this to the paramount role of the UNSC. Elsewhere, and especially in New Delhi,[11] there was one additional argument made with some emphasis. If the UNSC was going to be making decisions on interventions as an evolutionary adaptation of the Charter, then the question of reforming its structure and procedures becomes vitally important. Otherwise, more frequent interventions launched by an unreconstructed UNSC would erode the global legitimacy of the UN rather than imbue the interventions with international legitimacy.

There is also agreement among most Asian commentators that interventions cannot become the pretext for imposing external political preferences with regard to regimes and political and economic systems. Consequently, even though sovereignty may be violated, the cases justifying such action must be tightly restricted to such heinous crimes as genocide and mass murders,[12] it must always be the option of last resort, it must be temporary, intervening forces must withdraw as soon as possible, their actions while inside the target country must be guided by considerations of political impartiality and neutrality between the domestic political contenders as well as strict fidelity to international humanitarian law, and, above all, they must respect and ensure the territorial integrity of the target state.[13]

---

[11] Sripapha Petcharamesree, 'Rapporteur's Report, ICISS Round Table Consultation, New Delhi, 10 June 2001'; available on the Commission's website at www.iciss.gc.ca.

[12] Intriguingly, and presumably with the example of the Bamiyan statues in mind although also perhaps the destruction of the mosque in Ayodhya in 1992, one person in New Delhi also suggested that the responsibility to protect extended to cultural heritage. See also Ramesh Thakur and Amin Saikal, 'Vandalism in Afghanistan and No One to Stop It', *International Herald Tribune (IHT)*, 6 March 2001.

[13] At first glance, East Timor – an operation to which even China acquiesced – would appear to contradict this. But in fact, from a strictly technical point of view, East Timor

The New Delhi consultation was enriched by the many examples from within Asia that formed the historical backdrop to the more abstract discussion, from Bangladesh and Cambodia in the 1970s to Sri Lanka and the Maldives in the 1980s and East Timor (as also, inevitably, Kosovo) in the 1990s. New Delhi was notable also for the sympathetic reception that we got to the reformulation of 'humanitarian intervention' into the 'responsibility to protect', with the responsibilities to prevent and rebuild as integral components of it.

Frequent and intensive interactions with analysts and officials from the Asia-Pacific – at representative seminars with several speakers on the podium[14] as well as conversations that I have led as the sole or keynote speaker as an ICISS commissioner – lead me to the following three conclusions:

- most people in the region are yet to read the Report and engage with its main themes and arguments, and there has been little media coverage of it;
- there remains a generalised reluctance to accept the principal conclusions of R2P based on an instinctive resistance to the very word 'intervention' by the majority that has not read R2P;
- among those who have read R2P, there are in fact surprising sympathy and receptivity to its main thrusts and recommendations.

The general mood seems to be that R2P is needed but ahead of its time.[15]

Middle East

Not surprisingly, the double standards criticism was raised most forcefully by interlocutors in the Middle East with regard to the plight of the Palestinians. Mohammed Ayoob has articulated the argument with characteristic forcefulness: 'Israel's continued occupation and the continuing armed assault against the Palestinians is already a breach of

was not a coercive intervention in the internal affairs of a member state. For one thing, the UN had never given formal consent to Indonesia's annexation of the territory and so the question of requiring Indonesian consent did not arise. For another, Indonesian consent was in fact secured.

[14] Tokyo, 16 December 2002, Bangkok, 19 March 2003, Singapore, 20 March 2003, 17th Asia-Pacific Round Table, Kuala Lumpur, 6–9 August 2003, Jakarta, 23–25 February 2004.

[15] See Landry Subianto, 'The Responsibility to Protect: An Indonesian View', and Mely Anthony, 'The Responsibility to Protect: Southeast Asian Perspectives'; papers delivered at the 17th Asia-Pacific Round Table, Kuala Lumpur, 9 August 2003.

international security that makes it obligatory for the Security Council to intervene under Chapter VII of the charter.'[16] Ambassador Omran el-Shafie of the Egyptian Council for Foreign Affairs noted the tension between the principles of maintaining territorial integrity and the right of self-determination. Emphasising the sanctity of existing borders, he nevertheless acknowledged that in cases of extreme abuse like slavery, genocide and apartheid, the doctrine of sovereignty must yield to international norms. He expressed the dominant Arab belief that the Palestinians' exercise of the right to self-determination had been met with 'excessive and disproportionate force'. Yet he also acknowledged that internal armed conflicts can compel the government to use excessive force, and that it was difficult to establish the conditions under which this could justify international intervention.[17]

Others acknowledged that, in some cases, earlier intervention might be preferable and less costly in saving lives than later intervention. Still others noted that the results of Western intervention had not always been beneficial and sometimes had aggravated the crises and created fresh problems. Many expressed reservations regarding the term 'humanitarian', saying it should never be associated with war. There was considerable support for the involvement of regional and civil society organisations in close coordination with the UN, particularly with respect to early warning and conflict prevention.[18] The principles, safeguards and issues of the threshold and lawful agency for authorisation of intervention expressed by Middle East interlocutors were remarkably similar to those we heard in Asia and are very largely reflected in R2P.

Africa

Article 4(h) of the Constitutive Act of the new Africa Union, adopted in Lomé on 11 July 2000, explicitly spells out the principle of intervention: the 'right of the Union to intervene in a Member State' with respect to the commission of 'war crimes, genocide and crimes against

---

[16] Mohammed Ayoob, 'Third World Perspectives on Humanitarian Intervention and International Administration', *Global Governance* 10:1 (2004), p. 112.

[17] Omran el-Shafie, 'Intervention and State Sovereignty', discussion paper for the ICISS Round Table Consultation in Cairo, 21 May 2001.

[18] See Ambassador (retired) Ahmed T. Khalil, 'Rapporteur's Report, ICISS Round Table Consultation, Cairo, 21 May 2001'; available on the Commission's website at www.iciss. gc.ca.

humanity'.[19] There are many possible explanations for the greater willingness of Africans to accept intervention. Their greatest fear is state failure leading to humanitarian crises, where the sensitivity to intervention is less. Asia and Latin America have been more successful in state consolidation and for them the trigger to intervention is more likely to be alleged human rights violations, on which there is far more international disagreement.

Sovereignty is elusive in the African context of tensions and polarisation between state and society. In effect sovereignty has been 'alienated' from society and become restricted to an international relational dimension (the negative conception of non-interference rather than the positive one of enabling attributes and assets). Also, many weak African states lack empirical sovereignty, being subject instead to warlords, robber barons, gun and drug runners, etc.[20] The greater African openness to interventions may be explained also by recent African history.[21] Far too many regimes – Haile Mariam Mengistu in Ethiopia, Idi Amin and Milton Obote in Uganda – had used the shield of sovereignty for their abusive records, treating people, African people, as objects rather than actors. In response, civil society groups had concluded that, in the midst of egregious and massive atrocities and abuses, sovereignty should be subordinated to international concerns and humanitarian assistance.

But African civil society representatives were just as uncomfortable with the association of the term 'humanitarian' with 'war' as their counterparts elsewhere. Moreover, African interlocutors were appreciative of the fact that the shift in terminology from 'humanitarian intervention' to the 'responsibility to protect' embraced preventive and post-conflict peace-building as integral elements.[22]

The more challenging question was not whether sovereignty should be an absolute shield, but who has the authority to speak and act on behalf of the people when their sovereign interests are no longer represented by their own governments, or when there is no functioning government at all, or when minorities are subjected to extreme oppression by the

---

[19] The text of the Constitutive Act is available online at www.africa-union.org/home/Welcome.htm.

[20] Adonia Ayebare, 'Regional Perspectives on Sovereignty and Intervention', discussion paper prepared for the ICISS Round Table Consultation, Maputo, 10 March 2001.

[21] Ibid.

[22] Emmanuel Kwesi Aning, 'Rapporteur's Report, ICISS Round Table Consultation, Maputo, 10 March 2001'; available on the Commission's website at www.iciss.gc.ca.

government in the name of the majority community. The important points were to ensure that interventions result from the explicit authority of a mandated multilateral organisation and to link them to a political strategy that allows for a strategic engagement with the country subject to intervention.

Latin America

In the twentieth century, Latin America was the most frequent target of intervention by its great and powerful neighbour to the north. At the same time, the continent had its share of rogue regimes (often backed by Washington) that brutalised their own people as recently as the 1970s and 1980s. The dual experience has shaped its response to the tension between sovereignty and intervention more sharply than in Africa and Asia.[23]

Chilean Foreign Minister Maria Soledad Alvear acknowledged that 'humanitarian intervention' is one of the most controversial and hotly disputed topics on the international agenda that highlights 'a disturbing vacuum in our collective humanitarian system' in coping effectively with massacres and other tragedies. The fundamental ethical premise must be that we are fellow human beings united by solidarity across borders. At the same time, the value of sovereignty is rooted in painful historical encounters and many have understandable fears that generalising a supposed right to intervention could be abused by the great powers to launch unilateral interventions. Hence the tension between the two must be approached and resolved with sensitivity and caution. 'For Chile, the United Nations Charter constitutes the only possible legal framework, the condition sine qua non, governing humanitarian intervention.' In turn this ties the topic to UN practice, the role of the UNSC and the use of the veto. 'We must respect the prerogatives of the Security Council, but at the same time we must remember that our interests do not always coincide with those of the permanent members, and that international law and United Nations practice are not frozen in time', she concluded.[24]

---

[23] See Jorge Heine, 'The Responsibility to Protect: Humanitarian Intervention and the Principle of Non-intervention in the Americas', in Ramesh Thakur, Andrew F. Cooper and John English, eds., *International Commissions and the Power of Ideas* (Tokyo: United Nations University Press, 2005), pp. 221–45.

[24] Maria Soledad Alvear, 'Humanitarian Intervention: How to Deal with Crises Effectively', introductory remarks at the ICISS Round Table Consultation, Santiago, 4 May 2001 (unofficial translation).

In the discussion generated by Alvear's introduction and other prepared papers, participants agreed on the principles that subsequently
found their way into R2P.[25] It was noted that geography and history
ensured that in Latin America, 'the contrast between [US] hard power
and [UN] legitimacy is viewed in even more vivid colors than in other
regions of the globe'. The UN reflected and depended on the interests of
member states, was not organised to make quick decisions and needed
innovations to permit a global oversight system. Participants agreed that
the UNSC is the most acceptable institution for authorising intervention,
but disagreed on what was permissible when circumstances called for
intervention but the Council failed to act.

R2P, the United Nations and the new normative architecture

Military intervention for human protection purposes is a polite euphem-
ism for war: the use of deadly force on a massive scale. Power politics is
at the core of the contested aspects of such interventions, including
threshold of abuse, legal authority for the intervention and replacement
of the repressive with a progressive regime. For example, if law and order
is to be restored, whose law and whose order will it be? Answers to all
such questions are profoundly political in content and are made by
political actors on the basis of political judgements.

During the twentieth century there was growing isomorphism among
states with respect to international human rights norms. But there is
neither a homogeneous international society with respect to human
rights and humanitarian concerns, nor a unifying normative architecture. Rather, the reality of norm variation attests to the existence of a
polymorphic international society. Human rights regimes are most successful when they try to harmonise respect for human rights among
nations that already provide effective guarantees on human rights and
least successful when introducing human rights to new jurisdictions.[26]
The claim that the human rights norm protects citizens from the state[27]

---

[25] Luis Bitencourt, 'Rapporteur's Report, ICISS Round Table Consultation, Santiago, 4 May
2001'; available on the Commission's website at www.iciss.gc.ca.

[26] Andrew Moravcsik, 'Explaining International Human Rights Regimes: Liberal Theory
and Western Europe', *European Journal of International Relations* 1:2 (June 1995),
pp. 157–89.

[27] Thomas Risse, '"Let's Argue!": Communicative Action in World Politics', *International
Organization* 54:1 (Winter 2000), p. 5.

is truer of Western than developing countries. For in the latter case, the threat of a failed state would be a major derogation of human rights. 'The role of the state is essential in the need to ensure respect for and . . . the realisation of human rights.'[28]

With independence, the newly decolonised countries engaged simultaneously in state-building, nation-building and economic development. Sovereignty was the critical shield behind which the triple pursuit was attempted. The path-dependence of their colonial history offers a clue as to why sovereignty and its correlative norm of non-intervention are more deeply internalised in the developing country elites than their counterparts in the West. As memories of colonialism dim and become increasingly distant, the salience of sovereignty correspondingly diminishes. Domestic groups instead begin to use the international human rights norm to subject the actions of their own governments to increasingly harsh scrutiny. In parallel with this, fewer and fewer Western leaders are impressed any longer with charges of neo-imperialism by historical association.

At this stage human rights advocacy groups inside the target state can forge alliances of convenience with foreign and international counterparts. Norm-violating governments can choose to deny the validity of global norms and reject critics as agents or stooges of ignorant or ill-intentioned foreigners. But if vulnerable and subjected to sufficient pressure, they may begin to make tactical concessions in order to mollify domestic and international critics, lift aid suspensions and so on. The discourse has shifted from denying to accepting the validity of the norm, but rejecting specific allegations of norm-violation by questioning the facts and evidence presented by critics, or else insisting that these are isolated incidents and the cases will be investigated and perpetrators will be punished, etc. By such a process of 'self-entrapment',[29] the war for human rights is won though many battles might remain to be fought.

---

[28] Danilo Türk, 'Humanitarian Interventions: Balancing Human Rights and National Sovereignty', *International Policy Perspectives*, No. 2002.1 (St. Louis: University of Missouri–St. Louis, January 2002), p. 20.

[29] Risse, '"Let's Argue!"' p. 32. In a subsequent refinement with colleagues, Risse developed the five-stage spiral model of norm generation, diffusion and domestication by the target state: repression, denial, tactical concessions, prescriptive status (when the state accepts the international norm and incorporates it into domestic legislation), and rule-consistent behaviour. Thomas Risse and Kathryn Sikkink, 'The Socialisation of International Human Rights Norms into Domestic Practices: Introduction', in Thomas Risse, Stephen

Normative inconsistency and incoherence

The norm of non-intervention is underpinned by a cluster of auxiliary norms. To replace it with a new norm of intervention carries the risk of producing, not a norm cascade, but a bursting of the dam. One of the peculiar aspects of the NATO countries' handling of the Kosovo conflict was their stress on the formal sovereignty and territorial integrity of Yugoslavia even while violating the same. Designed to deny any normative incoherence between state sovereignty and 'humanitarian intervention', the formula fell into the related trap of normative inconsistency. Sovereignty in effect became 'fluid and contingent'.[30]

Normative coherence requires compatibility among a cluster of cognate norms, for example among the norms of the use and non-use of force, non-proliferation of weapons, arms control and disarmament, and intervention and non-intervention in the internal affairs of sovereign states. *Normative inconsistency* refers to unevenness in the application of any one particular norm, for example non-intervention or non-proliferation (cf. Iraq, Israel and North Korea), either in different locations or cases around the same time, or in like cases and even the same place over time.

Whether it was Britain in Kenya[31] or Belgium in the Congo,[32] the colonial powers were brutal in dealing with dissent and rebellion. The displacement and ethnic cleansing of indigenous populations was carried out with such ruthless efficiency that the place of settler societies like Australia, Canada and the USA in contemporary international society is accepted as a given[33] because, as Paul Keal notes, the 'criteria fixed by

---

C. Ropp and Kathryn Sikkink, eds., *The Power of Human Rights: International Norms and Domestic Change* (Cambridge: Cambridge University Press, 1999), pp. 17–35.

[30] Christine M. Chinkin, 'Kosovo: A "Good" or "Bad" War?', *American Journal of International Law* 93:4 (October 1999), p. 845.

[31] For two recent books that dramatically revise the severity and scale of British repression and what today would be termed atrocities, see David Anderson, *Histories of the Hanged: The Dirty War in Kenya and the End of Empire* (New York: W. W. Norton, 2005); and Caroline Elkins, *Imperial Reckoning: The Untold Story of Britain's Gulag in Kenya* (New York: Henry Holt, 2005).

[32] For an account of the scale of humanitarian atrocities committed by Belgium in its African colony, see Adam Hochschild, *King Leopold's Ghost* (Boston: Houghton Mifflin, 1999).

[33] Nor is the double standards discourse simply historical. Having led the international intervention in East Timor for humanitarian reasons, Australia found itself in a dispute with the independent government of East Timor over the maritime boundary separating the two countries. More important than the principles involved are the commercial

the inner circle' of powerful states 'articulate rules of legitimacy and norms of behaviour'.[34] Which rights that Westerners hold dear would they be prepared to give up in the name of universalism? Or is the concept of universalism just a one-way street – what we Westerners have is ours, what you heathens have is open to negotiation?

One hint of the answer lies in the following: 'the diffusion of international norms in the human rights area crucially depends on the establishment and the sustainability of networks among domestic and transnational actors who manage to link up with international regimes, to alert Western [sic] public opinion and Western [sic] governments'.[35] The philosophical antecedents of such beliefs lie in the eighteenth–nineteenth-century theory of evolutionary progress through diffusion and acculturation from the West to the rest. The implicit but clear assumption is that when Western and non-Western values diverge, the latter are in the wrong and it is only a matter of working on them with persuasion and pressure for the problem to be resolved and progress achieved.[36] The cognitive rigidity is shown again in the statement that 'Pressure by Western states and international organisations can greatly increase the vulnerability of norm-violating governments to external

---

opportunities to exploit the oil and gas reserves which lie on the East Timor side of the median line, the traditional demarcation line of maritime boundaries in international law. While East Timor's budget is A$100 million per annum, Australia has taken an average of A$1 million *per day* in contested oil and gas royalties since 1999. Moreover, two months before East Timor's independence in 2002, Australia withdrew from the maritime boundary jurisdiction of the two international bodies that could have adjudicated on the dispute, the International Court of Justice and the International Tribunal on the Law of the Sea, thereby demonstrating its level of confidence in its own case. See Peter Holding, 'The New Battle over East Timor', *Age* (Melbourne), 21 April 2005. The two countries reached an agreement at the end of April 2005 for sharing revenues while deferring the decision on the boundary delimitation for fifty years.

[34] Paul Keal, *European Conquest and the Rights of Indigenous Peoples: The Moral Backwardness of International Society* (Cambridge: Cambridge University Press, 2003), p. 188.

[35] Risse and Sikkink, 'The Socialisation of International Human Rights Norms into Domestic Practices', p. 5.

[36] Many in developing countries watched bemusedly from the sidelines when the same attitudinal divide opened up across the Atlantic in 2003 with respect to the US threat of war on Iraq and the stiff resistance from European citizens. The dominant view in Washington seemed once again to be that the European people could not possibly be right. The task was to show them the error of their ways or, failing that, to make sure that the European governments listened to the US administration rather than to their own people. That the administration could be wrong was a priori beyond the realm of possibility.

influences.'[37] Self-evidently, only non-Western governments can be norm violators; Western governments can only be norm setters and enforcers.

The rejection of the International Criminal Court (ICC) by Washington – described by Sweden's ambassador to the UN as reminiscent of George Orwell's immortal line in *Animal Farm* that 'we are all equal but some are more equal than others'[38] – highlights the irony that the USA 'is prepared to bomb in the name of human rights but not to join institutions to enforce them'.[39] In other words, even if we agree on universal human rights, they still have to be constructed, articulated and embedded in international conventions. The question remains, therefore, of the agency and procedure for determining what they are, how they apply in specific circumstances and cases, what the proper remedies might be to breaches, and who decides, following what rules of procedure and evidence. Under present conditions of world realities, the political calculus – relations based on military might, economic power and media and NGO dominance – cannot be taken out.

As far as many Afro-Asians are concerned, *that* is the problem. The resilience of the opposition to the internationalisation of the human conscience lies in the fear that the lofty rhetoric of universal human rights claims merely masks the more mundane and familiar pursuit of national interests by different means. As the 2001 UN world conference on racism at Durban showed, human rights comprise one of the most fiercely contested sectors on the terrain of ideas. The contestation reflects competing conceptions of the good life, the proper relationship between citizen and state, historical wrongs and present rights, and correlative rights and obligations.

Besides, overriding the norm of non-intervention erodes another major contemporary norm, namely the non-use of force to settle international disputes. The rule of law ideal has been diffused from the West to become an international norm. It asserts the primacy of law over the arbitrary exercise of political power by using law to tame power; the protection of the citizen from the arbitrary actions of the government by making both, and their relationship to each other, subject to impersonal and impartial law; and the primacy of universalism over

---

[37] Thomas Risse and Stephen C. Ropp, 'International Human Rights Norms and Domestic Change: Conclusions', in Risse, Ropp and Sikkink, eds., *The Power of Human Rights*, p. 277.

[38] Pierre Schori, 'What We Need is a Cooperative America', *IHT*, 6 August 2002.

[39] Chinkin, 'Kosovo: A "Good" or "Bad" War?', p. 846.

particularism through the principle of equal in law, whereby individuals coming before the law are treated as individuals, divorced from their social characteristics.[40]

Normative contestation

Norms do not simply collide; they are contested, sometimes fiercely so. At any given time, incompatible norms may exist in different segments of human society around the world. New norms must make the case that they are either logical extensions of the existing law or necessary changes to it. Successful norm promotion requires the attributes of norm entrepreneurship. Conversely, success in vetoing or blocking the replacement of one norm with another also depends on a combination of structural power and coalition-forming skills: international 'spoilership' as the corollary to international leadership.

When there are contested norms, the selection made from them will depend on the relative prominence of each, their relative compatibility or coherence with other prevailing norms and the extent to which they fit the existing environmental conditions. Two of the major norm shifts since the Second World War are multilateralism ('meaning that all relevant actors are expected to play by the same set of rules') and restrictions on the use of force.[41] On both counts, many developing countries had problems with NATO going to war over Kosovo in 1999, let alone Iraq in 2003.

An order secures habitual compliance either through perception of legitimacy, in which case it is a just order; or through fear, in which case it rests on coercion. While the West wants to proscribe the unconstrained use of force to maintain domestic order, developing countries want to proscribe the use of force by outsiders to enforce justice within errant member states. For many developing countries, the norm of non-intervention remains a moral imperative, not simply a legal inconvenience to be discarded at the whim and will of the West.

Since the international system is highly stratified, there is a high probability of interventions being seen as instruments of depredation by the strong against the weak. For developing countries they conjure

[40] Ellen S. Cohn and Susan O. White, 'Legal Socialisation Effects on Democratisation', *International Social Science Journal* 152 (June 1997), p. 165.
[41] Ann Florini, 'The Evolution of International Norms', *International Studies Quarterly* 40:3 (September 1996), pp. 377–8 and 382–3.

up visions of the nineteenth-century doctrine of the 'standard of civilisation', with human rights being the new standard.[42] But the Western
construction of the new standard is ahistorical, airbrushing the role
of violence in the making of most Western states. Americans may be
innocent of the role of violence, conflict and conquest in the historical
enterprise of constructing modern US society as a paragon of amicable
multiethnic society; but war made the modern European states as well.[43]
The claim of developing-country governments to monopoly over the
legitimate use of violence is resisted by many armed groups from within;
is the state in the contemporary developing world to be denied the
right to use force against those who would challenge its authority as
the lawful guardian of domestic order? And of course, outside intervention on behalf of groups resisting state authority by force encourages
other recalcitrant groups in other places to resort to ever more violent
challenges, since that is the trigger to internationalising their power
struggle. Ayoob asks how seriously delayed or distorted the Western
state-making enterprise would have been if the likes of Amnesty International, Human Rights Watch, the UN Human Rights Commission and
the UNSC had been monitoring their actions during the violent phases
of their state-making process, for example in the US civil war.[44]

There is a logical slippage between normative idealism and realpolitik
in picking and choosing which elements of the existing order are to be
challenged and which retained. If ethical imperatives and calculations
of justice are to inform, underpin and justify international interventions, then there is a powerful case for reforming the composition of
the UNSC and eliminating the veto clause with respect to humanitarian
operations. To self-censor such calls for major reform on the grounds
that they are unacceptable to the major powers and therefore unrealis-
tic, is to argue in effect that the motive for intervention is humanitarian, not strategic; but the agency and procedure for deciding on
intervention must remain locked in the strategic logic of realpolitik.
'Eroding the existing normative basis of international society in order
to provide major powers the facility to intervene selectively in the

---

[42] Gerritt W. Gong, *The Standard of 'Civilisation' in International Society* (Oxford:
Clarendon, 1984).
[43] For the role of violence in state-making, see Youssef Cohen, Brian R. Brown and A. F.
K. Organski, 'The Paradoxical Nature of State-Making: The Violent Creation of Order',
American Political Science Review 75:4 (1981), pp. 901–10.
[44] Ayoob, 'Humanitarian Intervention and International Society', p. 227.

domestic affairs of weaker states ought not to form a part of the humanitarian intervention argument.'[45]

The rise and fall of developing countries as norm entrepreneurs

But is anyone listening any more to developing-country charges of double standards and hypocrisy? In the 1960s–70s, the heady days of the post-colonial period, international conditions favoured narratives of griev-ance and claims for redress and assistance. The developing countries were the norm advocates and norm generators, via the UN General Assembly, in delegitimising colonialism,[46] criminalising apartheid and legitimising armed national liberation movements. They were less suc-cessful in efforts to delegitimise the existing international economic order and replace it with a new one. The end of the Cold War marked the triumph of liberal internationalism in economics. The command econ-omy, bankrupt conceptually and politically illegitimate, lost all attraction as a model for the South. In combination, these shifts led to the loss of Third World solidarity and to the search for US capital, credits, technology, management and markets.

The 'transformation of human rights inverts the concept, from one premised on the protection of people from the violence of states to one justifying the application of violence by the world's most powerful states against weaker ones. With this transformation, human rights betrays its own premises and thus becomes its own travesty.'[47] The humanitar-ians' moral imperative was on the march again with regard to Darfur. Those who quickly occupy the moral high ground are disdainful of diplomats on the low road to compromise solutions based on negoti-ations. For in the realm of righteous indignation and moral rectitude, principles are not for sale, values are not for bargaining. As discussed in chapter 5, there is a crisis of horrific proportions in Darfur. But the record of Westerners as peace-makers among their wards in Cyprus, Palestine, the Indian subcontinent and southern and western Africa is a

[45] Ibid., p. 229.
[46] See Robert H. Jackson, 'The Weight of Ideas in Decolonisation: Normative Change in International Relations', in Judith Goldstein and Robert O. Keohane, eds., *Ideas and Foreign Policy: Beliefs, Institutions, and Political Change* (Ithaca: Cornell University Press, 1993), pp. 111–38.
[47] Robert M. Hayden, 'Biased Justice: "Humanrightism" and the International Criminal Tribunal for the Former Yugoslavia', in Raju G. C. Thomas, ed., *Yugoslavia Unraveled: Sovereignty, Self-determination, Intervention* (Lanham: Lexington Books, 2003), p. 280.

sorry one. A history of smouldering sectarian conflicts and ethnic hatred as one of the principal legacies of colonialism should induce a sense of caution, diffidence and humility.[48] The size of Sudan, the historical roots of the crisis,[49] and the ease with which any Western intervention can be exploited as yet another assault on Arabs and Muslims,[50] means that the prospects of a successful outcome of the use of unilateral military force are questionable. Moreover, deadlines set by outsiders have the perverse effect of reducing rebels' incentives to negotiate an end to conflict.[51] Then there is the moral hazard of encouraging rebel groups everywhere to internationalise their crisis by intensifying violence. The Darfur rebels are alleged to have rejected two peace proposals because 'the compromises would mitigate humanitarian suffering and thereby reduce the likelihood of decisive international intervention'.[52] In his monthly report to the UNSC in August 2005, Kofi Annan criticised the Khartoum government for failure to disarm the militias and hold them accountable for earlier atrocities. But he also criticised the rebels for a substantial rise in abductions, harassment, extortion and looting during July 2005 that had intensified insecurity in Darfur.[53]

A group of former foreign ministers believe a better approach is that NATO, 'strengthened by the warrant of Security Council legitimacy,

---

[48] In January 2005, speaking in Sudan's assembly, President Thabo Mbeki of South Africa launched a withering attack on Winston Churchill and other historic figures, calling them racists who ravaged Africa and blighted its post-colonial development. He charged the British imperialists of the nineteenth and twentieth centuries with treating Africans as savages and having left a terrible legacy of countries divided by race, colour, culture and religion. Rory Carroll, 'Mbeki Attacks "Racist" Churchill', *Guardian*, 5 January 2005.

[49] A good short introduction is Alex de Waal, 'Counter-insurgency on the Cheap', *London Review of Books* 26:15 (5 August 2004).

[50] Meeting in Tripoli in May 2005, seven African countries (Chad, Egypt, Eritrea, Gabon, Libya, Nigeria and Sudan) rejected 'any foreign intervention in the Darfur problem', insisting that it must be dealt with 'through its African framework'; *Globe and Mail* (Toronto), 17 May 2005.

[51] On 25 November 2004, the UN Special Envoy Jan Pronk took the rare step of publicly blaming solely the Sudan Liberation Army for restarting the fighting in north Darfur; 'UN Blames Rebels in Darfur', *Guardian*, 26 November 2004; 'Sudan Rebels Violating Pact', *Daily Yomiuri*, 26 November 2004.

[52] Alan J. Kuperman, 'Threat of Retaliation Fuels Sudan Fighting', *Japan Times* (reprinted from the *Washington Post*), 2 October 2004. Kuperman claims that the Bosnian Muslims and the Kosovo Liberation Army followed the same strategy to internationalise their conflict by provoking ruthless retaliations in a remarkably cold calculation whereby they sacrificed their own civilians in order to gain political leverage.

[53] Edith M. Lederer, 'Annan Accuses Sudan Rebels of Banditry', *Washington Post*, 17 August 2005.

could do much more to bring a halt to Darfur's horrific humanitarian crisis'. Accordingly they urged NATO to provide immediate logistical support to the small AU force and seek the establishment of a no-fly zone over Darfur in the UNSC and 'put a brigade-sized element at the disposal of the United Nations to augment the AU force until it can build up sufficient strength of its own'.[54]

'Cherry picking' norms and laws to suit the partisan interests of the powerful will undermine respect for the principle of world order founded on law. That is to say, the normative consensus on which law rests will begin to fray and the international order will risk collapse. Much of the twentieth-century advances in globalising norms and international law have been progressive and beneficial. But their viability will be threatened if developing countries are not brought more attentively into the process of norm formation, promulgation, interpretation and articulation; that is, made equal partners in the management of regimes in which international norms and laws are embedded. Otherwise, norms will become the major transmission mechanism for embedding structural inequality in international law, instruments and regimes. In the construction of the normative architecture of world order after the end of the Cold War, developing countries have been ringside observers, not members of the project design or implementation team.

That said, it is also important that leaders of the global South examine their own policies and strategies critically. If the impetus for action in international affairs usually appears to come from the North, this is partly due to a failure of leadership from the South. Instead of forever opposing, complaining and finding themselves on the losing side anyway, developing countries should learn how to master the so-called 'new diplomacy' and become norm entrepreneurs. Otherwise in practice they risk simply being dismissed as the international 'nattering nawabs of negativism'.

The examples of the ICC and the US–UK war on Iraq show that the depiction of a binary divide along the North–South axis is too simplistic, lacking in nuance. Europe has been as sharply divided from the USA on these issues. The key difference is that where developing countries simply oppose, the Europeans also propose creative alternatives as well that are often far more progressive than Washington's preferences. And

---

[54] Madeleine Albright, Robin Cook, Lamberto Dini, Lloyd Axworthy, Ana Palacio, Erik Derycke and Surin Pitsuwan, 'NATO to Darfur', *IHT*, 26 May 2005.

they are able to do so because they have a strategic vision for the collective advancement of the welfare and security of their peoples, unencumbered by a reflexive resistance to initiatives that stifle progress for the sake of protecting the ruling elite's privileges.

Conclusion

The survey of views and opinions on the heavily contested subject of international intervention to protect populations at risk of serious harm leads to some unexpected conclusions. Nowhere is there an absolute rejection of intervention. In all consultations, people were prepared to concede that sometimes, outsiders may indeed have to step in with military force to protect innocent victims from perpetrators of mass killings and ethnic cleansing. In every single case, when pressed, people preferred the option of 'No more Rwanda' where genocide took place with no intervention, to 'No more Kosovo' where there was intervention outside the framework of UN authorisation.

Second, the weight of historical baggage is too strong for a new consensus to be formed around the concept of humanitarian intervention. If commentators, scholars and major powers wish to help victims instead of helping themselves, they should embrace the conceptual vocabulary of R2P instead.

Third, in all our consultations people emphasised the central importance of the UN. The organisation embodies the existing international moral code and political consensus on the proper rules of conduct. If the code and consensus have become obsolete, then the UN is still the only proper forum and arena for renegotiating the terms of engagement of individual states with a single international standard of civilisation. Any one intervention does not simply violate the sovereignty of any given target state in any one instance; it also challenges the *principle* of a society of states resting on a system of well-understood and habitually obeyed rules. Those who insist on retaining veto power but want to permit extra-UN enforcement of community norms insist on keeping the very rules that produce the outcomes they wish to reject. They cannot then claim legitimacy: there is far too serious a problem of *normative incoherence* (between intervention and procedural restrictions on the use of force).

Fourth, all parts of the developing world (as well as others) are seriously concerned with issues of double standards and selectivity. The Palestinian issue is the most blatant example of *normative inconsistency* (discriminatory application of the same norm). No one expects or demands that the UN must act everywhere or nowhere. But the choice between action or no action must be based on 'objective' factors like the feasibility of an operation, not on political relations with the different potential targets of intervention.

Fifth, there is unanimous opposition to the idea of Western military interventions unauthorised by the UN. There is far too much historical baggage for suspicions and fears to be allayed simply on assurances of good faith and intention. And yet, paradoxically, there is reluctance to rule out the idea that sometimes some individual or groups of states may have to take military action in the face of a paralysed UN.

Sixth, developing countries are united in the insistence that external intervention must never lead to territorial breakup. Protection of at-risk peoples must not lead to new political or territorial arrangements imposed by external actors.

All this suggests that a new consensus on the tension between intervention and sovereignty is possible. If developing-country governments and critics can move beyond their reflexive hostility to and suspicion of the very word 'intervention' itself, they are likely to find that 'the responsibility to protect' contains all the safeguards they need, and all that they are going to get, with respect to threshold causes, precautionary principles, lawful authorisation and operational doctrine. If R2P is to be the basis of a new international consensus, this can only come about in the UN forum.

Living in a fantasy world is a luxury we can ill afford. The real choice is no longer between intervention and non-intervention, but between different modes of intervention: ad hoc or rules-based, unilateral or multilateral, and consensual or deeply divisive. To interveners, R2P offers the prospect of more effective results. The question is not whether interventions should be forbidden under all circumstances, but whether the powerful should respect procedural safeguards if interventions are to be justified. To potential targets of intervention, R2P offers the option and comfort of a rules-based system, instead of one based solely on might. It would be far better to embed international intervention within the constraining discipline of the principles and caution underlying R2P than to risk the inherently more volatile nature of unilateral interventions. Absent an agreed new set of rules, there will be nothing to stop the powerful from intervening 'anywhere and everywhere'.

The High-Level Panel, borrowing from R2P, proposed five criteria of legitimacy instead: seriousness of threat, proper purpose, last resort, proportional means and balance of consequences.[55] With respect to internal conflicts, the panel explicitly endorsed the ICISS argument that 'the issue is not the "right to intervene" of any State, but the "responsibility to protect" of *every* State'.[56] In a significant breakthrough for the growing acceptance of the new norm, China's official paper on UN reforms, published on 7 June 2005, noted that 'Each state shoulders the primary responsibility to protect its own population . . . When a massive humanitarian crisis occurs, it is the legitimate concern of the international community to ease and defuse the crisis.' It went on to list the conditions and safeguards, including UNSC authorisation, which form the core of R2P.[57] In the meantime in the USA the Gingrich–Mitchell task force too endorsed R2P, including the calls for the norm to be affirmed by the UNSC and the General Assembly, as compatible with and supportive of US efforts to reform UN policy tools.[58]

The legitimacy criteria will simultaneously make the Security Council more responsive to outbreaks of humanitarian atrocities than hitherto, and make it more difficult for individual states or ad hoc 'coalitions of the willing' to appropriate the language of humanitarianism for geopolitical and unilateral interventions. Annan made an explicit reference to ICISS and 'the responsibility to protect' as well as to the HLP, endorsed the legitimacy criteria, and urged the Security Council to adopt a resolution 'setting out these principles and expressing its intention to be guided by them' when authorising the use of force. This would 'add transparency to its deliberations and make its decisions more likely to be respected, by both Governments and world public opinion'.[59]

In the event, 'the responsibility to protect' was one of the few substantive items to survive the brutal negotiations towards the very end of the pre-summit negotiations in New York in September 2005. The agreed document contained clear, unambiguous acceptance by all UN members of individual state and collective international responsibility to protect populations from genocide, war crimes, ethnic cleansing and

---

[55] High-Level Panel on Threats, Challenges and Change, *A More Secure World: Our Shared Responsibility* (New York: UN, A/59/565, December 2004), para. 207.

[56] Ibid., para. 201, emphasis in original.

[57] *Position Paper of the People's Republic of China on the United Nations Reforms* (Beijing: 7 June 2005), downloaded from http://news.xinhuanet.com/english/ 2005-06/08/content_3056817_3.htm, Part III.1, 'Responsibility to Protect'.

[58] *American Interests and UN Reform: Report of the Task Force on the United Nations* (Washington, DC: US Institute of Peace, 2005), p. 15. Available at www.usip.org.

[59] Annan, *In Larger Freedom*, paras. 122–35.

crimes against humanity, and willingness to take timely and decisive collective action for this purpose, through the Security Council, when peaceful means prove inadequate and national authorities are manifestly failing to do it. The concept was given its own subsection title.[60]

Our ability and tools to act beyond our borders have increased tremendously and thereby increased demands and expectations 'to do something'. Consider an analogy from health policy. Rapid advances in medical technology have greatly expanded the range, accuracy and number of medical interventions. With enhanced capacity and increased tools have come more choices that have to be made, often involving philosophical, ethical, political and legal dilemmas. The idea of simply standing by and letting nature take its course has become less and less acceptable.

Similarly, calls for military intervention happen. The continuing tragedies of Liberia, Burundi, the Congo and Sudan,[61] and potential tragedy in Myanmar, come readily to mind. 'Regime change' lies at the intersection of minimum standards of human rights within borders, minimum standards of civilised international behaviour, and circumstances in which outsiders may legitimately suspend sovereignty and use military force to intervene in internal affairs. Because human nature is fallible, leaders can be weak and corruptible and states can be frail and vulnerable to outbreaks of multiple and complex humanitarian crises.[62] R2P will help the world to be better prepared, normatively, organisationally and operationally, to meet the challenge, wherever and whenever it arises again, as assuredly it will.

---

[60] Draft Outcome Document, 13 September 2005, paras. 138–40.

[61] For a call by one of the ICISS co-chairs for the international responsibility to protect to be honoured in the deteriorating conditions of western Sudan, see Gareth Evans, 'The World Should Be Ready to Intervene in Sudan', *IHT*, 15 May 2004.

[62] Gareth Evans and Mohamed Sahnoun, 'The Responsibility to Protect', *Foreign Affairs* 81:6 (Nov/Dec 2002), p. 100.

PART IV

Institutional developments

13

Reforming the United Nations

In a number of key meetings during and after the Second World War, world leaders drew up rules to govern international behaviour and established a network of institutions to work together for the common good. Both the rules and institutions – the system of global governance with the United Nations as the core – are under serious challenge. The Iraq War brought to a head the larger question of the changing nature of threats in the modern world, the inadequacy of existing norms and laws in being able to address such threats and the need for new 'rules of the game' to replace them. Too often has the UN been shown to be proof against occasions of the larger kind. The United Nations is the arena for collective action, not a forum where nations who are unable to do anything individually should get together to decide that nothing can be done collectively.

How can the United Nations be so restructured as to empower it to enforce resolutions against recalcitrant regimes like Saddam Hussein's but not take any action against Israel? Unless and until this is done, will Washington re-commit to the international organisation? Conversely, if and when it is done, how many others will walk away from the world body,[1] viewing it 'not as an independent broker but as a glorified sub-contractor to the United States'?[2] Can the UN square this particular circle of the circumstances in which it is right and wrong to use force across (and, increasingly, within) borders in today's world? Or is it the case that the several countries have become so disparate that the gap

---

[1] For a sense of the raw passion and fury in the Arab and Muslim world at the double standards in US policies towards Iraq and Israeli treatment of Palestinians, and the perception that after the Iraq invasion, the UN Security Council 'subsequently legitimized a war and occupation that most of the rest of the world had clamorously opposed', see Salim Lone (a Muslim from Kenya who worked with the UN for twenty years), 'One More Casualty of the War on Terrorism', *Washington Post*, 29 August 2004.

[2] Quoted in Thalif Deen, 'UN Warned of Iraqi "Deathtrap"', *Asia Times* (www.atimes.com), 13 May 2004.

between them simply cannot be bridged by any one organisation? How true is it to say that 'As a pre-cold-war organisation operating in a post-cold-war world, the UN has struggled to be relevant and effective'?[3] In his commencement address at Harvard University on 10 June 2004, Secretary-General (SG) Kofi Annan noted that 'The United Nations was never meant to be a suicide pact. But what kind of a world would it be, and who would want to live in it, if every country was allowed to use force, without collective agreement, simply because it thought there might be a threat?'[4]

The more serious threat to the UN's viability may come not from the USA, but from developing countries who have become disillusioned with the organisation as the forum for legitimising American dominance over the rest of the world. So far, most developing countries have viewed the UN as a partner in the joint quest for development and security, not an adversary trying to impose an American agenda or ideology. But if the UN becomes for the rest of the world what the old Warsaw Pact was for the former Soviet satellites, it will be a threat to the autonomy and security of most member states, not the collective instrument for protecting them through strength in unity.

This chapter proceeds in four parts. First, I will review the record of the UN through 'on the one hand, on the other hand' views. Next I will outline the reforms implemented in the UN system since 1997 largely on the initiative of the SG himself. I will then examine the difficulties associated with reforming the UN Security Council (UNSC). In the final part, I will discuss the report of the High-Level Panel on UN reforms.

The UN record: helpful or baleful?

The UN opened up new horizons in 1945, but the steps taken since then have been small, hesitant and limited. This is not to deny the organisation's many real accomplishments: decolonisation, elimination of apartheid, peacekeeping missions, behind the scenes peace-making, the development and extension of the rule of law, human rights promotion, gender empowerment, assistance to refugees, collective action for such common problems as resource depletion and environmental degradation,

---

[3] Ivo Daalder and James Lindsay, 'Divided on Being United', *Financial Times Weekend*, 6–7 November 2004.

[4] Kofi A. Annan, 'Three Crises, and the Need for American Leadership', UN Press Release SG/SM/9357.

and so on. The League of Nations died in the horrors of the Second World War a mere twenty years after its establishment, the UN has survived into the new millennium. It has to operate today in a global environment that is vastly more challenging, complex and demanding than the world of 1945. It has proven to be remarkably agile on some occasions but not up to the task on others.

On the one hand, the UN promised much but accomplished little. Set up as a many-splendoured forum for realising humanity's loftiest aspirations, it has often been reduced to a many-splintered organisation mired in petty squabbles. The founders created the General Assembly (GA) as the forum of choice for discussing the world's problems, resolving disputes and articulating global norms; the UNSC for keeping the peace and enforcing the norms; the specialised agencies to address transnational technical problems; and the office of the SG to run this vast machinery smoothly and efficiently. In fact the GA has become a forum for public recriminations more than public diplomacy, the Cold War against the 'evil empire' was won by the USA and its allies, and countries that have moved from poverty to prosperity have done so by embracing market principles rather than relying on UN handouts. The United Nations has played a scarcely discernible role either in keeping the peace, promoting successful development or defeating the worst enemies of freedom and human rights since the end of the Second World War.

The Rwanda genocide was a stark reminder of how major powers set the agenda and lay down the parameters within which the Council operates, and of the need 'for a great power patron if the Council is to engage in a conflict'.[5] The Council failed to represent international society. Canadian Major-General Roméo Dallaire, Force Commander of the UN Assistance Mission in Rwanda (UNAMIR), famously observed that with 5,000 properly equipped and appropriately mandated troops, he could have stopped the slaughter of hundreds of thousands of Rwandans – a view to which he still holds ten years after the event.[6] Instead the UNSC, in an act of eternal and surreal infamy, adopted Resolution 912 which ordered UNAMIR strength to be cut from 2,558 to 270. Even after Resolution 918 of 17 May authorised a force strength of 5,500 for UNAMIR-II, it took three months for the first troops to arrive in Rwanda.

---

[5] Howard Adelman and Astri Suhrke, 'Rwanda', in David M. Malone, ed., *The UN Security Council: From the Cold War to the 21st Century* (Boulder: Lynne Rienner, 2004), p. 496.
[6] Personal conversation, New York, 26 March 2004.

Colin Keating, president of the Council at the time, has written of his futile efforts to persuade the Council to call what was happening 'genocide'.[7] The USA would have none of it for fear that the word would increase international and domestic political-cum-legal pressure, under the Genocide Convention, to intervene to stop the carnage.[8] China in private was also strongly averse to the introduction of any human rights language in the Council and interpreted the Genocide Convention in that light. Despite Nigeria's best efforts, the non-aligned caucus proved impotent as well. Ambassador Ibrahim Gambari, who represented Nigeria on the UNSC at the time (and followed Keating as its president in May 1994), describes the Council as 'first and foremost a political institution that functions in concentric circles of interest and influence'. The core comprises the United States as the P1 member, followed by the circle of the P3: the US, France and the UK. The next circle is the P5, followed by the Non-aligned Movement whose members meet on a regular basis to try to harmonise their positions on matters before the Council. The outer ring consists of the elected members who do not even belong to the Non-aligned Movement and are thus all on their own.[9]

Equally, however, one could argue that, on balance, the world has been a better and less bloodier place with the United Nations in being than would have been the case without the organisation's existence. That existence in turn has been sustained by the UN's ability to manage change by implementing reforms. Set up to manage the world in the revolutionary conditions prevailing after a major world war, the organisation has had simultaneously to reflect, regulate and respond to the changing circumstances all around it since 1945, and in particular since the end of the Cold War. At a time when George W. Bush, president of the organisation's most powerful and influential member, threw down the gauntlet of relevance, the demands on the organisation continued to be great and urgent, the expectations of it compelling and poignant. It was, after all, to the UN and the Europeans that Bush turned for 'nation-building' in Afghanistan after the military defeat of the Taliban

---

[7] Colin Keating, 'Rwanda: An Insider's Account', in Malone, ed., *The UN Security Council*, p. 508.

[8] It was not until 25 March 1998 that, during a stopover in Kigali on 25 March, President Bill Clinton acknowledged the genocide and apologised for the US share of the blame in the ensuing humanitarian crisis.

[9] Ibrahim A. Gambari, 'Rwanda: An African Perspective', in Malone, ed., *The UN Security Council*, p. 519.

government; it was to the UN that he turned to buttress his campaign against Iraq; it is the UN that is left to face the unimaginable task of alleviating HIV/AIDS in Africa; it is the UN that led the efforts at humanitarian relief operations after the devastating earthquake and tsunami that struck across the Indian Ocean at the end of 2004; and it is the UN that must keep alight the flame of human rights.

Internal reforms

There are two different ways of conceptualising UN reform. The first is to think of reform in terms of the relations among the different parts of the UN system. In public perception, the UN is a collective entity. In reality, the organisation is a collection of discrete entities, each with its own set of rules, members and interests. From a reform perspective, three distinctions are especially pertinent: between the intergovernmental organs, which are served by UN officials and whose members are the political masters of the Secretariat; the Secretariat, of which the SG is the chief administrative officer; and the interaction between the two. The SG and UN officials cannot prescribe to their political masters how to reform the intergovernmental organs; that remains the prerogative of the member states themselves. The 1997 report on reform focused mainly on those changes in the Secretariat that lie within the SG's purview. The 2002 report, while recalling earlier efforts at reform and their continuing implementation, completion and fine-tuning, focused also on the interface of the work by the Secretariat and the intergovernmental processes.

The second way to conceptualise UN reforms also starts with public perceptions. For most people, the mention of the subject conjures up either one of two scenarios: reforming the structure, composition and procedures of the UNSC; or eliminating waste, inefficiency, bureaucratic rigidity, costliness and so on associated with the world organisation.

The 1997 reform report outlined a programme of reform that featured a new leadership and management structure.[10] To streamline coordination, strengthen cohesion and ensure strategic coherence and direction in the work of the organisation, the SG established a Senior Management Group which meets under his chairmanship at regular intervals. UN

---

[10] *Renewing the United Nations: A Programme for Reform. Report of the Secretary-General* (New York: UN, A/51/950, 14 July 1997).

departments, offices, funds and programmes were grouped into four core activities of the organisation: peace and security, economic and social affairs, development cooperation, and humanitarian affairs. An executive committee was established for each of these four areas to facilitate communication among departments with common interests and cognate programmes of work. The Office of the High Commissioner for Human Rights and the Centre for Human Rights were consolidated into a single Office of the High Commissioner to strengthen the institutional basis from which to lead the organisation's mission. Mary Robinson was remarkably successful during her tenure as High Commissioner in lifting the profile of the office and promoting the human rights norm. The new post of Deputy SG was meant to assist the SG in attending to issues involving multiple departments within the UN. The Department of Disarmament Affairs was reconstituted. A new Strategic Planning Unit was established within the Executive Office of the SG. Anti-crime efforts were consolidated into a new Office for Drug Control and Crime Prevention based in Vienna. At the field level, the UN has moved increasingly to a common framework for the provision of services and adopted the concept of unified country teams and strengthened the capacity of resident coordinators to serve the whole system.

In 1999 the SG urged global business leaders to make globalisation work for all people of the world. They responded to this challenge, and the resulting Global Compact provides the UN with a framework for involving the private sector in its various development goals. It calls on companies to embrace ten universal principles in the areas of human rights, labour standards and the environment. The Global Compact has the potential to be an important instrument for instilling civic virtue in the global marketplace. With more than 1,500 companies from seventy countries, it is the largest corporate citizenship initiative in the world.

There were five principal messages in the 2002 report.[11] The organisation must be clear on what to do before it can learn how to do it well. There is a need to shed some accumulated responsibilities that are no longer relevant in today's world, in order to devote more focused attention on today's urgent issues like terrorism, water scarcity, HIV/AIDS,

---

[11] I was a senior adviser on reforms and the principal writer (but not the author: it was not my report but that of the Secretary-General) for the 2002 reform report. The exercise is discussed in more detail in Ramesh Thakur, 'Reforming the United Nations: Changing With and For the Times', *International Peacekeeping* 10:4 (Winter 2003), pp. 40–61.

human rights, ageing, etc. Second, the UN must simplify and rationalise its rules of procedure and processes in order to reduce complexity, cut paperwork and time, and increase efficiency and cost-effectiveness. The UN cannot become captive to the tyranny of trivia. It needs fewer meetings, simpler processes and shorter documents written in clear and crisp language. Within two years of the reform report, there was a 13 per cent reduction in paperwork.[12] Third, the UN system is dispersed across the world, comprising a number of different units often working together with partners from government, civil society and the private sector. This places a premium on coordination, joint programming and common databases and knowledge networks. Fourth, there is a serious disconnect between the establishment of programme priorities and the allocation of resources to achieve common goals. The four-year medium-term plan was replaced with a two-year strategic framework, with the first due to be presented to the General Assembly in Autumn 2005. Finally, the report looked at how to attract and keep the best people as UN staff by offering them a rewarding career as international civil servants. The work ethos of the organisation must be transformed from a culture of entitlements and automatic increments to a culture of results-based performance and rewards. But while the UN has to be lean, it must not be mean. Cost-cutting must not be driven by ideological extremism to the point where relentless shedding of 'excess' fat turns the organisation into 'UN Lite'.

Efforts to emphasise reform as an ongoing process are reflected also in a number of reviews, initiatives and developments outside the Secretariat. The Brahimi Panel looked back on the half-century's experience of peacekeeping in order to bring it into line with the realities of the new century.[13] Other reports have underlined the UN's new-found capacity and willingness to engage in serious introspection with regard to some painful episodes in its history and draw the necessary lessons from them. In an externally commissioned report on the genocide in Rwanda,[14] and through a report of the SG himself on the fall of Srebrenica,[15] the

---

[12] Kofi A. Annan, *Report of the Secretary-General on the Work of the Organization* (New York: UN, 2004, document A/59/1), para. 256.

[13] For an earlier comment on the Brahimi Report, see Ramesh Thakur, 'Cambodia, East Timor and the Brahimi Report', *International Peacekeeping* 8:3 (Autumn 2001), pp. 115–24.

[14] *Report of the Independent Inquiry into the Actions of the United Nations during the 1994 Genocide in Rwanda* (New York: United Nations, 15 December 1999).

[15] *Report of the Secretary-General Pursuant to General Assembly Resolution 53/35 (1998)* (New York: UN Secretariat, November 1999).

UN offered candid and critical accounts for public debate and reflection of the shortcomings in UN peacekeeping. The GA has adopted measures and procedures to simplify its agenda, better focus the work of its committees and begin reducing its extensive documentation. The Monterrey Conference on Financing for Development (2002) helped to bring together the different parts of the international system, including the international financial institutions, to forge a partnership for development. The combined result of the cycle of reforms and reviews, and the implementation of many of their recommendations,[16] has been to enhance the UN capacity to act with more unity of purpose and coherence of efforts.

On the other hand . . .

Yet the responses to date to calls for UN action have been neither as prompt, effective nor uniform as they need to become. If the UN fails to accommodate its structures, processes and agendas to the transformations sweeping the world, it will risk atrophy and fade into irrelevance. The UN is charged with the neutral stewardship of the world's collective destiny. The gap between promise and performance remains unacceptably large, so that few can be confident that the next group turning to the UN for protection will not be cruelly betrayed because the world body lacks the ability to make critical decisions quickly, or the mandate and resources to act: the story of Darfur in 2004 is proof enough of this. Structural reforms in the UNSC remain stalemated and most countries see it as having been captured by the major powers. The main donors are frustrated with the protracted, wasteful and counter-productive posturing in the GA. Summit conferences become battlegrounds for vested groups to carry on ideological trench warfare by other means.

In November 2004, the UN staff associations in New York (the global headquarters of the organisation) and Geneva (the site of most UN agencies) adopted resolutions critical of the organisation's senior management.[17] UN staff surveyed for an internal report believed that

---

[16] The UN as such under Kofi Anan has been more open to reforms than the collective membership of the organisation. A report prepared by the General Accounting Office of the US Congress found that of the 1997 reform proposals, those that did not require approval from member governments had achieved a 70 per cent implementation rate, while those requiring governmental approval had only a 44 per cent implementation rate. Jess Bravin, 'UN Gets Mixed Grades on Streamlining Effort', *Asian Wall Street Journal*, 18 February 2004.

[17] 'UN Staff Prepare to Vote against Annan', *Weekend Australian*, 20–21 November 2004.

integrity and ethical behaviour are not taken into account adequately in decisions on selection and promotion, and expressed concerns about the consequences of 'whistle blowing' or reporting misconduct.[18] Howard Adelman and Astri Suhrke note that 'despite the apologies and inquiries and efforts to describe, explain, recommend, and allocate blame, no one was in the end held accountable for possibly the greatest failure of the UN in history . . . Overall, the weak accountability mechanisms in relation to disasters like Rwanda constitute a fundamental structural weakness of the UN system.'[19] On the other hand, it clearly cannot be the case that managers are left open to blackmail by staff on trumped-up charges because they were denied promotion, for example.

Report of the High-Level Panel

In order to forge a new consensus on the norms and laws governing the use of force in world affairs in relation to contemporary threats, Annan brought together a group of sixteen distinguished experts to probe the nature and gravity of today's threats and recommend collective solutions to them through a reformed UN. The panel was given a threefold task: to develop a shared analysis of current and future threats to peace and security, prepare a rigorous assessment of the contribution that collective action can make in meeting these threats, and recommend the changes needed to make the UN an effective instrument for collective response.

The composition of the panel was initially ridiculed for its average age (around 70) when the task was to look to the future: 'Alzheimer's commission',[20] 'relics trying to reform a relic'[21] and 'a cross between déjà vu and amnesia'[22] were among the choice descriptions.[23] The choice of an American as research director, a Canadian as his deputy, and then an American again to coordinate the SG's response, further underlined the lack of sensitivity within the UN Secretariat to the widely held perception

---

[18] Warren Hoge, 'Report Criticizes the Way UN Fights Corruption', *International Herald Tribune (IHT)*, 16 June 2004.

[19] Adelman and Suhrke, 'Rwanda', pp. 495–6.

[20] Personal conversation, 2004.

[21] Unnamed UN ambassador quoted in 'United Nations: Fighting for Survival', *Economist*, 20 November 2004, p. 23.

[22] Brabara Crossette, quoting a former high-ranking UN official, 'Sixteen Wise People and the Future of the UN', *UN Wire* (www.unwire.org), 1 December 2003.

[23] No one has questioned the eminence and distinction of any one of the members individually; it is the balance among the group that raised many eyebrows.

around the world that the UN is unduly deferential to its host country, constantly exposed to US-centric world-views and analyses by the dominant US media, prone to pre-emptive appeasement of US concerns and sensitivities, and insufficiently attentive to developing-country views and aspirations.[24]

In the event the panel's report confounded most sceptics. The report is both comprehensive and coherent, presenting a total of 101 recommendations.[25] It provides a brief survey of the sixty-year history of the UN, a useful analysis of the challenges confronting it today and a set of broad and specific proposals to improve its performance and relevance. The overarching themes are our shared vulnerability and the primacy of the rule of law embedded in universal institutions and procedures that are efficient, effective and equitable. The central thesis, albeit a contestable one,[26] is that no country can afford to deal with today's threats alone, and no threat can be dealt with effectively unless other threats are addressed at the same time.

Conceptual and normative advances

The report's four major conceptual-cum-normative advancements are the interconnectedness of today's threats; legitimacy criteria for the use of military force; an agreed definition of terrorism; [27] and the need to

---

[24] There was similar dissatisfaction at the choice of an American professor to head the Millennium Development Goals (MDGs) project. When very good people with experience of living and working in poor developing countries are readily available, it struck some as curious that the project should be led by someone whose knowledge of poverty is solely academic and whose record as policy adviser has produced more shock than awe. For a commentary attacking the HLP brief and report as being unduly tilted towards Northern-centric security concerns at the cost of Southern interest in the development agenda, see Muchkund Dubey (a former foreign secretary and thus neither uninformed nor an insignificant voice), 'UN Report on Threats, Challenges and Change', *Economic and Political Weekly* (5 February 2005), pp. 502–6. In making this attack, Dubey ignores the MDGs. The point is not to question the individual credentials and quality of any one of these people, but their combined optical distortion when the rest of the world is already suspicious of the extent to which the UN has become a forum for the pursuit of Western human rights and 'humanitarian intervention' agendas.

[25] High-Level Panel on Threats, Challenges and Change, *A More Secure World: Our Shared Responsibility* (New York: UN, A/59/565, December 2004).

[26] For a sharp criticism of much of the High-Level Panel's assumptions, see the review of its report by Michael Glennon, 'Idealism at the UN', *Policy Review* 129 (2005).

[27] Its analyses and recommendations on terrorism and nuclear weapons have already been discussed in earlier chapters.

extend normative constraints to non-state actors. It identifies the major threats as war and violence among and within states; the use and proliferation of weapons of mass destruction; terrorism; transnational organised crime; and poverty, infectious disease and environmental degradation. The threats can come from state and non-state actors and endanger human as well as national security. Collective security is necessary because today's threats cannot be contained within national boundaries, are interconnected and have to be addressed simultaneously at all levels. This is all very well, but it does not address the real challenge of how to institute and operationalise a workable collective security *system*, as noted in chapter 1.

According to the panel, the primary challenge to the international community is to ensure that imminent threats do not materialise, and distant threats do not become imminent. This requires early, decisive and collective action against all the threats before they can cause the worst devastation. Such a prophylactic approach must emphasise development as a structural prevention approach while including the possibility of preventive military action. The panel endorses UN-authorised but not unilateral preventive action.

Security Council restructuring

The report has some useful comments on how to streamline, strengthen and revitalise the roles and functions of the GA, ECOSOC (Economic and Social Council) and the SG. The GA's committee structure is badly dysfunctional with respect to focus, size and mandate. Yet universal membership gives the GA a unique role and legitimacy in building global consensus on security, development and human rights issues. It also has failed to exercise its power of purse to telling effect. The panel calls sensibly for the deletion of the enemy clauses that cause unnecessary resentment, for example in Japan; the formal disbanding of the Trusteeship Council; and the abolition of the Military Staff Committee through appropriate Charter amendments (paras. 298–300). But it shied away from recommending the abolition of ECOSOC, even though the body 'is perceived nearly universally as ineffective, poorly structured, and not up to the task of taking decisive action'.[28] The 2005 summit's outcome

---

[28] *Capturing the 21st Century Security Agenda: Prospects for Collective Responses* (Muscatine, Iowa: Stanley Foundation, 2004), p. 50. This is the report of the discussions of a very high-level and experienced group of UN hands.

document agreed to delete the anachronistic enemy clauses from the UN Charter and to wind up the obsolete Trusteeship Council, but with regard to the equally anachronistic Military Staff Committee, faced with unexpected and surprising resistance from some quarters, it merely asked the UNSC to consider the Committee's composition, mandate and working methods.[29]

The most critical section is the one dealing with the UNSC. The call for reforming it is justified by the need for greater credibility, legitimacy, representation, effectiveness, and enhanced capacity and willingness to act in defence of the common peace. As well as geographical balance, membership criteria should include contributions to the regular budget, voluntary contributions to UN activities and agencies, and troop and other personnel contributions to UN peace operations. Those who contribute the most to the regular budget, specialised agencies and peace operations should have a commensurate say in making decisions; those who make the decisions should contribute commensurately.

The five permanent members of the Security Council (P5) have certain characteristics in common. They were victors in the Second World War and all of them possess nuclear weapons. They created the UN and gave themselves exalted positions at the time. Washington, anticipating a Nationalist triumph against the communists, ensured China's seat at the high table as a means of having an important ally in the Pacific. This arrangement was ossified by the Cold War. With the Cold War over and the UN now espousing democratic principles, the UN needs to be reformed to reflect the changes. A static permanent membership of the Council undermines the logic of the status, erodes the legitimacy of the Council, diminishes the authority of the organisation and breeds resentment in the claimants to the ranks of the great powers.

The legitimacy of the UNSC as the authoritative validator of international security action has been subject to a steady erosion as it has been perceived as being unrepresentative in composition, undemocratic in operation, unaccountable to anyone 'below' (e.g. the GA) or 'above' (the World Court), and ineffective in results. The Security Council's record is relevant to an assessment of the claim that it has exclusive authority over military intervention.[30] It suffers from a quadruple legitimacy deficit: performance, representational, procedural and accountability.

---

[29] Draft Outcome Document, 13 September 2005, paras. 176–8.
[30] Aryeh Neier, 'The Quest for Justice', *New York Review*, 8 March 2001, p. 34.

Its performance legitimacy suffers from two strikes: an uneven and a selective record. It is unrepresentative from almost any point of view.[31] Its procedural legitimacy is suspect on grounds of lack of democratisation and transparency in decision-making. And it is not answerable to either the General Assembly, the World Court or the nations of the world.

Western countries often fret at the ineffectual performance legitimacy of the Council. Their desire to resist the Council's role as the sole validator of the international use of force is the product of this dissatisfaction at its perceived sorry record. But the moral authority of collective judgements does depend in part on the moral quality of the *process* of making those judgements.[32] The collective nature of the decision-making process of the UNSC is suspect because of the skewed distribution of political power and resources among its members. If the UNSC were to become increasingly activist, interventionist and effective, the erosion of representational and procedural legitimacy and the absence of any accountability mechanisms would lead many countries to question the authority of the Council even more forcefully.

UNSC reform is held hostage to a curious oddity. While there is consensus on the need for reform, the agreement breaks down as soon as any one particular formula or package is proposed. Once people see the details of a concrete proposal, losers and opponents always seem to outnumber winners and supporters. One major explanation for this is that 'representation' can have many different meanings.

To start with, fifty-one member states were represented in the UNSC in 1945 by five permanent and six non-permanent members. Today a total of 191 member states are represented by five permanent and ten non-permanent members.

One can represent the interests of one's constituents, as with members of elected parliaments.

Or the Council could be so composed as to reflect population distributions: many people are surprised to learn that India's population is bigger than all of Africa and almost double that of Latin America.

The heavy financial burden in the UN system borne by Germany and Japan without permanent membership amounts to taxation without representation.

---

[31] See Ramesh Thakur, ed., *What is Equitable Geographic Representation in the Twenty-first Century?* (Tokyo: United Nations University, 1999).

[32] Amy Gutmann and Dennis Thompson, *Democracy and Disagreement* (Cambridge, MA: Harvard University Press, 1996), p. 4.

Or representation could refer to the need for the UNSC to reflect the major cultures, religions and civilisations of the world. There is, for example, no Islamic permanent member at present.

A fifth possible meaning of representation would be to favour membership of representative democracies at the expense of others.

Many developing countries remain worried that the forces of globalisation impinge adversely on their economic sovereignty, cultural integrity and social stability. 'Interdependence' among unequals can mean the dependence of some on international markets that function under the dominance of others in norm setting and rule enforcement. To the extent that the UN is the central coordinating agency of the global commons, developing countries need to be drawn into its key management bodies so as better to protect their interests.

The most common meaning given to representation is in terms of the different regions of the world. Asia is under-represented and, unconscionably, Africa and Latin America have no permanent members at all.

Or one could argue that the Council's permanent membership, in terms of its original logic, reflect the military power of states. The problem with this is the moral hazard of rewarding countries for being bad international citizens. It is unfortunate also that the permanent membership is coterminous with the five nuclear-weapons powers.

Alternatively, should permanent membership be a reward for good international citizenship to countries who make the UN system work, pay their dues on time and in full, contribute diligently to peacekeeping operations and in myriad other ways work hard to keep the UN system ticking?

There is need also to provide a platform for the views of NGOs and the private sector in the UN. They make up two important layers of international civil society. Yet there is no official formula for their representation on the UNSC. While there has been great effort in recent years to give NGOs a voice in UN debates without giving them a vote in UN decisions, multinational corporations, despite their considerable role in world affairs, are totally disenfranchised in the UN.

There is surprisingly broad agreement already on the leading candidates: Germany, Japan, India and Brazil, and two of Egypt, Nigeria or South Africa. Opposition comes from three groups: those with a vested interest in the status quo, especially the P5; the regional rivals of each of the leading candidate countries; and a large group who would see their status diminished still further with the growth of permanent members from five to ten. All three groups have found it expedient to adopt the tactic of divide-and-rule, convincing the leading contenders to compete with one another. Only very recently have Brazil, Germany, India and Japan (the Group of 4 or G4) awakened to the realisation that either they will all become permanent members in one major round of reforms, or none will. In 2004 they finally presented a combined pitch for their joint cases.[33] In the following year their opponents (Algeria, Argentina, Mexico, Pakistan, South Korea, Spain) lobbied under the 'Uniting for Consensus' banner.

The High-Level Panel noted that a decision on Security Council enlargement 'is now a necessity' (para. 250). But, unable to agree between them, the panellists outlined two models. Neither model was radical, revolutionary, new or free of flaws. More crucially, if sixteen distinguished world citizens acting as individuals cannot choose between the two models, can 191 separate governments do so? The answer from the September 2005 summit was a resounding 'No'. The world leaders expressed their support for 'early reform of the Security Council as an essential element of our overall effort to reform the United Nations, in order to make it more broadly representative, efficient and transparent, and thus to further enhance its effectiveness and the legitimacy and implementation of its decisions'. They committed themselves to continue the efforts to achieve a decision.[34] That is, after a decade of talks, they agreed to talk some more. And they wonder why the UN is falling into disrepute.

Reforming the UNSC procedures

The push for democratisation in the world has been led by the three Western members of the P5 (Britain, France and the USA, the P3). Yet the P3 have been the most fiercely resistant to bringing democracy and transparency to the workings of the Council itself. Only very recently have some of these operational shortcomings been remedied, for example through such steps as briefings by the Council president; meetings between the members, troop-contributing countries and the

---

[33] Ramesh Thakur, 'A Refitted Security Council', *Japan Times*, 29 August 2004; Mark Turner, 'Four Frontrunners Combine to Push Campaign for UN Role', *Financial Times*, 20 September 2004; 'Japan Seeks to Join P-5 Club', *Daily Yomiuri*, 23 September 2004; 'Heavyweights Battle for Seats in Expanded UN Security Council', *Japan Times*, 23 September 2004.
[34] Outcome Document, para. 153.

Secretariat on peacekeeping operations; daily publication of the Council's agenda, including informal consultations; monthly circulation of the forecast of work of the Council; and holding open sessions at the request of any country, even a non-UNSC member. These advances need to be consolidated. The UNSC has also been more daring and imaginative in tackling threats to peace and security on a broader front, for example with respect to the trade in conflict diamonds and a special session on HIV/AIDS.

The UN is usually attacked for doing too little, too late. Has the UNSC been doing too much and too soon? In recent times the UNSC has been co-opting functions that belong properly to legislative and judicial spheres. Iraq was put under international receivership by means of time-unlimited sanctions. The UNSC determined the borders of a supposedly sovereign state; told it how much of its export earnings it could keep; how many observers it had to admit, as well as where and when; and what weapons it could keep and develop. Similarly, the Security Council imposed sanctions on Libya for its failure to extradite two citizens accused of being the brains behind the Lockerbie bombing. That is, without a trial and conviction, the Council was bent on compelling one sovereign state to hand over its citizens to another sovereign state on the basis of allegations from the latter – which had itself, just a few years earlier, defied the World Court's verdict in a case brought against it by Nicaragua. In August 2004, the Council approved a US-backed resolution demanding the immediate withdrawal of all foreign forces from Lebanon – at a time when more than 100,000 US troops were occupying Iraq.

The UNSC has taken on a legislative role in its recent resolutions on terrorism and non-proliferation. This is intruding into the realm of state prerogatives as negotiated in international conferences and conventions. UNSC decisions are binding, so 191 legislatures are denied their right of review over international treaties. If and when the UN Charter is reformed, one item on the agenda should be curbs on untrammelled authority in the UNSC that is presently subject to no countervailing political check or judicial review.[35]

---

[35] In the *Namibia* and *Lockerbie* cases, the International Court of Justice cast doubts on the blanket immunity of the Security Council from judicial scrutiny but did not go so far as to enunciate a doctrine of judicial review. See Jose E. Alvarez, 'Judging the Security Council', *American Journal of International Law* 90:1 (January 1996), pp. 1–39; and

The veto clause symbolises a compromise between national and global interests. It ensures that the organisation will not construct a global interest in conflict with the national interest of any one of the P5. Thus the veto is a reconciling instrument designed to ensure that any global interest forged by the UN is in harmony with the common national interests of the five most important members. In the final analysis, the veto registers the power realities of the international political world. In most cases where UN efforts to deal with outbreaks of international violence are frustrated by a veto, it is the fact of great power opposition, not its expression in the form of a UNSC veto, which is the obstacle to peace.

Table 13.1 documents that the countries using and perhaps over-using the veto in the last two decades have been Britain and the USA. The High-Level Panel acknowledged the veto as being 'anachronistic' but saw 'no practical way of changing the existing members' veto powers'. Accordingly it recommended neither the expansion of the veto to new permanent members nor its elimination for the existing P5, although it did recommend a curtailment of the veto's use (para. 256). If the veto is a genuine contribution to correlating power to responsibility and facilitating the search for great power consensus necessary to international action, it should be held by all permanent members. If it is an obstacle to the effective functioning of the UNSC, it should be abandoned.

If power were to be correlated precisely to authority, the veto would be restricted to just one, the USA. But the remaining P4 will veto such a Charter change. If there was equal justice for all, there would be no further discrimination between existing and any new permanent members. But in fact there is very little stomach for extending the veto power to any more countries. Nevertheless, as a matter of principle, the African Union remained insistent (as of August 2005) that all new permanent members must have exactly the same veto rights as the P5. If the G4 can bridge the narrow divide with the African proposal – although time is rapidly running out – they might get sufficient votes in the General Assembly in support of their model. Countries aspiring to permanent membership would then test their support in the GA in successive rounds of voting until only six countries remained

Thomas M. Franck, 'The "Powers of Appreciation": Who is the Ultimate Guardian of UN Legality?', *American Journal of International Law* 86:3 (July 1992), pp. 519–23.

Table 13.1. *The changing patterns of Security Council veto use, 1946–2004*

	China*	France	USSR/Russia	UK	USA	Total
1946–49	0	2	46	0	0	48
1950–59	1	2	44	2	0	49
1960–69	0	0	18	1	0	19
1970–79	2	7	7	14	21	51
1980–89	0	7	4	15	46	72
1990–99	2	0	2	0	5	9
2000–04	0	0	1	0	8	9
Cold War (1946–89)	3	18	119	32	67	239
Post-Cold War (1990–2004)	2	0	3	0	13	18
TOTAL	4/5	18	122	32	80	257

* From 1946 to 1971, China's seat on the Security Council was occupied by Taiwan, which used the veto only once (to block Mongolia's membership application in 1955). The first veto exercised by the People's Republic of China was on 25 August 1972.
Source: UN data.

(two each from Asia and Africa, and one each from Europe and the Americas). They would then be able to present a full slate of six candidates for permanent members, making it difficult for any of the P5 to veto a package that had thrice been endorsed by the GA by a two-thirds majority.

The aspiring new members may well in the end agree to forgoing the veto power as the price of gaining permanent membership. The June 2005 draft resolution by the G4 contained a promise that none of the newer permanent members would exercise the veto at least until after the promised review in 2020. In that case, we may witness yet another twist in the legality vs. legitimacy debate. The equation and politics of legality vs. legitimacy is bound to be profoundly affected if there are six more permanent but veto-less members. For the very fact of permanence will enhance their stature and give them continuity, experience, expertise and institutional memory. Part of the identity of the P5 as an exclusive club includes 'a shared history and set of experiences. They have learned about each other from working together and have developed shared understandings.'[36] If the vote on a resolution is 24–1 or 23–2 in a twenty-five-member Council with eleven permanent members, but the resolution is defeated because one of the veto-wielding P5 (V5?) votes negatively, then the gap between legality and legitimacy could become a chasm. If China and Russia were the only two negative votes on a Kosovo or Darfur type crisis and a coalition of the willing launched military action after such an abortive resolution, it is hard to believe that the coalition would not claim and be conceded international legitimacy.

Peace-building Commission

The panel recommended the establishment of a new Peace-building Commission (PBC) under UNSC authority to identify countries sliding towards state collapse, institute measures to halt the slide and plan for and assist in the transition from war and conflict to peace and post-conflict peace-building (paras. 261–9). The simple facts are that about half of all countries emerging from conflict slide back into armed violence within five years, and that some of the worst outbreaks of violence in recent times – Angola in 1993, Rwanda in 1994 – came after the conclusion of peace agreements. Annan endorsed the call for a PBC and recommended that it report both to the Security Council and ECOSOC, but in sequence, as simultaneous reporting lines 'will create duplication and confusion'.[37] It would be a forum in which representatives from donor countries, troop contributors and the country being helped can sit together with leaders from other countries, regional organisations and international financial institutions to agree on a common strategy, offer policy guidance, mobilise the necessary resources and coordinate all the different efforts. It could be the central node for the promotion of peace-building strategies both in general terms and in country-specific situations.[38]

To assist with these tasks, the SG proposed the creation of a small and dedicated Peace-building Support Office that would prepare the

---

[36] Ian Johnstone, 'Security Council Deliberations: The Power of the Better Argument', *European Journal of International Law* 14:3 (June 2003), p. 460.

[37] Kofi A. Annan, *In Larger Freedom: Towards Development, Security and Human Rights for All*. Report of the Secretary-General (New York: UN, document A/59/2005, 21 March 2005), para. 116.

[38] Further details were supplied in 'Explanatory Note of the Secretary-General: Peacebuilding Commission' (New York: United Nations, 17 April 2005).

documentary inputs for the PBC meetings, work with relevant UN units at headquarters and in the field to provide quality planning inputs for peace-building missions and conduct best practice analysis and develop policy guidance. In addition, there should be a Standing Fund for Peace-building as a voluntary, replenishable fund. The September 2005 summit agreed to establish a PBC as an intergovernmental advisory body, but weakened its authority by not placing it under the UNSC. Instead it is to be tasked with reporting annually to the GA, and to make its discussions and recommendations available as public documents to all relevant bodies and actors. The idea of a Standing Fund was also endorsed.[39]

Quota politics in the Secretariat?

A senior former Asian ambassador to the UN commented at a regional seminar in Sydney in 2004 that it is difficult for Asians to connect with the UN when its senior officials dealing with Asia are not Asians. Other senior Asia-Pacific ambassadors and ministers in the room expressed agreement with this sentiment: 'Viewed from Asia, the UN still exhibits an Atlantic orientation, and the organs of the UN are felt to have very little impact on the way Asian governments behave.'[40]

The proportion of Asians in senior ranks in the UN system in general, and in the Department of Peacekeeping Operations (DPKO) in parti-cular, is shown in table 13.2. Asians contribute about half the total number of UN peacekeepers and one-quarter of the UN's regular and peacekeeping budget and have suffered around one-quarter of total UN peacekeeping deaths. But there was not a single Asian (and just one African) in the senior ranks of the DPKO, and overall they comprise a mere 17 per cent of senior UN staff [41] in an organisation that supposedly supports human security and popular sovereignty as well as national security and state sovereignty. Much attention is focused on promoting women to senior posts, which is good; but not enough on regional representation in the senior ranks, which is not so good. In point of fact, women do not fare as badly as Asians, comparatively speaking: 35

---

[39] Outcome Document, paras. 97–105.

[40] Vanessa Hawkins and Aaron Timms, *Asian Approaches to Peace and Security and the Role of the United Nations*. Report on a conference hosted by the Lowy Institute for International Policy (Sydney) and the International Peace Academy (New York), 1–3 September 2004, Sydney, p. 4.

[41] Director and above: D1, D2, Assistant Secretary-General and Under-Secretary-General.

Table 13.2. *Geographic distribution of populations, UN contributions and UN posts, 31 January 2004 (percentages)*

	No states (% UN total)	Population (% world)	GDP (% world)	Contribution to UN budget	Senior UN posts*** (n =331)	PKO contribution ($)	PKO contribution (personnel)	PKO fatalities	Senior PKO posts*** (n =12)
Africa	27.75	13.30	1.83	0.89	16.36	0.18	34.36	22.63	8.33
Asia	28.27	59.07	24.66	26.57	16.97	25.18	43.96	23.21	0.00
East Europe*	10.99	5.64	2.62	2.27	9.10	1.00	6.60	7.73	8.33
Latin America	17.28	8.63	6.19	5.34	10.91	1.20	5.31	3.40	16.67
West Europe and Others**	15.70	13.36	64.70	64.92	46.66	72.44	9.77	43.03	66.67

* Includes Russia.

** Others = Australia, Canada, New Zealand and USA.

*** Directors and above.

Source: UN data.

Table 13.3. *Geographic distribution of high-level representatives of Secretary-General,* 2004

	Africa	Asia	From Latin America & Caribbean	Europe	Canada & USA	Russia	TOTAL
Africa	11	0	1	3	4	0	19
Latin Am & Caribbean	0	0	4	1	1	0	6
Asia & Pacific	0	2	0	3	0	0	5
Europe	0	0	0	4	1	0	5
Middle East	0	1	0	3	0	0	4
Other High Level	3	4	3	3	5	2	20
TOTAL	14	7	8	17	11	2	59

* Special Adviser/Envoy/Representative.
Source: Compiled from information downloaded from the UN website (www.un.org/News/ossg/srsg/ table.htm), 30 December 2004.

per cent (from a worldwide pool of around 51 per cent). Moreover, of the senior staff, just under one-third (31 per cent) come from the P5, and indeed one-quarter come from the Western P3. Between them, Canada (9) and the US (47) have exactly the same number of senior staff (excluding the SG and Deputy SG) as all of Asia, when they account for 5 and 60 per cent of the world's population respectively.

It is worth slaying another myth, that the UN is top-heavy. Of the total of 2,493 professional staff in the UN Secretariat on 31 January 2004, 331 (13 per cent!) were in the senior ranks of director and above. (The total number of personnel in the UN system worldwide was 54,379 as of 31 December 2003, of whom 22,088 were in the professional category and the rest general service.)

The distribution of high-level representatives of the SG at the end of 2004 is shown in table 13.3. Just seven of the fifty-nine high-level posts were held by Asians. The two tables together confirm the extraordinary neglect and marginalisation of Asia and Asians who account for more than half the world's population, contain some of the world's oldest civilisations and are not short of experienced and sophisticated diplomats. It is worth recalling that Asians tend to be high-, even over-achievers. Thus US census data for 2004 show that Asian-born Americans had the highest median income at US$62,551, compared to $55,714 for European-born, $33,962 for Latin American-born, and $42,677 for all foreign-born.[42]

The under-achievement of Asians in the UN system is at best a curiosity that needs investigation and explanation, at worst a scandal. It reflects badly on the system of UN senior appointments and on Asians as being the least united and cohesive of all the regional groups in the UN system. Making a public fuss is alien to the Asian way. But in the context of a culture of self-serving and self-advancing arguments at the United Nations, the result is a failure by Asian governmental representatives to promote the interests of their people in the UN system. They need to become more aggressive in proposing professionally competent Asian names for suitable senior posts, and then lobbying for them.

There is another aspect to this, namely the pressure from governments for their appointees – often former diplomats with a career devoted to serving the national interests of their own country rather than the general international interest – to assume key posts. The success of the pressure is directly proportional to the location of the countries in the international power and wealth hierarchy (table 13.2); and to some extent also to their numbers as groups in the organisation. The result:

> is a human resources crisis in the United Nations. An entrenched bureaucracy, fuelled by counterproductive quotas, nepotism and outlandishly generous tenure policies, impedes the rise of talent and excellence through the ranks. This system hinders the rise of talented junior officers, limiting the quality of the system's middle management and ultimately making senior appointments a challenge.[43]

But the above tables show the quota system to be a myth. And, if the general conclusion about senior management being less than the best is correct, then the quota system serves as a scapegoat for the failings of mainly Western senior managers (half in the general category in the Secretariat, including two-thirds in DPKO which was the main target of

---

[42] Ela Dutt, 'Asian-origin Americans Have Highest Earnings in US', *Economic Times* (Mumbai), 26 February 2005.

[43] Ludovic Hood, 'The UN Must Let Talent Rise', *IHT*, 13 August 2004. Hood served with the UN in East Timor from 2001 to 2004.

the above-cited analyst). In addition, almost all the powerful and big budget senior posts in the Secretariat and in the UN system are filled by Westerners, including peacekeeping, political affairs,[44] management, development and environment programmes, children's fund, human rights, refugees, etc. If we take the last item, about three-quarters of the world's refugees are to be found in Asia and Africa and only one-quarter in Europe and North America. Yet of the ten UN High Commissioners for Refugees so far, only one, Sadruddin Agha Khan (1965–77) was from a developing country.

Higher rank can correlate as much to one's nationality as competence, ability and seniority. Moreover, the donor countries emplace their appointees and implement their agendas as often through tied extra-budgetary financing, which can exceed the regular budget resources (for example for the High Commissioner for Human Rights). Senior appointments (Assistant and Under-Secretary-General) are a mix of power politics and money politics through lobbying by the powerful and the wealthy countries, and personal connections (people known to the SG or his senior advisers). In practice, the most critical criteria in appointing the senior people would appear to be the major donor governments and their choices, the major powerful countries (P5, but not just them), the united and vocal geographical groups, and personal knowledge of people. Thus competence and ability often come a distant fourth. The result is that subordinate staff can end up being more competent and have to 'carry' their seniors. Not surprisingly, this leads to demoralisation and cynicism and encourages the growth of a time- and self-serving mentality. An important reform would be to give far more discretion and authority to the SG to hire the best professional staff available; for the SG to professionalise the recruitment of senior UN staff[45] and be held accountable for the performance of the Secretariat overall; and for such managerial authority and performance accountability to cascade down from the SG to the different rungs of the managerial ladder as well.

---

[44] In 2005 an African replaced a European as head of the UN Department of Political Affairs.

[45] Priorities are somewhat skewed when the senior official in charge of security for the UN system is an Under-Secretary-General and the person in charge of human resources is an Assistant SG.

Conclusion: a San Francisco or an Albert Einstein moment?

The most optimistic had hoped for a San Francisco moment in New York in September 2005, one no less decisive and momentous than the signing of the United Nations Charter sixty years earlier in the city by the bay. This would have been a fitting culmination to the momentum built up since Secretary-General Kofi Annan's speech two years earlier where he proclaimed that the organisation had come to a fork in the road, a moment no less decisive than 1945 when the UN was set up. The most critical concluded that instead the UN had an Albert Einstein moment, recalling the man of the century's famous description of madness as doing something over and over again and expecting a different result each time. This is otherwise known as the triumph of hope over experience. The UN Charter was written in another age for another world. The High-Level Panel's report had revived the flagging momentum for serious institutional reform. Yet the UN has been a graveyard for almost all previous major reform proposals. Saying that he had 'resisted the temptation to include all areas in which progress is important or desirable' in order to concentrate on items on which 'action is both vital and achievable', Annan presented 'an agenda of highest priorities' for September 2005 for forging a new consensus on key challenges and priorities and converting the consensus into collective action.[46] The major debate and evidence of international opinion will come in the annual session of the General Assembly starting in September 2005. An extensive process of outreach and consultations will be necessary. Building a political consensus and generating the necessary momentum will require accommodating the divergent perceptions of the broad range of threats by different segments of the international community. Losers will have to be compensated, opponents neutralised and, of course, winners strongly mobilised.

One of the more interesting things to watch for will be whether the differences of opinion, based on competing interests, help to break the pattern of voting by consensus in some of the key groups in UN politics. If so, this 'reform' might in itself be of lasting benefit to the UN, for the insistence on consensus has produced the politics of the lowest common denominator, allowing the most recalcitrant to hold any progress to ransom. Too often have too many member states refused to let

---

[46] Annan, *In Larger Freedom*, paras. 5, 7.

majority group interests come in the way of the principle of an artificially preserved consensus. As Annan remarks, somewhat courageously, 'consensus (often interpreted as requiring unanimity) has become an end in itself'.[47] Instead of providing an effective mechanism for reconciling divergent interests, it has prompted the GA to retreat into generalities as a means of avoiding action. The fear remains that if the reform agenda is stalled or thwarted yet again, many other countries will join the USA in taking the UN less seriously.

Canadian Prime Minister Paul Martin expressed 'profound disappointment' about the summit's failure to agree on an operational and powerful human rights council and criticised the fondness for 'empty rhetoric' over concrete results.[48] He was blind to the Canadians' spoiler role in joining the uniting for dissensus group whose prime motivation was to thwart the G4's plan to expand the permanent membership of the Security Council. South African President Thabo Mbeki criticised 'rich and powerful nations' for allegedly blocking attempts to widen the Security Council to include more developing nations.[49] He chose to ignore Africa's role in bringing to a halt the momentum that had been built up by the G4 campaign because the African Union insisted on full veto powers for all new permanent members. Had the AU combined with the G4, they might well have had the votes. The Western countries blamed the developing countries for blocking efforts at management reform, that would have given greater discretionary authority to the Secretary-General in hiring and firing UN personnel, for fear that Americans and Europeans would stand to gain if the General Assembly surrendered its prerogatives in this regard. This ignores the existing severe distortions in the senior ranks of the UN system that are disproportionately dominated by Westerners.

Washington wanted to focus on non-proliferation and management reform, but betrayed an instinct for mismanaging international diplomacy in presenting a list of demands for 750 amendments at the eleventh hour to a text that had been under negotiation for months, and in the refusal to link non-proliferation to disarmament. For their part, Americans have yet to receive a convincing answer as to why the world's only superpower should acquiesce in its own 'Gulliverisation', bound

---

[47] Ibid., para. 159.

[48] Terry Weber, 'Martin Blasts "Empty" UN Reform Efforts', *Globe and Mail* (Toronto), 16 September 2005.

[49] *BBC News*, 17 September 2005, http://news.bbc.co.uk/2/hi/americas/4253358.stm.

and tethered by the many fine strands of international treaties and conventions. Or why they should not seek to refashion institutions to reflect their pre-eminence. Or why indeed the growing circle of democratic countries should accept moral equivalence with regimes which are anything but when it comes to collective decision-making.

The politics of perception on this count were also mishandled in the reform push, with an American as research director, a Canadian as his deputy, an American as the point man again in coordinating the Secretary-General's response, and a Canadian again as the seniormost UN official in charge of reform. Every one of these people is extremely well qualified and competent individually, but the optics of their combined effect is disastrous in allaying suspicions of a Western-dominated agenda. In turn, the developing countries demand handouts and greater say in decision-making but are fiercely resistant to institutionalising responsibility and accountability for acts of commission and omission.

Hypocrisy and overblown rhetoric are no monopoly of the First, Second or Third World. The ideals and workings of the UN were subverted by the major Western powers in the first decade of the organisation's existence, when the West held a commanding majority of votes. During the Cold War, the Soviet Union happily mouthed the rhetoric of democracy, self-determination and non-intervention while repressing its own people and subjugating Eastern Europeans. Washington was fiercely critical of Soviet human rights violations while supporting abusive dictatorships in Africa, Asia, Europe (Franco's Spain) and Latin America. The GA annually accepted the credentials of the slaughtering Khmer Rouge over that of the Vietnamese-installed regime that put a halt to the Cambodian killing fields.

Hidden in the details of reform proposals and in the vitriol of UN-haters is the reality that the struggle for UN reform is a battle over policy, not just process nor even a simple management upgrade. In particular, should the UN be the forum of choice or last resort for collective-action solutions to global problems: less or more environmental regulation, non-proliferation and disarmament or just non-proliferation, counter-terrorism or human rights, a strong state that provides social protection and regulation or an unobtrusive state that lets capital and markets rule the roost, etc.? That is, it is a struggle between international Keynesianism and neo-liberalism.

A twenty-three-nation poll of over 10,000 people commissioned by the BBC holds some surprising and encouraging results for the beleaguered organisation. Almost two-thirds of the respondents would react

Table 13.4. *Cross-national views on UN reforms, 2004 (N=23)*

	UN more powerful*		More permanent members**		Eliminating veto***	
	Positive	Negative	In Favour	Oppose	In Favour	Oppose
Argentina	44	22	–	–	–	–
Brazil	–	–	73	12	62	19
China	69	18	54	33	47	36
France	54	37	67	25	47	43
Germany	87	07	–	–	–	–
India	55	23	87	06	–	–
Indonesia	–	–	–	–	73	13
Italy	–	–	86	09	–	–
Japan	–	–	–	–	46	13
Lebanon	58	18	72	07	84	09
Russia	57	11	44	28	25	29
S. Africa	–	–	76	16	–	–
Spain	–	–	–	–	71	13
Turkey	40	24	–	–	–	–
UK	75	20	74	21	56	35
USA	59	37	70	23	57	34
Average of 23	64	19	69	–	–	–

* What view would you take if the UN were to become significantly more powerful in world affairs?
** There are five permanent members of the UN Security Council. Would you favour or oppose additional countries becoming permanent members?
*** Would you favour or oppose a rule change that meant no single permanent Security Council member could veto a decision backed by all the others?
Other responses have not been included in the table. Polling was conducted between 15 November 2004 and 3 January 2005. The sample size was 10,842.
Source: 'BBC Poll Backs Call for UN Reform', *BBC News,* 21 March 2005, at http://news.bbc.co.uk/2/shared/spl/hi/pop_ups/05/world_un_reform_poll_findings/html.

positively to a more powerful UN; more than two-thirds favour an enlargement of permanent membership of the UNSC, including a majority in four of the five present permanent members, and a plurality in the fifth (Russia); but most want the Council to be able to override a solitary veto (table 13.4).

To be faithful to the nations and peoples of the world who have kept faith with it for six decades, the United Nations must persevere in its efforts to consolidate its strengths, fill in the gaps and eliminate wasteful habits and procedures. For its performance has been patchy and variable. It has been neither uniform in its response nor consistent in the quality of services provided. Without the United Nations, in the last sixty years the world would have been a more, not less, dangerous place. But with the United Nations remaining essentially unchanged in structure, authority and powers, the world is unlikely to be a mainly free, healthy, prosperous and peaceful place in the next sixty years.

14

The political role of the United Nations Secretary-General

The establishment of a secretariat with a chief executive at its top converts ad hoc intergovernmental conferences into an international organisation. During the Cold War, the failure of the principal political organs to function as originally envisaged placed a disproportionate burden on the shoulders of the Secretary-General (SG). As a result the office became one with little power but considerable influence. The burden of pacific settlement under chapter 6 of the UN Charter as often as not fell on the office of the SG. It was an SG who conceived the novel institution of UN peacekeeping operations and became the lynchpin of their management and the critical channel of communication between the several actors. Because the UN pursues the two great agendas of peace and development simultaneously, it is not surprising that human security, with roots equally deep in both agendas, grew in fertile UN soil. The SG has had an important role to play in promoting the new concept of human security and the notion of institutionalising the prosecution of humanitarian atrocities and crimes against humanity.

Since the end of the Cold War, the SG is looked to in many quarters almost as an alternative voice of dissent in a US-dominated United Nations, when in fact the Cold War ended in a triumph of American values and destroyed the institutional checks on the exercise of US power globally. To be effective, the SG must retain US confidence at a time when a rampant USA does not find it easy to brook any opposition. But to be credible and respected in the rest of the world, the SG must be able to demonstrate independence of Washington, embraced but not suffocated by it. The challenge has been only too apparent with respect to Iraq, Kosovo and the threats of international terrorism and weapons of mass destruction. On all these, the SG has often found himself in the eye of the storm, sometimes having to defend the UN position against attacks from various quarters, at other times capturing the mood of the UN collective interest ahead of any resolutions adopted by its major political organs. He also has responded to the new circumstances and challenges by trying to broker norm shifts, initiating reforms and reviews and indicating new directions in which member states may wish to take the organisation.

For all these reasons, the political role of the SG is an apt metaphor of the UN's changing peace and security agenda. Member states control the UN, its professional staff represent it. The political science literature informs us of the fallacy of the rational actor model of state decision-making. This is even truer of the UN. It is not a unitary actor. There is no such thing as *the* United Nations. Instead, there are several United Nations, each with its own balance of composition and political interests. The UN Security Council, the General Assembly and the International Court of Justice are the geopolitical, normative and legal centres of gravity respectively. The political masters are member states, not UN officials, not even the SG. The UN in consequence is first and foremost a political organisation. As such, its decisions result from political bargaining and accommodation based on power equations and competing national interests. The hope is that the international interest will somehow emerge from this interplay of hard negotiations among member states, that any significant resolution coming out of the main deliberative and executive organs will somehow capture the collective interest from the assertion and reconciliation of national interests. Against all that, the Secretary-General of the United Nations – not the president or prime minister of any member state – is the personification of the international interest and the voice of world conscience.

The political role of the SG was a novel phenomenon of post-1945 international politics.[1] The 2003 Iraq crisis – when some American commentators implicitly compared Kofi Annan to Neville Chamberlain and his policy of appeasement of dictators – showed how far we still have to go before the concept of a spokesman for the world is firmly established and widely accepted. The SG is required to be a politician, diplomat and international civil servant all rolled into one. This is why Trygve Lie, the first SG, as he met his designated successor Dag Hammarskjöld at the airport in New York on 9 April 1953, remarked famously that Hammarskjöld was about to inherit 'the most impossible

---

[1] For earlier commentaries, see Leland Goodrich, 'The Political Role of the Secretary-General', *International Organization* 16:4 (1962), pp. 720–35; Leon Gordenker, *The UN Secretary-General and the Maintenance of Peace* (New York: Columbia University Press, 1967); and C. S. R. Murthy, 'The Role of the Secretary-General since the End of the Cold War', *Indian Journal of International Law* 35 (1995), pp. 181–96.

job in the world'[2] – certainly one that is impossible to fill to the satisfaction of all in an increasingly fractious community of states. Because of the nature of the responsibilities and burdens placed on the shoulders of the SG, he is bound to attract critical scrutiny and harsh judgement from one quarter or another.

In this chapter, I will begin by outlining the bases of the SG's authority and then describe the five key constituencies surrounding his political role. Next, I will highlight the importance of personal attributes in underpinning, finally, the international leadership role of the SG.

Bases of power and authority of the SG

The job may be impossible because it is trapped in several paradoxes. The SG is elected to office as an individual, not as the representative of a government or a region; yet the regions demand 'their' turn at the office. He must have the backing of almost all governments but owe no allegiance to any in an organisation of, by and for states. Is the SG the 192nd member state of the UN, or the 16th member of the UNSC? What are the bases of his – we are yet to be graced with a woman SG – power and authority, and what means of action does he have? Is he mainly a symbolic figurehead or an influential actor in the turbulent world of international politics?

The origins of the office in both its administrative and symbolic roles lie in the League of Nations whose first SG was Sir Eric Drummond.[3] A product of the British civil service culture, he was influential on policy issues, but largely from behind the scenes. He viewed his role as a career civil servant, faithful to the wishes of whichever political party was in government. He did not address the Assembly, and addressed the Council in public session solely as Secretary. The first Director General of the International Labour Organisation (ILO), by contrast, was a leading French politician, Albert Thomas. He became a public leader in a highly political manner, outlining programmes like a head of government, often

---

[2] The incident is described in www.un.org/Depts/dhl/dag/time1953.htm. The phrase was used in the subtitle of a major study of the office: Benjamin Rivlin and Leon Gordenker, eds., *The Challenging Role of the UN Secretary-General: Making 'The Most Impossible Job in the World' Possible* (Westport: Praeger, 1993). For a study of the various Secretaries-General, see Edward Newman, *The UN Secretary-General from the Cold War to the New Era: A Global Peace and Security Mandate?* (London: Macmillan, 1998).

[3] See James Barros, *Office without Power: Secretary-General Sir Eric Drummond 1919–1933* (Oxford: Clarendon, 1979).

joining in the ILO debates and constantly cultivating constituencies outside the formal governmental structures (including trade unions). After the Second World War, the pattern was repeated with the Commonwealth, in the form of Arnold Smith as an efficient but unobtrusive chief administrative head, and Shridath Ramphal as an articulate and dynamic leader in policy formulation who went beyond being just a secretary.

While some drafters of the UN Charter would have preferred to restrict the SG's role to the traditional model of an apolitical head of a civil service, obedient and deferential to the political masters, others argued for a more clearly political and activist conception. In the end both conceptions found expression in the Charter, though they do not necessarily cohabit all that easily. The status, authority and powers of the SG are derived chiefly from the clauses of the UN Charter, but depend also invariably on the skills and personality of the incumbent and the state of relations among the major powers of the world. The political role of the SG in turn is a function of the interplay between the Charter functions and powers, the personal attributes and the political equations among the member states.

On the one hand, the SG's authority is less than that of a cabinet minister, for he does have member states as his political bosses and is not a political minister himself. The SG has neither the trappings nor 'the accoutrements of power' of a state,[4] but is instead an aide to governments. His role is to assist and facilitate the principal political organs in making informed and sound decisions, not to make decisions himself; and then to implement their decisions faithfully and report to them accordingly. Thus the SG can raise uncomfortable questions but may not prescribe the correct answer, influence events without being able to control them and appeal to member states' better instincts to realise the hopes and aspirations of the peoples of the world without pointing the finger of judgement when they fall short.[5]

On the other hand, the SG has greater authority than the head of a national bureaucracy, in that he has no cabinet and minister as the final political and policy boss. He also has greater scope to expand his power and influence through allocating resources among the departments and activities, appointing senior staff and mediating the pulls and pressures

---

[4] Alan James, 'The Secretary-General as an Independent Political Actor', in Rivlin and Gordenker, eds., *The Challenging Role of the UN Secretary-General*, p. 24.
[5] Shashi Tharoor, 'The Role of the Secretary-General', United Nations, 2004.

of member states through creative interpretations that maximise his scope for privileging his own preferences and priorities. Moreover, as the UNSC and GA are often split, the SG can sometimes manoeuvre his way through those divisions to advance his own priorities by indicating possible points of agreement. The SG has the right to be present and take part in the debates in the political organs and often does. He provides the logistical and intellectual basis for many UNSC and GA resolutions and may urge particular courses of action. The SG is expected to implement the most controversial of decisions with the most scrupulous impartiality, exercising political judgement while avoiding the twin temptations of inflating or deflating the role of the office. The SG is also at the nerve centre of a sensitive communications network, often speaking directly to governments, civil society representatives and business leaders, and required to submit reports and analyses on a vast range of topics. As well as using the budget as a vehicle for inserting priorities into the organisation's work agenda, the SG submits an annual report on the work of the organisation that gives him a guaranteed instrument for outlining his vision for the UN. All these avenues allow the SG to shape the institutional context and normative milieu within which personal influence must be wielded.

The process of selecting secretaries-general has been haphazard and ad hoc. The GA appoints an SG on the recommendation of the UNSC (Article 97). 'Appointment' supposedly stresses the administrative function, while 'election' would have suggested a more clearly political role. The Council vote is subject to veto by a permanent member. This immediately changes the thrust from selecting someone who commands the widest following to someone who is least unacceptable to the major powers and places a premium on a non-activist, if not passive, SG. Undue deference to the major powers by an SG is reinforced if the incumbent should be interested in re-election.

Rosemary Righter notes that 'In the history of the United Nations, not one UN secretary-general has been appointed because he was expected to provide outstanding leadership . . . In Dag Hammarskjöld, the five permanent members simply made a mistake of judgment.'[6] Shirley Hazzard remarked of Kurt Waldheim that he was 'proof against every occasion of a larger kind'.[7] Of another incumbent it was said he was so

---

[6] Rosemary Righter, *Utopia Lost: The United Nations and World Order* (New York: Twentieth Century Fund Press, 1995), p. 270.

[7] Shirley Hazzard, *Countenance of Truth: The United Nations and the Waldheim Case* (New York: Viking, 1990), p. 73.

self-effacing, he would not make waves even if he fell out of a boat. As US ambassador Max Finger put it, member states want of their SG 'excellence within the parameters of political reality'.[8]

The SG is the chief symbol of the international interest, advocate of law and rights, general manager of the global agenda and a focal point in setting the direction of world affairs. Some of the built-in disadvantages of the office could be overcome by altering the term from five to seven years and making it non-renewable.

The chief constitutional basis of the powers and authority of the SG is the Charter status of the Secretariat as one of the principal organs (Article 7), headed by the SG as its chief administrative officer (Article 97).[9] Any SG can interpret the dignity so conferred on the office to claim a responsibility to uphold the principles and purposes of the Charter independently of the mandates of the UNSC and the GA. Article 98 requires the SG and the Secretariat to discharge normative and operational mandates entrusted by the other principal organs. In practice this has evolved into the delegation of considerable authority to the SG in the implementation of those (burgeoning) mandates. Moreover, the SG is required by the Charter to submit a report each year to the GA on the work of the organisation (Article 98). Thus his single most important annual report has constitutional status and protection. Article 99 of the Charter authorises the SG to bring to the attention of the UNSC 'any matter which in his opinion may threaten the maintenance of international peace and security'. Articles 98 and 99 are further reinforced by Article 100 which seeks to protect the independence and impartiality of the SG.

Article 99 and other clauses can be interpreted expansively by an incumbent SG under the doctrine of implied powers. Absent this independent determination and possible initiative, and absent the opportunity to report every year to the GA on the work of the organisation for the year just past and in so doing to outline the vision and requirements for the forthcoming year as well, the post of SG in the League had rested on a purely administrative conception. The interwar period had demonstrated a dangerous void in the League system of collective security. Major powers base their policies on their respective national interests.

---

[8] Quoted by Brian E. Urquhart and Erskine Childers, *A World in Need of Leadership: Tomorrow's United Nations* (Uppsala: Dag Hammarskjöld Foundation, 1990), p. 18. See also the revised edition published in 1996.

[9] See James S. Sutterlein, 'The UN Secretary-General as Chief Administrator', in Rivlin and Gordenker, eds., *The Challenging Role of the UN Secretary-General*, pp. 43–58.

When this produces dissent and disarray in the Council because the major powers or groups of member states are bitterly divided on what to do, without Article 99 there is no one who can stand above the fray and be the champion and voice of the international interest.

Article 99 vests the SG with an explicitly political responsibility.[10] The discretionary authority vested in the SG links the chief executive of the UN constitutionally and symbolically to its central ideal. The carefully crafted language is instructive: *any* matter, without limitation; *matter*, not dispute or conflict; *in his opinion*, not in the judgment of others; *may* threaten, not actually threatening. Article 99 confers on the SG both a broad reservoir of authority and a wide margin of discretion, requiring, in the words of the 1945 UN Preparatory Commission, 'the exercise of the highest qualities of political judgment, tact and integrity'.[11] Between them, Articles 98 and 99 have helped to move the office of the SG from the periphery closer towards the centre of UN decision-making. Article 99 was augmented by Security Council Resolution 1366 (30 August 2001) which invited the SG to refer 'cases of serious violations of international law' to the Council. This reaffirmed the SG's role as 'a key member of an interpretive community associated with the implementation and elaboration of charter-based law'.[12] As either the GA or the UNSC may repudiate a particular interpretation of his or her role by an incumbent SG, the interpretation does not become authoritative until after a period of deliberation and accepted practice.

This section would not be complete without noting that the body of practice built up by the several SGs includes also an occasional example of the limits to the powers of the SG. Thus in 1963 U Thant was clear that he could not launch peacekeeping operations under his own authority. In a matching vein, in 1980 Waldheim declined a request from Thailand to place on observer team on the Thai side of the border with Cambodia under his personal authority, as this authority properly belonged to the UNSC.[13]

---

[10] See Stephen M. Schwebel, 'The Origins and Development of Article 99 of the Charter: The Powers of the Secretary-General of the UN', *British Year Book of International Law* 28 (1951), pp. 371–82.

[11] Quoted in Roberto V. Lavalle, 'The "Inherent" Powers of the UN Secretary-General in the Political Sphere: A Legal Analysis', *Netherlands International Law Review* 37:1 (1990), p. 25.

[12] Ian Johnstone, 'The Role of the UN Secretary-General: The Power of Persuasion Based on Law', *Global Governance* 9:4 (October–December 2003), p. 441.

[13] Lavalle, 'The "Inherent" Powers of the UN Secretary-General', p. 32.

The key UN constituencies

In order to maximise his influence and expand his role, the SG must be attentive and sensitive to five key constituencies and must demonstrate a grasp and command of intergovernmental processes. First, he must ensure that his corps of international civil servants are in broad sympathy with his vision for the organisation, responsive to his wishes and commands and motivated as well capable and competent. International secretariats, more so than national bureaucracies, can be riven by factional jealousies, jurisdictional turf wars and national loyalties. Equally, though, the staff look to the SG to articulate UN values, be the voice of moral clarity on behalf of the international community as a whole and issue clarion calls for action in defence of the international interest. If an SG fails to do this, his staff are demoralised and their motivation is weakened. As Inis Claude comments, 'A Secretary-General who scorns his responsibilities as chief civil servant in favour of political ambitions neglects his major opportunities for his minor ones.'[14] In recent times the authority of the SG as the chief administrative officer of the organisation has been corroded by budgetary micromanagement, excessive politicisation of appointments and promotions and a refusal to grant independent intelligence assessment and analytical capacity.

Second, the SG must retain the confidence of the member states who constitute the voting majority in the GA as the plenary body of the organisation.

Third, the SG must ensure he has the support of member states who control the resources without which the UN cannot implement its mandate and carry out its necessary operations.

Fourth, he must not alienate those who control the UNSC, in particular the five permanent members (P5), and in particular the USA (P1). He must be attentive to the priorities of the UNSC even while remaining sensitive to the passions of the GA. The UNSC has the primary responsibility for maintaining peace and security (Article 24.1), the GA has a residual responsibility (especially under Articles 10, 11), and the SG has a discretionary responsibility (Article 99). During the Cold War, deadlock in the Council often produced an authority and policy vacuum that only the SG could fill through creative interpretations of his role and

---

[14] Inis L. Claude, 'Reflections on the Role of the UN Secretary-General', in Rivlin and Gordenker, eds., *The Challenging Role of the UN Secretary-General*, p. 259.

expansion of his remit to include the establishment and oversight of peacekeeping operations and mediation efforts,[15] in particular through the inherently undefined good offices role of the SG.[16]

Peacekeeping requires leadership by the SG precisely because it falls conceptually between war-fighting and diplomatic negotiations, both of which are undertaken primarily by states. Dag Hammarskjöld played a key role in the development through UNEF-I in 1956 in the Middle East. The report produced by him a mere two days after the GA resolution still stands as a remarkable tribute to the core principles of classical consensual peacekeeping. In Lebanon two years later, faced with deadlock in the UNSC, Hammarskjöld acted on his own to augment the UN Observer Group in Lebanon (UNOGIL), saying to the Council that if it disapproved, he would of course accept the consequences.[17] In the Congo crisis in 1960, he led the UNSC by nine months in describing the collapse of institutions as constituting a threat to international peace and security and the Council found itself reacting to the SG's initiatives.[18] The division of responsibilities is for the UNSC to establish (and renew or terminate) the peacekeeping operations and give them their mandate, for the GA to appropriate funds for them, and for the SG to exercise oversight through directions to the Special Representative and Force Commander. But occasionally circumstances may arise where the SG has to exercise independent judgement with little or no time to seek the guidance of the Council or the Assembly. One of the most intense controversies concerned the decision by Thant to accede to Egypt's formal request to pull out UNEF in 1967, an act which paved the way to the Six Day War.

[15] See Kjell Skjelsbaek, 'The UN Secretary-General and the Mediation of International Disputes', *Journal of Peace Research* 28:1 (1991), pp. 99–115.

[16] See Thomas M. Franck, 'The Good Offices Function of the UN Secretary-General', in Adam Roberts and Benedict Kingsbury, eds., *United Nations, Divided World* (Oxford: Clarendon, 1988), pp. 79–94; and Bertrand G. Ramcharan, 'The Good Offices of the United Nations Secretary-General in the Field of Human Rights', *American Journal of Human Rights* 76:1 (1982), pp. 130–41.

[17] Recounted in Franck, 'The Good Offices Function of the UN Secretary-General', pp. 87–8.

[18] In the Tehran hostage crisis in 1979, Kurt Waldheim similarly described it as a threat to international peace and security before the UNSC had so decided. And after the terrorist attacks of 9/11, Annan was often ahead of the UNSC in capturing and articulating the sense of UN solidarity with the USA and the justification of self-defence for the ensuing war on the Taliban regime of Afghanistan.

With the end of the Cold War, great power agreement in the UNSC translated into a greatly expanded agenda of the UN and a multiplication of peacekeeping and conflict resolution missions and activities. Javier Pérez de Cuéllar is credited with having mainstreamed human rights protection in the El Salvador peace operation and thereby ushered in the new generation of peacekeeping tasks.[19] Boutros Boutros-Ghali oversaw the gradual incorporation of police and civilian elements into peace operations to the point where the missions typically became civilian-dominant. As their nature changed to reflect the more demanding challenges of complex humanitarian emergencies, the SG found himself at the heart of a complex web of several peace operations, directing the military and humanitarian operations, engaging in conflict prevention and resolution activities, and supervising elections and post-conflict reconstruction efforts.

The rise in activism and agenda of the UNSC coincided with the decline of the role and influence of the GA. The fate of the UN's peace and security agenda then hinged on the relationship between the UNSC and the SG as its two principal organs. Boutros-Ghali accused the Council of 'micromanaging' peacekeeping operations at the expense of his authority and that of ground commanders.[20] In the Balkans, he was given an overly ambitious mandate against his advice and not given the resources to implement it. When things went wrong, he was an easy target by the very same members of the UNSC who bore the primary responsibility for the messy response by the international community to the atrocities being committed. Nevertheless, personality differences also are part of the explanation, for Pérez de Cuéllar had an 'easy and confident relationship while Boutros-Ghali had a comparatively difficult one'.[21] (Other elements of the explanation would include the tripling of the number of resolutions being adopted by the UNSC and the vastly expanded number and missions of peace operations during Boutros-Ghali's term compared to his predecessor's.)

The increased and expanded UN missions produced a commensurate enlargement of the SG's day-to-day operational responsibilities and political judgement calls and decisions. A good example is the decision

---

[19] Johnstone, 'Role of the UN Secretary-General', pp. 447–8.
[20] Barbara Crossette, 'UN Chief Chides Security Council on Military Missions', *New York Times,* 6 January 1995.
[21] Marrack Goulding, 'The UN Secretary-General', in David M. Malone, ed., *The UN Security Council: From the Cold War to the 21st Century* (Boulder: Lynne Rienner, 2004), p. 277.

by Annan to withdraw all international UN staff from Baghdad after the tragic bombing in August 2003 and his determined resistance to returning to Iraq until the prior question of the status of governing authority in the country was first resolved. The proper political balance between the UN's major member states and different principal organs proved impossible to strike amidst the passions stirred by the Iraq War. Annan was left to improvise as best he could, seeking to chart a steady course for the organisation amidst the transatlantic clash of civilisations between Old Europe and the New World.

Fifth and finally, the SG must mobilise the support of civil society – a ready and powerful resource and reservoir of political support and goodwill for the UN. The rise of civil society numbers, networks and activism has effectively broadened the UN's constituency. Some in civil society say that the Iraq crisis has heightened the need for a global peoples' assembly to counter the repeated betrayals by an intergovern-mental organisation. Others look to the SG as the last line of defence of Charter principles. But this places an impossible burden on the world's top international civil servant. If the UNSC is united, the SG cannot be an alternative voice of dissent. If it is divided, he cannot be a substitute for inaction by a splintered Council.

Personality

The SG is the symbol and representative of the UN. The personal qualities required are integrity, independence of mind and the ability and willingness to set the collective interest of the UN above the partisan interests of member states. He must provide intellectual leadership, managerial ability, negotiating skill and, in an age of mass communi-cations, the ability to establish a rapport with an international audience. The SG must know when to take the initiative in order to force an issue and when to maintain a tactful silence; when courage is required and when reticence is welcome; and when commitment to the UN vision must be balanced by a sense of proportion and humour. The personal skills and attributes that are most crucial include charisma, the ability to articulate bold visions and complex arguments in crisp and clear sound-bites, powerful oratory, patience almost beyond human tolerance, the ability to listen and keep confidences, an instinct for grasping the big picture without neglecting the necessary details and a strong sense of the demands and expectations of the organisation against the limits of the possible.

Often, in the most volatile and conflict-riven areas of the world, the SG is the only channel of communication between the parties concerned and the only interlocutor between them and outside actors. This vests in the SG the responsibility to exploit the clauses of the Charter under chapter 6 for the pacific settlement of disputes and thereby to expand the gamut of his political role.[22] The practical manifestation of this is the appointment of special representatives of the SG for the world's many trouble spots, such as Cyprus, Cambodia, the Great Lakes in Africa, the Korean Peninsula, Myanmar and East Timor.[23] Through his network of special envoys, the SG is engaged in the process and substance of multilateral diplomacy on a 24/7 basis around the world. Examples of successful mediation by SGs include Hammarskjöld's negotiations with China for the release of captured American airmen in 1955, and Thant's role in easing the control of West New Guinea from the Netherlands to Indonesia in 1962 and guiding Bahrain to independence from Britain against competing claims from Iran in 1970–1.

Pérez de Cuéllar argued that multilateral diplomacy by the SG is quite different from traditional diplomacy.[24] Reflecting the UN Charter principles, it attenuates the disadvantages of the weaker party. It seeks an objective and lasting solution to the dispute based on principles of justice and equity within the parameters of the prevailing power equations but not confined to the expediencies of the day. And it gives all member states a stake and role in shaping the peace.

Sometimes the office of the SG is useful to member states as a face-saving means of resolving a dispute where they themselves have identified the major points of resolution but need the UN imprimatur to 'sell' it to their separate domestic constituencies. Elevating the dispute to the UNSC risks an unnecessary and unwanted internationalisation of the conflict. Seeking the good offices of the SG is an easier process to manage, more expeditious and less susceptible to unpredictable risks. Such an example occurred in New Zealand in the mid-1980s with respect to the sinking of the Greenpeace boat *Rainbow Warrior* in Auckland.[25]

[22] See Mark W. Zacher, 'The Secretary-General and the United Nations' Function of Peaceful Settlement', *International Organization* 20:4 (1966), pp. 724–49.

[23] See Donald J. Puchala, 'The Secretary-General and His Special Representatives', in Rivlin and Gordenker, eds., *The Challenging Role of the UN Secretary-General*, pp. 81–96; and Connie Peck, 'Special Representatives of the Secretary-General', in Malone, ed., *The UN Security Council*, pp. 325–39.

[24] Javier Pérez de Cuéllar, 'The Role of the UN Secretary-General', in Roberts and Kingsbury, eds., *United Nations, Divided World*, pp. 68–9.

[25] See Ramesh Thakur, 'A Dispute of Many Colours: France, New Zealand and the "Rainbow Warrior" Affair', *The World Today* 42:12 (December 1986), pp. 209–14.

Trygve Lie (1946–53) fell foul of the Soviet bloc in the context of the
Korean War, and Dag Hammarskjöld (1953–61) suffered a similar fate a
decade later in the Congo. U Thant (1961–71) is often said to have left
no mark at all, whereas the allegations and revelations of Kurt Waldheim's (1972–81) links to the Nazi regime left a sour aftertaste that
survived his departure. Nor was Thant very popular in Washington for
his vain efforts to search for a solution to the Vietnam War, any more
than Waldheim was for his equally futile effort to secure the release of
American hostages in Tehran in 1980.

Pérez de Cuéllar (1982–91), the UN's first Latin American SG, had to
confront the thorny issue of the Falklands/Malvinas war between the UK
and Argentina. Sir Marrack Goulding, who served both him and Boutros-Ghali as Under-Secretary-General, has written that the SG almost
succeeded in mediating an interim agreement which, if it had been
accepted and signed, would have averted the war.[26] Pérez de Cuéllar
used his inherent authority under the Charter to begin a process of
negotiation on the Iran–Iraq War that culminated in a successful UNSC
resolution within six months (January–July 1987). In Central America,
he exploited a tiny window of opportunity under a UNSC resolution to
insert the SG into a peace process that achieved success over six years in
1989 and greatly enlarged the UN role and presence in the 1990s. And he
used his own judgement also to back the advice of his Special Representative Martti Ahtisaari against the counsel of his senior advisers in New
York to save the day in Namibia during that country's transition to
independence.[27]

Boutros-Ghali (1992–6) responded with enthusiasm to the request
from the UNSC summit meeting of January 1992 – at the very start of his
turbulent tenure – on recommendations for strengthening the UN capacity for preventive diplomacy, peacekeeping and peacemaking. But his
prickly personality and propensity to censure, in public, the rich and the
powerful for neglecting the needs of the weak and the poor alienated him
from the key members of the UNSC, while a marked reluctance to
delegate decision-making authority to subordinates meant that his circle
of admirers within the Secretariat dwindled. In the end the USA blocked
his re-election.

By contrast, Kofi Annan (1997–2006) was so successful at cultivating
his constituencies and protecting an inherently narrow political base of

---

[26] Goulding, 'The UN Secretary-General', p. 271.
[27] Ibid., pp. 273–4.

support that he was reappointed unanimously, and that, too, six months earlier than necessary. His legacy will include a series of reforms of the Secretariat in his capacity as chief administrative officer of the UN. The more lasting political legacy will be his unsuspected but deep commitment to universal human rights and human security. On the first point, he has been openly critical of the lack of good governance in Africa in a way that only an African SG could be. On the second point, he has successfully articulated the African continent's desperate plight with respect to the new or soft threats of poverty, disease and HIV/AIDS.

Leadership

The single most important political role of the SG is to provide leadership:[28] the elusive ability to make others connect emotionally and intellectually to a larger cause that transcends their immediate self-interest. Leadership consists of articulating a bold and noble vision for a community and establishing standards of achievement and conduct, explaining why they matter and inspiring or coaxing others to adopt the agreed goals and benchmarks as their personal goals. Of the SGs to date, only two are generally thought to have combined the qualities of inspirational and aspirational leadership: Dag Hammarskjöld and Kofi Annan. Annan reminds the world often that the UN is a unique font of international legitimacy. No person is in a better position to reflect that international legitimacy in his public statements than the SG. Nevertheless, just as the legitimacy of the organisation can be enhanced or eroded by a combination of factors, so too can the legitimacy of the SG's pronouncements.

It is worth distinguishing three types of legitimacy underpinning the SG's political role in world affairs: constitutional, performance and representational. We have already discussed the constitutional basis of the power of legitimacy vested in the SG. Clearly, if the SG exceeds expectations in his actual performance, he will greatly expand the scope for independent initiatives. Conversely, perceptions of poor performance will eat away at his authority to function as the chief spokesperson for the international interest and the chief administrative officer of the UN.

The SG's representational legitimacy is twofold. On the one hand, the election of the SG has rotated among the world's major regional

---

[28] For an early article on this subject, see Robert W. Cox, 'The Executive Head: An Essay on Leadership in International Organization', *International Organization* 23:2 (March 1969), pp. 205–30.

groupings. To the extent that the principle of equitable geographical representation pervades the entire UN system, such a rotational principle is essential to preserving the legitimacy of the office. On the other hand, the SG represents the international community as a whole and not any particular continent, region or constellation. If the SG is seen to favour the interests of any one particular group at the UN, his ability to sway the others will be correspondingly diminished. The SG must simultaneously avoid alienating and being captured by the only remaining superpower. At times Annan appears to have lost the confidence of Washington even as he is attacked for being their pliant tool elsewhere. Sometimes he gently chides Washington, for example with respect to Iraq, even while urging others to understand why particular states should feel the urge to act unilaterally when existing institutions fail to confront today's changed threats.

Annan has also been uniquely skilled in norm generation and entrepreneurship. One technique for the transmission of ideas into international policy is by means of blue-ribbon international commissions.[29] Annan has used this technique to record changed ideas about familiar institutions and practices, as with the Brahimi Panel on Peace Operations,[30] or to call for fresh thinking on how the UN can remain the centre of collective action to respond to changing circumstances and threats, as with the High-Level Panel on UN reforms.[31]

At times there have been undercurrents of unease, apprehension and outright hostility towards Annan from sections of American neo-conservatives, developing-country governments and the left-liberal NGO community. To the first group, he represents an organisation that they loathe, and they tried to use the oil-for-food scandal in 2004 to discredit both the UN as an organisation and Annan personally. The second group was angered by his articulation of the challenge of humanitarian intervention. They recall that he became America's choice for SG when Washington turned on Boutros-Ghali and decided to support Annan because in 1995, 'as acting Secretary-General', he had departed from Boutros-Ghali's restraint and 'authorised the NATO bombing of the

---

[29] See Ramesh Thakur, Andrew F. Cooper and John English, eds., *International Commissions and the Power of Ideas* (Tokyo: United Nations University Press, 2005).

[30] *Report of the Panel on United Nations Peace Operations*, UN doc., A/55/305-S/2000/809 (21 August 2000).

[31] High-Level Panel on Threats, Challenges and Change, *A More Secure World: Our Shared Responsibility* (New York: UN, A/59/565, December 2004).

Bosnian Serbs that paved the road to the Dayton Peace Agreement. That action, more than anything else, convinced American officials, including me, that he was the best possible person to lead the UN.'[32] The Arabs would have liked stronger public statements from him in defence of the beleaguered Palestinians under relentless assault from the Israeli government of Ariel Sharon.

Many commentators from civil society still hold Annan responsible for the Rwanda genocide and do not believe he has paid an appropriate price for it: 'Kofi Annan, who was head of the DPKO at the time, went on to become Secretary-General, taking with him his closest staff, who had been central in the decisionmaking process in Rwanda.'[33] Annan himself confessed, in a speech at the UN on 26 March 2004 to mark the tenth anniversary of the genocide, that at the time, he thought he had done everything possible to rally the international community and mobilise support for the UN force in Rwanda. But now he believes he could and should have done more.[34]

It was in relation to the impending Iraq War that many governments and NGOs – and even UN officials[35] – felt most keenly disappointed, almost to the point of feeling that the SG had betrayed the Charter principles and UN values in not standing up to Washington boldly and publicly. They believe that Annan should have adopted a more robust position on the illegal and illegitimate invasion of Iraq.[36] It was not until after the attack on the UN compound in Baghdad on 19 August 2003 that killed his Special Representative and friend Sergio Viera de Mello that Annan began to speak clearly against the US war policy in Iraq. The

---

[32] Richard C. Holbrooke (US ambassador to the UN, 1999–2001), 'Kofi Annan', *Time* magazine, 26 April 2004, p. 59. In fact there is no such formal function as 'acting SG'. Presumably SG Boutros-Ghali was on leave at the time, and Annan was the senior official in charge.

[33] Howard Adelman and Astri Suhrke, 'Rwanda', in Malone, ed., *The UN Security Council*, pp. 495–6. See also Per Ahlmark (former deputy prime minister of Sweden), 'A Culture that Rewards Failed Leadership', *Japan Times*, 18 April 2004. The article was distributed worldwide by Project Syndicate and published, for example, as 'UN Chief's Career Clouded', *Australian*, 3 May 2004.

[34] My own notes from that event.

[35] Thus the former director of communications for the UN in Iraq: 'It was astonishing that Mr Annan backed the US position on elections and the June sovereignty date when it was so overwhelmingly opposed by Sistani and the majority of Iraqis . . . The UN ended up intensifying the crisis it needed to resolve, again appearing pro-US, anti-Iraqi and anti-democratic to boot . . . The UN . . . must correct its excessive pro-US tilt'; Salim Lone, 'An Uprising in Support of Democracy', *Guardian*, 13 April 2004.

[36] Even a serving Australian military officer in uniform said this to me in April 2003.

clearest statement of opposition came on 10 June 2004 in a commencement address at Harvard University referred to in the last chapter.[37]
According to the critics, his failure to speak such verities before and
during the Iraq War brought no benefit to the UN and failed to
soften the contempt of the Bush administration for it. During Annan's
watch the UN's role in Iraq was reduced to an 'after-sales service provider
for the United States'.[38]

The strength of passions on this is such that a few things need to be
said in defence of the SG. The political environment in which Annan has
to operate is unique. Previous SGs, operating within the overall umbrella
of the Cold War bipolar world, did not have to face the problem of a world
of only one superpower. The problems posed by this began to emerge
during Boutros-Ghali's term but the full scope and magnitude became
apparent only after 9/11 and the triumph of the neo-conservatives within
the Washington policy community. Thus, on the one hand, Annan has
often been seen as unduly, even pre-emptively, accommodative of US
concerns and interests. On the other hand, at the end of 2004 a group of
senior American foreign policy experts, described as Annan admirers and
UN supporters, met with him for over three hours to plead that he should
do more to repair relations with Washington.[39]

Very few governments were able to withstand US bilateral pressure – a
mix of coercion and blandishments – in Washington's unipolar
moment.[40] It is easy to overlook the fact that elected members comprise
a two-thirds majority on the UNSC and developing countries form the

[37] Kofi A. Annan, 'Three Crises and the Need for American Leadership', commencement
address at Harvard University, 10 June 2004, UN Press Release SG/SM/9357.
[38] Alexander Cockburn, 'Stupid Leaders, Useless Spies, Angry World', *The Nation*, 17 May
2004, p. 8.
[39] Warren Hoge, 'Frank Words for Annan in Effort to Revitalize UN', *International Herald
Tribune (IHT)*, 3 January 2005. One could raise two questions about this meeting.
Would Annan have agreed to a similar meeting with experts from any other country,
or does the meeting in itself prove that the USA is more equal than others in the UN?
And, if the cause of the increased political distance between New York and Washington is
that American policy-makers have chosen to walk away from the UN, then was the
group's message being delivered to the right audience?
[40] A number of small and vulnerable countries did of course stand up to Washington and
refused to be bribed or bullied on the crucial second resolution authorising military
action against Iraq. But it is still the case that if the community of nations wanted to
declare emphatically in advance that military action would be illegal and illegitimate,
they should have introduced such a resolution in the UNSC and/or the General Assembly, and not shifted the entire burden to the SG. Such a resolution, even if vetoed, would
have made military action that much more problematic.

overwhelming majority in the GA. For them to demand courage of conviction on the SG's part is to shift the burden of courageous decision-making solely on to his shoulders, when it should fall more properly on theirs. They appointed him SG, and reappointed him unanimously, knowing he was Washington's preferred choice. No SG can make up for the shortcomings of member states. On 30 March 2000, the UNSC went to Washington and paid a courtesy call on the US Senate Foreign Relations Committee. Not only was this without precedent in the annals of the UN; such a tribute at the court of the imperial middle kingdom is unimaginable with respect to any other member state. The visit was reconciled with the integrity of the UN as an international organisation by claiming that all fifteen UNSC ambassadors had decided to visit Capitol Hill on the same day in their private capacity. In July 2002 the Council granted the USA a second year's exemption from the jurisdiction of the International Criminal Court, and in May 2004 the Council unanimously adopted a resolution calling on states to criminalise the transfer of proliferation-sensitive nuclear material and skills: in the one case frustrating and in the other usurping the treaty-making powers of sovereign states. What are the SG and his staff to make of all this? Should the SG be commended for accurately anticipating the power equation in the UNSC or condemned for losing his way at the crossroads of power and principle? Is he to be a modern-day Don Quixote, tilting ineffectually at the windmills as they are caught in the crosswinds of the prevailing gusts from the north-westerly direction against the gentle puffs from the south-easterlies?

By refraining from indulging in one-finger diplomacy, the SG kept open channels of communication with Washington until such inevitable time as the administration came to the conclusion that it does, after all, need UN help to extricate itself from a mess entirely of its own making. The choice between short-term and long-term effectiveness and fidelity to the Charter was Annan's judgement call and he has to be judged on it in the fullness of time.

The charges levelled at Annan ignore his occasional public disagreements with the USA on some issues before the 2003 Iraq crisis and the fact that the impact of his public disagreements would diminish if they became habitual. In 1998 he acted independently to obtain an agreement from Saddam Hussein (which was characteristically violated by Iraq in due course) for the return of UN weapons inspectors to Iraq, to the evident annoyance of the Americans and British; on 3 July 2002 he sent, and made public, a formal letter to Secretary of State Colin Powell protesting that the US threat to veto the extension of the Bosnia peace-keeping mission unless US peacekeepers were exempted from ICC juris-diction risked undermining both the institution of peacekeeping and the cause of international criminal justice;[41] and in 2004–5 he reiterated his intention to campaign for the requisite ratifications and entry-into-force of the ICC.

Annan did speak out after the war. He did not use shrill and strident language. That is not his style. But with his inimitable courtesy, he remarked, for example, that 'all parties in Iraq' should refrain from violence, respect international humanitarian law and give the process of transition a chance, that the Falluja uprising was 'a resistance against occupation' and that 'violent military action by an occupying power against the inhabitants of an occupied country will only make matters worse'.[42] Later still, in an interview with the BBC in September 2004, he described the war as having been illegal,[43] and in a letter to the leaders of Iraq, Britain and the USA in early November 2004, he warned that a forcible assault on Falluja would risk alienating Iraqis when their support for elections was vital.[44]

The timing of that letter and the characterisation of the war as illegal – in the middle of the US presidential campaign – showed a lapse of judgement that became more pronounced as the oil-for-food scandal gathered pace in 2005. During his first term, Annan was a Teflon-coated leader who could do no wrong, commonly described as an international diplomatic rock star who was wined and dined by the glitterati of Washington and New York. Glowing profiles recalled his noble African ancestry, his soft charisma, his glamorous Swedish wife who was herself the niece of the legendary Raoul Wallenberg, and his deft diplomatic skills and immense global moral authority. While the developing

---

[41] I was working on the SG's second reform report at the time. Certainly the impact of the SG's letter was dramatically evident in conversations with UN colleagues and national diplomats alike.

[42] Jim Wurst, 'Annan Warns Against Further Violence in Iraq', *UN Wire* (www.unwire.org), 28 April 2004; Evelyn Leopold, 'Annan Warns Against Violence in Iraq', Reuters (www.reuters.co.uk), 28 April 2004.

[43] 'Iraq War Illegal, Says Annan', *BBC News*, 16 September 2004, at http://news.bbc.co.uk/go/pr/fr/-/1/hi/world/middle_east/3661134.stm.

[44] 'Annan Plea as Iraq Assault Looms', *BBC News* (http://news.bbc.co.uk), 6 November 2004.

countries praised him for his focus on Africa and activists applauded his courage in highlighting AIDS as a global priority, Western governments backed his campaign to reform the unwieldy world body and the humanitarian community was elated at his willingness to champion the protection of people being killed by their own abusive governments. This culminated in Senator Jesse Helms agreeing to release $1 billion in US backpay to the UN, the award of the Nobel Peace Prize jointly to the UN and Annan and his unanimous re-election to a second term.

Midway into his second term, Annan seemed to be walking on eggshells as his world started falling apart. The interim report of the Volcker Committee inquiring into the oil-for-food scandal faulted him for lax managerial oversight and a cursory investigation of possible conflict of interest when his son's employment with Cotecna, a company bidding for a lucrative UN contract, was first disclosed in 1999. But it found no evidence that the SG had knowingly steered the UN contract towards Cotecna. When Annan claimed to have been 'exonerated', one of the three principal investigators, Mark Pieth, publicly disagreed, saying that a certain mea culpa from the SG would have been appropriate. The SG's son Kojo Annan was found to have engaged in significant improprieties and traded on his surname to advance the company's interests and his own fortune. Having been told by his son that he had severed his connection with Cotecna at the end of 1998, Annan had to face the public humiliation and a father's personal devastation in learning that Kojo had stayed on Cotecna's payroll until February 2004, had received more than double the amount disclosed for his services during this period, had tried to disguise the financial payments by channelling them through several different routes and had stonewalled the Volcker Committee's efforts to establish the facts and follow the trails. Some of the SG's aides have been criticised for lax and sometimes unethical behaviour. Five separate Congressional committees were investigating the plethora of charges and allegations, with some of their chairs not being shy in calling for Annan's resignation as the head of an organisation that was rife with scandal and broken of spirit. When the Volcker Committee submitted its main report in September, Annan accepted full responsibility for the failings of maladministration pointed out in the report. Critics wondered privately, especially against the backdrop of Rwanda and Srebrenica, if he knew the difference between taking responsibility and paying lip service to it.

Conclusion

The temper of the times condition expectations of the role of the office of Secretary-General of the United Nations. The changing contours of world politics provide the context in which opportunities, requirements and constraints on the scope for the UN's role and independent action by the SG are shaped. For example Kofi Annan is personally credited with reaching out to the business sector through his Global Compact and to civil society representatives who have found the United Nations a far more hospitable place under his stewardship. Yet both of these were made possible by major changes in a much larger context. The end of the Cold War marked the triumph of liberal economics over the command economy and the concurrent rise of civil society activism within and across borders. This was reflected in the abatement of reflexive hostility to market capitalism and non-governmental activism by many UN member states. Annan's genius lay in channelling the historic ideational transformations into new institutional linkages.

The role of the SG expands and contracts in direct correlation with the standing of the organisation itself at any given time. The UN is still the forum of choice for debating the great issues of the day. A considerable amount of the world's important business gets done in its corridors and chambers. Rare is the country that does not send a senior and skilled diplomat or politician as its permanent representative to the UN mission. The respect and attention commanded by the SG as the head of the organisation reflects this reality. While the P5 may treat him 'merely as a Foreign Minister',[45] the rest accord him the status virtually of a head of state.

The exercise of international leadership by the SG is still subject to the systemic and structural constraints of a unipolar world order whose bedrock organisational principle is state sovereignty. The SG does not have the luxury to act in isolation from the shifting power structures of world politics. The fundamental issue underlying the political role of the office always has been and remains whether the SG 'is more an adjunct of the intergovernmental system or part of a wider process of global governance that transcends state structures'.[46] The SG can unquestionably use the office as an international pulpit to shape policy and shift norms. But the latitude and impact will usually depend as much on

[45] Kurt Waldheim, *In the Eye of the Storm* (London: Weidenfeld and Nicolson, 1985), p. 140.
[46] Edward Newman, 'The Post-Cold War Secretary-General: Opportunities and Constraints', *Global Dialogue* 2:2 (Spring 2000), p. 107.

exogenous forces beyond the SG's control, most notably the state of relations between the key political constituencies at the United Nations, as on personal traits of charm, courtesy, judgement and persuasion.

Under modern conditions the UNSC and the SG, as two principal UN organs, must understand and respect each other's powers, prerogatives and responsibilities in order to establish a harmonious relationship. The SG must play a political role that is complementary to that of the UNSC and never in competition with it; respectful of the pivotal role of the Council in maintaining peace and security while mindful of the political temper in the GA which is the truer barometer of the sentiments of the international community at large. When the UN's major powers and groups are bitterly divided, the SG must strive to forge a fragile agreement by identifying common elements, reminding member states of the Charter principles, nudging them towards face-saving formulations that can recreate a sense of common purpose and appealing for calm and unity. The SG cannot direct and order: he is the company secretary to the P5's permanent board of directors.

In such circumstances, the most important requirement is for the SG to exercise the skills of soft leadership. The SG has the power to advise, encourage, caution and warn. He does so with the benefit of having access to all sides of an argument and all parties to a dispute or conflict; being the confidant of governments or, in Hammarskjöld's words, 'the trustee of the secrets of all the nations'.[47] This is why member states with the requisite technical capacity may well seek to eavesdrop on his conversations in order to glean information on what he may be contemplating and others may be saying to him. By the same token, once it is widely believed that conversations with the SG are not assured of confidentiality, one of the major assets and roles of the SG is effectively destroyed.

Quiet diplomacy within the confidential confines of the SG's private office can be supplemented or substituted by the public diplomacy of the UN's bully pulpit. The establishment and conduct of peacekeeping operations, as also the innumerable requests by the other principal organs for special reports of the SG, provide an additional source of political leverage. Dissatisfaction with US capture of the UN agenda promotes wishful thinking about expanded independent powers for the SG. On the other side, those impatient to rush to enforcement often fail

---

[47] Cited in James, 'The Secretary-General as an Independent Political Actor,' p. 28.

to appreciate that any public endorsement by the SG of the coercive instruments of international statecraft can damage his credentials as the vital core of conciliatory diplomacy. And, potentially, the pacific settlement of disputes under chapter 6 of the Charter is among the SG's most valuable political roles with respect both to conflict prevention and constructive collaboration. The ease and frequency of international travel brings the SG into contact with representatives of many governments, chief executives of international organisations and multinational corporations and civil society organisations. This is a multi-textured milieu of international relations far removed from the elegant simplicity of the rational actor model of foreign policy decision-making. It provides the SG with many opportunities to probe and explain, test and tease, persuade and dissuade; to engage in diplomatic parlance but also to exercise ideational leadership.

Conclusion: at the crossroads of ideals and reality

The record of the United Nations shows a surprising capacity for institutional innovation, conceptual advances, policy adaptation and organisational learning. This can be shown with respect to peacekeeping and peace operations, human security and human rights, sanctions and the use of force, and so on. Yet in 2005, when this book was completed, the United Nations was an organisation in turmoil. On the one hand, there were efforts to initiate the most far-reaching, comprehensive and bold reforms in the UN's sixty-year history. On the other, the organisation was struggling to cope with a string of allegations of fraud and misconduct by foot soldiers and senior officials. A high-profile inquiry into the deeply damaging oil-for-food scandal fingered the son of the Secretary-General (SG) and faulted the SG for failure to conduct a proper investigation of possible conflict of interest. His former chief of staff was accused of shredding documents in relation to the scandal shortly after the inquiry was launched. The explanation that these were duplicates that had been destroyed in order to free up office space did not pass the 'smell test' for many American critics. The High Commissioner for Refugees had to resign in the aftermath of allegations of sexual harassment. The chief of the UN's internal oversight office – meant to oversee accountability and integrity in the organisation – left under a cloud with respect to oversight and recruitment lapses. An externally commissioned report found a culture of management abuses, sexual innuendoes and public humiliation of staff in the UN's Electoral Assistance Division whose head seemed to believe in impunity because of her gender and developing-country identity.[1] And there were allegations of grave sexual crimes committed by UN personnel on peacekeeping duty. All this produced calls by some US critics for the SG to resign. When

---

[1] Judith Miller, 'Review Finds Abuses by Management at the UN's Election-monitoring Office', *New York Times*, 30 March 2005.

many of his long-time aides left instead, one reporter accused him of sacrificing them as scapegoats in order to save his own skin.[2]

A wag is said to have remarked that 'The interesting thing about Richard Wagner's music is that it ain't as bad as it sounds.' The same might be said of the United Nations: it is not quite as bad as often believed. In Shashi Tharoor's metaphor, the United Nations is both a stage on which member states have the starring roles and work out their relationships, partnerships and rivalries; and an actor implementing the decisions made on the stage by the member states.[3]

If the UN is in crisis, it is a crisis of contradictory expectations. Its Charter begins with the grand words 'We the peoples of the world'. The reality is that it functions as an organisation of, by and for member states. Alexander Solzhenitsyn observed that at the UN, the people of the world are served up to the designs of governments.[4] The UN needs to achieve a better balance between the wish of the peoples and the will of governments; between the aspirations for a better world and its performance in the real world; between the enduring political reality enveloping and at times threatening to suffocate it and the vision of an uplifting world that has inspired generations of dreamers and idealists to work for the betterment of humanity across cultural, religious and political borders.

During the UN's lifespan, both the economic, political and military realities and the vision of a good international society have changed. But it remains the focus of the hopes and aspirations for a future where men and women live at peace with themselves and in harmony with nature. The idea of a universal organisation dedicated to protecting peace and promoting welfare has survived the death, destruction and disillusionment of armed conflicts, genocide, persistent poverty, environmental degradation and the many assaults on human dignity of the twentieth century.[5] Based on human solidarity and transcending

---

[2] Thalif Deen, 'UN Chief Tries to Boost Staff Morale, Faults Media Attacks', Inter Press Service News Agency (www.ipsnews.net), 18 April 2005.

[3] Shashi Tharoor, 'Saving Humanity from Hell', in Ramesh Thakur, Edward Newman and John Tirman, eds., *Multilateralism under Challenge? Power, International Order, and Structural Change* (Tokyo: United Nations University Press, forthcoming).

[4] Quoted in Rosemary Righter, *Utopia Lost: The United Nations and World Order* (New York: Twentieth Century Fund Press, 1995), p. 85.

[5] For an account of the role of the United Nations at the intersection of ideas and public policy, see Louis Emmerij, Richard Jolly and Thomas G. Weiss, *Ahead of the Curve? UN Ideas and Global Challenges* (Bloomington: Indiana University Press for the UN Intellectual History Project, 2001).

national perspectives, the UN provides and manages the framework for bringing together the world's leaders to tackle the pressing problems of the day for the survival, development and welfare of all human beings everywhere. Yet multilateralism is under unprecedented challenge, from arms control to climate change, international criminal justice and the use of military force overseas. At such a time, it becomes especially important to reaffirm the UN's role as the principal embodiment of the principle of multilateralism and the main forum for its pursuit. The causes and consequences of public policy challenges and decisions are international, but the authority for addressing them is still vested in states. The UN's mandates are global, while its staffing and financial resources are less than that of major municipal authorities. National governments are vested with more authority than they can exercise in today's world, but the authority of the international policy-maker is limited to less than might otherwise be accomplished. 'As a result, national governments retain the authority to disable international policy making, but not the capacity to resolve problems on their own.'[6] Hence the UN's dilemma of doing too little and too late, or being over-committed and over-stretched.

In this final chapter, I would like to organise some concluding thoughts around the five themes identified in the introduction: guide-lines on the use of force, the legality–legitimacy gap, the UN–US relationship, the developing–industrial countries divide and the rule of law. I will then finish with the suggestion that the United Nations has to come to terms with being both a stage for realism where the cynics can feel vindicated, and an actor pursuing ineluctable ideals so that the sense of excitement and romantic adventure is not lost.

The use of force

The provision of security imposes two requirements: those not author-ised to use force should renounce its use and threat in their social relations, while the authorised agents of any community with the mono-poly on the legitimate use of violence must have the capacity and the will to use force when required. For any international enforcement action to be efficient, it must be legitimate. UN Security Council (UNSC) decision-making procedures may be defective and flawed, but

[6] David Kennedy, *The Dark Sides of Virtue: Reassessing International Humanitarianism* (Princeton: Princeton University Press, 2004), p. 133.

at least they are regulated and subject to international oversight. For enforcement action to be effective, it must match resources to mandates and be based on a unity of purpose and action in the international community so as to avoid fracturing the existing consensus. For it to be equitable, it must balance the competing interests among the many constituencies that make up the international community and avoid privileging the interests and viewpoints of one over the others. To achieve freedom from fear, citizens must be assured that national authorities with the legal monopoly of the means of violence will not unleash the agents and instruments of violence on the people, and states must be assured that the most powerful will aim to settle differences of opinion around the negotiating table and not at the point of tank turrets, helicopter gunships and missiles.

Like the League of Nations in the interwar period, the United Nations embodied the idea that aggressive war is a crime against humanity, with every state having the interest, right and duty to collaborate in preventing it. But the UN has not lived up to demands and expectations in securing a disarmed and peaceful world. For the UN to succeed, the world community must match the demands made on the organisation by the means given to it. Sometimes force must be used, even in the cause of peace. Only the UN can legitimately authorise military action on behalf of the entire international community, instead of a select few. But the UN does not have its own military and police forces. A multinational coalition of allies can offer a more credible and efficient military force when robust action is needed and warranted. What will be increasingly needed in future is partnerships of the able, the willing and the high-minded with the duly authorised. Anything else risks violating due process. Moreover, as Iraq's continuing crisis demonstrated, if force is used recklessly, prematurely and unwisely, then support for it will decline both among those who must provide the soldiers and the international community in general. That is, like crying wolf, misuse of the option of force compounds the difficulty of mobilising support for that option when it is genuinely needed and warranted.

The major powers need to return to the shared management of a troubled world order. To avoid the appearance and charges of double standards, the UN system needs to be ready, willing and able to confront humanitarian catastrophes wherever they occur. The unavoidability of selectivity should not become an alibi for the strong using force against the weak. That will only heighten disorder. One veto should not override the rest of humanity. Otherwise we might see more unilateral actions with less or no UN involvement – and thus less order and less justice in the global community.

Legality and legitimacy

The Kosovo and Iraq interventions underlined widespread perceptions that powerful countries can break the rules of the Charter regime with impunity. This has widened the gulf between law and legitimacy. The humanitarian community has had a critical role in this. As David Kennedy notes, war has always been with us, and so has humanitarianism: 'an endless struggle to contain war in the name of civilization'.[7] He argues that the humanitarian community has by and large failed to confront the reality of bad consequences flowing from good intentions, preferring to retreat into denial, or intensifying efforts to do good, or pointing the finger of accountability at others. The reason for much of the first part of Kennedy's argument lies in the growing influence and power of humanitarian actors as a result of which they have effectively entered the realm of policy-making, at the same time as their emancipatory vocabulary has been captured by governments and other power brokers. International humanitarians are participants in global governance as advocates, activists and policy-makers. Their critiques and policy prescriptions have demonstrable consequences in the governmental and intergovernmental allocation of resources and the exercise of political, military and economic power. With influence over policy should come responsibility for the consequences of policy. When things go wrong or do not happen according to plan, the humanitarians share the responsibility for the sub-optimal outcomes.

The explanation for the second part of the argument – the denial of responsibility – is the refusal to acknowledge that they have crossed over from the world of ideas and ideals into the realm of power and policy-making. Human rights has become the universal vocabulary of political legitimacy and humanitarian law of military legitimacy. But rather than necessarily constraining the pursuit of national interests in the international arena by military means, human rights and humanitarian law provide the discourse of justification for the familiar traditional means of statecraft. Much as humanitarians might want to believe that they still hold up the virtue of truth to the vice of power, the truth is that the

---

[7] Ibid., p. 323.

vocabulary of virtue has been appropriated in the service of power. The fault line between activists and policy-makers is no longer as sharp as it used to be.

Moreover, both the military strategist and the humanitarian activist retreat into abstract principles at the very point where the application of rules (humanitarian law) and standards (human rights) become conceptually and operationally interesting. For instance, if an Iraqi insurgent is hiding among the civilian populace in Fallujah, how many civilians may a US soldier kill without violating the principles of distinction between soldiers and non-combatants? And how many Iraqi civilians may legitimately be killed in order to save one American soldier without violating the principle of proportionality? This is a contemporaneous restatement of the dilemma familiar from the atomic bombings of Hiroshima and Nagasaki in August 1945: were they justified on the twin principles of distinction and proportionality? Rather than answer these difficult questions with any degree of clarity, both the humanitarian and the strategist retreat into restatements of abstract rules and standards, or the vocabulary of absolute normative commitment: the use of force must always be proportional; civilians may never be targeted; we will do our utmost to protect our soldiers; etc.

The subject of international intervention to protect the victims of humanitarian atrocities is a particular manifestation of the more general paradox. The central objective of traditional humanitarian policy-making has been to reduce the frequency and violence of war. Now many humanitarians demand the use of violence and war in order to advance the humanitarian agenda. But how can one 'intervene' in Kosovo, East Timor, Iraq or Darfur and pretend to be detached from and not responsible for the distributional consequences with respect to wealth, resources, power, status and authority? This dilemma is inherent in the structure of interventions and has nothing to do with the false dichotomy between multilateral interventions in one context and unilateral interventions in another. 'The effort to intervene . . . without affecting the background distribution of power and wealth betrays this bizarre belief in the possibility of an international governance which does not govern.'[8]

Kennedy's solution is to engage in a rigorous calculation of the costs as well as benefits, of the areas illuminated by the shining light of idealism

---

[8] Ibid., p. 130.

but also the darker sides of virtue, of alternative strategies and policy options.[9] Instead of a priori enchanting multilateral processes and institutions, we must weigh them and their long-term project against immediate and long-term humanitarian outcomes. Is it worth bombing Belgrade to save Kosovo or ousting Saddam to save Iraq, given the consequences that can *reasonably* be predicted? Maybe, maybe not. The answer requires a rigorous empirical assessment and cannot be derived from a priori norms. In all such policy choice frameworks, there are winners and losers, virtuous outcomes and horrendous costs. Because the darker sides can sometimes swamp the benefits of humanitarian work, it must be tempered by a sensibility of pragmatism that focuses the searchlight of critical reasoning on the noble goals and aspirations of humanitarianism.

International organisations that are perceived by their members as legitimate are governmental in the way in which they exercise social control through the promulgation of norms (standards of behaviour) and laws (rules of behaviour). The United Nations, not unlike national governments, represents a structure of authority that rests on institutionalised state practices and generally accepted norms. But 'governmental bodies are expected to be accountable and open to opposition',[10] otherwise they will suffer an erosion of their legitimacy.

There is another problem with claims of UN legitimacy. The bases of its legitimacy include its credentials for representing the international community, agreed procedures for making decisions on behalf of international society and political impartiality. But sometimes this elides into claims of legitimacy based on the technical identity of the Secretariat as an international civil service, which is quite problematic.[11] For example, when post-war Iraq requested UN assistance for training Iraqi judges and prosecutors who would be trying Saddam Hussein and his senior associates, the response from Kofi Annan was that the organisation would not assist national courts that can impose the death penalty.[12] Similarly, in

[9] See also David Rieff, *A Bed for the Night: Humanitarianism in Crisis* (New York: Simon and Schuster, 2003), and Fiona Terry, *Condemned to Repeat? The Paradox of Humanitarian Action* (Ithaca: Cornell University Press, 2002).

[10] Ian Hurd, 'Legitimacy and Authority in International Politics', *International Organization* 53:2 (Spring 1999), p. 383.

[11] See Robert Keohane, 'The Contingent Legitimacy of Multilateralism', in Thakur, Newman and Tirman, eds., *Multilateralism under Challenge?*

[12] Marlise Simons, 'Iraqis Not Ready for Trials; UN to Withhold Training', *New York Times*, 22 October 2004.

his report on transitional justice, Annan again affirmed that the UN would not establish or participate 'in any tribunal for which capital punishment is included among possible sanctions'.[13] But whose pre-ferred political morality is this? What proportion of the world's people live under governments that have capital punishment on their statutes, including China, India, Indonesia and the USA? Who sets the relevant international standards and benchmarks? Does the UN somehow have a state of grace above its member states?

The UN–US *pas de deux*

Because of the sustaining belief in being a virtuous power, the USA is averse to domesticating international values and norms, be they with respect to greenhouse gas emissions, the death penalty, landmines or the pursuit of universal justice. But this self-image of exceptionalism is neither congruent with how others see it nor conducive to securing their cooperation. The American revolutionaries defined tyranny as the fusion of legislative, executive and judicial powers in one authority and founded the USA on the principle of separation of powers as the main safeguard of freedom. It is thus ironic that many Americans seem to want to use the UNSC as a forum of concentrated power to control the actions of all other countries. 'It is part of the pathology of US power today that the evident need for a constitutional check on the world's most powerful state – a constraint the United States would welcome if it were true to its political heritage – is now seen to stem from spiteful anti-Americanism.'[14]

The UN must manage its most critical bilateral relationship without compromising its independence and integrity by appeasing Washington. In the case of the International Criminal Court (ICC), the initial multi-lateral commitment by the USA faltered as its partners went farther than the US comfort zone. There is general acceptance and support for the claim that the US position in the world is unique, its military is stationed and called for duty around the world, and exposure to the risk of mischievous allegations against its soldiers would unduly inhibit its

---

[13] Kofi A. Annan, *The Rule of Law and Transitional Justice in Conflict and Post-conflict Societies.* Report of the Secretary-General (New York: UN document S/2004/616, 23 August 2004), para. 64(d).

[14] Robert W. Tucker and David C. Hendrickson, 'The Sources of American Legitimacy', *Foreign Affairs*, 83:6 (November/December 2004), p. 26.

global security role. Accordingly a number of modifications were made to the Statute of Rome to accommodate legitimate US concerns on the scope of the statute and the discretion of the prosecutor. But ultimately 120 countries refused to accept that the world's only policeman should enjoy a blanket legal immunity from the Court's universal jurisdiction. The two sides reached contrary conclusions from the experience. Many Americans drew the lesson that it was better to formulate their opposition early and forcefully. Many others concluded that instead of making concessions to Washington which fail to secure their compliance anyway, it was better to move faster to create international regimes without US participation if necessary.[15] The quarrel over ICC exemption in the Summer of 2002 was a defining moment for US relations with its closest traditional allies. Securing the exemption may have convinced Washington that pressure would bring it victory in the UNSC on almost any issue. In fact Washington had used up its political capital, and the ICC experience strengthened the determination of many Western governments 'not to let the Council again bend to such pressure'.[16]

At a major international conference on UN reforms in Waterloo, Ontario in April 2005, many participants expressed concern that Washington had no real interest in reforming the organisation. While many countries believed reform to be necessary and desirable, Americans were worried that the real reform agenda was to constrain US power, for example by adopting guidelines on the use of force. It would therefore be foolish to invest too much time and effort into satisfying American demands. Instead, participants said, the better strategy would be to work with Washington where possible but work around it where necessary.[17]

Contrary to the instant explanations offered after 9/11 that the USA is the terrorists' target of choice because of its success, dynamism and openness, the core basis of international *respect* for the USA, albeit with reservations and caveats, is its extraordinary success as a society, economy and polity. The basis of dissatisfaction is the overseas policies and

---

[15] Georg Nolte, 'The United States and the International Criminal Court', in David Malone and Yuen Foong Khong, eds., *Unilateralism and US Foreign Policy: International Perspectives* (Boulder: Lynne Rienner, 2003), p. 89.

[16] Paul Heinbecker (Canada's ambassador to the UN at the time), 'Washington's Exceptionalism and the United Nations', *Global Governance* 10:3 (July–September 2004), p. 276.

[17] The papers have been published in Paul Heinbecker and Patricia Goff, eds., *Irrelevant or Indispensable? The United Nations in the 21st Century* (Waterloo: Wilfrid Laurier University Press, 2005).

actions. Americans fret over a nettlesome UN and the Hamlet-like allies who agonise over moral qualms when Washington has determined that military action is vital to US security interests. In Old Europe, the great powers had accepted the existing balance of power as a foundational value and a prerequisite to a functioning system of legal rules. If it was disturbed or threatened, the legal rules could be set aside temporarily until the balance of power was restored. The US commitment to the post-1945 order had emphasised the protection of the democratic community through rules constraining the use of force by 'the other side'; the impact of 9/11 in the moment of unipolar triumph saw an expansion in the use of force to promote and export the democratic franchise.

In world affairs the focus on form over substance, structure over outcome means that governance is often dislocated from governing. Authority is the right to make policy and rules, while power is the capacity to implement the policy and enforce the rules. The UN has authority without power. It symbolises global governance but lacks the attributes of international government. The USA has global power but lacks international authority. Often it acts as a de facto world government but disclaims responsibility for the distributional outcomes of its actions with regard to resources, environment, labour and justice. Power buttresses authority, and authority is reinforced with power. The exercise of power is rendered less effective and generates its own resistance if divorced from authority. The latter in turn is corroded when challenges to it go unanswered by the necessary force. Lack of capacity to be the chief enforcer acting under chapter 7 means that the UN remains an incomplete organisation, one that practises only parts of its Charter.

That being the case, Luck asks, 'Is it tenable for the UN to say that it only wants to walk on the soft side of the street but nevertheless wants to have some degree of control over what happens on the other side as well?'[18] The USA has found it difficult to comprehend why the UN does not accept the history of the exercise of American power being virtuous in intent and beneficent in results. But authority is also weakened when it becomes just a handmaiden to power. Progress towards the good international society requires that force be harnessed to authority rather than lawful authority being hijacked to pursue the agenda of power politics.

[18] Edward C. Luck, 'Another Reluctant Belligerent: The United Nations and the War on Terrorism', in Richard M. Price and Mark W. Zacher, eds., *The United Nations and Global Security* (New York: Palgrave Macmillan, 2004), p. 105.

The UN, headquartered in the USA, is universal in membership. The USA is global in reach and power. We begin the twenty-first century with the convergence of US global dominance in military might, economic dynamism and information technology that is without precedent in human history. To this list can be added the soft power hegemony in the major multilateral institutions, especially the International Monetary Fund (IMF), the World Bank and the UN; the collective action dominance of the G7 and the North Atlantic Treaty Organisation (NATO); and the many globally influential media and non-governmental organisation (NGO) conglomerates located in the USA.

By their bitter separation over Saddam Hussein's Iraq, the USA and the UN provoked a mutually reinforcing legitimacy crisis of American power and UN authority. The lack of a sense of moral clarity – values that it espouses and principles in defence of which it is prepared to stand up and be counted – diminished the UN's moral authority and hence its legitimacy. The certainty of moral clarity put the Bush administration on a course that seriously eroded its moral authority in the exercise of world power. The charitable view is that Washington set about undermining the existing bases of world order without having any alternative system as its replacement. The more critical interpretation is that the war on terror is a diplomatic strategy for imposing and exercising US dominance.

Nevertheless, it would be a mistake to fault the Bush administration rather than a broader tendency to unilateralism. Multilateral rhetoric notwithstanding, the Clinton administration scapegoated the UN for the Somalia débâcle, never put its full weight behind the Chemical Weapons Convention (CWC), launched a tardy campaign for the ratification of the CWC and the Comprehensive Test Ban Treaty (CTBT), and presented the ICC to the Senate for signature in the dying days of the administration. While the Clinton administration launched missile strikes on Afghanistan and Sudan in 1998 without even the pretence of going through the UN, Bush at least tried to rally the UN to the cause of ousting Saddam Hussein and went his own way only when rebuffed.

Two distinguished American professors have argued that post-1945 US foreign policy had rested on four pillars of legitimacy: a commitment to international law, an acceptance of consensual decision-making, a reputation for moderation and an identification with the preservation of peace above all other goals. The free world recognised that the long peace had been preserved by the perseverance and stability of US power married to a moral vision. The world was duly grateful and in return held fast to the belief that American power was both necessary and right, that is, legitimate. The administration of President George W. Bush, particularly in relation to the war on Iraq, has produced a 'startling loss of legitimacy'[19] on all four counts separately. Their combined effect has been to strike the world with terror: the world 'now sees the United States increasingly as an outlier – invoking international law when convenient, and ignoring it when not; using international institutions when they work to its advantage, and disdaining them when they pose obstacles to US designs'.[20]

Post-Westphalia?

The sense of unease about the UN being an after-sales service provider for American train wrecks was evident in relation to Iraq. The US–UK policy on Iraq was a multiple assault on the foundations and rules of the existing state order as well as the transatlantic relationship.[21] It seeks to replace self-defence and wars of necessity with preventive defence and wars of choice,[22] the successful strategy of containment with the untried doctrine of pre-emption,[23] deterrence with compellence, a multilateral system of global governance centred on the UN with a unilateral system of global dominance by the USA, and leadership by consent-cum-persuasion with one by command and control; to abort the European search for a new world order based on the Kantian transition from barbarism to culture through liberal institutionalism and revert instead to the old world order that Europe discarded after several centuries of warfare, based on force of arms; and to supplant the Westphalian order of equal sovereign states with a post-Westphalian system of one pre-eminent if virtuous power. One of the central dynamics of international

---

[19] Tucker and Hendrickson, 'Sources of American Legitimacy', p. 23.

[20] Ibid., pp. 24, 32.

[21] See Ramesh Thakur and W. P. S. Sidhu, eds., *The Iraq Crisis and World Order: Structural, Institutional and Normative Challenges*, and W. P. S. Sidhu and Ramesh Thakur, eds., *Arms Control after Iraq: Normative and Operational Challenges* (Tokyo: United Nations University Press, forthcoming).

[22] For an argument that this reverses two centuries of American tradition on global diplomacy, see Arthur Schlesinger, 'Seeking Out Monsters', *Guardian* (London), 19 October 2004.

[23] For a critical Chinese perspective, see Zhaojie Li, 'The Doctrine of Preemptive Self-defense: A Legal Justification for the Use of Force against Iraq?', *University of Tokyo Journal of Law and Politics* 1 (Spring 2004), pp. 108–20.

relations is the interaction between the structural constants of the primacy of the state as an actor and the condition of international anarchy, and the variable of the distribution of power. When the latter is transformed into unipolarity, it moves the system from a concert towards an imperial order. The most profound and long-lasting significance of 9/11 might thus be that it tipped us into a post-Westphalian world. Ironically, in this it is synchronous with the religiously fired project of al Qaeda which also challenges the Westphalian secular state-based authority structure of the international order.[24]

US policy is full of contradictions within the Westphalian paradigm. 'The United States sees itself spreading its gifts, inspiring a global tide of liberty, but often it is seen as the symbol not of opportunity but of a threatening modernity: trampler of tradition, mouther of hypocrisies, poor listener, bully, robber baron disguising its intent in a cloak of noble convictions.'[25] How can the most prominent dissident in many global norms and regimes claim to be the world's most powerful enforcer of global norms and regimes? How can the most vocal critic of the very notion of an international community anoint itself the international community's sheriff? How can London and Washington claim to enforce UN resolutions by denying the authority of the UN?

The answer lies in a conception of world order rooted outside the Westphalian framework of sovereign equality. This also explains why some of today's most potent threats come not from conquering states within the Westphalian paradigm, but from failing states outside it. In effect the Bush doctrine implies that the gap between the fiction of legal equality and the reality of power preponderance has stretched beyond breaking point. Washington is no longer bound by such fiction. The USA will remain as fundamentally trustworthy, balanced and responsible a custodian of world order as before, but of a post-Westphalian imperial order centred on Washington.[26]

---

[24] Daniel Philpott, 'The Challenge of September 11 to Secularism in International Relations', World Politics 55:1 (October 2002), p. 92. Richard Falk distinguishes between the 'imperial globalisation' of the Bush administration and the 'apocalyptic globalisation' of al Qaeda; Richard A. Falk, The Declining World Order: America's Imperial Geopolitics (London: Routledge, 2004), p. viii.

[25] Roger Cohen, 'Globalist: Paying a Deadly Price for US Global Hubris', International Herald Tribune (IHT), 4 May 2005.

[26] Although Falk describes 'the idea of a global empire administered from Washington' as 'a dead end'; Falk, Declining World Order, p. 25.

As Jonathan Schell puts it, recalling the example of Rome:

> A powerful republic gives birth to an empire, which in turn destroys the republic . . .
>
> The Administration's across-the-board hostility to the constraints of law, domestic and international, is not accidental. The constitutional structure that is the backbone of the republic is a stumbling block to the empire. The republic requires a single standard, to which all are subject – the law. But the empire requires a double standard – one set of regulations for others, and another set, or none, for the imperial ruler. In the imperial conception, 'law' is a set of rules dictated by the ruler for everyone else to obey. In this conception, other countries are not permitted weapons of mass destruction, but the United States may have them (and use them to stop the others from getting them). Other countries must obey the Geneva Conventions, but the United States is exempt. Other countries must wage war only defensively; the United States may do so pre-emptively.[27]

This explains why the risk to the soldiers of the intervening, warring-by-choice countries is minimised by transferring the burden of danger to the civilians and soldiers of the other side. And it also explains the refusal of the USA, which wields enormously destructive power well beyond its borders, to permit such a global exercise of power to be accountable to international institutions, let alone to those who suffer its consequences. That is, repressive regimes can be held accountable by foreign governments for their use of force internally by countries that insist on exempting their own use of force internationally from any independent international accountability. Kathy Ferguson and Phyllis Turnbull explain the US imperial expansion with the help of three 'fruitful oxymorons': 'portable sovereignty' that allows Washington to project its power to any spot in the world; 'national internationalism' as the basis of US exceptionalism; and 'the peaceful arms trade' that selects the proliferation of weapons of mass destruction as the core threat to international peace and security as a tactic of denying the role of these and conventional weapons in ensuring US military supremacy.[28]

Intriguingly, during his seventeen-minute second inauguration speech on 20 January 2005, President Bush mentioned liberty and freedom

---

[27] Jonathan Schell, 'Empire Without Law', *The Nation*, 31 May 2004, p. 7.

[28] Kathy E. Ferguson and Phyllis Turnbull, 'American Portable Sovereignty', *Peace & Policy* 9 (2004), pp. 31–46.

more than forty times, but human rights only once.[29] The rhetoric is immensely attractive to millions who do want to overthrow their own despotic governments. Yet 'never has imperial America . . . been as rampant and detested as it is today'. The comment that 'imperial America will not like the democratic Arabia that missionary America will have helped to spawn'[30] is applicable far more generally than just to the Arab world. The empirical record of the strange marriage of neo-conservatives and liberal human rights activists is largely one of failure, which has led at least one former interventionist to retrench from a new imperial role for the US seventh cavalry/marines.[31]

To the extent that Rwanda's genocide in 1994 remains one of the most shameful, painful and defining moments in the UN's sixty-year history, it is worth returning to that for illuminating US–UN relations. The skill, speed and logistical efficiency displayed by Belgium, France and the USA in evacuating their soldiers and nationals during the early days of the genocide reinforced General Roméo Dallaire's firm conviction at the time that the rapid deployment of just 5,000 well-trained and well-armed professional troops in the first days of the genocide (6–22 April) would have stopped or substantially reduced the tragedy. He sadly concluded that serving the UN goals is not high on the foreign policy priority of most countries. Instead, 'What they want is a weak, beholden, indebted scapegoat of an organization, which they can blame for their failures or steal victories from.'[32]

While Nye notes the paradox that even the most supremely powerful country cannot achieve its goals acting alone,[33] Sorensen poses a pertinent question:

> what is more unrealistic than to believe that this country can unilaterally decide the fate of others, without a decent respect for the opinions of mankind, or for the judgment of world institutions and our traditional

---

[29] President Bush 'has promoted democracy when it has coincided with other US interests . . . When opposition to tyranny has been at odds with security or economic policy . . . the Bush administration of the past four years consistently chose to ignore and excuse oppression'; 'The Rhetoric of Freedom', editorial, *Washington Post*, 21 January 2005.

[30] David Hirst, 'Dangerous Democracy', *Guardian*, 20 April 2005.

[31] David Rieff, *At the Point of a Gun: Democratic Dreams and Armed Intervention* (New York: Simon and Schuster, 2005).

[32] Roméo Dallaire, *Shake Hands with the Devil: The Failure of Humanity in Rwanda* (Toronto: Random House Canada, 2003), p. 90.

[33] Joseph E. Nye, *The Paradox of American Power: Why the World's Only Superpower Can't Go It Alone* (New York: Oxford University Press, 2002).

allies? Only the arrogance of power and the ignorance of history could lead any American to believe that our vast military superiority confers upon us moral superiority as well.[34]

American policy-makers cannot construct a world in which all others have to obey universal norms and rules, but Washington can opt out whenever, as often, and for as long as it likes on global norms with respect to nuclear tests, landmines, international criminal prosecution, and climate change regimes – all of which, incidentally, were negotiated in and reflect the post-Cold War world. Conversely, a world in which every country retreated into unilateralism would not be a better guarantee of US national security than multilateral regimes.

Yet all states are *not* equal in status, capacity, legitimacy and morality. On most objective criteria, there is the USA, and there are the rest. The fact that some 'legitimate' governments (meaning recognised as such) are engaged in criminal activities indicates the troubling degree to which the very word has been corrupted. Why should the community of democracies willingly submit its actions to the restraining discipline of the judgement of self-serving regimes? It seems intuitively plausible to posit that the structure of global governance, including international organisations, must bear some relationship to the underlying distribution of power (the final disconnect of the seven listed in the introduction).[35] Is the weight of anomalies now too heavy for the Westphalian fiction to be sustainable for much longer? Imperialism is not a foreign policy designed to promote, project and globalise the values and virtues of the dominant centre, but a form of international governance based on an unequal hierarchy of power.[36] The reality of inequality structures the relationship between the imperial centre and all others. This is not a matter of malevolence on the part of a particular administration in Washington, but an artefact of the reality of a unipolar world that will shape the foreign relations of any administration.

---

[34] Theodore C. Sorensen, 'JFK's Strategy of Peace', *World Policy Journal* 20:3 (Fall 2003), p. 4.

[35] See Thakur, Newman and Tirman, eds., *Multilateralism under Challenge?*

[36] 'We treat UN Security Council members like ingrates who offend our princely dignity by lifting their heads from the carpet'; Robert C. Byrd, 'The Arrogance of Power', 19 March 2003, available at http://byrd.senate.gov.

The United Nations as a bridge between the North and the global South

Ironically, while Washington has become exasperated at efforts to turn the UN into an organisation to thwart US international policy, many developing countries have become disillusioned with the UN for having been reduced to a front organisation for the USA. They are likely to be perturbed when the newly appointed American Under-Secretary-General for Management, Christopher B. Burnham, openly declared that his 'primary loyalty is to the United States of America'.[37] As the East–West divide ended with the passing of the Cold War, some of the underlying differences between North and South became relatively sharper. They are also more acute to the extent that the North coincides largely with the West while the global South corresponds largely with non-Western countries. The industrialised North demands tighter fiscal discipline, better governance, more respect for human rights, greater adherence to international regimes and more positions at senior policy levels in international organisations to ensure greater donor accountability. The developing countries demand more aid, better access to rich markets, greater international labour mobility, a more equitable sharing of wealth and resources across the globe and more positions at senior policy levels in international organisations to redress a serious representational deficit. While one group is still trapped in the colonial past with scant regard to joint management of the future, the other is fixated on a future that disowns responsibility for aspects of the past best forgotten. As the UN conference on racism held in Durban in August–September 2001 showed, there is an industrialised–developing countries divide on some basic principles underpinning international relations. And it was the rich–poor country divide that wrecked the world trade talks in Cancun, Mexico in September 2003.

Considering the ill-fated history of the League of Nations, the UN founders would have felt pride and satisfaction that their creation is still intact, embracing virtually the entire international community. Yet their vision of a world community equal in rights, bound by a common vision and united in action is still to be realised. As the sun rose on the new century it illuminated some of the darker legacies of the last one. It is simply not acceptable:

---

[37] Quoted in Colum Lynch, 'At the UN, a Growing Republican Presence', *Washington Post*, 21 July 2005.

- that millions of people should continue to be condemned to a life of poverty, illiteracy and ill-health;
- that the combined GDP of the forty-eight least developed countries should be less than the assets of the world's three richest people;
- that the annual income of 2.5 billion – almost half – of the world's poorest people should be less than that of the richest 250;
- that the brunt of these misfortunes should fall on women.

The two major sets of controversies dividing industrial from developing countries in the context of UN policy have been the relative priority to be accorded to development and security, and the circumstances in which sovereignty can be suspended in order to honour the collective responsibility to protect. The UN Intellectual History Project concluded that the intellectual contributions to ideas, analysis and policy-making in the economic and social arenas, including setting development goals, 'have been among the UN's most important achievements'.[38] Two contributions are particularly notable. The UN was instrumental in clarifying the statistical indicators of development – what is to be measured – and in establishing the professional ethic of statistical independence and objectivity.[39] And second, the UN was instrumental in broadening the concept of development to make it more human and environment-friendly,[40] and sensitive to regional complexity and nuance.[41] Since the 1980s this has taken the form of constructive dissent to the prevailing Washington consensus among the World Bank, the International Monetary Fund and the US Treasury. The high priority given to development is evident in the efforts being devoted to mobilise the world in support of the Millennium Development Goals.

With regard to the second set of concerns, the reason for much disquiet around the world with the precedent of NATO action in Kosovo was not because their abhorrence of ethnic cleansing is any less. Rather, it was because of their dissent from a world order which permits or tolerates unilateral behaviour by the strong and their preference for an

---

[38] Richard Jolly, Louis Emmerij and Thomas G. Weiss, *The Power of Ideas: Lessons from the First Sixty Years* (New York: UNIHP, 2005), p. 3.

[39] This story is told in Michael Ward, *Quantifying the World* (Bloomington: Indiana University Press for UNIHP, 2004).

[40] Richard Jolly, Louis Emmerij, Dharam Ghai and Frédéric Lapayre, *UN Contributions to Development Thinking and Practice* (Bloomington: Indiana University Press for UNIHP, 2004).

[41] Yves Berthelot, ed., *Unity and Diversity in Development Ideas: Perspectives from the UN Regional Commissions* (Bloomington: Indiana University Press for UNIHP, 2004).

order in which principles and values are embedded in universally applicable norms and the rough edges of power are softened by institutionalised multilateralism. Institutionalisation puts limits on policy autonomy, gives others a voice in policy and places restraints on the arbitrary and indiscriminate exercise of power that is indispensable. The lesson has been strongly reinforced by the Iraq War.

Many of today's wars are nasty, brutish, anything but short, and mainly internal. The world community cannot help all victims, but must step in where it can make a difference. Not being able to act everywhere can never be a reason for not acting where effective intervention is both possible and urgently needed. Selective indignation is inevitable, for we simply cannot intervene everywhere, every time. But community support for selective intervention will quickly dissipate if the only criterion of selection is friends (where the norm of non-intervention has primacy) versus adversaries (where the right to intervene is privileged). Instead of selective, we must still pursue policies of effective indignation. Intervention must be collective, not unilateral. And it must be legitimate, not in violation of the agreed rules which comprise the foundations of world order.

The rule of law

The rule of law has been defined by the Secretary-General as 'a principle of governance in which all persons, institutions and entities, public and private, including the State itself, are accountable to laws that are publicly promulgated, equally enforced and independently adjudicated'.[42] Questions of the lawfulness and legitimacy of overseas military action by individual or groups of states cannot be separated from the question of the authoritative determination of just cause and justified response. International law, like all law, is an effort to align power to justice. Politics is about power: its location, bases, exercise, effects. Law seeks to tame power and convert it into authority through legitimising principles (e.g. democracy, separation of powers), structures (e.g. legislature, executive and judiciary) and procedures (e.g. elections). Law thereby mediates relations between the rich and the poor, the weak and the powerful, by acting as a constraint on capricious behaviour and setting limits on the arbitrary exercise of power. It is our one big safety net for

---

[42] Annan, *The Rule of Law and Transitional Justice*, para. 6.

civilised conduct. Conversely, the greater the gap between power and authority, the closer we are to anarchy, to the law of the jungle where might equals right, and the greater is the legitimacy deficit. Equally, the greater the gap between power and justice in world affairs, the greater is the international legitimacy deficit.

Much as smaller economies seek protection from the big economic powers in rules-based regimes like the World Trade Organisation (WTO) or bilateral/regional free trade agreements that embed agreed codes of conduct and dispute settlement mechanisms, so the weak and vulnerable countries seek protection from the predatory instincts of the powerful – an abiding lesson of history, if ever there was one – in a rules-based world order that specifies both the proper conduct to be followed by all states and the mechanisms for reconciling differences between them. In the words of Chile's Foreign Minister Maria Soledad Alvear, 'saving lives must always take precedence over institutional concerns. Nevertheless, the truth is that over the long term, respect for institutions is a better guarantee of survival for the human species than a disorderly world in which unilateral solutions and the law of the jungle prevail.'[43]

The UN lies at the centre and indeed symbolises a rules-based order. The binding character of contracts does not rest on the reliance of one party to a contract on the word or signature of the other party. Rather, it rests on the institution of the contract itself.[44] The same argument holds with respect to the UN Charter which regulates *when* force may be used and international humanitarian law which regulates *how* force may be used. Similarly, sovereignty as the organising principle of international society is not the property of any particular state, but an international institution, 'the foundational principle on which the rest of international relations is constructed'.[45] Progress requires the creation and maintenance of a rules-based world order that specifies both the proper conduct to be followed by all states and the mechanisms for reconciling differences between them.

Those who challenge or evade the authority of the UN as the sole legitimate guardian of international peace and security in specific instances thus contribute to an erosion of its authority in general and

---

[43] Maria Soledad Alvear, 'Humanitarian Intervention: How to Deal with Crises Effectively', introductory remarks at the ICISS Round Table Consultation, Santiago, 4 May 2001 (unofficial translation).

[44] Friedrich V. Kratochwil, *Rules, Norms, and Decisions: On the Conditions of Practical and Legal Reasoning in International Relations and Domestic Affairs* (Cambridge: Cambridge University Press, 1989), p. 28.

[45] Hurd, 'Legitimacy and Authority in International Politics', p. 393.

undermine the principle of a world order based on international law and universal norms. Those who would challenge and overthrow the existing order must therefore indicate which is their preferred alternative *system of rules, including dispute resolution*; simply rejecting an existing rule or norm, no matter how unsatisfactory or unjust, in order to overthrow a particular ruler, no matter how odious, is not enough.

When applied to humanitarian atrocities, the bottom-line question remains: faced with another Holocaust or Rwanda-type genocide on the one hand and a Security Council veto on the other, what would we do? This cannot be separated from the question of the authoritative determination of just cause and justified response: who, under what rules of evidence and procedure, can rightfully decide on what is to be done? Reducing the entire debate simply to a question of UN authorisation as a necessary condition for overseas military action is simply not good enough. If UN authorisation is not a necessary condition, then either we accept the resulting international anarchy and the law of the jungle in world affairs, or we spell out the preferred alternative set of rules and the institutions and regimes in which they are embedded. Logically, there are six alternatives:

1. Any one country can wage war against any other.
2. Any one coalition of states can wage war against another country or group.
3. Only NATO has such a right with respect to launching military action against a non-NATO country.
4. Only NATO has the right to determine if military intervention, whether by NATO or any other coalition, is justified against others outside the coalition.
5. A regional organisation can take in-area military action against errant members of the organisation (e.g. the African Union against deviant AU members, or NATO against deviant NATO members), if they have agreed in advance to such rules of the game for governing internal relations, or if they seek and get ex post facto authorisation from the Security Council; but not against non-members in out-of-area operations.
6. Only the United Nations can legitimately authorise armed intervention.

The first and second are recipes for international anarchy. Indeed the challenge of 'humanitarian intervention' arises from the increasingly clear recognition that we no longer cede the right to any one state to use massive force within its borders free of external scrutiny or criticism, whether it be Serbia in Kosovo, Indonesia in East Timor, India in Kashmir or Russia in Chechnya; claims for reversing the progressive restrictions on the right to interstate armed violence will be met with even more scepticism. The third is a claim to unilateralism and exceptionalism that will never be conceded by the 'international community'. The fourth was unwittingly implicit in the argument that NATO's actions in Kosovo cannot be construed as having set a precedent. The assumption underlying the claim is both demonstrably false, and almost breathtakingly arrogant in setting up NATO as the final arbiter of military intervention by itself and every other coalition. The fifth and sixth options pose the fewest difficulties, although the history of the Warsaw Pact (Hungary 1956, Czechoslovakia 1968) and that of the Organisation of American States (OAS) should inject elements of caution even with respect to the fifth. The UN Charter, like no other regional or international document, encapsulates the international moral code and best-practice international behaviour. The urge to 'humanitarian intervention' by powerful states, coalitions of the willing or regional organisations outside their own area of operations must be bridled by the legitimating authority of the international organisation.

The romantics and the cynics

Observers of the United Nations may be divided into two broad groups: the romantic and the cynical. For the former, the global organisation can do no wrong and is the solution to all the world's problems. They do not believe it is possible for some nations to have wealth and jobs while laying waste to the human spirit of many peoples in other parts of the world. They point to the UN Charter as the moral compass that identifies the international civic with the global human community. They do not deny the reality of the failures of Bosnia, Rwanda and Darfur. Rather, they insist that the failures must be seen in context. First, a lot of good is done even in some 'failed' operations, resulting in the saving of hundreds of thousands of lives. Second, there are many other operations that are acknowledged to be overall, if partially flawed, successes, such as Namibia and Cambodia. Third, there are other parts of the UN system that are generally efficient and worthwhile. Most importantly, say the ardent UN groupies, the failures of the UN are really failures of its member states who find in it a convenient scapegoat for their own shortcomings, weaknesses and lack of political will.

To the cynics the UN seems only too willing to claim credit for any success while shifting the blame for all failures to the lack of an elusive 'political will' on the part of member states and the major powers. In the cynics' view, the UN is itself a symptom of many of the world's problems. It suffers from exaggerated claims, inflammatory rhetoric, inept leadership, a bloated and excessively politicised agenda, bureaucratic sclerosis, uncontrolled expansion of economic and social programmes, jurisdictional squabbles, wasteful spending habits, lack of accountability and the inability to formulate and implement meaningful reform.

The romantics, their eye firmly on the prized UN ideal of a just and humane world without borders, fail to see the sordid wheeling and dealing driven by personal ambition, venality and naked power politics. The cynics, overwhelmed by perceptions of pervasive waste, corruption and inefficiency, fail to raise their eye to the prize of a better world that beckons over the horizon.

In all its operations, the United Nations is required to navigate its way through the policy 'trilemma' of needs, mandates and reality: the needs of the people or situation, the normative and operational mandates given to it by the Security Council and the General Assembly, and the political realities of demands and expectations of member states and peoples, the tolerance thresholds of other member states and peoples, and the availability of human, financial and material resources.

Ready availability as a convenient scapegoat may be a valuable if unappreciated UN contribution. There will be occasions when political leaders will welcome the UN's ability to provide a 'golden bridge' across which national governments can retire to safety, as well as a 'lightning rod' for deflecting and burying the more violent political reactions at home to international events.

The UN Charter was a triumph of hope and idealism over the experience of two world wars. This is a creative tension that must be resolved in specific cases without abandoning either the sense of realism or the aspiration to an ideal world. The flame of idealism flickered in the chill winds of the Cold War, but refuses to die out with a stubbornness that is worth noting. In the midst of the swirling tides of change, the UN must strive for a balance between the desirable and the possible. It is still the symbol of our dreams for a better world, where weakness can be compensated by justice and fairness, and the law of the jungle replaced by the rule of law.

As such it has to strike a balance between realism and idealism. Its decisions must reflect current realities of military and economic power.

In a world in which there is only one universal international organisation but also only one superpower, the UN must tread a fine line so as neither to become irrelevant to the security imperatives of the USA nor become a mere rubber stamp for US designs. The unilateralist impulse in Washington has posed a major challenge to the international organisation. It will lose credibility, its very raison d'être, if it compromises core values.[46] The United Nations is the repository of international idealism; Utopia is fundamental to its identity. Even the sense of disenchantment and disillusionment on the part of some cannot be understood other than against this background.

If the humanitarian community needs to temper its idealism with a smallish dose of realism, the reverse might be true of the USA. In any given year since the end of the Second World War, the balance sheet of American support for and opposition to dictatorships has usually been negative. In pursuing such short-term tactical policies, US governments have betrayed not just the people yearning to overthrow their local tyrants, but also their own ideals. Many Americans fail to grasp the power of the metaphor of the shining lights in the city on the hill, the hypnotic pull of the ringing American Declaration of Independence, the stirring inspiration of Abraham Lincoln's Gettysburg address. These are not just American treasures; they are the common heritage of mankind.

The UN, too, has been guilty of compromising core values. No objective historian of the past sixty years could credibly claim that victory in the great battles for defeating the evil of communism or promoting the onward march of human rights and freedoms (apartheid excepted), has been won by the world body rather than by America. Moral clarity and backbone, essential for courage of convictions, do not sit easily alongside institutional timidity and instinctive risk-aversion.

History's learning curve shows that the UN ideal can neither be fully attained nor abandoned. In Dag Hammarskjöld's words, 'the constant struggle to close the gap between aspiration and performance . . . makes the difference between civilisation and chaos'.[47] The real challenge is to ensure that the gap does not widen. The global public goods of peace,

---

[46] Some commentators, while agreeing with the need 'to combine power with principle', nonetheless believe that the High-Level Panel's report 'ends up bowing more to the raw distribution of power than to international principles'; Satish Kumar, 'Global Threats and UN Reforms', *Hindu* (Chennai), 24 March 2005.

[47] Quoted in Brian Urquhart, *A Life in Peace and War* (London: Weidenfeld and Nicolson, 1987), p. 378.

prosperity, sustainable development and good governance cannot be achieved by any country acting on its own. The debate over Iraq in 2002–4 demonstrated the true test of UN relevance: both as a brake on an unjustified and unilateral resort to war, and as a forum for legitimising the collective decision to enforce community demands on outlaw regimes.

While discussing Iraq, Elizabeth Wilmshurst's caution about a possible crime of aggression was noted. She is hardly alone in this view: 'In effect, Blair secretly colluded with a foreign power to carry out a war of aggression. That was a crime' based on 'the flimsiest of intelligence and the most equivocal of legal advice'.[48] Should Tony Blair, George W. Bush and John Howard then be prosecuted for war crimes? After all, Germany's leaders were put on trial after the Second World War not for having lost the war, but for having started it, on the grounds that no grievances or policies can justify the resort to aggressive war. Clearly, this could be done only in the full knowledge that even the attempt at it would destroy the UN system. Knowing this, should the ethic of responsible consequences be trumped by the ethic of moral conviction? Must international interest not be allowed to come in the way of international principle? Countries justify pragmatic compromises with principles by calling it realism, whereas the same instinct for survival by the UN is labelled hypocrisy. Given that all three countries are vibrant and robust democracies, is it necessarily such an unmitigated disaster to let the electorates have the final say, as happened in Spain? Certainly by Spring 2005 it was difficult to dispute that the war was a net political liability for all three administrations. In Britain, in the words of a prominent commentator who did not hide her Labour Party sympathy, 'When Blair goes, his departure will cauterise the angriest wounds of the war and much else: the million marchers will have their scalp and Iraq will be his epitaph.'[49]

Conclusion

Confronted with a world they cannot change, reasonable people adapt their behaviour to reality. But the turning points in human history have come from the efforts of those unreasonable people – Gautama Buddha,

---

[48] Roy Greenslade, 'No Vote for a Criminal', *Guardian*, 4 May 2005.

[49] Polly Toynbee, 'Tony Blair's Time is Over', *Guardian*, 4 May 2005. See also Alan Cowell, 'British Grow Less Unflinching on Warfare', *IHT*, 4 May 2005.

Jesus Christ and Mahatma Gandhi among them – who set out to change the world instead. Peter Benenson, the founder of Amnesty as an international movement, died on 25 February 2005. While he 'did not change the world, he didn't leave it as he found it either'.[50] The long walk to freedom from war draws inspiration from this thought. The causes of war are many and complex, the call to end it is single-minded and simple. Cynics insist that war is an inherent part of human society. To end war would indeed be to end history. Maybe. But so too have crime and poverty always been part of human history. Any political leader who admitted to giving up on the fight to end crime or poverty would quickly be returned to private life by voters. Paradoxically, in the case of war it is those who seek to abolish it who are considered to be soft in the head.

The establishment of the United Nations was a small but symbolically important step on the journey to tame the use of aggressive, unlawful and unjustified force as a means of settling quarrels among different members of the human family scattered across the globe. Towards the end of his report on the package of UN reform proposals, Annan observes that 'We are united both by moral imperatives and by objective interests.' Wondering whether member states will have the courage to fulfil their responsibilities and the wisdom to transcend their differences, he argues that 'it is for us to decide whether this moment of uncertainty presages wider conflict, deepening inequality and the erosion of the rule of law, or is used to renew our common institutions for peace, prosperity and human rights'.[51] Sustained, coordinated efforts *can* turn killing fields into playing fields and rice fields. Success comes from having the courage to fail. If one has never failed, then one has not tried enough: one has not pushed oneself hard enough, not tested the limits of one's potential.

The United Nations remains our one and best hope for unity in diversity in a world in which global problems require multilateral solutions. It is the embodiment of the international community and the custodian of world conscience. It represents the idea that unbridled nationalism and the raw interplay of power must be mediated and moderated in an international framework. It is the centre for harmonising national interests and forging the international interest. Of course the UN is an international bureaucracy with many failings and flaws; and a

---

[50] Jonathan Power, 'Meanwhile: A Shining Light for Human Rights', *IHT*, 4 March 2005.

[51] Kofi A. Annan, *In Larger Freedom: Towards Development, Security and Human Rights for All*. Report of the Secretary-General (New York: UN, document A/59/2005, 21 March 2005), paras. 220–2.

forum often used and abused by governments – who control it, not the other way round – for finger pointing, not problem solving. There is a proclivity in UN circles to seek fresh legislation as the solution to problems of implementation. Too often has the UN demonstrated a failure to tackle urgent collective action problems due to institutionalised inability, incapacity or unwillingness. These are the three facets – an international bureaucracy, a politicians' talkshop and a spineless-cum-toothless cop on the beat – that oftentimes have drawn the most serious criticism, much of it warranted.

Yet the world body remains the focus of international expectations and the locus of collective action. The reason for this is that more, much more, than the attributes of bureaucratic rigidity, institutional timidity and intergovernmental trench warfare, the United Nations is the one body that houses the divided fragments of humanity. It is an idea, a symbol of an imagined and constructed community of strangers. It exists to bring about a world where fear is changed to hope, want gives way to dignity, and apprehensions are turned into aspirations. In the words of the illustrious Secretary-General Dag Hammarskjöld, the United Nations was 'not created in order to bring us to heaven, but in order to save us from hell'.[52] The concept of hell is incomplete without the concept of heaven.

---

[52] Quoted in Brian Urquhart, *Hammarskjöld* (New York: W. W. Norton, 1994), p. 48.

INDEX